Empire and Local Worlds

Publications of the
Institute of Archaeology, University College London

Series Editor: Ruth Whitehouse
Director of the Institute: Stephen Shennan
Founding Series Editor: Peter J. Ucko

The Institute of Archaeology of University College London is one of the oldest, largest and most prestigious archaeology research facilities in the world. Its extensive publications programme includes the best theory, research, pedagogy, and reference materials in archaeology and cognate disciplines, through publishing exemplary work of scholars worldwide. Through its publications, the Institute brings together key areas of theoretical and substantive knowledge, improves archaeological practice, and brings archaeological findings to the general public, researchers, and practitioners. It also publishes staff research projects, site and survey reports, and conference proceedings. The publications programme, formerly developed inhouse or in conjunction with UCL Press, is now produced in partnership with Left Coast Press, Inc. The Institute can be accessed online at www.ucl.ac.uk/archaeology.

Encounters with Ancient Egypt Subseries, Peter J. Ucko, (ed.)
Jean-Marcel Humbert and Clifford Price (eds.), *Imhotep Today*
David Jeffreys (ed.), *Views of Ancient Egypt since Napoleon Bonaparte*
Sally MacDonald and Michael Rice (eds.), *Consuming Ancient Egypt*
Roger Matthews and Cornelia Roemer (eds.), *Ancient Perspectives on Egypt*
David O'Connor and Andrew Reid (eds.), *Ancient Egypt in Africa*
John Tait (ed.), *"Never Had the Like Occurred"*
David O'Connor and Stephen Quirke (eds.), *Mysterious Lands*
Peter Ucko and Timothy Champion (eds.), *The Wisdom of Egypt*

Critical Perspectives on Cultural Heritage Subseries, Beverley Butler (ed.)
Beverley Butler, *Return to Alexandria*
Ferdinand de Jong and Michael Rowlands (eds.), *Reclaiming Heritage*
Dean Sully (ed.), *Decolonizing Conservation*

Other Titles
Andrew Gardner (ed.), *Agency Uncovered*
Okasha El-Daly, Egyptology, *The Missing Millennium*
Ruth Mace, Clare J. Holden, and Stephen Shennan (eds.), *Evolution of Cultural Diversity*
Arkadiusz Marciniak, *Placing Animals in the Neolithic*
Robert Layton, Stephen Shennan, and Peter Stone (eds.), *A Future for Archaeology*
Joost Fontein, *The Silence of Great Zimbabwe*
Gabriele Puschnigg, *Ceramics of the Merv Oasis*
James Graham-Campbell and Gareth Williams (eds.), *Silver Economy in the Viking Age*
Barbara Bender, Sue Hamilton, and Chris Tilley, *Stone World*
Andrew Gardner, *An Archaeology of Identity*
Sue Hamilton, Ruth Whitehouse, and Katherine I. Wright (eds.), *Archaeology and Women*
Gustavo Politis, *Nukak*
Sue Colledge and James Conolly (eds.), *The Origins and Spread of Domestic Plants in Southwest Asia and Europe*
Timothy Clack and Marcus Brittain (eds.), *Archaeology and the Media*

Janet Picton, Stephen Quirke, and Paul C. Roberts (eds.), *Living Images*

Tony Waldron, *Paleoepidemiology*

Eleni Asouti and Dorian Q. Fuller, *Trees and Woodlands of South India*

Russell McDougall and Iain Davidson (eds*.), The Roth Family, Anthropology, and Colonial Administration*

Elizabeth Pye (ed.), *The Power of Touch*

Miriam Davis, *Dame Kathleen Kenyon*

Marcos Martinón-Torres and Thilo Rehren (eds.), *Archaeology, History, and Science*

John Tait, *Why the Egyptians Wrote Book*

Peter J. Ucko and Rachael Thyrza Sparks (eds.), *A Future for the Past*

Ruth D. Whitehouse (ed.), *Gender and Italian Archaeology*

Simon Hillson, *Mammal Bones and Teeth*

Nick Merriman, *Beyond the Glass Case*

Paulette M. McManus (ed.), *Archaeological Displays and the Public*

Sally-Ann Ashton, *Petrie's Ptolemaic and Roman Memphis*

Norah Moloney and Michael J. Shott (eds.), *Lithic Analysis at the Millennium*

Mark Nesbitt, *Identification Guide for Near Eastern Grass Seeds*

Christopher Tilley, *The Dolmens and Passage Graves of Sweden*

Sarah L.R. Mason and Jon G. Hather (eds.), *Hunter-Gatherer Archaeology*

Jon G. Hather, *The Identification of the Northern European Woods*

Jon G. Hather, *Archaeological Parenchyma*

D. F. Clark, M. M. Roxan, and J. J. Wilkes (eds.), *The Later Roman Empire Today*

Nicholas Balaam and James Rackham (eds.), *Issues in Environmental Archaeology*

Rob Sands, *Prehistoric Woodworking*

David R. Harris and Kenneth D. Thomas (eds.), *Modelling Ecological Change*

Shmuel Ahituv and Eliezer D. Oren (eds.), *The Origin of Early Israel-Current Debate*

A. J. Ammerman (ed.), *The Acconia Survey*

Hans-Gert Bachmann, *The Identification of Slags from Archaeological Sites*

Anthony J. Barham and Richard I. Macphail (eds.), *Archaeological Sediments and Soils*

D. R. Brothwell, K. D. Thomas, and Juliet Clutton-Brock (eds.), *Research Problems in Zooarchaeology*

Beatrice de Cardi, *Archaeological Surveys in Baluchistan, 1948 and 1957*

J. C. Mann and M. M. Roxan (eds.), *Legionary Recruitment and Veteran Settlement During the Principate*

Martin Millett (ed.), *Pottery and the Archaeologist*

D. Price Williams, *The Tombs of the Middle Bronze Age II Period from the "500" Cemetery at Tell Fara (South)*

Richard Reece, *Excavations in Iona 1964 to 1974*

Jonathan N. Tubb (ed.), *Palestine in the Bronze and Iron Ages*

Paula J. Turner, Roman Coins from India

Margaret M. Roxan, *Roman Military Diplomas 1985 to 1993*

Margaret M. Roxan, *Roman Military Diplomas 1978 to 1984*

Margaret M. Roxan, *Roman Military Diplomas 1954 to 1977*

Empire and Local Worlds
A Chinese Model for Long-Term Historical Anthropology

Mingming Wang

Left Coast Press inc.

Walnut Creek, California

LEFT COAST PRESS, INC.
1630 North Main Street, #400
Walnut Creek, CA 94596
http://www.LCoastPress.com

ISBN 978-1-59874-404-0 hardcover
ISBN 978-1-59874-405-7 paperback

Library of Congress Cataloguing-in-Publication Data:

Wang, Mingming.
Empire and local worlds : a Chinese model for long-term historical
anthropology / Mingming Wang.
p. cm.—(Publications of the Institute of Archaeology, University
College, London.)
Includes bibliographical references and index.
ISBN 978-1-59874-404-0 (hardback : alk. paper)—ISBN 978-1-59874-405-7
(pbk. : alk. paper)
1. Ethnology—China—Guangzhou. 2. Ethnohistory—China—Guangzhou. 3.
Guangzhou (China)—Historiography. 4. Guangzhou (China)—Social life and
customs. 5. China—History—Ming dynasty, 1368-1644. 6.
China—History—Qing dynasty, 1644-1912. I. Title.
GN635.C5W357 2009
306.0951'27—dc22
2009013031

Printed in the United States of America

∞™ The paper used in this publication meets
the minimum requirements of American
National Standard for Information Sciences
—Permanence of Paper for Printed Library
Materials, ANSI/NISO Z39.48–1992.

09 10 11 12 13   5 4 3 2 1

Contents

Figures and Tables

Foreword

Stephan Feuchtwang

Wang Mingming is a Chinese anthropologist well versed in English-language anthropology. He is China's most prolific published writer of anthropological studies, essays, and histories. He has written this book in English rather than in his mother tongue after the publication of his earlier work on the city of Quanzhou in Southeast China (Wang Mingming, *Shiqu de Fanrong: Yizuo Laocheng del Lishi Renleixue Kaocha [The Bygone Prosperity: A Historical Anthropological Study of an Old City]* Hangzhou: Zhejiang Renmn Chubanshe, 1999). The argument is a continuity, but the focus is now different. The book now frames its narrative in a narrower and thoroughly explored space: a system of territorial neighborhoods locally known as *pujing* [wards and precincts], engaging, as broadly as the earlier book did, world system, dynastic, and regional histories.

In it, Wang Mingming reverses the perspective of historical anthropologists who, even when they are as enlightened as Marshal Sahlins, still take European civilization as a template. Wang Mingming takes Chinese civilization as his template and comments on Sahlins, Norbert Elias, Eric Wolf, and many others as he writes the city of Quanzhou into a history of China and its maritime trade.

For the structure of conjunctures, or events, he substitutes the pulse of civilization in a highly important margin, from its absorption as a principality to its defense against hostile empires, showing how this city became one of the biggest ports in the empire and how its life as a city of commerce and culture was in turn fostered and suppressed, deemed chaotic in positive and negative senses—to be fostered, because chaos is creative, to be restrained and purified, because chaos is disorder. In these pulses of change, the city's elites changed from outward-looking and cosmopolitan rulers of a city of many religions to sponsors and patrons of local territorial temples and their rival festivals who affected the center of empire not just by channeling new religions into it, or just bringing to it luxury products and money, but also as neo-Confucian statesman themselves, promoted to the center of the empire.

As an historical ethnography, this book focuses on the forms of the city, the layout and cosmology of its divisions and its shape. It describes the maturation of city walls into that of a regional capital and ends with their destruction by modernizers seeking to strengthen China by ridding themselves of the weight of a defeated empire. It describes the changing cartography of the world seen from its (Chinese) civilizational and imperial center as the city changes in its constant triple functions, as military, ritual, and mercantile central place.

Another historian of China, David Faure, corrects anthropologists of localities by showing how the local—be it of lineage, of temple, of trade, or of ethnicity—has imperial origins and, in the other direction, that the empire is a state built of localities in all their variety, according to the time and the condition in which they were incorporated into the state. Wang Mingming does this, too, but adds the vital anthropological counterpoint of local re-appropriation of centrally projected institutions.

For Wang Mingming, a long historical view is essential, to see how assertions of central authority turn to local assertions of own authority and in turn central responses to lower-level re-appropriations of their own initiatives, back and forth across centuries. It is also necessary to correct the rather glib analytic category of "elites" by greater specification into representatives of the imperial court, regional powerful personages, and local social groups and their leaders. Most vital, we need to grapple with the idea of civilization as an active noun or a verb [*jiaohua*], a project, or rather a projection, correcting "degeneration" and revitalizing its localities. Civilization is organized projection and installation of low-level urban place organization in a long-term pattern of open, tributary, and colonial expansion, then a closure of borders and always a civilizing effort from an imperial center. It is also the appropriation of this organization into eccentric and protodemocratic territorial cults, in turn revitalized and brought under control, a pulse of the ordering of chaos and the creativity of chaos. Each, the center and the locality, projects its own hierarchies of authority. Each is reliant on the other for its imagery. The civilizing project can be specified, for instance, in alternating projections of the category "ghosts" [*gui*] from benign to morally punitive, from effective and responsive soldiers to frightening agents of catastrophe (plague, piracy, invasion). The book ends with the city's leaders mounting, out of its usual season and on a far greater scale, a ritual of Universal Salvation, held in 1896, a year after the imperial defeat by Japan, in which the whole population was mobilized to mourn, cleanse, and strengthen itself by caring for the orphan souls of soldiers and neglected ancestors, a reconnection to its defeated past.

Chinese historians and other literary producers and recorders of the Chinese empire's civilizing project have produced many terms for describing its cosmology and its historical processes of change. Anthropologists need to take these into account at many levels, not just by regarding them as emic or native concepts but by working through them to produce adequate descriptive concepts. Wang Mingming has in this book gone a long distance with this work. For instance, he uses his analysis of Quanzhou to take issue with Eric Wolf's concept of a tributary mode of production by showing how imperial China is both feudal and Asiatic and neither. He shows how the same concept, in the hands of another historical anthropologist of China, Hill Gates, cannot accommodate the cosmological or civilizational aspects of empire and furthermore fixes it wrongly as an enemy of trade and commerce, whereas often and in large areas of its regime the empire encouraged commerce as an expansion of its tax base.

Wang Mingming shows how we need to develop a comparative study of civilization. By way of comparison, Wang Mingming demonstrates how Chinese civilization became an equivalent of Norbert Elias's civilizing process and how it differed from it: Chinese civilization was not the civilizational project of absolute monarchs presiding over the tensions between nobility and an emergent bourgeoisie after the breaking up of the Holy Roman Empire. It was similarly "modern"—indeed it was, now referring to Michel Foucault, a kind of governmentality. But Chinese civilization was that of ritual governmentality, of what Wang Mingming calls "bureaucratic spectacles." This kind of civilization—the active noun—consisted in empire-building, similar to nation-building, except that it started much earlier in the tenth century and was most forcefully implemented by the first Ming emperor in the fourteenth century. This civilization was government by exemplary rites, accompanying surveillance plus punishment, levies, labor-service, and tax but not surveillance for the husbanding of productivity even though it often encouraged commerce and always left open the possibilities of formally illegal but not prevented trade. Chinese civilization in the late imperial period was a drawing and a garrisoning of borders of the Divine Prefectures [*shenzhou*] and the rule of justice or equity, a rule of differential reciprocity, which can itself be described as a ritual economy of mutual obligation and respect. It was education through ritual performance to turn subjects within those borders into the civilized [*huanei*] and keep at bay and as tributaries various degrees of the uncivilized [*huawai*], whereas before the tenth century there was no such clear differentiation of the civilized in one bordered territory. Until this impulse of homogenization, there were simply the civilized and the uncivilized in the world Under Heaven [*Tianxia*].

This is a history of a civilization with three related patterns of time. Imperial time is an alternation in which sage rule by sage emperors and sage ministers replaces and is followed by confused rule by confused emperors. Regional time is a pulse of closure or opening, a mythical or folkloric pulse of the city, of Quanzhou as a carp flourishing or being caught in imperial nets of control. Local time is transformation and appropriation, turning garrison command into militia of local families and their strong men organized around cults and festivals of gods. Each scales up from the local in different ways: to the civilizing cosmos of orthodox neo-Confucianism; to the cosmological image of a landscape and its *fengshui*; or up in the command hierarchy of gods and congregations of gods. None of this is apparent unless seen through a long-term historical glass. History is not visible simply as culture, however structural, or as a counterpoint of great and little traditions, or as a place-for-itself or as a place-as-part of something far bigger (empire or nation). It has to be seen historically as phases of the reordering of Chinese society and politics.

A long view such as this is written against the grain of presentism, which emphasizes the discontinuity of modern and national from premodern imperial. It is written against a museum nostalgia for Quanzhou's heyday as a maritime, cosmopolitan metropolis, of the city as a tourist brand. Instead, it demonstrates a patterned history that includes the present and all the phases through which the genealogy of the neighborhood territorial division of the city can be traced in archives, living materials such as festivals, archaeological materials such as commemorative steles and the remains of city walls, and copious documents and publications.

This is a pioneering work of urban and historical anthropology. It is the work of a highly accomplished and refreshingly non-Western anthropologist.

London, April 2008

Acknowledgments

In my many years of researching Quanzhou, I have benefited a great deal from my teachers, including the archaeologists Zhuang Wei Ji and Ye Wen Cheng and the anthropologists Chen Guo Qiang, Huang Shu Min, David Parkin, Stuart Thompson, and Elizabeth Croll, as well as from a great number of senior colleagues, including the anthropologists Fei Xiao Tong, Stephan Feuchtwang, Marshall Sahlins, and James Watson and the local historians Fu Jin Xing and Wang Lian Mao, whose inspiration, encouragement, and support have been invaluable.

The Chinese Ministry of Education and the British Council sponsored my studies in London between 1987 and 1993. The Central Research Fund of the University of London funded the period of my fieldwork back home in Quanzhou between 1989 and 1991, and Beijing University granted me time to make many return visits during the past fifteen years. I would like to take this opportunity to express my gratitude to these organizations.

In 2000, the University of Chicago provided me with a six-month visiting professorship, during which I began to write this book. My time there was very rewarding. In particular, I would like to thank Professor Marshall Sahlins for arranging my visit and making me feeling at home in a foreign place.

Besides local gazetteers and dynastic histories, I have used several collections of archival materials compiled by local historians, to whom my tributes should be paid.

I have used some of the materials I had used elsewhere—for instance, those in "Quanzhou: The Chinese City as Cosmogram," *Cosmos*, 16(1) (1994): 3–25; "Place, Administration, and Territorial Cults in Late Imperial China: A Case Study from South Fujian," *Late Imperial China*, 16(2) (1995): 33–78; and "Mapping 'Chaos': The Dong Xi Fo Feuds of

Quanzhou, 1644–1839" in Stephan Feuchtwang, (ed.), *Making Place: State Projects, Globalization and Local Responses*, pp. 33–60 (London 2004a). I thank Professors William Rowe, Emily Lyle, and Stephan Feuchtwang, the editors of these articles, who helped a lot in my earlier efforts of analyzing these data.

Professors Stephan Feuchtwang, Mayfair Yang, Andrew Strathern, and Dr. Pamela Stewart read the earlier draft of the book and gave important suggestions for revision. I thank them for their support of my work and for their efforts in helping me to produce the final draft. My gratitude is also due Professor Mike Rowlands, whose encouragement has been invaluable. John Osburg, a Ph.D. candidate in the Department of Anthropology at the University of Chicago, carefully read through a later draft of this book and made many important corrections and provided useful suggestions for wording and sentencing; Zhang Fan, a graduate student at Beijing University, helped me create the index. I thank them for their important support.

Beijing, March 2009

Notes on Transliteration and Bibliography

1. I follow the official Chinese *pinyin* system in transliterating most Chinese personal and place names. There are exceptions: for instance, for widely known and accepted forms such as "Confucius" and "China," I have followed popular usages. In transliterating personal names, I assign each character a "word"—for instance, Fei Xiao Tong—but the names of the authors who have published in English are transliterated in the manner in which they appear in the publication.

2. For technical considerations, when quoting from official histories and gazettes, I indicate only the specific *juan* (volume or sections) to which I have referred. A few exceptions are those of the new editions of the histories and gazetteers from which I cite particular sentences. The compiling work of most imperial official histories and gazetteers was led by senior scholar-officials whose statuses were somewhat different from that of "editors." In order to acknowledge this distinction, I have chosen to refer to them as "compilers" instead of "editors," both in the text and in the bibliography.

3. Most of the widely known classics I cite, such as *The Analects*, are not included in the bibliography. I simply indicate the source at the end of the quotation—for example, (*Analects*: 3).

4. Chinese journals published on the mainland are not organized into "volumes." Instead, they are categorized as certain issues published in particular years. I follow this mainland system of classification when citing from these journals throughout the book.

Prelude

In September 1997, a group of specialists went to Leiden to participate in a conference on maritime trade and socio-economic development in Song-Yuan (tenth to fourteenth centuries) Quanzhou. They made a wide range of contributions, covering "socio-political, economic, and archaeological topics, and referring to local contemporary developments in Quanzhou, to interregional trade relations such as the trade between Quanzhou and India or Thailand, and also to carrying out investigations into developments in areas overseas."[1] By engaging Quanzhou from a distance, they were to rethink the distinction between the East and the West. Following a recent critique of the Euro-Centrism of the "world system,"[2] they presented a number of perspectives from which the coastal Chinese city can be viewed as one of the central metropolises of pre-European "world trade" and "industrialism." With the support of abundant materials, they demonstrated that from 1000 to 1400 C.E., Quanzhou's commerce was greatly advanced. It featured "international" and supraregional trade ties, a highly commercialized city, and an industrialized hinterland. The city itself was a space in which merchants from different parts of the world frequently interacted. Furthermore, given that the central government and members of the ruling elites engaged in trade, the demarcation between official tributary trade and "illegal private" trade was ambiguous. All these

---

[1] Angela Schottenhammer, Introduction to her edited, *The Emporium of the World: Maritime Quanzhou, 1000–1400* (Leiden 2001), p. 3.

[2] Janet Abu-Lughod, *Before European Hegemony: The World System in A.D. 1250* (New York 1989).

factors, proving the city to be "the emporium of the world," seem to have questioned the widely accepted perception that Chinese, by contrast with Europeans, were never interested in trade as a commercial undertaking.[3]

Around the same time, the bureaucrats in the local government of Quanzhou were spending lengthy days on a large conservation project. Not concerned with the intricacies of academic debate, they simply showed a firm belief in history. They aimed to preserve an assortment of relics honoring "Quanzhou's tradition of openness" [Quanzhou *de kaifang chuantong*]. In accordance with China's "open door policy," previously the Bureau of Culture of the municipal government had made efforts to promote local culture for purpose of "letting the world know Quanzhou, letting Quanzhou go to the world" [*rang shijie liaojie* Quanzhou, *rang* Quanzhou *zouxiang shijie*]. Now, the bureaucrats and technocrats of urban planning put forward a clearly formulated set of political guidelines for the same purpose. Following these guidelines, various historical sites related to the history of maritime trade, to Quanzhou's role as the "starting point of Maritime Silk Roads," and, in a word, to Quanzhou's exemplary history of China's "open past" were enlisted to receive special care.

Today, visitors to Quanzhou would be guided to such monuments of maritime trade, the relics of the "golden age." What the visitors are told is not all unconvincing. But when presented with the "truth" of the official account, a thoughtful person may be skeptical. Were we to look a little more closely at the cultural landscapes of Quanzhou, we would soon discover that local history is more complex than it is represented.

A few years ago, for purpose of making Quanzhou a truer "coastal city" [*haibin chengshi*], the designers working in the Municipal Office of Urban Planning took the task of making use of their skills in re-orienting the city toward the Bay of Quanzhou. They hoped that by placing the city closer to "oceanic civilization" it would embrace the "blue" and "transparent" maritime world together with its energy and modernism radiating from the West. They re-envisaged the history of the city. They redefined what had just been endorsed as a local expression of ancient China's "liberalism" paradoxically as a "feudal enclosure."

Mr. Huang, the director of the Office, once told me: "Without direct openings to the maritime world, old Quanzhou did not deserve the name of a port city." It was true that even in the heyday of its commerce, the city kept a fairly large distance from the harbor. Not located on the coast, it

---

[3] Several years later, these papers were collected and edited by Angela Schottenhammer and published in a volume entitled *The Emporium of the World: Maritime Quanzhou 1000–1400* (Leiden 2001). Some of their arguments are echoed by Jack Goody's recent critique: "the impressions derived from 'Orientalism' often treat the East and the West as following totally different trajectories in the medieval period." Especially see Jack Goody, *Food and Love: A Cultural History of East and West* (London 1998), pp. 272–274.

was not really a "port city." It was at pains to maintain a balance between the coast and the inland. Ancient Quanzhou did have some linkages and openings to the outside world, but as an imperial city it was, after all, an enclosure. Established on a plain already protected by the mountain range in the north and the Jinjiang River in the south, it was further enclosed by long city walls and moats that functioned to shield off external challenges. The city was founded in the early eighth century. It was bounded by a rectangular wall, shaped to symbolize the Earth (and thus the presence of imperial power) and to ensure the safety of the government. Expanded in the tenth century, the outer shape of the city became irregular. The government compound remained at the city center. Rebuilt and consolidated in later periods, the city walls appeared to have had a majestic look to them, described in classical Chinese as *wei* [power and prestige].[4] Looking at the imperial maps of Quanzhou region, we could also agree with the theory that a fear of the sea always dominated the minds of the imperial official-scholars. In the imperial maps of the region, the sea was depicted with a threatening aspect, "its violent wave and undulations and fierce splashes of surf," which, as the Western historian of China Richard Smith argues, was in sharp contrast with Western cartographies. In Western cartographies, the distant waters are represented as symbols of the exploration of the unknown. By contrast, "Chinese cartographers have devoted their primary attention to rivers and inland waterways. Even Chinese coastal waters reflect predominantly administrative concerns—in particular the suppression of smuggling and piracy."[5]

My book is written in an age of paradox. Given the many major social, political, and intellectual problems of our time, the problem of how to understand the history of Quanzhou—one of the modern world's "peripheral places"—sounds radically trivial. However, the history of Quanzhou has attracted a great deal of attention not only locally but also nationally and internationally. Consequentially, the history of the city has been narrated into several stories. As an assemblage of facts and artifacts, it has been used to critique Orientalist comparisons in the West, and it has been deployed as a model for revitalizing local tradition in the East, just as its imperial architectures has been taken as a reminder of "Oriental despotism." These narratives have enveloped certain big issues sufficiently typical of the paradox of the contemporary world. In the twenty-first century, the care for the local worlds has continued to "enhance" the energy of the larger world. Orientalism, Occidentalism, and, more usually, the synthesis of the two have survived the violence of

---

[4] So, Kee-long, *Prosperity, Region, and Institutions in Maritime China: The South Fukien Pattern, 946–1368* (Cambridge, MA: 2000), pp. 164–165.
[5] Richard Smith, *Chinese Maps* (Hong Kong 1996), p. 5.

time to work as conceptual forces feeding on and transcending the same realms of the local.

History is like the "other" in anthropology; it can be conceptualized into different "mirrors" that often distort the "original." I cannot pretentiously exempt myself from this tendency. But noting the fact, I dare claim to be more aware of our own intellectual paradoxes. In my mind, one of such paradoxes has resulted from our own conceptualizing endeavors. The problem is not that we have not paid sufficient attention to historical specificities; rather, it is that many of us have sought too anxiously to derive monolithic concepts from complexly related historical processes. Because we are different persons and with different worldviews, the conceptual types we have constructed are self-contained and diverse and, in many cases, mutually conflicting. I am not suggesting that conceptual types as "historical metaphors" merely reflect the "mythical realities" of intellectuals (despite that in a lot of cases they do).[6] Nor am I intending to argue that all types are useless. I am simply pointing to the fact that "inducing" a singular conceptual type from complexly related historical processes is often not all that different from deducing a metaphysical concept. Paying attention to the fact, and trying to draw from it something for our learning, I turn to a possibility: to make sense of the history of a place such as Quanzhou, we need to focus on its "confusion," the blend of different orders in a sort of spatial propensity, "a type of types" offering us opportunities for a different sorts of deduction.

Perhaps anthropologist Marshall Sahlins's redefinition of the idealized *polis* as the "publicly authorized discourse" can be a good beginning of our discussion. As Sahlins puts it:

> In the *polis*, "an organization constituted by its self-awareness as a human community, the *arche* (sovereign power) "came to be everybody's business" (women and slaves, as usual, excepted). Rotating the authority among the several groups of citizens, thus making domination and submission alternating sides of the same relationships, rendering its decisions by public debate among equals in the public square, hence as open covenants openly arrived at, so elevating speech to preeminence over all other instruments of power, speech that was no longer the compelling ritual word pronounced from on high but an argument to be judged as persuasive in the light of wisdom and knowledge verifiable by all as something called truth, the *polis*, by these and many other means, subjected social action to the collective will and made men conscious of their history as human action.[7]

---

[6] Surely, by "historical metaphors" and "mythical realities," the anthropologist Marshall Sahlins's vocabulary refers to the cultural and cosmological quality of history, but not simply to intellectual representations. See Marshall Sahlins, *Historical Metaphors and Mythical Realities: Structure of the Early History of the Sandwich Islands Kingdom* (Ann Arbor 1981).

[7] Marshall Sahlins, *Islands of History* (Chicago 1985), p. 34.

In classical China, as in ancient Greece, there were several definitions of the city. But in the Chinese definitions, historical action had been portrayed differently from the *polis*. Unlike the Greek *polis*, which referred to the sphere wherein "the most talkative of all body politics" gained independence,[8] the Chinese concept of the city had little to do with the "sphere of freedom" in discourse. In classical Chinese, three pictographs were used to refer to the city. These were *yi*, *guo*, and *cheng*. *Yi* denotes an enclosed space situated above and surrounded by people on their knees below. *Guo* depicts the enclosure itself and is composed of two elements, a square of city walls and a group of soldiers with weapons to guard the enclosed space. *Cheng* refers to the completed city walls. Furthermore, the classical Chinese city is different from the *polis* in that it is more akin to an extended castle that enclosed all the populace of the city under its own protection. The ambition to encompass the guarded subjects as expressed in all the three pictographs makes the classical Chinese city distinct from the *polis*, whose "sovereignty" relies heavily on public action in the realm of discourse.

In translating the word *city*, modern Chinese intellectuals have struggled to rediscover the closest counterparts in classical Chinese characters that best convey the modern notion of the city. Apart from *guo* (in classical periods referring to both a city and a state), two characters have been found to make up a dual pictograph word: *cheng* [garrison] and *shi* [market].

As we just said, the term *cheng* originally refers to "walls," "enclosures," or "defensive structures." Referring to "urban centers," it also carries the meaning of "powers residing in force," in which the distinction between governed civilization [*wen*] from ungoverned wilderness [*ye*] is also conveyed. The term *shi*, which also appeared in classical periods, instead refers to a location selected by people for its convenience in communication and to a nexus point in space where social exchanges are concentrated. Surely, the "elementary form" of *shi* is a marketplace. But it is not merely such. The notion of *shi* transcends the idea of a marketplace to encompass a large collection of things, including moving people, flowing goods, reciprocated gifts, and alternating symbols.

In his *China's Gentry*, Fei Xiao Tong, one of the greatest Chinese anthropologists of the twentieth century, postulates that *cheng* and *shi* can be differentiated conceptually as two types of towns, "the garrison-town as the seat of traditional bureaucratic authority and the wealthy gentry, and the market town as a link between the peasants' local industry and more highly developed commerce and manufacturing."[9] In his book, Fei brings forward much evidence to support his typology.

[8] Hannah Arendt, *The Human Condition* (Chicago 1958), pp. 30–31.
[9] Fei, Xiao Tong (Hsiao-tung Fei), *China's Gentry: Essays in Rural-Urban Relations* (Chicago 1953), p. 104.

We can find in Fei's work the usefulness of sociological typology, but we should not be led by it to turn away from the observation that the two "types" are virtually inseparable from each other. In remote areas distant from the locations of *cheng* [garrisons], "townization" could have been achieved through the evolution of *shi*. But in most other examples, even a small *shi* was not isolated from a *cheng*, and, conversely, a *cheng* is dependent on a *shi*, which it was installed to incorporate, protect, control, and/or enact, and it was built so that it could feed itself from it. In a larger town, the two "gestures" of *cheng* and *shi* often came simultaneously to distinguish, not only in politico-economic terms but also in symbolic-cosmological ways, the urban from the rural. And it should be emphasized that in the dual composition of *chengshi*, the sense of *cheng* usually outweighed the sense of *shi*, in the way in which the former encompassed the latter as to what was to be protected and enhanced as a lower member of its designated hierarchy.

Historical Quanzhou was such an example.[10] In the third century, smaller rural settlements and market towns created by Chinese migrants living on the southeast coast began to "crystallize" into larger places.[11] Soon, the Wu (221–280 C.E.), one of the three contesting kingdoms centering on the Lower Yangze River, conquered the area and established Fengzhou [Harvest Town], a county seat situated to the northwest of the current city.[12] The small walled town of Fengzhou was the beginning of Quanzhou's urban history. But the transition that occurred in the fifth year of Wude Reign (623) of the Tang Dynasty was even more important. In that year, the region was formally designated a prefecture, "Wurong Zhou" ["Prefecture of Military Glories"].[13] By 700 C.E., the area had changed from a loosely administered prefecture centered in the garrison-town of Fengzhou into a higher level administrative region. In the process, the urban center also moved southward to the current location. In 711, the name *Quanzhou* [literally, Spring Prefecture] was

---

[10] For a comprehensive survey of documents about the changes of Quanzhou's historical geography, see *Quanzhou Fangyu Jiyao [Materials of Historical Geography of Quanzhou]*, Office of Local Gazetteers (Quanzhou 1985).

[11] See Hugh Clark, *Community, Trade, and Networks: Southern Fujian Province from the Third to the Thirteenth Century* (Cambridge 1991).

[12] Wu Kingdom was one of the three contesting states emerging in the Chinese world after the decline of the Han empire in 220. The other two states were Wei (220–265) and Shu (221–263). The three states respectively controlled the southeast (Wu), southwest (Shu), and the north (Wei) of China.

[13] The connotation of *Wurong* was in line with the spirit of the elegiac title of the great Tang conqueror and founder Li Yuan's reign—*Wude*, or "Military Virtue." The place name *Wurong Zhou* suggests by itself that in most decades of the seventh century the Quanzhou was more or less a garrison-town.

first endorsed.[14] The term has since also been used to officially refer to an extensive municipal region.[15]

Quanzhou as a regional city for imperial administration emerged well before the heyday of maritime trade. This fact does not imply that interregional trade had become possible only after the State established garrisons and sites of civilization; rather it merely suggests that the enclosed spaces of *cheng* were important factors in the "marketization" of the town. With this point in mind, we are not surprised to see that after having spent long years in studying Song-Yuan Quanzhou, an economic historian specializing in the study of Song-Yuan Quanzhou has concluded that "the State played an important role" in the making of the commercial city.[16]

I do not mean to suggest that the two conjoined elements of the Chinese city have not remained in a stable hierarchical structure. In my understanding, despite that *cheng*'s dominance over *shi* was ideologically "the usual way," in the historical processes of a particular place, or even in those of the actual alternating dynasties of the empire, interactions between *cheng* and *shi*, including the rise and fall (described in Chinese as *xiaozhang*) of the relative strengths of them were encompassed as flexible propensities of the *cheng*.

In *The City in Time and Space*, Aiden Southall expresses his viewpoint on the Chinese city, which as a synthesis of two equally remarkable aspects, has obviously fascinated him for a long time:

> The sublime grandeur and vast expanses of the city's cosmic symbolism, displayed in its physical structure of walls, gates, temples, altars, and palaces, enacted in its splendid imperial processions and awesome sacrifices, heavy with ritual, more and more infused with power; on the other hand, the ongoing bustle of townsfolk and merchants, the immerse variety of goods, the colorful cosmopolitan crowds, the paralleled richness of exquisite dishes, irresistible aromas, fabled delights, and voluptuous pleasures unstintingly offered with sumptuous profusion and enchanting grace.[17]

---

[14] During the 940s, the municipality was upgraded to the level of Jun, or command-province, and was renamed Qingyuan [Clear Source], previously referring to the springs in the mountains to the north of the city. In the year of 985 (the early Song), the name Quanzhou was once again adopted, and it has since continued to refer to both the prefecture and the city. See *Licheng Quzhi* [*The Gazette of Licheng Borough*] 2 Vols., Office of Local Gazetteers, Quanzhou (Beijing 1999), Vol. 1, pp. 3–12.

[15] Currently, Quanzhou Municipality comprises six rural counties, four newly established "county-level cities" [*xianji shi*] and three central urban districts (two of which were established just a few years ago). All are administered by the municipal government whose office compounds are situated at the center of the city of Quanzhou.

[16] As he argues, the Song and the Yuan governments adopted a policy favoring overseas trade. This "opened a much wider range of economic opportunities for coastal communities" and "generated a new source of revenue for the government at both the central and the local levels." So, *Prosperity, Region, and Institutions in Maritime China*, p. 282.

[17] Aidan Southall, *The City in Time and Space* (Cambridge 1998), p. 151.

Adding to Southall's point, I would say that although the splendor of convergence continued to characterize the Chinese city, in different historical periods, the blending of the two aspects or, more symbolically, "gestures" of the city yielded different compositions of urban form. But how did the interactions of the two "gestures" come into play and make history? To what extent can we describe the different compositions of urban form as historical transformations? What do the conjunctures implicate for our anthropological pursuit of history? The questions remain to be answered.

The Carp, the Imperial Nets, and Its Loopholes

Anthropologists in the West are principally concerned with "other histories" far away from the *polis* and equally distant from locations such as the Chinese *chengshi*. Many of them have agreed that history as envisaged and re-enacted with the image of the *polis* should be situated among other cultural orders and modes, especially "mythologies." From "mythologies," anthropologists draw a comparison, as Levi-Strauss suggests in his *Tristes Tropiques*, to show that the basis of human existence is not to be discovered in Western civilization but to be found in the timelessness of remote peoples.[18] Recently, they have also admitted that the "type" discovered through investigation of remote peoples, admittedly a never realized form, has been in contact with the expansive civilization of the *polis*. To understand the relationship between "mythologies" and "histories" in the modern age, Sahlins has dwelt on "islands of history" (or, in fact, "cultures without cities") with the enlightenment of which he has sought to discover a kind of historical anthropology that is needed to show the privilege of the civilizing.

I venture to claim to be also a historical anthropologist. But I have derived my perspective from my own country but not a remote island. The lengthy distance between the *polis* and Quanzhou city should be admitted. Were we to adopt traditional Chinese cosmography, the "other" for the Chinese would be the *polis*, which, together with all the island peoples and kingdoms in the maritime world, had come to be known as "island barbarians" [*daoyi*] for the millennium between the tenth century and the end of the Qing Empire. However, I have chosen a different viewpoint. Locating China at the ambiguous space, I hope to work with a comparison, applying it to adapt historical anthropology into a new departure: a step toward an understanding of the transformative combinations in the Chinese city as a new mode of historiography.

---

[18] Claude Levi-Strauss, *Tristes Troipiques* (New York 1997 [1973]), p. 477.

I go into detail later about what this attempt implies. At this preliminary stage, let me briefly note a few things about Quanzhou, from which I hope to draw out a new mode of narration.

First, I should note that Quanzhou has been known by several other names. One of these was Jinjiang, which often appeared in imperial official gazetteers of the region.[19] Another was Zaitun, originally a Persian and, later, Italian (mis)translation of the flower, thorny paulownia, which Liu Congxiao, one of the most powerful municipal governors of the tenth century, planted all around the city.[20] In most decades of the twentieth century, the prefecture was officially designated as the Municipal Region of Quanzhou [*Quanzhou Diqu*], an exception being the Maoist years (1949–1976). During Mao's time, the city continued to be called "Quanzhou," but the municipality was redefined as Jinjiang (after the name of a rural county situated to the south of the city). Between the late 1950s and the 1970s, the city comprised several urban "communes" [*gongshe*], a system of "administrative and productive places" that first appeared in the countryside and then transplanted into the city.

Quanzhou, Zaitun, Jinjiang, and so forth have been used by different regimes to name the same place, and these names contain their own stories of origin and characterization. Each of these has a genealogy of historical linkages. For instance, the Maoist regime's redefinition of Quanzhou as Jinjiang, together with its installation of communes in the city, simply reminds us of several historical moments—such as those that we will encounter later—in which the "ruralization" of a commercial town named Quanzhou and Zaitun was deemed central to those who (such as, Zhu Yuan Zhang, the first emperor of the Ming) despised the "moral decay" of the city and hoped to build their own "power centers" on the same foundation.

In an inspiring way, Sahlins argues for us that "people act upon circumstances according to their own cultural presuppositions, the socially given categories of persons and things" with which people also respond to the "worldly circumstances of human action."[21] With the point in mind, we pay attention to the "signs" with which people envisage the world as social categories in places. Place names turn out to be good examples. So

---

[19] Jinjiang originally referred to the river running from northwest to southeast outside the southern city walls. Most often, it was used to designate the county seat of Jinjiang situated to the south of the river. But sometimes, the prefecture of Quanzhou was also called Jinjiang. When it was called Jinjiang, it had a dual role: it was at the same time the capital of the prefecture and the town center of the county called Jinjiang.

[20] Meanwhile, in the essays and poems written by the literati, Quanzhou has often appeared as *Wenling*, or "Warm Hills." See *Licheng Quzhi* [*The Gazette of Licheng Borough*] 2 Vols., Vol. 1, p. 3.

[21] Sahlins, *Historical Metaphors and Mythical Realities*, p. 67.

to begin with, let us focus on a recent event in which their histories have been re-enacted as patterns of transformation.

In the early 1980s, in order to reform the system of local administration (and perhaps also to restart the engine of urbanization), the State changed all the urban "communes" into "street offices" [*jiedao ban*]. Also, to distinguish the municipal city from its surrounding regions, it decided to change the names of municipal boroughs. The State Council instructed all municipalities and boroughs to abandon their Maoist place names. Having received the instruction, the municipal government in Quanzhou transferred this task downward. Several local historians were called to work in the newly established Office of Place Names [*Diming Ban*], toward a new name. After having completed some detailed studies, they rediscovered the old name of "Carp City" and proposed that the city of *Quanzhou* should be replaced by *Licheng*, or "Carp City."[22]

The historians said that the term "Carp City" sounded most consistent with the tradition of the historical city.[23] The name "Carp City" was ancient. Together with other place names, it had been used to refer to Quanzhou in ancient times (indeed it began to be used as one of the alternative names of Quanzhou approximately seven centuries ago).[24] They also said that Carp City was quite special. Compared with the place's other names, it was more of a loan-word from the local dialect, and, as such, it could help revitalize the cultural character of ancient Quanzhou. Their superiors accepted their proposition.

It is a fact that in the local dialect of Quanzhou the meaning of Carp City is especially rich. If a visitor asks why their place is called Carp City, locals would say that it is because the city looked "exactly like a tail of carp." Pointing to the Clear Source Mountain [*Qingyuan Shan*] to the north of the city, they would advise him or her to make an excursion up to the peak, where, on one of mountain rocks they would be able to get a birds-eye view of the town. Looking down from there, they would notice that the town did indeed form the shape of a carp. On our own, we might fail to distinguish the carp shape, but with the help of local guides, we would be urged to put our imaginations to work: "Look, and see how clear this picture is! The East Gate [*Dongmen*] of the city is the mouth of the carp. It leans toward the East Lake [*Donghu*], like the mouth of the

---

[22] The results of their research can be found in the following publication: *Quanzhou Diming Zhi* [*The Gazette of Place Names in Quanzhou*], Office of Place Names (Quanzhou 1983).

[23] To the present local government, the name "Carp City" may just be meaningful because of its "selective authenticity" as an old name. But to historians, the carp, the net devised to confine or catch it, and the holes in the net that the twin pagodas created to free the carp vividly reveal some historical shifts and turns through which Quanzhou underwent many historical upheavals.

[24] *Licheng Quzhi* [*The Gazette of Licheng Borough*] 2 Vols., Vol. 1, pp. 2–3.

carp reaching for a pearl. The city and the lake come together to form a picture of the "Carp Playing with the Pearl" [*liyu xizhu*].

Different place names are based on different stories, and each story has its own significance. But the fact has not prevented locals from paying more attention to the metaphor of the Carp. The image of carp fish is an auspicious sign for the Chinese. In classical China, rendered as imperial bestowals, carp were used to honor the capable princes and scholars. A story goes that when the son of Confucius was born, the King of Lu bestowed him with a few tails of carp as an expression of his regard. So Confucius gave his son the name of Carp [*Li*]. Although we have no evidence to support the story, it is undeniable that from the classical periods to the present day, images of carp have often appeared in Chinese New Year prints [*nianhua*]. In the renowned folktale of "The Carp Leaping over the Dragon's Gate" [*Liyu Yue Longmen*] (Figure P.1), it is suggested that if a carp leaps over the Dragon's Gate it would become a dragon, and if it failed it would remain a fish. As a symbol of upward mobility and competence, a carp's tail is depicted as a trickster-destroyer of obstacles (the imperial passage of the Dragon's Gate) whose metamorphosis depends on its own capabilities. Ambiguously, the image of carp is treated as what bestows success for upwardly mobile individuals,

Figure P.1 Mural painting of *The Carp Leaping over the Dragon's Gate* (undated) (discovered in a small local temple in a neighborhood in the East Street of Quanzhou) (photo by Wang Mingming 2004).

such as traditional scholars who sought their fortunes through the imperial degree examination system [*Keju*].

The association of Quanzhou with carp partly derives from the symbolic connotation of carp as suggested in the folklore of "The Carp Leaping over the Dragon's Gate." But a more local explanation of why carp has been used to name the city of Quanzhou is also available. Folklore in Quanzhou maintains that the city had originally been planned in accordance with an excellent geomantic order. Shaped like the tail of a carp, the city's urban spaces flourished. The flow of geo-energy [*diqi*] made it possible for the city's commerce to prosper in the distant past. For the same reason, in the ancient times, the city cultivated many capable men, who had, at different stages of history, become successful and powerful scholars, officials, and merchants. Potentially also, like those carp that could leap over the Dragon's Gate and become dragons, these capable local men could even become emperors.

In ancient times, emperors realized that Carp City was a place with exceptionally good geomancy. In order to limit the city to its local confines and prevent its hidden *fengshui* [geomantic] propensities from surging into political realities, they established a new prefecture, Yongchun,[25] next to Quanzhou, envisioning it as an extensive geomantic fishing net. The net was intended to catch the Carp in Quanzhou. But the plan failed because of two tall pagodas: the Eastern and the Western Pagodas in the Buddhist Monastery of Kaiyuan Si (Figure P.2), which were constructed in the Song Dynasty and which penetrated the net and allowed the Carp to swim into the river. Local commerce continued to flourish, and Quanzhou continued to produce successful men after the emperors' failure to capture the Carp. The result was that Quanzhou enjoyed a lengthy period of prosperity.

As historians and archaeologists have revealed, from the tenth century to the early fourteenth century, the harbor in the Bay of Quanzhou, a few miles to the east of the city, was opened to trade, and the city became an important way-station on the imperial tributary-trade route, which connected a large part of China with the maritime world. In its heyday, local official and popular attitudes toward commerce were open. Local people had rather exceptionally cosmopolitan worldviews. The city enjoyed an expansion, and the hinterland became industrialized. Public life became so unrestricted that several of the world's great civilizations found their own footings in the city.

The folktale of the Carp also reveals a lot about Quanzhou's decline. As it goes, by the beginning of the Ming Dynasty (1368–1644)—which historically was the starting point of Quanzhou's decline as a commercial

---

[25] Yongchun is now one of the several counties attached to the Quanzhou Municipality.

Figure P.2 The Eastern and Western pagodas in the city of Quanzhou (photo by Wang Mingming 2004).

city (Figure P.3)—the *fengshui* propensities of Quanzhou began to concern Zhu Yuan Zhang, the founding emperor of the Ming. He feared that Carp City had the potential to yield an emperor capable of supplanting him. He sent the general and geomancer, Zhou De Xing, to re-order the original *fengshui* order of Quanzhou. As a set of *fengshui* maneuvers, Zhou De Xing built up several garrison-towns along the coast and established a great number of the imperial War God temples [*Guandi Miao*] and bridges to block the flow of energy [*qi*] in and around Carp City. These garrisons, temples, and bridges were supposed to confine the Carp to the smallest possible area. Zhou De Xing also set fire to the two great pagodas, which, to his great frustration, were preventing the fishing net from its effective operation. But the fire failed to burn down the pagodas. According to legend, the Heavenly Master of Rain [*Yushi*] was angered by Zhou De Xing's actions and released a massive rain shower to extinguish the fire. As a result, the Carp was saved from its enemies and became as energetic as ever.[26]

Zhou De Xing was in fact a real historical figure in the early Ming Dynasty. According to official historical records, he was sent by Zhu Yuan Zhang (Emperor Hongwu) as the Baron of Jiangxia [*Jiangxia Hou*] to

---

[26] This folktale of geomantic struggle was recorded by a Republican Era local intellectual, Wu Zao Ting in the 1940s. See Wu, Zao Ting, *Quanzhou Minjian Chuanshuo Ji* [*A Collection of Folk Tales and Legends in Quanzhou*] (Fuzhou 1985 [1940]), pp. 1–5.

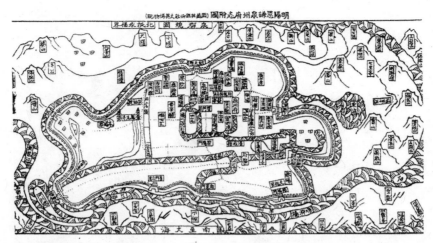

Figure P.3 The official map of Quanzhou in the Ming Dynasty (the *juan* of maps, the 1612 edition of *Quanzhou Fuzhi* [*Quanzhou Prefecture Gazette*] compiled by Yang Ming Qian).

build a line of garrison-towns along the southeast coast. In and around these garrison-towns and the militarily consolidated walled cities such as Quanzhou, Zhou De Xing sought to implement the emperor's policy of banning maritime trade [*haijin zhengce*], to draw a borderline between the Chinese world and the barbarians (including the "pirate dwarfs," *wokou*, supposedly Japanese merchant-warriors) and to pacify the coastal society.[27]

Ming Shi [*The History of the Ming Dynasty*] has a full biography of Zhou De Xing, in which the imperial historians describe him as a military general who accomplished several military campaigns against separatist rebellions in the southwest (Guizhou province) and in the southeast (Fujian province). As a reward for his loyalty and military contributions, he was called back to the imperial palace by the emperor, where he continuously received great imperial honors. In the imperial palace, he was bestowed with great personal prestige and power. Nonetheless, his good fortune did not last to the end of his life. In his later years (the twenty-fifth year of Hongwu Reign, 1393), his son plotted a conspiracy of rebellion and failed. Zhou De Xing was prosecuted along with his son

---

[27] Elsewhere, I have compared in more detail the folktale with the official biography of Zhou De Xing. As I have argued, the difference between the official and folkloric biographies of Zhou De Xing lies in the fact that the former treats Zhou De Xing as a loyal imperial hero, whereas the tale of the Carp treats him as a "folkloric bad guy." See Wang, Mingming, *Shiqu de Fanrong: Yi Zuo Laocheng de Lishi Renleixue Kaocha* [*Prosperity Bygone: A Historical Anthropology of an Old Town*] (Hangzhou 1999), pp. 154–161.

and all his family members, except for a handful who managed to escape to remote areas.[28]

A part of the folktale of the Carp also reflects on the death of Zhou De Xing. But unlike *The History of the Ming Dynasty*, it says nothing about the Zhous' conspiracy against the State. Instead, the emphasis is placed on the ways in which Zhou De Xing received the "imperial honor of suicide" bestowed by Emperor Hongwu (Zhu Yuan Zhang) as punishment for his unsuccessful campaign to destroy Quanzhou's *fengshui* order. Local folktales also say that Zhou De Xing's life ended in Quanzhou in an inauspicious geomantic "cave" [*xue*], where he lost all his potency.

The diverse inhabitants of Quanzhou have remembered their history of imperial dynasties, modern revolutions, political campaigns, and reforms from a wide array of perspectives. In contemporary Quanzhou, more and more young people have become attracted to Western fashions, fast-food restaurants, luxurious hotels, and Karaoke bars—in a word, to "the new." Nonetheless, people of different generations in Quanzhou still talk about the story of the Carp, and many are aware of the connection between the name of the town and the story of the Carp (although only a small few have mastered the full details of the story).

Undoubtedly, to many, stories of the old days such as this one have become mere comic tales that help local people form their "joking relationships." But this observation does not imply that such "fish stories" are entirely devoid of historical references and implications. As some local historians have told me, the tale of the Carp at the very least captures a moment in Quanzhou's past and offers a local representation of the emperor's fear of the local tradition of commerce that "we, the people of Quanzhou, had long ago." Historical and archaeological findings that local historians have amassed have indicated that in the dynasties prior to the Ming, Quanzhou enjoyed several centuries of prosperity. From the Tang to the Yuan dynasties, merchants from Quanzhou traveled to Southeast Asia, South Asia, the Middle East, and even to Europe. Meanwhile, locally, the people of Quanzhou were host to crowds of foreign merchants, missionaries, travelers, and explorers without reacting strongly to their foreign appearance and customs. To them, commodities flowed smoothly from place to place. In the Ming and Qing Dynasties, an official anti-maritime trade ideology was formulated and imposed on the local populace to create ideal communal order in the city.[29] The State

---

[28] *Ming Shi* [*The History of the Ming Dynasty*], compiled by Zhang, Ting Yu (1974 [1739] Beijing), *juan*, p. 132.

[29] Timothy Brook has shed important light on the ideal of "rural order" and its failure in the commercialization of late Ming. See Timothy Brook, *The Confusions of Pleasure: Commerce and Culture in Ming China* (Berkeley and Los Angeles 1998).

also imposed policies against regional "world trade"[30] that sought to re-establish the moral orthodoxy and tributary hierarchy for China. In reaction to these late imperial policies, some of the people from Quanzhou escaped into the maritime world and organized their own "kingdoms of piracy" [*haidao wangguo*].

In this study I am not pursuing a history of place-naming politics. But I do consider such a history to be relevant to our "commemoration" of the interactive drama of *cheng* and *shi*. In my view, the folktale of interactions says something about the vitality of coastal commerce and reveals "the worth and humanity of the 'inferiors' who supplied their superiors' needs."[31] In associating the city with the energetic Carp, the failed "imperial fisherman" (Zhou De Xing), and the ambivalent role of the emperor (Zhu Yuan Zhang), the folktale entertains a legend that is figured as an interactive drama of local society and supralocal powers. Not without a sense of paradox, the legend is also in a complex way conjoined (or "confused" in its neutral sense) with a popular wish to move "upward" (for example, to become "destined-to-be emperors"), including the desire to surround oneself with the "trappings of official status"[32] or to join the historical cycle of emperor-rebel reversals. Looking closely into the details of history, I find that the tales depicting the interaction of these three forces tell us a great deal about how the three main social powers in the city interacted and made history.

History and Senses of History

Excluding a great number of migrant laborers, over 200,000 residents now inhabit the urban area of 8.2 square kilometers in the borough of Carp City.[33] Such a large population is by no means homogeneous; it is divided by distinctions of gender, status, bureaucratic rank, and wealth, as well as other social, political, and economic differences. There are also ethnoreligious distinctions, with several hundred Hui (Muslim Chinese) households, a hundred or so Menggu (Mongolian), She Minority households, and other State-identified "ethnic minorities" [*shaoshu minzu*] living in the city. However, despite their diversity

---

[30] In my view, the concept "world trade" can actually be applied to pre-Ming Quanzhou's regional transcultural networks, especially when we believe that "world systems" existed prior to the Western world system of the modern age. See Janet Abu-Lughod, *Before European Hegemony: The World System in A.D. 1250* (New York 1989).

[31] Hill Gates, *China' Motor: A Thousand Years of Petty Capitalism* (Ithaca 1996), p. 176.

[32] David Faure, The emperor in the village: Representing the state in South China, in Joseph P. McDermott (ed.), *State and Court Ritual in China* (Cambridge 1999), pp. 267–298.

[33] The other districts that have now been attached to the city area as administrative units equivalent to counties include Luojiang, Fengze, and Fengzhou, all in the outskirts of Licheng.

locals proudly introduce themselves as *Quanzhou Ren* [the people of Quanzhou].

Expressing their sense of history, the people of Quanzhou speak of their city as having been an old-time seaport where commerce was highly advanced. At the same time, they also feel honored by their town being dubbed one of the "famous cities of the archives" [*wenxian mingbang*]. Another relic of local pride can be found on the front gate of Kaiyuan Temple, the largest Buddhist Monastery in Quanzhou, where it's inscribed that "the streets of Quanzhou are full of sages" [*manjie doushi shengren*]. To many inhabitants of Quanzhou, the sense of "sage" that the sentence—supposedly uttered by the great Song Neo-Confucian mentor Zhu Xi (1130–1200)—is intended to convey suggests that for centuries Quanzhou was saturated with a rich scholarly and literary culture.

In a book entitled *Reviews of the Writings by the Sagacious Persons from Quanzhou*, local historian Fu Jin Xing confirms this point by listing some 950 authors from Quanzhou. He calls them "Quanzhou's sagacious men" [*Quan xian*]. According to him, these "sagacious men" published some 2,400 books (exclusive of several hundreds missing in the turmoil of history and a nearly equal number written by modern writers). In his book, Fu Jinxing, inheriting the legacy of his forerunners in imperial times, concludes that Quanzhou deserves the name "coastal home of Confucius" [*haibin zhoulu*], which earlier inhabitants had given to their city.[34]

The ways in which writing has been perceived in Quanzhou are different from how anthropologists have seen it. Levi-Strauss, for example, saw writing as "what seems to have favored the exploitation of human beings rather than their enlightenment."[35] Following Levi-Strauss, some may read Quanzhou's literary tradition as an indication that it has long been "contaminated" by the civilizing power of the "Oriental empire." However, at least to some local historians, writing is nothing other than a virtue, derived from Quanzhou's history of social mobility and openness.

Local historians all say that the coastal city is distant from China's "central plains" [*zhongyuan*]; and for that reason, it had, in its earlier episodes of history, avoided many of the frequent catastrophes of war and dynastic replacements that plagued the north. Indeed, the ways in which Quanzhou gained good fortune by being peripheral has remained what has explained its centrality. In the events of what historians have now described as the late Tang warlord-induced "chaos" [*luan*], the

[34] Fu, Jin Xing, *Quanxian Zhuzuo Shuping* [*Reviews of Works by the Sagacious from Quanzhou*] (Xiamen 1994), p. 6

[35] Levi-Strauss, *Tristes Tropiques*, p. 361.

region accommodated many "high scholars" who fled the north to seek refuge in the south. The people of Quanzhou benefited greatly from the teachings of these migrant scholars. Furthermore, under the influence of several generations of Neo-Confucianism, starting with the Northern Song (960–1125), Quanzhou gained opportunities to give itself "more culture." Zhu Xi, one of the founders of Neo-Confucianism, was born in the hinterland of Fujian. In the middle of his career he served as a bookkeeper in one of the rural counties attached to the Quanzhou Prefecture and then as a traveling lecturer. He exerted a strong influence on the regional tradition of Quanzhou by founding several Confucian academies. For that reason, Quanzhou has also been known as "the place where "Zhu-cius passed through and brought civilization" [Zhu Zi *guohua*].

Let us take it as a challenge to identify what is contained in notion of "sage"— the personified perspective of civilization and the internalized pattern of moral order—as part of the urban form. But in so doing, we should not mean to say that one should ignore the difference that obviously exists between our own neatly defined notion of culture and local people's taken-for-granted "confusion."

In the city of Quanzhou, people have cherished their own culture as a "mixture" [*hunhe*]. Despite that several advocates of civilization in imperial times had perceived the "mixture" as harmful to the moral integrity of the Chinese, many people in Quanzhou have re-appropriated the maritime trade that flourished between the tenth and the early fourteenth centuries as perfectly consistent with the "sagacious civilization." For them, the metaphor of the Carp, which I have dwelled on at some length, embodies a perfect union of commerce and civilization.

The union, or what I referred to, somewhat disparagingly, as the "confusion," or more neutrally, as the "conjuncture," can be related to the tradition of the Song-Yuan South Fujianese merchants. These merchants supposedly shared a mentality of what economic historian So Kee-long has defined as "bounded rationality in action."[36] The content of this sort of "rationality" seems rich. So has applied it to reconsider Douglas North's concept of an "institution."[37] In his comparative study of the driving forces in economic history, North has confined his perspective to formal institutional frameworks determined by the State. By contrast, So finds himself deeply intrigued by the "informal institutional structure" in Song-Yuan Quanzhou. The notion of "informal institutional structure" derives from new institutional economics in the West. But interestingly, So argues that it was deeply rooted in the so-called informal institutions of

---

[36] So, *Prosperity, Region, and Institutions in Maritime China*, p. 275.
[37] Douglas North, *Structure and Change in Economic History* (New York 1981).

Confucian ethics, religious beliefs, and coherent lineages that contributed greatly to the prosperity of Song-Yuan Quanzhou.[38]

However, scholars interpret the "union," its local expression can be best understood locally. The spirituality of the energetic Carp can still be detected in the mood and atmosphere of social life in Quanzhou. A visitor will be surprised at how local town folks often present themselves to the outsiders by making a reference to the local proverb that "everyone in Quanzhou is fiercely competitive" [*Quanzhou Ren gege meng*]. Nobody knows when such a saying came about, but many know about its implications. Implicitly, "fiercely competitive" [*meng*] denotes the same dual implications represented by the energetic Carp, although it does not directly refer to it. It conveys the sense of competitiveness in social mobility as exemplified by the sagacious men's success in imperial exams and in different forms of higher learning, and the merchants' success in commercial affairs.

In my belief, this not only is intriguing but also is useful to our efforts to understand the long interactive drama of *cheng* and *shi*. I am an anthropologist who set out to write a history for my discipline. I have no doubt that the tales of the Carp are the stuff of legend, not history. Are they not simply dreams of *fengshui* potency? Do they not represent a certain Chinese phantasm of power? One who has sufficient academic sensitivity would be able to question the ways in which the official renaming of boroughs has echoed the vernacular histories whose interpretive power had been denounced by the same regime as "cultural survivals" to be terminated in the process of modernization. But in spite of all this, I remind myself that a history written about the city in the spirit of the Carp may be so locally engaging that it could satisfy our own curiosity for "local knowledge."

In studying local history, I have found Marshall Sahlins's works particularly enlightening in two aspects. First, Sahlins has pointed out for us the pitfalls of treating local histories simply as expressions of utilitarian rationality or as the symbolic supplies satisfying the nationalistic demands. Second, closely related to the first point, his notion that cultures exist as cosmologies of related social beings, divinities, and "natural phenomena" has profound implications for our identification of senses of history. These are especially useful for our study of Quanzhou whereby both utilitarian rationality and nationalism have been applied to "convert" local history into modern "beliefs."

However, in my analyses of specific processes, I have paid attention to the changing situations of the empire that have struck me as important. Two aspects of historical time, the cycle of separation and reunion and

---

[38] So, *Prosperity, Region, and Institutions in Maritime China*, pp. 285–286.

the rotation of open and closed empires, have come to characterize the dynastic cycles. Moreover, in the dynastic cycles, a dramatic transition took shape in the early Ming. It has drawn our attention to an analysis of the "civilizing process" concerning which European experiences have proved to be greatly more useful as a comparison.

My overall study can be regarded as an ethno-historiography of Quanzhou. Specifically, it is an anthropological interpretation stemming from a historical consideration of how the "mixture" conveyed in the metaphor of the Carp—and in the blending of *cheng* and *shi* in the concept of the city—has been achieved through time. Growing out of research focused on public life in the neighborhoods of the municipal city, the study deploys its own analysis of historical materials to map the world of time. Here, I consider senses of history (such as those expressed in the folktales surrounding the Carp) to be richer than "subjective histories." In my mind, senses of history are locally informed "narrative frameworks" in which history as process "writes itself" into several interrelated patterns.

Most economic historical studies of Quanzhou have focused on the "heyday" of the city. These authors have been obsessed with the question of what made Song-Yuan Quanzhou so prosperous. The question is not trivial. But for us, it is less eye-catching than the process by which Quanzhou emerged as an economic and administrative center, developed into a prosperous regional city (still controlled and mobilized by imperial bureaucratic apparatuses), changed into a target for the imperial civilizing project, and then fell into "chaos" [*luan*] in the period after the Mid-Ming (the fifteenth century).

G. William Skinner's inspiring synopses of Quanzhou-centered cycles suggest that the regional history of Quanzhou consists of the following stages. First, from the third century onward, gradual development and commercialization enhanced the urbanization of the region. By the twelfth century, the economy of the southeast coast was highly commercialized and made up of an extensive overseas trade network that became centered in Quanzhou but reached as far as India, the Middle East, Africa, and the margins of Europe.[39] Throughout most of the thirteenth and fourteenth centuries, owing to government encouragement and the further expansion of merchant power, the economy of Quanzhou reached its heyday. Religious life was characterized by a famous plurality. Urban culture was

---

[39] Concerning these prosperous centuries, local historians have published extensive studies. In the past decades, foreign historians (especially see Yoshinobu Shiba, *Commerce and Society in Sung China* [Ann Arbor 1970]; G. William Skinner, Presidential address: The structure of Chinese history, *Journal of Asian Studies*, 42(2) [1985]: 271–292) and archaeologists (Richard Pearson, Li Min, and Li Guo, Port city and hinterland: Archaeological perspectives on Quanzhou and its overseas trade, in Angela Schottenhammer [ed.], *The Emporium of the World*, pp. 177–236) has also produced enlightening studies.

cosmopolitanism in outlook. But in the transition from the Yuan to the Ming, and especially after the establishment of the Ming Dynasty, coastal maritime trade was banned. As a consequence of this change, the center of regional economy shifted out of Quanzhou. From the perspective of the macro-region, it was replaced, in the late sixteenth century, by the newly established Moon Harbor [*Yuegang*] in Zhangzhao Prefecture, which was in turn replaced by a Xiamen-Fuzhou-centered cycle "inspired" by foreign imperialism—in the mid-nineteenth century.[40]

In terms of the Carp folktale, what Quanzhou experienced during the early Ming was a reversal of fortune. Historically, the turning point could be understood as Quanzhou's change from a cosmopolitan city into an object of monarchical civilization.[41] The legend of the Carp emerged in the fourteenth century while the city was undergoing a sequence of drastic changes.[42] The emperors of the early Ming launched several civilizing campaigns. In the process, orthodox Neo-Confucian ideology was advocated, ethico-political guidelines for daily practices were imposed, the local merchants' activities were restricted, and visits by foreign traders were prohibited. Trade from the old harbor gave way to small scale "smuggling" in the fishing villages. Consequentially, Quanzhou's "good fortune" was altered.

When collated, historical records and oral tradition indicate that the imperial model of civilization did not enter Quanzhou without obstacles. On the contrary, it was constantly challenged from both within and without the regional officialdom. During the Ming and Qing transition, undercurrents reversing Quanzhou's fortune powerfully reinvented Quanzhou's bygone prosperity in the spectacles and stories of the Carp. But from the "orthodox" imperial perspective, public life in Quanzhou was characterized above all by "chaos."

As Timothy Brook has argued, in historical studies, imperial China has been regarded as evolving from rural self-sufficiency and "high" imperial control in the early and middle periods of the empire to the decadence of commerce and "public sphere" in the post-agrarian centuries of "petty capitalism."[43] By contrast, the perspective we can gain by studying Quanzhou indicates that "rural self-sufficiency" was the ideal model adopted by the imperial court as late as the Ming to as a corrective to commercial chaos. In the late imperial period, the cosmopolitan city struggled to survive the late imperial "ruralization" (also civilization in this particular period). In the process, what concerned the regional

---

[40] Skinner, Presidential address.

[41] Compared with the early and middle ages of the city, the transformation in the late fourteenth century has received much less attention.

[42] Wang, *Shiqu de Fanrong* [*Prosperity Bygone*], pp. 154–178.

[43] Timothy Brook, *The Confusions of Pleasures*.

elites—politicians, scholars, and merchants—was not so much what could set themselves corporately and socially apart from the populace as how they could maintain their mediating role between the imperial State—the political, economic, and symbolic universe of empire—and local worlds. To a great extent, elites were those who at once helped extend the imperial net and created holes in the net to free the Carp.

Toward the end of the book, the important role of urban elites in Quanzhou will become more apparent. Here I set out to investigate the historically varied ways of political interaction. I take a long view of history to show how the drama of the Carp, the imperial net, and its loopholes was performed and replayed in varied historical contexts. The duration of historical time to be considered will span from the early phase of the centering of Quanzhou to the end of the empire. In those long centuries, desirable geopropensities—the outer shapes and inner energies of place and landscape—continued to be what the altering State powers, urban elites, and local communities struggled to achieve. They also served as arenas in which different social forces came to interact. I pay special attention to the preceding processes and the consequences of the fourteenth century transition (which obviously was not a total break with the previous stages), which is reflected in the folklore of that time. Around the transition, the reconstitution of urban form became central.

CHAPTER 1

Introduction

To make my narrative more concise, I have chosen to approach the larger story of Quanzhou by way of organizing available materials around a smaller genealogy. This is a history of an institution of spatial organization, that of *pu* and its Ming-Qing version *pujing*. The changing institutions specified by the terms of *pu* and, later, *pujing* were core to the making of the outer form and the inner dynamics of place and landscape in imperial Quanzhou. It was central to both the imperial arts of control, to the regional urban elites' strategic tactics, and to popular religious/cultural practices and conceptions. It was installed in the city in the thirteenth century, during Quanzhou's commercial heyday, and evolved into, in terms of its political and social roles as well as its cultural conceptions, diverse patterns of ritual landscape and social activity in late imperial dynasties of the Ming and the Qing. After having spent more than a decade studying them, I have found that changing spaces of *pu* and *jing* reflected most clearly the changing nature of politics, commerce, public life, and landscape in historical Quanzhou.

First, let me provide a brief explanation. The main character in the word *pujing* is *pu*. *Pu*, originally meaning "ten *li*,"[1] is used in both

---

[1] *Li*, a Chinese "mile," approximately equal to 500 meters.

classical Chinese and Quanzhou's local dialect—which is locally perceived to be one of the rare intact linguistic relics of the former—to mean also "wards," "stations," "shops," "brigades," "offices," or "watch posts." It is, in its older and narrower sense, the word for guarded focal points in the place hierarchy of the empire. At the same time, *pu* also refers, in its extension from administrative and military nodal points, to "low-level places," for example, "villages," "neighborhoods," "communities," and "guarded areas" (especially, areas guarded by gods and their "soldiers").

There is no character that means exactly the opposite of *pu*, but the above-mentioned connotations of *pu*, in one way or another, contrast with the greater landscapes of civilization and supralocal spatial entities. Paradoxically, as such, *pu* was, in the very beginning of its existence, devised to accomplish official "supralocal" tasks. Unlike maritime trade from Quanzhou, which came to the attention of the court only after having created an attractive channel of resources, the institution of *pu* was installed with an explicit political rational by the court. *Pu* in this sense were spatially segmented units for networked information transmission and superintendent local control.

Originally termed *putu* [wards and charted areas], the institution of *pujing* first emerged as a system of territorial administration during the Yuan (1271–1368), which replaced the Song *fangxiang* system of urban districts. Chen Si Dong, a prominent local historian, wrote in his extremely succinct discussion to argue that *pujing* emerged as a system of urban neighborhood division in the late thirteenth century.[2] According to him, during the thirteenth century, the magistrate divided Quanzhou into of 36 territorial units called *pu* [wards], which were in turn integrated into three urban boroughs called *yu*. By the Ming, the term *jing* [precincts] had been added to describe subward divisions of precincts. Around 1700, another *yu* (borough) was added, and Quanzhou then consisted of four urban districts. In the mid-eighteenth century, two more *pu* were added, thus making a total of 38 *pu* divisions of the city.

Obviously, the core of *pu* and *jing* was an institution of spatial organization. Relevant to this, in historical and anthropological studies of China, two sorts of approaches have been advanced: (1) G. William Skinner's approach to the hierarchies of "central places" as functionally related networks of commerce, transportation, and imperial local administration[3]

---

[2] Chen, Si Dong, Qianyan [Foreword], to Chen Chui Cheng and Lin Sheng Li (eds.), *Quanzhou Jiu Pujing Jilue* [*An Investigation into the Old Pujing in Quanzhou*] (Quanzhou 1990), pp. 1–2. See also *Licheng Quzhi* [*The Gazette of Licheng Borough*] 2 Vols., Office of Local Gazetteers, Quanzhou (Beijing 1999), pp. 81–102.

[3] G. William Skinner, Marketing and social structure in rural China, *Journal of Asian Studies*, 24(2–3) (1964–1965): 195–228; 363–399; Cities and the hierarchy of local systems, in G. William Skinner (ed.), *The City in Late Imperial China* (Stanford 1977), pp. 275–353.

and (2) Ch'u T'ung-tsu,[4] Brian McKnight's,[5] Timothy Brook's,[6] Michael Dutton's,[7] and many others' approaches to regional administration and surveillance. In local contexts, the aspect of Chinese spatial organization as shown in the approach of imperial field administration is central to *pu* and *pujing*'s official designation.[8] But in the city of Quanzhou, *pu* and *pujing* did not merely signify an institution of "central place" and local administration. In fact, while the concepts of *pu* and *jing* continued to serve as apparatuese of imperial local administration, already by the early Ming *pujing* had been re-invented as a radically different system from the previous prototype of local administration in the Yuan. Merged with a set of imperial regulations of sacrifice and conduct consciously devised for the people to obey, in the Ming *pujing* became a space for disciplining and civilizing. Even more dramatically, starting in the mid-Ming, the territorial divisions and sacrificial rituals of *pujing* were re-appropriated into territorial worship practices that consisted of ritual activities that were by that point understood as "licentious cults" [*yinci*], oppositional to the Ming's official notion of civilization.

The transformation of *pu* from a kind of bureaucratic apparatus in the Yuan into Ming civilizing rituals and then, by the mid-Ming, into local communities of popular "licentious cults" suggests a complex history whose spirit is apparent in the folklore of the Carp. I will dwell on this history in greater detail.

When I began to focus on studying Quanzhou, I had been trained as an anthropologist. I was working toward an approach to the mystics of the State and regional culture as seen in the co-existing calendars and spectacles of ritual activity.[9] Since then, I have been fascinated with the politics associated with the concepts of *pu* and *jing*. Ultimately, the process whereby the same institution absorbed different functions has struck me as important. I have sought to bring it into the forefront of the anthropology of "Chinese territorial cults," which has been the focus

---

[4] Ch'u, T'ung-tsu, *Local Government in China under the Ch'ing* (Cambridge, MA 1961).

[5] Brian K. McKnight, *Village and Bureaucracy in Southern Song China* (Chicago 1971).

[6] Timothy Brook, The spatial structure of Ming local administration, *Late Imperial China* 6 (1) (1985): 1–55.

[7] Michael Dutton, Policing the Chinese household, *Economy and Society* 17(2) (1988): 195–224.

[8] *Licheng Quzhi* [*The Gazette of Licheng Borough*] 2 Vols., Vol. 1, pp. 81–82.

[9] During the period of my research, culture in Quanzhou was undergoing a process of re-invention. While the new calendar continued to function as a temporal guideline of work and leisure, the Chinese lunar calendar was undergoing a resurgence in both official and popular ritual cycles. Several government departments were assigned the task of renewing old Quanzhou's transnational ties through museum displays, tourism, and the organization of traditional festivals. The lunar calendar was deployed to regulate regional rhythms of cultural work. Among local households, the lunar calendar also re-emerged as an important institution. Numerous temples, festivals, and "gods' birthdays" were celebrated on "old calendars days."

of such anthropologists of China as P. Steven Sangren[10] and Stephan Feuchtwang.[11]

Had Sangren and Feuchtwang gone to study Quanzhou, they would have found that *pujing* provided a good example in which to examine, from an "emic" perspective, conceptions of social space in which peripheral small places and their own cultural patterns are distinguished from and related to imperial cosmology. "The production of culture" (Sangren) and the "bureaucratic metaphor" (Feuchtwang) are surely two guises through which the dialectics of empire-locality linkage are displayed. But through my own ethnographic and historical inquiries, I have found the concepts of "political economy of symbols" and "bureaucratic metaphor" inadequate.

Instead, what has intrigued me has been the ways in which *pujing* has been involved in multiple consciously organized dynastic and regional campaigns to bring local society back onto the "right track" of civilization. The purpose of these campaigns was the assertion of orthodox visions of order, but the result of these campaigns was far from successful. Thus, in the Qing Dynasty, two more efforts were made to turn the "licentious cults" into something that would be useful to imperial rulers and regional elites, in which what was associated with *pu* and *jing* was enhanced, in an open manner, as spectacles of regional vitality.

I began to study Quanzhou in the early 1980s. The first piece of work that I produced concerned the emergence of the harbor.[12] During the late 1980s and the early 1990s, as an anthropologist, I made both ethnographic and historical investigations into the city's public life as seen particularly in the practices of *pujing*. The emergence of the harbor and the invention of *pujing* took place in two different episodes of history, and they represented two different lines of development, the former economic and the latter bureaucratic and civilizational. The rise of the seaport in Quanzhou signaled the early expansion of regional prosperity. Institutions and politics related to the concept of *pu* were invented during the Song and the Yuan, when Quanzhou came into its prosperous age. But it was not a commercially and culturally liberating force. On the contrary, it was limiting and restrictive, ironically during Quanzhou's most prosperous period. We should not easily define such changing "places" in terms of a system of politically restrictive locales. In the history of *pu*, what is significant is a set of processes that vividly displays the active interplay

---

[10] P. Steven Sangren, *History and Magical Power in a Chinese Community* (Stanford 1987).

[11] Stephan Feuchtwang, *The Imperial Metaphor* (London 1992); Boundary maintenance: Territorial altars and areas in rural China, *Cosmos* 8(1) (1992b): 93–109.

[12] Wang, Mingming, Tangsong renkou de zengzhang yu Quanzhou gang de boxing [The increase of population and the surge of Quanzhou port in the Tang and the Song], *Fujian Renkou* [*Fujian Demography*], 1 (1987): 1–10.

between culture and commerce, integration and segmentation, civilization and the "wantonness" of popular cults, order and chaos, and state power and local propensity of energy. These processes are also reflected in the folklore of the Carp, which is indeed the very condensed story of the city. For me, such a set of processes, which were apparently connected with certain sets of relationships, provide a good example with which to illustrate the alternating pattern of political culture not only in the city of Quanzhou but also, by relation and implication, in imperial China and its world as a whole.

Pu, Pujing, and the History of Quanzhou

In the central portion of this book, I concentrate on:

1. The institutional evolution of *pu* as an administrative apparatus in the thirteenth century;
2. The administrative, ideological, and cultural perfecting of *pujing* in the early Ming between the late fourteenth century and the early fifteenth century;
3. The transformation of official *pujing* institutions into popular religious practices in the middle and late Ming, between the late fifteenth and the seventeenth century;
4. The imperial projects to re-enhance the energy of local worlds of *pujing* in the late Ming and the early Qing for two different ends:
   a. The installation in the late Ming the communal pact system, which demonstrated to be not quite effective;
   b. The installation of the "conferences of gods" by regional power elites, which yielded an unintended outcome—extensive feuds that could not be resolved by the court or the regional power elites;
5. The continued innovations surrounding the institution of *pujing* between the late eighteenth century and the nineteenth century in folklore and by the urban elite, and regional efforts to transcend local boundaries near the end of the nineteenth century.

The discussions that follow are historically specific. After Chapter 1's elaboration of our theme and its significance, Chapter 2 provides an historical outline of pre-Ming political economy and culture. I draw on historical studies to suggest a relationship between the coming of the age of commerce and the changing characteristics of the empire. A special emphasis is placed on the location of Quanzhou in the imperial and regional systems of hierarchical places whose history came much earlier than local history. Juxtaposing local history with imperial cosmology, I also draw and bear on Hill Gates's theoretical work, which views the Chinese tributary mode of production as central to the empire.[13] Gates, like her forerunner, the Marxist anthropologist Eric Wolf,[14] identifies the empire as characterized by a precapitalist mode of production. By contrast, I have argued strongly that this "Oriental empire" has its own cosmological structure of relationship. In historical Quanzhou, to become a central place in the empire, people first had to struggle to enter the imperial zoning of the world. But at the same time, as a marginal group, they also benefited from Quanzhou's liminal position. Situated between civilization and its outer realms, Quanzhou was able to advance into its heyday.

Except for Chapter 2's background history of the city, my study focuses on the story of *pu* and *jing*, whose multiple roles were manifest and transformative during the late imperial dynasties of the Yuan, Ming, and Qing (1270–1896) (for purpose of giving a clearer definition of the foundation of imperial order, I also touch on the pre-Yuan periods).

In the beginning, *pu*'s designated function was social control, information gathering, and document transmission. But by the early Ming, the territorial system had been deployed by officialdom to fulfill more tasks. To the Mongol colonial field administration of the Yuan, a new function was given to this institution. It became a means of symbolizing the presence of imperial power and cosmology in the local places. Gradually, the perfected Ming system of *pu* and *jing*, whose financial burden and social problems gradually came to trouble the government, was to be left in the hands of local inhabitants who, as socially and economically differentiated groups, reformed this political and cosmological order through ceremonial appropriations, storytelling, and daily practices. Through these processes, *pujing* evolved into a variety of things. Chiefly, as I argue, it was reshaped into a local institution of territorial guardian-gods' birthday festivals, in which official spatial conceptions were challenged.

Documentary materials in this subject are scarce. But taken as an analytical whole, they confirm that *pujing* played an important role in the public life of local inhabitants of Quanzhou during the Ming and the Qing. The significance of writing this history is apparent: Although there have been studies of imperial order and macro-scale political life in imperial Chinese cities, materials concerning the characteristics of "low places," such as *pu* and *jing* in urban Chinese communities, are rare as are materials that offer direct testimony of what the "dead interviewees" practiced, witnessed, and inscribed politics and customs. In themselves they

---

[13] Hill Gates, *China's Motor: A Thousand Years of Petty Capitalism* (Ithaca 1996).
[14] Eric R. Wolf, *Europe and the People without History* (Berkeley 1982).

reveal a historical pattern, in which a system of delineated neighborhoods was conjoined with other sources of social and political dynamics as a cycle of order and/or chaos.

The origination, authorization, transformation, and restrengthening of *pu* can be associated with the changes occurring in the broader context of Chinese society. Particularly, as I show in Chapter 3, during the Yuan, after serving in the Song as a system of courier-post networks, *pu* was inserted into local society by way of the Mongol colonial enterprise of neighborhood control, household registration, and economic exploitation. In the early fourteenth century, the Ming pacified this multicultural region. In order to turn the city into an outpost of the "Central Kingdom," a more appropriate translation of "China" [*Zhongguo*], the prefects and generals jointly consolidated the city walls and reformed the city's sacred landscape. A campaign of civilization, which was configured in terms of what Qian Mu calls "civilizing Confucianism" [*jiaohua zhi ru*], launched by the Ming court forced local merchants into the restricted positions of unofficial traders (or, sometimes, smugglers and pirates).[15] Within the walled city, a system of local administration, based on pre-existing models of territorial division, was imposed. It was central to the reorganization of the imperial outpost's spatial, social, and ethico-religious order[16] and had dual functions of surveillance and moral-religious sanction.

Chapters 4 and 5 illustrate the "reform" of *pu* in relation to the Ming court's "civilizing project" and, more specifically, to the assertion of "official religion" (or "institutionalized religion," as defined by C. K. Yang[17]). In defining the Ming court's "civilizing project," I rely heavily on a comparison between the Chinese civilizing project in the Ming and a particular sociological interpretation of modern European history.[18] Norbert Elias has argued for the central position of court aristocracy in European civilizing processes. By contrast, the diffusion of central ideology seemed to be more characteristic of the Ming's civilizing process. In the building of a Chinese society in the early Ming, the colonial rule of the Mongols in the Yuan was reinvented as a time-before in which both violence and commerce supposedly induced chaos. Thus the civilizing project was not targeted, as in the case of Europe, toward the making of bourgeois style of life in society but at, somewhat like the "national liberation" of the Han, the revitalization of "classical" Confucian social rationality. *Pujing* was therefore used as a system that was supposed to refine people's conduct. Another difference lies in the fact that the Ming

---

[15] Qian, Mu, *Guoshi Dagang* [*Outline of National History*] (Shanghai and Beiping 1939).
[16] Yang, Ching Kun, *Religion in Chinese Society* (Berkeley 1961).
[17] Ibid.
[18] Norbert Elias, *The Court Society* (New York 1983); *The Civilizing Process* (Oxford 1994).

notion of morality encompassed "punitive practices," a topic emphasized by Michel Foucault.[19]

In Chapters 6 and 7, my concern is with the 150 years of the middle and late Ming. I argue that during that period, owing to the partial decline of state control in the city, more autonomy was advanced, and *pujing* was transformed into a "popular religious" system of territorial cults, which in turn was connected with several regional developments, including the upsurge in piracy, the increased scale of emigration, and the quiet progress of commerce.

In 1928, the prominent Chinese folklorist and historian Gu Jie Gang visited the city of Quanzhou. In the same year, he published an article in *Minsu Zhoukan* [*Folklore Weekly*], an academic journal based in Zhongshan University in Guangzhou. To satisfy his curiosity for popular cults of the Earth God (Tudi Shen), as he termed it, Gu visited several *pujing* temples in Quanzhou. He understood all the *pujing* temples as local variations of the Earth God Temple, which, to him, were universally Chinese and "folkloric." But confused by their transformation, Gu said the following:

> Communal halls known as *she* were originally temples for the worship of sagacious and capable men who benefited the people with their contributions and moral exemplariness. . . . We know nothing about when such halls were turned into Earth God temples; nor do we know how the God of Community [*She Shen*] became the Earth God and termed *Fude Zhengshen* [Orthodox Divinity of Blessing and Virtue].
>
> But from a historical perspective, we understand that the Earth God used to have a very high position in the imperial pantheons. He was known as Houtu and was worshipped by the emperors together with Heaven and the Supreme Divinity (Shangdi). . . . Only by later times, was the Earth God worshipped in the small shrines like local Earth God Temples, which made the literati no longer interested in it. The literati thus established their own kinds of halls to commemorate great men. . . .
>
> The commoners' knowledge is indeed shallow, and their historical memory remains at the level of oral tradition. But they also demand that the names of sagacious and capable men be attached to their local shrines. Thus, in Quanzhou, they not only place Fude Zhengshen in their halls but also [imitating the literati] worship various great emperors, successful men, generals, and merciful mothers in the same halls.
>
> Locals give great honor to these great emperors, sage-kings, and the like. That is because the image of the Earth God gives people an impression of his weakness. It is also because [as the locals perceive it] he is only capable of performing ordinary miracles and not great ones. . . . The fierce and severe looking great emperors, heroic generals, handsome Crowned Princes [*taizi*], and beautiful female immortals all have strong individual

---

[19] Michel Foucault, *Discipline and Punish: The Birth of the Prison* (London 1977).

characteristics which satisfy local people's sensational demand more. Thus, the commoners have more profound feeling towards these deities; and as a result, their belief in the Earth God belief has declined.[20]

Gu Jie Gang neither provided clues to *pujing*'s imperial pasts, nor did he offer any clear argument concerning the important transformation of territorial patron cults. But he sensitively questioned how, central to *pujing*'s transformation, *pujing* halls as "communal halls" changed into territorial guardian-god temples in which fierce-looking generals and sage-kings were added to the Earth God shrines. In a sense, Chapters 5 and 6 can be seen as a consideration of social, economic, and ideological changes that contextualize this transformation in "popular religion."[21] In Chapter 7, I analyze the middle and late Ming ideological, politico-economic, and religious transformation in which official religion and popular cults actively intermingled in the realm of *pujing*.

In a historical discussion on Marshal Wen and other deity cults in late imperial China, Paul Katz argues for the presence of "civil society" in popular Chinese religious temples. He states:

> In considering the public nature of rituals performed at temples or during festivals, it might be helpful to treat these events as performances that brought differing representations and conflicting ideologies into a public space where they could be examined critically. Such performances had the potential to shape speech, influence behavior, and generally contribute to the construction and assumption of social power.[22]

Pujing popular rituals were quite different from the discursive practices of communicative action; but they did involve ceremonial expressions addressed as public. In Chapters 7 and 8, I relate these expressions to regional re-appropriations of imperial order. My analysis in these two chapters detects a nascent sense of "public space" in these re-appropriations. Here I also point out the connection between "folk cults" and official imperial advocacy of orthodoxy and the promotion of the sage-model, filiality, and martyrdom. Moreover, my own interest lies in these places as arenas in which different social and political forces converged in history. Thus, I dwell on the "restlessness" of popular celebrations.

After two long centuries of transformation, by the seventeenth century, the city of Quanzhou had changed from a site of civilization into a

---

[20] Gu, Jie Gang, Quanzhou de Tudi shen [Locality gods in Quanzhou], *Minsu Zhoukan* [*Folklore Weekly*], 28 March and 14 April 1928.

[21] Vague definitions of "Chinese popular religion" can be found in Sangren's *History and Magical Power in a Chinese Community* and in Feuchtwang's *The Imperial Metaphor*.

[22] Paul Katz, *Demon Hordes and Burning Boats: The Cult of Marshal Wen in Late Imperial Chekiang* (New York 1995), p. 185.

battlefield where the Qing troops were fighting to incorporate Taiwan into the new empire. Given all the ethnic and social confrontations prevalent at the time, Quanzhou became a place full of tensions between many different competing social forces, including regional warlords, scholar-officials, officials, scholar-gentry, merchants, and ordinary residents, some of whom, to different degrees, participated in the activities of secret societies, piracy, migration, and brotherhood associations. During this period, *pujing* continued to develop in the direction of "popular religion." But soon afterward, it was to undergo a dramatic change.

In Chapter 8, I begin with a synopsis of the early Qing transition and further analyze the ways in which the late Ming popular religious "conferences of gods" were adopted as strategic means by which regional elites and the court dealt with local order, their own interrelationships, and with the court. In Chapter 9, I consider popular responses to the regional power elites' project and analyze the unintended consequences of the projects in the light of the diffusion of feuds.

Along with the arrival of the expanding Western maritime empires, by the early eighteenth century, in the official regional maps, Quanzhou somehow returned to its early Qing frontier position. For a period, the expanding "modern Western world system" presented new opportunities for private traders and smugglers from Quanzhou to expand the scope and scale of their activities. By the 1830s, the Qing court and some local social groups were becoming wary of the economic forms, culture, and military forces from the Far West. From 1836 and 1838, opium trade in the coastal areas became a focal point of political debates that divided Qing ministers and regional magistrates into rival groups. After two years of court debate, the Throne received a moving memorial from a senior minister who had probed into the seriousness of the situation. A decision was reached in the court in the minister's favor. But from then to the late nineteenth century, the emperors who ruled China oscillated between a hard-line and a soft-line attitude toward the invading foreigners. In the vacuum left by the court and officialdom, the people of Quanzhou further turned *pujing* into units of local identity and arenas for status competitions and feud, much to the detriment of the efforts made by early Qing elites. Chapter 10 continues the discussion begun in Chapter 9, examining more closely how the strategic game of "conference of gods" was transformed into territorial festivity, "chaos," and popular redemptive discourse.

Places in the Maps of Local Worlds

The imperial functionaries installed in *pujing* have gradually declined since the 1920s. In the process, these "low-level places" have been replaced subsequently by Republican *Xianzhen* and *Baojia* institutions and then by postrevolutionary districts, urban communes, and street and neighborhood committees.[23] Important overlaps between the boundaries of the new urban neighborhoods and old *pujing* divisions have obviously existed, and local administration in the city has been no less "authoritarian" than its imperial counterpart. Nonetheless, *pujing* and their related activities (territorial festivals) have been constantly denounced and attacked by the two modern regimes in the twentieth century.[24]

Already by the 1920s, several organized campaigns had been launched to eliminate "superstition" [*mixin*], the modern term for imperial concept of "licentious cults" [*yici*].[25] As local people can still vividly remember, in Mao's time, "destruction" [*dapo*] as a "cultural revolutionary" keyword was painted on all the available walls of the city. Many temples that belonged to *pujing* divisions were torn down or used for new "public purposes" (such as clinics and schools); and activities with "superstitious color" were forbidden.

According to many locals, compared with those in the "mad years," people now have finally been allowed some "freedom" [*ziyou*]. Yet, the government still maintains a hostile attitude toward the deeply "superstitious" practices of *pujing*. Ironically, as I analyze further in the concluding chapter of the book, the antisuperstitious modern regimes of the twentieth century have drawn "historical lessons" only from the late Qing experience of territorial "chaos" in local neighborhoods.

By contrast, our study of the "premodern times" of Quanzhou begins by excavating a different layer of the past. Units of *pu* or *pujing* were devised as segments of space, and they had, paradoxically, conveyed something quite "supralocal," "civilizing," and "transcending." *Pujing* became only that which antagonized modern regimes in popular cultural movements, which, as this study will show, had offered certain "protodemocratic" foundations for modern Han-centric protonational consciousness.

Given that *pujing* represents a multitude of constructed and transformative settings for social and political existence in Quanzhou's neighborhoods, I regard it as deserving a total treatment in which

---

[23] Wu, Qi, Quanzhou baojia de jianli he xiangzhenbao quhua [The establishment of *baojia* and the divisions of *xiang, zheng,* and *bao* in Quanzhou], *Quanzhou Wenshi Zhiliao* [*Cultural and Historical Materials in Quanzhou*], 16 (1984): 117–138.

[24] Wang, Mingming, Flowers of the State, grasses of the people: Yearly rites and aesthetics of Power in Quanzhou, Southeast China (Ph.D. thesis, London 1993).

[25] Su, Tao, Dageming hou Quanzhou sanci pomi yundong [Three anti-superstitious movements in Quanzhou after the Xinhai Revolution], in *Quanzhou Wenshi Ziliao* [*Cultural and Historical Materials in Quanzhou*], 13 (1982): 172–180.

the perspectives of "central place," "administrative place," "symbolic community," and "senses of place" are combined.[26]

Little evidence is available that offers a portrait of the urban settlements (neighborhoods) on which the first local administrative institution was installed. But two things are clear. First, a larger scale history of the region can provide an account of the economic and social processes of community formation,[27] in which settlements and "central places" crystallized in the way that Skinner has outlined.[28] Second, and more important in this study, when *pu* were inserted into local society, they had consisted of artificial demarcations of boundaries that could be analyzed from the perspective of administrative spatial theory. Administrative spatial theorists have encouraged us to analyze state-society relations as they exist on the ground. In the present study, I have benefited from such a perspective. But these theorists have left local appropriations of administrative space to anthropologists of religion who, in turn, have succeeded in analyzing how conceptions of place and territorial cults were modeled on bureaucratic and ideological definitions of spatial hierarchies to become manifest as "Chinese senses of place." Thus in my work, I have also made references to these anthropological studies of Chinese religion.

In recent years, the term *place* has gained a dual connotation in the "postmodern shift" in anthropology.[29] Arjun Appadurai, most notably,

---

[26] A general theoretical reference for my perspective is Michael Hertzfeld's study of bureaucracy and its "symbolic roots" and performance (Michael Hertzfeld, *The Social Reproduction of Indifference: Exploring the Symbolic Roots of Western Bureaucracy* [Chicago 1992]). In invoking the historicity of *pujing*, I also draw and bear on Feuchtwang's notion of the symbolic derivatives of the Chinese bureaucratic metaphor (Feuchtwang, *The Imperial Metaphor*) and Watson's notion of "orthopracy" (James Watson, Rites or beliefs? The construction of a unified culture in late imperial China, in Lowell Dittmer [ed.], *China's Quest for National Identity* [Ithaca 1993], pp. 80–103).

[27] Hugh Clark, *Community, Trade, and Networks: Southern Fujian Province from the Third to the Thirteenth Century* (Cambridge 1991a).

[28] Skinner, Marketing and social structure in rural China; Cities and the hierarchy of local systems.

[29] Not long ago, places were still treated as locations of space-time universally existent as what accommodated culturally specific representations and social experiences. Recently, a reconceptualization has led some contemporary anthropologists to reverse the structural relationship. Contrary to the previous tendencies in which local communities were shaped as locations of protest against expanding nations and the "globe," the word *place* has been redefined and redeciphered as itself a forceful sensual and conceptual construction of attachment universally pervasive (or even determining). To "bring places back in," anthropologists have worked closely with cultural geographers and philosophers to give new qualities to place in which the universality of experience and structure of feeling in the "body-place matrix" take precedence over the materiality of local space-times (Edward Casey, How to get from space to place in a fairly short stretch of time: phenomenological prolegomena, in Steven Feld and Keith H. Basso [eds.], *Senses of Place* [Santa Fe 1996], pp. 13–52).

uses the notion of place to refer to the facts and events in ethnographers' travels that somehow bypass the departure and ignore the authorship. At the same time, he deploys it to mark out an arena of multiple "local voices" and "acts" that create discursively constructed settings in particular social modalities.[30] Under the influence of phenomenology and somewhat turning backward to interpretive anthropology, a new kind of "place-centered" anthropology has developed in studies of "senses of place"[31] and "anthropological locations,"[32] in which places are dealt with as meaningful displays of interpretation and ethnographic authorization.[33]

In writing the history of *pujing*, I also implicate my own sense of identity as an author and a "voice." But for me, in the particular analyses that unfold in the forthcoming chapters, the question of whether we can develop a new way of understanding determines how our intention of "self-authorization" can be fulfilled. As what connects administrative space and territorial cults, *pujing* offers an answer to the questions concerning the extent to which grass-roots ceremonial representations of place "reaffirm"[34] and/or "demonify"[35] the official state model of social spatial hierarchies and bureaucracy, as well as the extent to which political linkages and what we may call "symbolic relations" between the "center" and "periphery" in civilization were correlated as a setting in which our narratives could be regarded or absorbed as a part.[36] A point worth emphasizing is that our study of the transformation of *pu* and *pujing* is impossible without taking into account issues of territoriality and empire. Throughout the book, I contextualize *pujing* practices in the wider contexts of social and

---

[30] Arjun Appadurai, Introduction: Place and voice in anthropological theory, *Cultural Anthropology* 3(1) (1988): 16–20.

[31] Steven Feld and Keith Basso (eds.), *Senses of Place* (Santa Fe 1996).

[32] Akhil Gupta and James Ferguson (eds.), *Anthropological Locations: Boundaries and Grounds of a Field Science* (Berkeley 1997).

[33] Alessandro Dell'Orto, *Place and Spirit: Tidi Gong in the Stories, Strategies, and Memories of Everyday Life* (London 2002).

[34] 1 Emily Ahern, *Chinese Ritual and Politics* (Cambridge 1981).

[35] 1 Feuchtwang, *The Imperial Metaphor.*

[36] Today, anthropologists often say that a historical endeavor must be tripartite. In Ohnuki-Tierney's words, secifically it must consider historical processes, historicity (historical consciousness), and historiography, which "not only are all multiple but are also all contested by historical actors" (Emiko Ohnuki-Tierney, Introduction, to her edited *Culture through Time: Anthropological Approaches* [Stanford 1990], p. 23). As a historical endeavor, this study is also an intellectual project in the field of history. By way of conducting the study, I intend to open up a general discussion of the processes of civilization (and "decivilization"). I also anticipate a historical critique of "transcendence"—a notion that has not only defined the boundaries of Chinese social science but also frames foreign Sinological discourse of "China."

political experience, regional social change and dynastic transitions, which are also inscribed in the vernacular, in local folklore, and rituals of commemoration and authorization.

The history of urban prosperity has been narrated in oral tradition in terms of the interplay between "Carp City" and the expanding imperial "fishing net." *Pujing* had, for a period of time, been intended as the expanding net. Yet, through the performances of the Carp, the net was transformed into its opposite. Conscious efforts to "release the Carp from the net" appeared in the early Qing and the early twentieth century, respectively, in the Qing prefects' deliberate re-enhancement of the spirit of the Carp and in the Republican-Era destruction of the city walls as nexuses of the net.[37]

This study is primarily concerned with returning the Chinese city the original "confusion" of its two "tendencies": *cheng* [garrison] and *shi* [market]. As I explained in the prelude, I seek to use the blending of *cheng* and *shi* to bring to light the hidden patterns of imperial history in changing local situations. For me, the history of *pu* and *pujing* serves chiefly to illustrate this "confusion." But that does not mean that I will confine myself only to such "tendencies" and patterns.

I hope that this book also shows how historical processes unfolding around the concept of *pu* were at the same time modalities and actions in which different actors' lives became involved in larger history: the emperors' quest to conquer chaos, the magistrates' cultural re-invention of urban neighborhoods, the formation of unofficial translocal associations, the re-enacting of folk religious pilgrimages, and the scholar-officials' representations of "customs" all performed their roles and left their marks on the cultural politics of *pujing*. In my belief, probing into these politics, we will not only see how the court, regional powerful personages, local social groups, and communities have contributed to the formation of *pujing* as places, but we will also see the processes of civilization, its perceived "degeneration," and its revitalization. Embodied by the institution of *pujing*, these processes also transcended it and bring to view a sequence of interactive dramas of control and chaos. Thus, this study of *pujing* should not only draw on the center-periphery relationships but also engage and inform the anthropology of various civilizing projects.

---

[37] Unfortunately, neither of the revitalization campaigns resulted in prolonged good fortune for the city. And since history entered the twentieth century, although the nexuses of the net—the city walls—have been totally destroyed, the spirit of the Carp—as what we will see in the "conferences of gods" in the late Ming and the Qing—has continued to be condemned as what has induced chaos.

History as the Anthropology of Civilization

One of the most well-known names in the anthropology of China is Maurice Freedman.[38] In social anthropology in general, Freedman was one of the first—although so far unacknowledged outside the anthropology of China—to regard ethnographic places as limiting the competence of the anthropologist and to treat history as a gateway to the worlds of culture. Although he dubbed himself a "historical anthropologist," in his essay on "the politics of the old state," quoting extensively from historians, Freedman urged anthropologists to become sensitive to how the different "official" and "social" (unofficial) topographies of places, regions, and organizations could be linked into an "official map" in the history of Chinese civilization.[39]

For me, although the concepts of "official map" and linkages among the "segments," a term that Freedman borrowed from African and Oceanic anthropologists, seem obvious, several important questions spring from his formulation of "the politics of the old state": In what ways can we actually relate these so-called segments to the whole (society and state)? Was there a "map" that at once marked the boundaries and offered a linkage between the social and official imageries of place? If there was, then how, where, and by whom had it been drawn? Did the "authors" of the map not have different perceptions about which different landmarks should be emphasized? Can Freedman's general point about the "politics of an old state" be spoken about in historically specific terms?

---

[38] Since the 1980s, several other monographs based on first-hand anthropological field research in Hong Kong and Taiwan in previous decades have been published. Taking consideration of Freedman's notion of "sinological anthropology," these works have combined larger trajectories of cosmological, interpretive, and sociological developments in historical and contemporary China. More recently, studies written by a handful of social historians who have focused their attention on a historical anthropology of the Pearl River delta (David Faure and Helen Siu [eds.], *Down to Earth: The Territorial Bonds in South China* [Stanford 1995]) have further revealed the usefulness of Freedman's project with their vivid examples of local studies. But two decades after Freedman's essay was published, several village ethnographies were also published. In the mainland, since the late 1980s, a new generation of anthropologists and rural sociologists trained in and out of the country have relived the experiences of Fei Xiao Tong, Lin Yuehua, Francis Hsu, and, to a lesser extent, Tian Rukang. Forgetting what Freedman treated as unsuitable for a proper anthropological understanding of China, they have comfortably engaged themselves in the ethnographic separation of China into places (or pieces).

[39] Maurice Freedman, The politics of an old state: A view from the Chinese lineage, in G. William Skinner (ed.), *The Study of Chinese Society: Essays by Maurice Freedman* (Stanford 1999), pp. 334–350.

Apart from the problem of agency in his model,[40] Freedman offered an inadequate perspective on history. Deriving his models chiefly from the late Qing and the Republican experience, Freedman paradoxically insisted on a totality of traditional Chinese "social structure" that was far removed from the time in which he lived and studied. Under the influence of a twisted form of "semicolonialism," the celestial world was turning back to its own tradition in the pursuit of a coherent whole in order to combat expanding maritime empires from the outside—the West and Japan.[41] The pitfall of fictionalizing a perfect unity of "social structure" in an age of cultural contact and colonialism has been the negligence of the specificity of that historical time.[42] Moreover, in my view, even if we forget the century of the late Qing and the early Republican periods, in which Chinese perceptions of themselves had come to become one of what Marshall Sahlins has called "the cosmologies of capitalism,"[43] in the previous centuries, with which I am particularly concerned, the histories of official, intellectual, and local popular perspectives of place, region, and the imperial state were so complex and dynamic that a structural model could provide only a rough sketch at best.

I admire Freedman when he says that the anthropology of "complex societies" should dare to face "the politics of the old state." But I was disappointed by his treatment of politics as an official map of society. Not that I have been afraid to recognize the obvious effects of the totalizing maps of empire. Nor have I been overwhelmed by the assumption that resistance can account for all things "symbolic." In his *Historical Metaphors and Mythical Realities*, Sahlins has argued for "a world on which people act differentially and according to their respective situations as social beings, conditions that are as common to action within a given society as they are to the interaction of distinctive societies."[44] In my view, this statement accurately captures the situation in historical Quanzhou.

---

[40] From the perspective of Faure and Siu's, one way of filling the vacuum of agency in Freedman's model would be with the notion of regional nexuses of power, which, on the one hand, could manipulate symbols to local ends and at the same time "gentrify" local ethnic and communal cultures with the readily available patterns of orthodoxy. See Faure and Siu (eds.), *Down to Earth*.

[41] Anthropologists and historians concerning China should not easily look at formulations of modernity as representing a uniquely Western project impinging on China to drive it out of the "medieval darkness." But should we restrain ourselves from the heavily critiqued "impact-response" model of Fairbankian historiography? See Tanie Barlow (ed.), *Formations of Colonial Modernity in East Asia* (Durham 1997).

[42] Allen Chun, *Unstructuring Chinese Society: The Fiction of Colonial Practice and the Changing Realities of "Land" in the New Territories of Hong Kong* (Amsterdam 2000).

[43] Marshall Sahlins, Cosmologies of capitalism: The trans-pacific sector of the "world system," *Proceedings of the British Academy*, lxxiv (1988): 1–51.

[44] Marshall Sahlins, *Historical Metaphors and Mythical Realities: Structure of the Early History of the Sandwich Islands Kingdom* (Ann Arbor 1981), p. vii.

Despite my reservations concerning structural reproduction in Sahlins's model of the "structure of conjuncture," I have decided to start with the more dynamic and processual aspects of the same "structure." With them, I intend to reveal the interaction of the transforming modes of dynastic-cum-regional boundaries that established spaces for different "maps" to display themselves as significant patterns of social beings interacting under restricted and/or open conditions, a state of affairs that was a primary concern of Jacques Gernet's work on Chinese civilization.

Gernet outlines in *A History of Chinese Civilization* the "alternating modes" in imperial Chinese history. In his book, he shows how the history of late imperial China oscillated between an expansive empire and a self-bounded monarchy.[45] In several other recent studies of the early Qing, the open-endedness of the Manchu empire, which Gernet has alternatively seen as manifest in the "enlightened despot" form of the body politic, has been specifically examined from several different perspectives, such as the emperor's textual performance of the ceremonial order,[46] the world-constituting practices of guest ritual,[47] and the colonial enterprise of cartography.[48] These historical studies, although emerging from different theoretical concerns, have shed important light on the ways in which pre-Qing imperial Chinese cosmology was re-enacted to reconstitute a "world order" for the Qing. But they have not paid sufficient attention to the important differences between the Qing and its preceding dynasties, especially between the Qing and the Ming. Obviously, imperial China was by no means monolithic, and its history had a pattern. In the Chinese empire, which Gernet also refers to as of "the Chinese world," sometimes the country was opened as several inner zones in a nearly worldwide tributary system, in the ways which the above-mentioned studies have presented. But sometimes it was organized as a self-contained system in which "Sinicization" was excessively emphasized. The intention to build a bounded monarchy had been put, although only partially, into practice as early as the ninth century, during the Song Dynasty. What Gernet hinted at as "early modern China" in the Song Dynasty, was, however, terminated by the Mongols, one of the "Sinicized barbarians" from the North.

A reading of Gernet's narratives can show that the six centuries in which *pujing* existed as a changing institution was one such cycle of

---

[45] Jacques Gernet, *A History of Chinese Civilization* (Cambridge 1982 [1972]).

[46] Angela Zito, *Of Body and Brush: Grand Sacrifice as Text/Performance in Eighteenth-Century China* (Chicago 1997).

[47] James Hevia, *Cherishing Men from Afar: Qing Guest Ritual and the Macartney Embassy of 1793* (Durham 1995).

[48] Laura Hostetler, *Qing Colonial Enterprise: Ethnography and Cartography in Early Modern China* (Chicago 2001).

opening (the Yuan), closing (the Ming), and re-opening (the early Qing). This is not to suggest that the history of Quanzhou is a perfect reflection of the "Chinese world." Rather it means no more than that in our study Skinner's macro-region-centered history should come to terms with the type of dynastic chronology put forth by Gernet. In short, because of its regional characteristics, which many have singled out, the ninth and the tenth centuries belong to the phase of the open tributary empire, although accompanied at times by separatist regimes, whereas the later centuries, particularly the three hundred years of the Ming, were more closed.

In the imperial era, threads of continuity are apparent. But the interrelationship between official and popular topographies of place and region was patterned in different ways during different periods. In the periods of "open empire," cultural diversity flourished and commerce prospered. During the periods of "closed monarchy," orthodoxy ruled supreme. Patterns of regulation and displays of order also varied with time. In the periods in which the formation of the open empire facilitated expansive conquest and trade (for instance, the Yuan), boundaries were not emphasized. The "official map" of society that the court deployed was accordingly more inclined as a set of colonial functionaries that did not rely on the cultural boundaries of civilization. In the periods in which boundaries were strictly maintained for the stabilization of internal society, such as the Ming, the "official map" was deployed not only as the chart for administration but also as the pattern of ethico-moral and politico-legal sanctive practices (see Chapters 4 and 5).[49]

In correlation—but not neat correspondence—with changing imperial dynastic boundaries and the regional cycle, I regard the "official maps" of *pujing* as transformed in accordance with the patterns that I summarize as follows:

1. During the Northern and the Southern Song, while ideal models of "civil government" were emerging, the monarchy was confronted with expanding Sinicized empires from the North. Internally, the State first invented a set of civil surveillance institutions; but externally, it was pressed to survive in a world of competing empires. Under such conditions, urban neighborhoods were managed with civil means for the purpose of defending boundaries, and courier-post stations were consolidated and expanded.

---

[49] That is not to say that the "official map" was constantly redrawn; rather it suggests that it was redrawn during certain special historical epochs of dynastic history. In certain epochs, the older model for the interaction between state, region, and place was deemed out of date, and a newer pattern of social topography was necessitated.

2. During the Yuan, the Mongol empire became the real world power. Internally and externally, senses of dynastic boundaries gave way to extending frontiers and colonialism. Civil government gave way to militant means of control. *Pu* was inserted as an extension of the Mongols' military and semimilitary control over local places and units of exploitation.

3. In the Ming, the "Chinese Renaissance," previously envisaged and initiated among the Neo-Confucians and in the Song civil government, was revitalized. Meanwhile, along with the decline of the Mongol empire, the State adopted a strong measure to isolate China from the outside world. The mapping of places became important not only to the monarchy's pacification of earlier frontiers but also to the civilizing role of Confucianism. Within Quanzhou, *pu*, combined with *jing* to become *pujing*, and was re-installed for purpose of taxation, local administration, policing, information storage and transmission, and state rituals that extended the displays of order into local communities.

4. In the early Qing, after the conquest of the frontiers in the Southwest and the Southeast, the monarch began a new project of extending the empire. The tributary system was once again installed to allow trade. The "official map" that served to control local areas was redrawn as a chart for administrative functions. While the larger imperial ceremonies continued to honor the power of the emperor and his bureaucracy, lower-level rituals were left in the hands of local leaders and organizations who, together with local households, continued to transform these rituals into local cult festivals.

Furthermore, I should emphasize that from the perspective of landscape interpretation,[50] *pujing*, as a signifying system, was reinterpreted in each of these periods. Official interpretations changed dramatically over time, from the Mongol colonial maps of local society through to the Ming orthodox presentation of civilizing landscape and the early Qing regional elite replays of propensity, to the nineteenth-century reconfiguration of local self-government. In comparison, despite their transformative qualities, popular religious readings proved to be more continuous and persistent. These readings mostly fell into the category of boundary-maintenance through deity and ghost worship. Popular worship, like official imperial sacrifices, also performed the spectacle of authority and power. But these spectacles of authority and power differed from the orthodox

---

[50] James S. Duncan, *The City as Text: The Politics of Landscape Interpretations in the Kandyan Kingdom* (Cambridge 1990).

Ming definition of the sanctioning power of the City God and the Qing definition of propensity. Reliant on the popular concept of efficacy, it was closely related to local performances of competitiveness. In imperial and popular landscape readings, the local official, scholar, and merchant elites' readings played dual roles. Sometimes such readings, which were diverse as well, served as important points of reference for political strategies; sometimes they were deeply intertwined with local religious worship. And during most periods, even if they served the officialdom, like the official readings, they changed from time to time.

I regard it as important to relate these different types of reading to their constant interactions, which have the potential to recreate what Sahlins has defined as the "structure of conjuncture." As the case of the Qing illustrates in Chapter 7, factional politics in the court and the regional government often created possibilities for ideal-typic choices to be made as the official perspectives during different periods of time. Despite their being constrained by alternating visions of power's propensity, they could shift from a more open and locally engaged strategy to a less open and less locally engaged strategy. During the early Qing, the coastal region had been pacified, and the Manchu state adopted more or less an "open" strategy with which it sought to extend the Sinicized empire into the periphery. Under such circumstances, the remapping of places took advantage of locally prevalent traditions of "conferences of gods" with a more relaxed attitude toward neighborhoods and associations in competition and conflict with one another. However, by 1839, the same phenomenon came to be treated chiefly as a manifestation of chaos. To control chaos, a new "map," drawn through the joint efforts of local elites and imperial prefects, was devised to turn neighborhoods into mechanisms of local administration, moral teaching, and militia organization (Chapters 8 and 9).

From a "bottom-up" perspective, *pujing* were part of local festivals. These festivals created certain arenas in which "higher-level" statue-symbols were fought for in ceremonial and social patterns of order and chaos.[51] Such ceremonial and social patterns were themselves meaningful in more than one way, but they also relegated places in a politically and culturally constructed model of hierarchy. As such, they were characteristic of the sociologic of the politicians who were actors actively involved in the hierarchy's invention, maintenance, or reform.

Conversely, worth emphasizing is the fact that even if a strategy fitted well into the social conditions of a particular time, there was still a large

---

[51] In Chinese, *luan* has, through history, been defined in contrast and in relation to *zhi* [order]. In the official historiography of both the dynasties and regions of China, *luan* and *zhi* have been employed to account for the alternation of chaos and order. The ideal model is the apocalypse-like but cyclical replacement of *zhi* for *luan*.

space for its efficacy to be brought into doubt. For instance, the hierarchical value that was attached to it socially often could arouse sensations in the communal contests over the signs and patterns of the "official map." Consequentially, popular festivals became expressions of the sensations commonly felt for imperial recognition of local senses of place. They were so excessively popular that they, paradoxically, were beyond the control of the prefects who authorized them.

The dynamic interplay between the official and the unofficial can be seen in the different "maps" and ritual practices, and they were also conveyed in the changing connotations of a single category. As I show in parts of Chapters 4 and 5, the Ming founding emperor, Zhu Yuan Zhang, first turned the category ghosts [*gui*] into punitive officers who were to haunt people the government and police failed to catch. In the late fourteenth century, ghosts did serve as frightening sheriffs who punished criminals and moral wrong-doers in *pujing* communities. We know that in the Song, this category of divinity was also respected, but with a more merciful attitude. The Ming change was interestingly linked with the emperor's desire to construct a moral society. Equally interesting, as I illustrate more closely in Chapter 9, is that by the late Ming, the merciful attitudes toward ghosts re-emerged and became popular not only among the locals but also among the officialdom. The background to this change was the widespread fear of catastrophe, induced by epidemics, piracy, and earthquakes, which turned the category of ghosts into demons and those who died from demonic murder, who were to be expelled immediately.

These historical processes are multiply contextualized. Nonetheless, was I asked to offer a clearer line of *pujing*'s changes in meaning, I would venture to argue that there was a critical turn, and it occurred during the early Ming. As I pointed out earlier, it is from the Ming onward that *pujing* was gradually combined with the ceremonial institutions of "official religion." Moreover, during the same period, the "civilization" of *pujing* control, paradoxically, paved the way for its localization and popular movement of religious invention. Central to the transformation was the emergence of the spatial models of territorial cults and festivals, in which official spatial conceptions were altered. In these cults and festivals, the core facet of *pujing* consisted of its territorial dividedness, which did not contradict its horizontal and vertical linkages through cult alliances, pilgrimages, and pan-city celebrations.

This study seeks a cultural interpretation of local history. The folktale of the Carp and its related local understandings of history are the inspiration for this anthropological history of Quanzhou. My initial plan was to conduct an anthropology of history, but I have ended up with a genealogical approach to *pujing*. *Pu* and *pujing* subsequently emerged as spatial concepts referring to the same territorial divisions and boundaries, surrounded by stories about the origin of the city. The relative growth and decline of its prosperity and power, the extension of late imperial civilization, and the making and popularizing of local cults were absorbed into the matrix of urbanity as the interactive drama between imperial and local worlds. My ultimate argument for the methodology that I have come to propose is that the anthropology of history is impossible without a locally specific and comparatively implicative historical inquiry of institutions and practices, such as *pu* and *pujing*. This perspective is further discussed in the concluding chapter, in which I offer further consideration of how the pattern of Quanzhou's pasts could be presented in terms of the "natives' points of view" and how this pattern could help distinguish our history from the "official account," which is mostly the result of the synthesis of the late imperial Chinese cultural invention and twentieth-century Sinicization of the globalizing "Occidental" civilizing process. In my concluding remarks, I also bring back in the engines and settings of sinological anthropology. But before then, let me focus on a history of specificities.

CHAPTER 2

The Carp: Empire and the Culture of Commerce, 712–1368

In three dynasties of the classical period [Sandai, nameling Xia, Shang, and Zhou, from twenty-first century B.C.E. to 221 B.C.E.], the area outside the zones of the Nine Prefectures [*Jiuzhou*, namely, China] was uninhabited. During that period, Quanzhou did not exist. Stories suggest that long ago there was a small hamlet known as "Zhu Weng Zi Zhai" in the mountain to the north of current day Quanzhou. But we know nothing about whether this hamlet actually existed.

Written historical records clearly state that the region was opened up during the Qin [221–206 B.C.E.] and the Han [220 B.C.E.–220 C.E.] Dynasties, and during the Jin Dynasty [265–316] and the six dynasties [Liu Chao, 420–581], some small towns gradually emerged. But "civilization" [*shengjiao*] did not reach the fringe of the region until the end of the Tang (907). From the end of the Chen's separatist regime, and from the Song (960) till the Yuan (1271–1368) and the Ming Dynasties (1368–1644), the city expanded. Nonetheless, suffering from the rebellion of Pu Shou Geng (1357–1366), and from the warlord rule of Chen You Ding (1366–1367), the city was full of chaos. In the early years of the Qing the "boundary removal boundary policy" [*qianjie*] was implemented. The region fell into further chaos. Disintegration was seen everywhere. Not until the time when the present dynasty (the Qing) pacified the maritime rebels had the government begun to clear away disturbing elements in local society and change its policy . . . did the region began to open up. The past hundred years have been the most prosperous period. . . .[1]

This is a translation of a remark that Huai Yin Bu and Huang Ren, the compilers of 1763 edition of *Quanzhou Prefecture Gazette,* made regarding the history of Quanzhou. In the imperial historians' discourse, all the periods prior to the "heyday" of the Qing were understood as a "dark age." They acknowledged the post-Tang extension of "civilization" into the area, but in so doing they made it sound as if this area had begun to prosper only during the three "flourishing reigns" [*shengshi*] of the early Qing (the late seventeenth century and the early half of eighteenth century), during which they served as high-ranking officials.

Today, historical studies have moved away from Qing historians' sense of temporality. We can accept that prior to the Ming, the city of Quanzhou was situated far from the political and cultural centers of the empire and that in the pre-Qing periods, Quanzhou was frequently ruled by regional warlord regimes. We can also be sympathetic of their brief critique of the "boundary removal policy" implemented in the early years of the Qing. However, their sense of intellectual conscience seemed to be greatly downplayed by their insisting that later periods of the early Qing constituted the "heyday" of Quanzhou. Ample evidence indicates that Quanzhou's "heyday" should be traced back to a time well before the Qing. It was in fact during the long years of what the Qing historians viewed as "barbarianism" and "chaos" that the economy and the culture of the city flourished. During the early Qing, there was indeed an attempt to revitalize the pride of the Carp and its blend of energies. But, as we will see in Chapter 9, this attempt consisted of an officially organized spectacle of the Carp's ceremonial power, which came centuries after the era of Song-Yuan prosperity.

What led Qing historians to "distort" historical realities? Perhaps the combination of their desire to please the emperor whom they served and the political pressure under which they wrote constituted an important part of the explanation. Understandably, as scholar-officials, they were writing to replicate official Chinese historiographical tradition in a politically relevant and appropriate way.

Long before they wrote their remarks, a set of imaginaries had been available for scholars and officials to envisage the relationship between the "Central Kingdom" and the rest of the world. Despite the fact that China's rulers were not always Han themselves, these imaginaries persisted into later periods and continued to be used by different dynasties to assert their own sovereignty. The Qing was a non-Han dynasty. Most members of its

---

[1] *Quanzhou Fuzhi* [*Quanzhou Prefecture Gazette*], compiled by Huai Yin, Bu, and Huang, Ren (Quanzhou 1870 [1763]), *juan* 3.

ruling class were of Manchu descent. Although they strove to protect their own cultural identity, in order to claim the "Mandate of Heaven," they not only needed a command of the Han language and customs but also had to absorb the cosmological vocabularies of the "Central Kingdom" into their discursive repertoire. Gazetteer compiling, which greatly advanced in the early Qing, together with ethnographies and cartographies, were some of the means by which the Qing's achieved legitimacy and effective authority. Huai Yin Bu and Huang Ren were merely two of a great number of scholar-officials involved in this task for the court.

Heaven and Earth

The legacy of the archaic cosmological imaginaries had a long-standing history. It originated in the "rites and styles" of classical times. At its core was a geocosmology whose elementary framework was a system of "five zones" [*wufu*]. *Wufu* functioned at the same time both centripetally and centrifugally. Geographically, the boundaries of these zones changed from time to time.[2] Probably *wufu* emerged during the Kingdom of the Zhou (1125–256 B.C.E.) to refer to the five levels of its mapping of its own world. But from then on, this framework referred to modes of civilization, whereby the inner domain of the capital was defined as *dianfu* and the outer princes' domains as *houfu*. The princely domains were protected by the zone of pacification [*binfu*], which was in turn surrounded by the allied barbarians of the Yi and the Man, who formed a semicultured zone [*yaofu*], and by the Rong and the Di, who together formed the zone [*huangfu*] of savagery. The five zones were concentric squares radiating from the imperial city [*didu*], and at the same time they were described as different levels of culture oriented in a centripetal manner toward the capital. The different ceremonial structures in different zones were characterized hierarchically—*ji* for royal domains, *si* for princely domains, *xiang* for the zone of pacification, *gong* for semicultured zones, and *wang* for the zones of cultureless savagery.

The five zones constituted a complex system of relationships, a catalogue of peoples, and a structure of hierarchy deployed to know, describe, and manage the whole world under Heaven. In classical China, they delineated the cultural boundaries between the king and the rulers of principalities, and between the principalities and the barbarians. The concentric square was also a unity encompassing diversity, a system of "rites and styles" defined in terms of hierarchy. In such a new hierarchy, *gong* [tribute-paying], which later became a universal feature of the tributary mode, was applied to describe the interrelationship between the barbarians and princes.

---

[2] Gu, Jie Gang, and Shi, Nian Hai, *Zhongguo Jiangyu Yange Shi* [*History of the Changes of China's Borders*] (Beijing 2000 [1939]), pp. 56–57.

Figure 2.1 *Wufu*, the radiation of Chinese civilization from the imperial center (source: Joseph Needham, *The Shorter Science and Civilization in China*, Vol. 2, abridged C. A. Ronan, Cambridge 1981, p. 239).

Transcending the "map" of *wufu* was the conception of the "Great Unity" (Datong). Core to classical Chinese perceptions of the natural order and the human mind, which yielded the long-standing projection of social relations, the Great Unity was revealed as a means of government by ritual. As Confucius put it:

> Govern the people by regulations, keep order among them by chastisements, and they will flee from you and lose all self-respect. Govern them by moral force, keep order among them by ritual, and they will keep their self-respect and come to you of their own accord. (*Analects*: 3)

The Great Unity was never realized as concrete political formation. Around 900 B.C.E., the principalities loyal to the Zhou began to adopt their own model of royalty in order to realize their own political systems. Subsequently, a system of aristocratic cities, known as *guo* [cities enclosed by walls], replaced the archaic form of royalty. The emergence of *guo* had a great impact on the structure of the relationship between centers and margins. As one of the pioneers of Chinese anthropology, Lin Hui Xiang, pointed out long ago, "the contesting expansion of the principalities gradually resulted in the subordination and assimilation of the other ethnic groups besides the Huaxia," which by the Warring States period (453–221 B.C.E.) had produced a new phase of "Chinese culture." In that new phase, population mobility, inter-ethnic alliances, and military conquests led to the extension of the territory of China.[3] As part of the same process, the kingdoms that emerged from the former Zhou principalities gradually developed their own political philosophies. In their competition for dominance of the Chinese world, the princes sought to control territorial resources, military forces, and human capital. They reformed the class of officials and *shi* (scholars during the period) who in previous periods were concerned with sacrifices, war, and the management of palaces and estates, into a different stratum, and changed the nature of territorial control.[4]

Much of the change occurred around the concept of Xian (county). The idea of Xian emerged in the seventh century B.C.E. By the fourth century B.C.E., it had evolved into a local administrative system, especially in the Kingdom of Qin. Xian as an institutional measure was initially used to control the conquered territories. In the beginning, it referred to the newly acquired lands placed under the traditional power of high-ranking nobles. Gradually, it provided a new basis for the management of the country. Situating the new territories under the new condition, Xian later referred to a new type of territorial power, that is, the administrative districts controlled by the representatives of a central power. As such, it induced a radical transformation in China's political organization.

Starting in 314 B.C.E., after Qin's victory over the nomads of the north, victories in a series of wars against the Ba in Sichuan, the Han, Chu, Wei, and Zhao, brought Qin extensive territories that belonged to different principalities-turned-kingdoms. In 249 B.C.E., Qin finally put an end to the small realm of the Zhou. In 247 B.C.E., Prince Cheng of the kingdom came into power and, through ten years of military campaigns, eliminated all the other major kingdoms. In 221 B.C.E., having conquered all the lands, he took the title of "Huangdi" [August Sovereign]. With the help of his legal adviser Li Si, Shi Huang Di, or

---

[3] Lin, Hui Xiang, *Zhongguo Minzu Shi* [*History of Nationalities in China*] 2 Vols. (Beijing 1993 [1936]), Vol. 1, pp. 26–27.

[4] In the Warring States period, the class of Shi lost their status as nobility. Becoming more or less like a "floating stratum," Shi enjoyed more "freedom of speech," and they had the opportunity to explore various possibilities of social and political identification, including that of their becoming bureaucrats.

the "First Emperor" as the Huangdi of Qin (Qin Shi Huang) was later called, deployed a whole series of unifying measures to turn the entire Chinese world into a centralized state.

The unification of writing, transportation, money, and means of measurement was forcefully imposed on the vast country, which was divided up administratively into Jun (commanderies) and Xian (counties).[5] Within the central regions, the government undertook extensive public works to construct towns, roads, post houses [*yizhan*], canals, palaces, and so on. An extremely severe penal system was imposed on the country as well.

The harsh working conditions, severe penalties, and repression led to popular discontent and resentment from the aristocrats who lost their privileges and estates. Soon after the First Emperor's death, in 209 B.C.E., Chen Sheng and Wu Guang led a peasant uprising. The uprising was soon joined by an old aristocratic family, the Xiang from the old Chu kingdom. Xiang Yu became a strong force in the south. He created a quasi-empire on the line of noble fiefs, among which the Kingdom of Han was given to the command of Liu Bang. Along with the growth of his fame, Liu Bang also expanded his military force. In 206 B.C.E., he led his troops across the Qin river. After crushing the Qin army in 206 B.C.E., Liu Bang founded the Han Dynasty. In 202 B.C.E., he eliminated his rival Xiang Yu and proclaimed himself Emperor.

The empire of the Han lasted for some 200 years, ruled sequentially by twelve emperors who inherited in accordance with the royal line of descent from Liu Bang. The long history of the Han Dynasty is full of complex details. For our purpose here, it suffices to mention a lasting contradiction: to overthrow the Qin, the founders of the Han Dynasty not only mobilized the forces of the peasantry but also sought to revitalize the aristocracy of principality from the Zhou Dynasty (including the Warring States period). The new empire claimed its authority by promising a future of a non-Legalist state, which consisted of looser control, more "feudal" tradition, and more politics based in morality. Thus throughout the Han, a new synthesis of cosmological and ethical philosophies was made in the name of revitalizing the Zhou system of rites. Meanwhile, the fiefs (principalities) that Liu Bang distributed to his supporters during the war had to be placed in the proper slot of the political hierarchy. These fiefs and their aristocracy constantly became an issue for the emperor. Most of their rulers were descendants of the six old principalities from the late Zhou that were abolished by the Qin.

---

[5] Under the county level, Qin Shi Huang and his government also created a sort of autonomous self-governing bodies semi-attached to the higher level government.

The larger ones owned more than five or six Jun. To maintain the considerably federalized empire, the Han state, whose official ideologues constantly denounced the Qin, actually also reused much of the Legalist tradition that had been deployed by the Qin Shi Huang. Following the advice of several political thinkers, the Han court made a series of attempts to reduce the power of the aristocratic kingdoms. In the process, the system of local administration characterized by Jun and Xian administrative allocation was emphasized.[6] But the difficult task of managing the balance between the semikingdoms of the nobility and the centralized state continued to be unaccomplished until the end of the Han and later.

The Qin and Han constituted a period of great expansion for the Chinese state. From the perspective of political geography, prior to the Qin, the Chinese world was limited to the central principalities surrounding the capital and its royal zones. From the Qin to the Han, the "central kingdom" extended northward into Mongolia and Central Asia, eastward into Manchuria and Korea, southward into the Yue Lands and the territories of the tropical tribes and kingdoms of parts of Southeast Asia. Most of the expansion resulted in the abolishment of local noble and barbarian kingdoms and the founding of administrative Jun. These administrative districts were justified in Chinese history with reference to the disturbing and chaotic effects (*luan*) of the barbarians on the Chinese (Hua or Han), which in turn were regarded as demanding the completion of the peace and order of Heaven's Mandate.

In the process of expansion, the idea of Heaven also changed. In pre-Qin periods, "as dynastic Providence, Heaven was an all-seeing and justice-meting power" that authorized the king as Heaven's Son. The Son of Heaven studied ways "to identify his life with the Order of the Universe." The zones and the prefectures established throughout the empire were treated as earthly shadows of Heavenly Providence.[7] During the Han Dynasty, the ascending unitary orthodoxy fed on earlier textual representations of Heaven and Earth, but it reorganized the regional traditions of ritual, mythology, and seasonal rhythms of different principalities of the Zhou into a centralized political ideology. This ideology was characterized by "a vague belief that there was a connection between abnormal natural phenomena and social life," and it was concerned with the "practice of utilizing this belief as a tool in the political struggle."[8] In creating a unified order that encompassed a great deal of cultural

---

[6] Gu and Shi, *Zhongguo Jiangyu Yange Shi* [*History of the Changes of China's Borders*], pp. 77–78.

[7] Marcel Granet, *The Religion of the Chinese People* (Oxford 1975), pp. 68–70.

[8] Walfgang Eberhard, The political function of astronomy and astronomers in Han China, in J. K. Fairbank (ed.), *Chinese Thought and Institutions* (Chicago 1957), p. 70.

diversity, the court authorized a system of ceremonial centers for the imagined world. These had emerged as a mode of Great Unity in classical periods. They were a system encompassing some diverse worldviews in which the hierarchies of humans, lesser humans, and nonhumans were ordered in accordance with the classical sense of hierarchy. During the Han, the cosmology of unity encompassing diversity was reconstituted in the process of empire building into a system of imperial tributary relationships that were highly ceremonial. It promulgated teachings of civilization through ritual actions during the emperors' "pilgrimages" to the sacred sites linking Earth to Heaven.[9]

In what we may call "official religion," the model of radiating squares became the core content. The mountain-residences of divinities were understood as natural altars for the Son of Heaven to communicate with Heaven. The mountain divinities were turned into advisers and assistants to the emperor, and in later dynasties, ministries were established to house them as specialist-officials who offered the Son of Heaven advice in accordance with cosmological traces in Heaven.[10] Hierarchically defined zones and their rules of relationship were consolidated as the orthodox mode, in which empire was "cosmologically conceived as a territorial realm with tributary rulers at its fringes."[11] The regions on the outer zones of civilization that had their own distinctive lifestyles and worldviews were "tamed" into becoming "lands of princes," although their different styles of life were allowed to remain, in contrast to the orthodoxy of the imperial court's ceremonial space.

Tributary Systems

Quanzhou was absent from the long history of the evolution of classical imperial cosmology. The region where Quanzhou was later established as a central place was not formally incorporated into the central cosmic geography of the empire until the second century C.E. Prior its incorporation, several ethnic groups described in Chinese as the *Yue* lived in the region.[12] In the beginning, the identity of those who lived in the

---

[9] For a consideration of Tianxia, its imperial pilgrimage, and ethnography, see Wang, Mingming, Tianxia Zuowei Shiejie Tushi [Tianxia as the cosmography of the world], *Niandu Xueshu* [*The Annual Academic Review*], 2 (2004): 1–66.

[10] Gu, Jie Gang, *Qinhan de Fangshi yu Rusheng* [*Necromancers and Confucians in Chin and Han Dynasties*] (Shanghai 1998 [1955]).

[11] Stephan Feuchtwang, *The Imperial Metaphor: Popular Religion in China* (London 1992), p. 26.

[12] As we noted, prior to the third century, the major inhabitants in the area were non-Han. In spite of the First Emperor's (Qin Shi Huang Di's) efforts to unify all the known "nine prefectures" [*jiuzhou*] under Heaven, the region remained a region of the Minyue Kingdom (Minyue Guo).

region was conspicuously "ethnic." The Yue were the aborigines of the vast country of South China.

Regarding the "prehistory" of Quanzhou, Huai Yin Bu, Huang Ren, and their colleagues tell us the following:

> During the legendary period of Yugong, Quanzhou was situated within the territory of Yangzhou. During the Zhou, the region belonged to the Land of the Seven Mins (Qimin Di). During the Chunqiu and Warring States periods, it was part of the Country of the Yue (Yuedi). Having brought all the countries under Heaven into its realms of rule, the Qin Dynasty abolished the chieftains in the Kingdom of the Yue and established on the basis of it the Jun of the Central Min (Minzhong Jun). The area of Quanzhou was placed under the Jun of the Central Min. The Han rose, and in the course of its ascendance, Wu Zhu [the King of Minyue] followed the feudal princes in the overthrow of the Qin. Later, he led his army to attack the Chu and won many victories against them. In the fifth year of the Gaodi Reign [201 B.C.E.], Wu Zhu was bestowed with the title of King of Minyue and authorized to rule the old lands of the Min [by the Han]. [During Wu Zhu's rule], Quanzhou was part of his territory. Later, the people of Minyue rebelled. In the first year of Reign of Yuanfeng [110 B.C.E.], the Han pacified the area and moved most of the people to Jianghui [some parts of current Jiangsu and Anhui] and left the land of Minyue empty. The remaining inhabitants who escaped from this established their own county Ye Xian, which contained Quanzhou. Later, the Han court set up the Jun of Kuaiji under which a Commanding Region (Duwei) was established in its southern part to rule the country. During the Eastern Han [25–220 C.E.], the place name was changed to the Houguan Commanding Region (Houguan Duwei). But the region continued to be a part of the Jun of Kuaiji. Later, the Jun of Kuaiji was divided into the Eastern Part and Southern Part. Quanzhou belonged to the Southern Part.[13]

Three important points should be noted from this passage: First, prior to the Han, the area in which Quanzhou was later installed as a prefecture was not included in the official charts of prefectures in the "Central Kingdom"; instead, it belonged to the vaguely defined vast country of the Yue, who formed their own kingdoms during the Chunqiu and the Warring States periods.[14] Second, although the Qin established the Jun of Central Min in Fujian, local administration was obviously not put into practice. Thus near the end of the Qin, the King of the Yue in Fujian

---

[13] *Quanzhou Fuzhi* [*Quanzhou Prefecture Gazette*], compiled by Huai Yin, Bu and Huang, Ren, *juan* 3.

[14] Archaeological data accumulated during the past few decades have proved that the Yue had established their own cities by the Warring State period at the very latest. See Wu, Chun Ming, *Zhongguo Dongnan Tuzhu Minzu Lishi yu Wenhua de Kaoguxue Kaocha* [*Archaeological Investigations into the History and Culture of the Aborigines in Southeast China*] (Xiamen 1999), pp. 158–170.

was able to mobilize his own soldiers to support the Han and gain from his actions the recognition by the Han as a King. Third, in a rebellion against the Han, the Yue people were defeated, and the Han forced most of them to move to the Jianghuai region. After that, the Kingdom of the Yue was abolished, and the institutions of imperial administration began to be established.

From the end of the Han to the beginning of the centralized empires of the Sui and the Tang (from the third century to the end of the six century), the history of the region was multiple and complex. But two general tendencies seem apparent. The nomads to the north, northeast, and northwest of the "Central Kingdom" started to develop into sedentary peoples and advance southward. In the central plains, the defense against the northern "barbarians" and the need to expand into the south came together to push China toward a centralizing and statist direction. Unity was not the chief characteristic of this period. The frequently recurrent episodes of separation and "international" conflicts described in Chinese official histories as "ages of chaos" [*luanshi*] resulted in more interethnic contact, consisting of both violent conflicts and peaceful transactions. They also provided important opportunities for the politics of the state to be further experimented in some of the independent kingdoms. Interethnic contact and the politics of the State were absorbed in the Tang's political cosmology, which, however, was bound up with the synthetic legacy of the Han. During this complex period, the potential for a more cosmopolitan worldview was evident in such experiments. Tang monks went on pilgrimages to non-Chinese worlds (chiefly the Buddhist world of India) to discover "truth" in the remote.[15] But this cultural exchange soon gave way to the cosmology of a China-centered tributary system in which the Chinese empire defined both the terms of "trade" and civilization. In the process, imperial ceremonies once again became closely linked to the ceremonial sacrifices of emperors and officials and the guest rituals that received tribute-paying barbarians.

The tributary system relied itself on a hierarchical pattern of relationship that constituted China as the center of the world, concerning which, Richard Smith offers a succinct description:

> Tributary relationships rested on feudal principles of investiture and loyalty, with China as the lord and other states as the vassals. Non-Chinese rulers (and various groups of Chinese and foreigners under more direct Chinese rule) received a pattern of appointment, noble rank, and an official seal for correspondence with the Chinese "Son of Heaven." They, in turn, as loyal subjects of the emperor, dated their communications by the Chinese

---

[15] Wang, *Tianxia Zuowei Shiejie Tushi* [Tianxia as the cosmography of the world], pp. 44–45.

calendar, came to court, presented their "local products" as tribute, and performed all appropriate rituals of submission, including the standard three kneelings and nine prostrations known as the kowtow. These loyal tributaries received imperial presents and protection in return and were often granted certain privileges of trade at the frontier and at the capital.[16]

In the imperial tributary charts of the world, the relationship between the civilizing center and the periphery was also depicted as that between the "cooked" [shu] and the "raw" [sheng], which gradually was extended to distinguish the half-civilized barbarians from their "uncooked" counterparts.[17] In every dynasty, scholars with their own senses of intellectual conscience existed, but willingly or unwillingly, those appointed to compile official histories mostly devoted their efforts to writing a "raw prehistory" for their own "cooking" dynasty. From their perspective, the earlier inhabitants of Quanzhou had first been "raw" and then "cooked."

When this tributary system was such that the uncooked or "half-cooked" "barbaric" chieftains contributed their characteristically local produce—sometimes including "strange humans" such as magicians [huanren] and artists [yiren]—to the center, the exchange was called gong [tribute] or xian [devotion]. When the flow of products and objects ran in the opposite direction, from the center to barbarians, it was called "responsive disposal" [en] or "bestowal" [ci]. Coupled with this exchange system was a constant cultural process of civilization that maintained the center-to-periphery relationships. "Transformation" [hua] actualized by "education" [jiao] was core to the civilizing process. Those barbarians who were to be "transformed" were "converted to civilization" [guihua], while those who were yet to be transformed were viewed as outside the realm of the transformed [huawai].[18] As Sahlins notes: "Trade fits into the tribute system, normally, as the sequitur, since the 'tribute system' in its most general sense referred to the material mode of integration into civilization. Barbarians' tributes were signs of the force of attraction of imperial virtue, objectifications of the Emperor's civilizing powers."[19]

---

[16] Richard Smith, *Fortune-Tellers and Philosophers* (San Francisco 1991), pp. 13–14.

[17] Magnus Fiskesjo, On the "raw" and the "cooked" barbarians of imperial China, *Inner Asia* 1 (1999): 139–168.

[18] One of the core aspects of civilization was household registration, which served to distinguish the "cooked" from the "raw" not only in terms of their levels of education but also their attachment to tax payment and redistributive systems. See Liu, Zhi Wei, *Zai Guojia yu Shehui Zhijian: Mingqing Guangdong Lijia Fuyi Zhidu Yanjiu* [*Between the State and Society: A Study of Lijia Taxation-Labor Service Institution in Guangdong in the Ming and the Qing*] (Guangzhou 1997).

[19] Marshall Sahlins, *Culture in Practice* (New York 2000), p. 426.

In practice, the separation and reunion of political powers through imperial Chinese history conveyed a different sense of space and time. Imperial Chinese history can be seen as a number of temporal cycles rotating between two situations corresponding to the two polar conditions that Marxist historians have characterized as the "Asiatic mode of production" and the "feudal mode of production." In Marxist histories, the former has been usually ascribed to China, the latter to Europe. In Eric Wolf's view, in the "Asiatic mode of production," power was concentrated strongly in the hands of a ruling elite standing at the top of the power system. In the "feudal mode," by and large power was in the hands of local overlords, and rule at the apex was fragile and weak.[20] In the former situation, the central rulers deployed strong networks of irrigation, communication, and military conquest to facilitate their dominance over local overlords who were encouraged to fight against themselves so that the center could act as the supreme judge of right and wrong. In the same situation, the apex—the State—and the bottom of the power hierarchy—the peasants—were linked by a common antagonism toward the power-holding elite and surplus-taking intermediaries. In the case of the "feudal mode," the strategic elements of production and the means of coercion were in the hands of local surplus takers. Under such conditions, local elites intercepted the flow of tribute to the center. Local alliances were frequently directed against the center and their own counterparts.[21]

Hill Gates argues that throughout the past millennium what I would describe in terms of the "oscillating modes of Heaven" resulted in the copresence of the "tributary mode of production" and "petty capitalism." She maintains that in none of the historical periods were Chinese producers of commodities (petty capitalists) emancipated from the dominant tributary mode managed by state officials "who put their own requirements for reliable revenues, stable class relations, and continued hegemony above any perceived need for economic expansion.[22] Gates's observation is acceptable as one of the possible patterns of Chinese history. But I should emphasize that the oscillating modes have more to themselves than simply "relations of production."

Eric Wolf, on whose works Gates has based her interpretation, tends to treat the two situations as subcategories of the "tributary mode of production" in what he calls "historical societies." For those who are familiar with Chinese history, it is apparent that the two polar conditions co-existed in the same society and took turns dominating the Chinese world, or All under Heaven. The disunity that occupied more than half of the imperial era was the extreme outcome of the "feudal mode," whereas

[20] Eric R. Wolf, *Europe and the People without History* (Berkeley 1982), p. 81.
[21] Factionalism emerged as characteristic of the "feudal mode."
[22] Hill Gates, *China's Motor: A Thousand Years of Petty Capitalism* (Ithaca 1996), p. 7.

the condition of unification that characterized the "Central Kingdom" for the rest this era ran more or less on the track of the "Asiatic mode."

Chinese historians who have focused on the oscillating modes of unity and division have shown how division, paradoxically, contributed to the expansion of the territories of the unified empire.[23] Furthermore, it is more important to note that the tributary conception of the Chinese world, an invention of the unified empire, was also accepted as the prime virtue [*de*] of the ideal super-overlord among Han and non-Han rulers of both unified and divided states. Conversely, during times of unification, the tension between the center and the regional "feudal potentials" was always felt as a threat to unity and civilization.

The paradoxical character of the tributary mode resulted in paradoxical outcomes. In the late imperial period, several major non-Han dynasties— the Liao, Jin, and Yuan (916–1368)— squeezed the Han Chinese into marginal areas by taking over the "Central Plains" (Zhong Yuan). Changes in rulers sometimes also altered the center-to-periphery relationship, but they did not bring a "revolution" to the relationship's essential structure. Notwithstanding that dynastic lordship was from time to time displaced, establishing a central position in the hierarchy of zones was the common goal for both the Han and the "Hanized (or 'Sinicized') barbarians."[24] Likewise, when what is now known as China was broken into several states, the ideal of a "Central Kingdom" continued to obsess the rulers of separate regimes. Thus, during periods such as the "Five Dynasties and Ten States" (Wudai Shiguo, 947–979), separation often ended in contests for dominance in the overall space of the empire and was, without exception, replaced by the re-establishment of a unified empire.

The other side of the coin is that throughout all the periods of unification the centralized state often needed to cope with the contradiction between regional "feudal potentials" and the tributary system. The successful centralizing elite of surplus takers usually sought to extend their ideological model of civilization into the "barbarian regions." Although such a model might become dominant over a given period of time, imperial civilization was often contested by a number of other discourses stemming from the same central discourse.

Migration and Administration

The imperial inclusion of Quanzhou owed much to Han migrants to the region. Historical documents indicate that the earliest Han migration into Fujian occurred during the Three States Period. This migration was

---

[23] Gu and Shi, *Zhongguo Jiangyu Yange Shi* [*History of the Changes of China's Borders*].
[24] Jacques Gernet, *A History of Chinese Civilization* (Cambridge 1982 [1972]), pp. 174–201.

arranged by the rulers of the Wu Kingdom, centered in current-day Jiangsu province, and had the purpose of raising the number of troops. However, more significantly, migration took place in later periods, especially in the "chaotic ages" [*luanshi*] in North China—the "Yongjia Chaos" (Yongjia Zhi Luan) in the early fourth century, the North and South Dynasties (Nan Bei Chao, 420–589), the "An-Shi Chaos" (An Shi Zhi Luan) in the middle of the eighth century. The replacement of one dynasty by another was another important reason for social instability in the north that contributed to southward migrations.[25]

Let me briefly mention that today, local awareness of northern origins is extant in many forms of historical commemoration. Among local households, they are especially evident when a new house is built. In Quanzhou, it is still a local custom to fix a horizontal plaque above the main gate of the house. On this plaque [*bian*], the native-places [*yanpai*] of the families who live in the house are indicated. On these gate plaques, the most frequently used place names include Fenyang (Shanxi), Gushi (Henan), Taiyuan, and Shaanxi. The Jin River was named after the migrants from Shanxi (Jin) who initially settled along its banks.

Most of the north-to-south migration came about as demographic reactions to political disintegration in the northern central prefecture. But from the perspective of South Fujian, the destination of migrants, migration facilitated urbanization of the region. Skinner has conceptualized this in terms of "central place crystallization"—namely, the concentration of human and material resources in emergent local market towns and regional metropolises. The process initially took place in the surrounding areas along the valleys of the Jinjiang and Mulanxi Rivers.[26]

The formation of a central town was not simply a "natural outcome" of migrants' rational economic choice of settlement. In addition to what Skinner has defined as "regional economic integration," a gradual extension of the imperial administrative apparatus that accompanied north-to-south migration played an important role in the making of Quanzhou as a city. In 260 C.E., the Wu Kingdom set up Dongan County in the area and started to treat the area as a separate prefecture. Between the third and the seventh century, marketing and administrative systems had already matured in the area, but Quanzhou did not become the area's political and economic center until the eighth century. Earlier, the center of the region, subsequently named Dong'an (260), Jin'an (282), Jinping (486), and Nan'an (586), was located in today's Nan'an county on the

---

[25] Wang, Mingming, Tangsong renkou de zengzhang yu Quanzhou gang de boxing [The increase of population and the surge of Quanzhou harbor in the Tang and the Song], *Fujian Renkou* [*Fujian Demography*], 1 (1987): 1–10.

[26] Hugh Clark, *Community, Trade, and Networks: Southern Fujian Province from the Third to the Thirteenth Century* (Cambridge 1991).

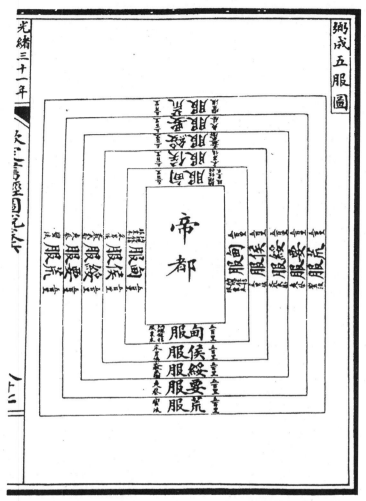

Figure 2.2 Qing map of Quanzhou Prefecture (source: Maps, *Quanzhou Fuzhi* [*Quanzhou Prefecture Gazetteer*], compiled by Huai Yin, Bu, and Huang, Ren, Quanzhou, 1763).

upper reaches of the Jin River.[27] Around the mid-Tang Dynasty (roughly 718), Jinjiang County, centered in today's Licheng (Carp City) area, was administratively separated from other counties belonging to the same prefecture (named Quanzhou). From then on, Quanzhou has served as the capital of the prefecture comprising the regional metropolis itself

---

[27] Zhuang, Weiji, *Jinjiang Xinzhi* [*A New Gazetteer of Jinjiang*] 2 Vols. (Quanzhou 1985), Vol. 1, pp. 92–97.

and a few attached rural counties. Further development occurred not in the prosperous periods of the centralized Tang Dynasty, but in the later periods of disunity—the Five Dynasties and Ten Kingdoms.

In the same process, many intellectuals and resigned high officials who escaped from the northern chaos found a haven in the frontier region of Quanzhou. Between the sixth and the ninth centuries, many famous scholars lived nearby the Mountain of the Nine Suns (Jiuri Shan) to the northwest of the city. There they established their own hamlets, academies, and temples and left great legends of their good deeds.[28]

As the Ming scholar He Qiao Yuan describes, Quanzhou is a region whose natural climate and land are not suitable for agriculture. So from very early on, seafood collection and plantation had progressed as alternative means of livelihood to grain production. Along with the expansion of population, even the joint enterprise of grain and seafood production could not meet the growing demand. Thus, many locals took advantage of commerce.[29] Maritime trade developed during the periods prior to the eighth century. By the latter half of the Tang, an occasional port had emerged in Quanzhou Bay. However, as Clark argues, the whole Minnan region had not yet developed into the final destination of trade. Instead, it was a station where goods passed and were transported to other ports. Trade volume was quite limited, too. Only by the tenth century did the situation change.

The Heyday

Quanzhou as a city emerged during the centralization campaign of the Tang. Even then, it was possessed an ambiguous status. Situated on the coastal frontiers of the "Central Kingdom," Quanzhou was, on the one hand, a marginal area distant from the central imperial capitals, especially during the unification periods of the Han, Tang, Song, and Yuan. Its earlier trajectory of civilization was that of the transformation of the "raw barbarians"—the Yue—to a blend of migrant Han and local ethnic groups.[30] On the other hand, during its heyday of regional development during the post-Tang periods, Quanzhou became an important transitional point on the empire's maritime tributary route.

During those periods, the local worlds were seen as parts of "All Under Heaven." The phrase "All Under Heaven" referred to an empire without sovereign boundaries. As we pointed out earlier, the geographic relationship patterned in All Under Heaven was mapped in terms of

---

[28] Ibid., Vol. 1, pp. 103–105.

[29] He, Qiao Yuan, Min Shu [The Book of Fujian] (Fuzhou 1994 [1628–1632]), juan 38.

[30] Lin, Hui Xiang, Zhongguo Minzu Shi [History of Nationalities in China] 2 Vols., Vol. 1, pp. 100–138.

the hierarchical order of the radiating zones surrounding the center. In the hierarchical order, the "Central Kingdom" fed on the barbarians as a corollary, and it defined its own centrality through representing the "barbarians" as external to itself.[31] The "Central Kingdom" constantly created its centricity from the ethnic becoming of the marginal groups such as the Qiang.[32] The relationship between itself and the outer layers was usually mapped with the figuring power of a tributary system that was supposedly or historically an extension of the Zhou Dynasty's classical political and social order.

Following the decline of the Tang Dynasty, Quanzhou, together with other prefectures of Fujian, entered a period of regional autonomy at the beginning of the tenth century. During this period, the Central Kingdom disintegrated. A number of separate states emerged. While disintegration worried many officials and political thinkers who adhered to the ideology of unification, it was probably warmly welcomed in Quanzhou, which, in the earlier half of the tenth century, was successively ruled by three different lineages, the Wangs (907–944), the Lius (944–962), and the Chens (962–978). During this period of decentralization, Quanzhou became an ever more central place in the "national" geography of the regional state. The regional regimes implemented a number of progressive policies to lighten taxes and accelerate regional economic expansion. Such policies likely sprang from the regimes' demand for tax revenue, which was needed to strengthen their own power against the northern regimes, but their implementation contributed considerably to local economic development. As Clark puts it: "Confronted with this independence, the autonomous rulers of Minnan were forced to find revenues in order to support themselves. Trade levies were among their most important resources. Consequentially, through both periods the rulers encouraged the development of trade, transforming Quanzhou from an occasional port of call into a regular destination."[33]

The growth of Quanzhou as a regional metropolis was part of the development of maritime trade on the China Coast, whose beginnings could be dated back to as early as the third century.[34] Archaeological

---

[31] The "barbarians" were not of the same kind. They were perceived as the peoples of Man, Yi, Rong, Di, Qiang, Fan, Hu, and Yue, the "to-be-civilized races" dispersed in the non-places outside the middle zones.

[32] Wang, Ming Ke, *Huaxia Bianyuan: Lishi Jiyi yu Zuqun Rentong* [*The Peripheries of Huaxia: Historical Memory and Ethnic Identity*] (Taipei 1997).

[33] Hugh Clark, Overseas trade and social change in Quanzhou through the Song, in Angela Schottenhammer (ed.), *The Emporium of the World: Maritime Quanzhou, 1000–1400* (Leiden 2001), p. 50.

[34] *Quanzhou Haiwai Jiaotong Shiliao Huibian* [*A Collection of Materials of Quanzhou's Overseas Communication History*], Quanzhou Museum of Maritime History (Quanzhou 1983), pp. 6–10.

discoveries of some foreign artifacts in the area indicate that Quanzhou
had been involved in frequent contacts with foreign cultures by the
fifth century at latest.[35] By the Tang Dynasty, Quanzhou was familiar
with merchants and migrants from abroad. By the ninth century, local
merchants were actively exchanging locally produced porcelain, copper,
and iron for foreign goods. Between the eleventh century and the early
fourteenth century, the government's promotion of maritime trade from
Quanzhou allowed commercial expansion to take more organized forms.
In 1087, the Northern Song set up a Trade Superintendent Office (Shibo
Si) in Quanzhou and sought to place regional foreign trade under its
control. The political background against which Shibo Si was installed
was complicated.[36] But the implications of it were far reaching. Shibo Si
endorsed maritime trade from Quanzhou, which had existed long before it
was officially recognized despite the importance of South Fujian merchants
in maritime trade.[37] Seizing this opportunity, Quanzhou developed into
the second largest seaport in China at the time and supplied, in the form
of upwardly flowing tribute, exotic luxury goods such as spices, shells,
ivories, and fragrant resins to the imperial court.[38]

In 1126, the capital of the Song felt under the attack by the Jin
imperial army. Part of the Song imperial family moved southward and
established their capital in Hangzhou, establishing the South Song
Dynasty (1127–1279). Between 1127 and 1130, the Southern Capital
Branch of the imperial family (Nai Wai Zong Zheng Si) moved into the
city of Quanzhou.[39] They settled there and intervened in the work of the
Trade Superintendent Office. In the end, they became intimately involved
in local maritime trade. As Chaffer argues: "With its imperial connection
the clan set the prefecture off from others (except Fuzhou of course) and

---

[35] For a comprehensive survey of religious relics and cultures in Quanzhou, see Wu You
Xiong's *Quanzhou Zongjiao Wenhua* [*Religious Culture in Quanzho*] (Xiamen 1993).

[36] Fu, Zong Wen, Songdai Quanzhou Shibo Shi sheli wenti tantao [An inquiry into some
issues concerning the establishment of Trade Superintendents in Quanzhou in the Song
Dynasty], *Quanzhou Wenshi* [*Quanzhou Culture and History*], 8 (1983): 1–10.

[37] So, Kee-long, *Prosperity, Region, and Institutions in Maritime China: The South Fukien
Pattern, 946–1368* (Cambridge, MA 2000), pp. 49–50.

[38] In 1974, an ocean-going junk abandoned in the 1270s as it was about to discharge its
cargo was unearthed in the port of Quanzhou. The cargo included small amounts of
three kinds of imports, tortoiseshell, frankincense, and ambergris. Each had come from
a number of possible sources, including Africa. See Wang, Lian Mao, Quanzhou haiwai
jiaotong shi yanjiu gaishu [A survey of historical studies of overseas communication in
Quanzhou], in *Zhongguo yu Haishang Sichou Zhilu* [*China and the Maritime Silk Route*]
2 Vols. (Fuzhou 1994), Vol. 2, pp. 18–30.

[39] The history of this branch is detailed in the recently discovered genealogy of a subbranch
of the clan in Quanzhou. See *Nanwai Tianyuan Zhaoshi Zupu* [*The genealogy of the Zhao
Family of Tianyuan Origin of the Southern Capital Branch*], Research Association of the
Southern Capital Branch of the Zhao Clan (Quanzho 1994).

brought in resources in the form of support payments from outside that were then spent in the prefecture. . . . To the end the clan participated in the overseas trade with the resources to indulge in its luxurious imports and exports."[40] The royal clan of the Song later created a huge economic (tributary) demand. The demand stimulated much regional economic expansion in the beginning, but gradually it became a burden for the expansion of trade.[41] Near the end of the Southern Song, the Mongols reached the outskirts of the city. Pu Shou Geng, a non-Han official who was trusted by the Song, defected together with his fellow merchants. They massacred the members of the Song Royal Clan and took over their maritime trade monopoly.

During the Song, Neo-Confucianism enjoyed a great diffusion. Zhu Xi, who spent most of his life in Fujian, taught some 160 students, who together made the "Fujian School" of Thought (Minxue).[42] A general characteristic of so-called Minxue was that it emphasized *yili* [righteousness and propriety], which broke away from the earlier Confucian emphasis on the hermeneutics of the classics [*xungu*]. The connotation of "righteousness and propriety," which was merely a re-invented Confucian idea of governing the people by rites, consisted of notions of just and proper conduct that had important implications for an emerging civilizing project targeted at transforming class-divided social groups into a cultural unity of kinship and bureaucratic performance. More important, in the Fujianese version of Neo-Confucianism, an unprecedented emphasis was placed on asserting the boundaries of civilization. Zhu Xi himself argued that "the distinction between Chinese and barbarians cultures is more important than the differentiation between the monarch and his subjects" [*huayi zhibian gaoyu junchen zhifen*].[43] Interestingly, however, given such discrimination against cultural others, Zhu Xi and his disciples were not opposed to Chinese trading with foreign merchants. Part of what can explain this "contradiction" might be the fact that Confucianism of any sort "contained ethical elements that could strengthen the observance of the virtue of trust."[44] Another factor might be that the Song version of Neo-Confucianism was more pragmatic than its previous forms. Neo-Confucians such as Zhu Xi had to face

---

[40] John Chaffer, The impact of the Song imperial clan on the overseas trade of Quanzhou, in Angela Schottenhammer (ed.), *The Emporium of the World: Maritime Quanzhou, 1000–1400* (Leiden 2001), p. 42.

[41] Zhang, Jia Ju, Songshi nandu hou de dushi shenghuo [Urban life after the Song court moved to the South], *Shihuo* (*Economic History*), 1(10) (1935): 36–43.

[42] Gao, Ling Yin, and Chen, Qi Fang, *Fujian Zhuzi Xue* [*The Fujian School of Zhu Xi's Philosophy*] (Fuzhou 1986), p. 4.

[43] C.f., Gao, Ling Yin, and Chen, Qi Fang, *Fujian Zhuzi Xue* [*The Fujian School of Zhu Xi's Philosophy*], p. 10.

[44] So, *Prosperity, Region, and Institutions in Maritime China*, pp. 49–50.

the historical situation that for the Song was the most serious challenge of their time (chiefly the Southern Song)—the "Sinicized barbarians" to the north. The "barbarians" in the south and the South Seas in fact supplied financial resources for the Chinese to defend themselves against the northern "barbarians."

Some of Zhu Xi's disciples became officials who were able to promote his Neo-Confucian ideals of social order and culture. But the Song court in Hangzhou obviously did not have the time to consider the significance of their ideas. To survive all its crises, the Song emperors, like the kings of the Min State, focused their attention on finding revenue. In the city of Quanzhou, the government's reliance on merchants' economic power dramatically increased. By the early thirteenth century, large merchant groups, who had accumulated great wealth, had cultivated their own style and manners. Dressed in pearls and silk, these merchants used gold and silver utensils in their households.[45] Powerful non-Chinese merchants, who were trendsetters among the elite in Quanzhou, also began to intervene in the government affairs. In 1211, these merchants approached the prefect of Quanzhou and offered to sponsor repair of the city walls. The prefect petitioned the court, and having gained the court's approval, collected donations with which he consolidated the walls.[46] The merchants not only sponsored public projects such as city wall rebuilding but also invested in the organization of a coastal military watch system.

Foreign merchants' influences in Quanzhou continued to expand during the Yuan Dynasty, which overthrew the South Song in 1279. It has been well documented that the Yuan rulers classified their subject populace into four classes: the Mongols, the Semu peoples (Semu Ren, literally "colorful-kinds of people"), the Northern Han (Han), and the Southerners (Nan Ren).[47] In this castelike system, the Mongols and foreign "colorful-kinds of people" were regarded as the superior classes, and the Han Chinese were placed in the lower classes of Han Ren and Nan (Southern) Ren.

For the Han Chinese, such a "racial caste," if we may use the phrase, amounted to a reversal of the hierarchy of peoples that Chinese conventionally adopted to locate their own position in the world. During the Yuan, the four racial class divisions indeed also created more ethnic tensions within Quanzhou and led some individuals to leave home for

---

[45] Gu, Yan Wu, *Rizhi Lu* [*Record of Daily Accumulated Knowledge*] (Changsha 1994 [1670]), *juan* 48.

[46] *Quanzhou Prefecture Gazetteer*, compiled by Yang Ming, Qian (Quanzhou 1612), *juan* 4. See also *Quanzhou Jiufengsu Ziliao Huibian* [*A Collection of Materials on Old Customs in Quanzhou*] (Quanzhou1985), Gazetteer Office of Quanzhou, pp. 6–24.

[47] Lin, *Zhongguo Minzu Shi* [History of Nationalities in China] 2 Vols. Vol. 2, pp. 50–85.

lands overseas.[48] But for the merchants, the Yuan's hospitable attitude toward foreign visitors and traders was beneficial to Quanzhou's regional tradition of commerce. The Yuan government continued to treat Quanzhou as a major station for the supervision of trade. Foreign merchants were encouraged to visit and stay in the city. Thus, during the Yuan, Quanzhou's economy continued to grow. The number of foreign countries and regions trading with Quanzhou increased from something between thirty and forty in the Song to ninety-eight in the Yuan. The city was described as the place where "maritime merchants from the four seas and all sorts of luxurious goods presented by many barbarians concentrated" and, as an imperial recognition of its important position, the rank of the city itself was upgraded to the capital of a province [*xingsheng*] in 1277.[49]

All that did not simply mean that local people felt less oppressed than did their fellow subjects in other regions governed by the Mongols. It meant only that the merchants who had gained recognition as a higher class had begun to influence the political life of the city. The Family of Pu Shou Geng came from a merchant group of Persian origin, whose ancestors supposedly traveled through the South China Sea to settle in China and migrated from Guangdong to Quanzhou during the Southern Song. (The family name Pu was a Han transliteration of Abu in Arabic.) The Pu family controlled the extremely busy maritime trade from Quanzhou for a lengthy period of time.[50] To direct the many vessels coming and going, Pu Shou Geng even constructed a large building called "Wangyun Lou" or the "Watching Clouds Tower" on the coast.[51] During the Song-Yuan transition, the Pu family turned against the Song, and they continued to dominate Quanzhou's overseas trade for most periods of the Yuan Dynasty.[52]

The high mobility of the Pu family during the Song-Yuan period is vividly represented in a rare genealogy of one of its branches discovered by Zhuang Wei Ji in 1955 in south Quanzhou:

---

[48] *Quanzhou Haiwai Jiaotong Shiliao Huibian* [*A Collection of Materials of Quanzhou's Overseas Communication History*], pp. 334–337.

[49] Zhuang, Jing Hui, *Haiwai Jiaotong Shiji Yanjiu* [*Archaeological Studies of Overseas Communication History*] (Xiamen 1996), pp. 99–101.

[50] For a summary of research and controversies surrounding Pu Shou Geng's role in the politics and commerce of Quanzhou, see So, *Prosperity, Region, and Institutions in Maritime China: The South Fukien Pattern, 946–1368*, pp. 301–305.

[51] *Quanzhou Haiwai Jiaotong Shiliao Huibian* [*A Collection of Materials of Quanzhou's Overseas Communication History*], p. 24.

[52] Zhuang, Wei Ji, Quanzhou songchuan wei Pu jia Sichuan kao [An investigation into the interrelationship between the Song boat and the Pu family], *Zhongguo yu Haishang Sichou Zhilu* [*China and the Maritime Silk Route*] 2 Vols. (Fuzhou 1991), Vol. 1, pp. 344–354.

Our founding ancestor Pu Meng Zong was the prefect of Hunzhou during the early reign of Renzong [1023;1063] during the Song. During Jiayou Period (1056–1063), and he was appointed as you-zheng in Western Shu [Sichuan], where he settled.

Our second-generation ancestor, Pu ke, made an agnatic tie with Su Zi Shan, and he served once as the professor of Pingyuan County.

Our third-generation ancestor Pu Yao Ren was appointed magistrate of Taihe County in the Ji'an Prefecture of Hexi during the Shaoxing Reign (1132–1162).

Our fourth-generation ancestor Pu Xu studied with Zhu Xi.

Our fifth-generation ancestor Pu Guo Bao lived in Fushun County in Xuzhou Prefecture in Sichuan during the Kaixi Reign (1205–1207). He followed his son into Fujian.

Our sixth-generation ancestor Pu Shi Bin was appointed magistrate of Jinjiang County in the Quanzhou Prefecture of Fujian Province for his contribution to the dynasty. He brought his family there when he was in office. After finishing his period of office, his family became registered locals, and they settled in Fashi Xiang of Jinjiang County. His wife had the surname Cai, and she had three sons.

Our seventh-generation ancestors included the three brothers, Pu Shou Cheng, Pu Shou Geng, and Pu Shou. Shou Cheng served as prefect of Puzho for nine years during the Xianchun Reign (1265–1274). He was thrifty and simple in character. He took nothing from the people. He dug a well and named it Zeng Jing. From the well he fetched two bottles of water and placed them beside where he was seated. He was praised by the people: "The heart of the Pu family is as transparent as the water from the well of Zeng Jing, which will continue to flow for thousands of years [*Zengshi Jingquan qiangu lie, Pujia xinshi yiban qing*]. He registered his household in Taizhou in the Gongchang Prefecture in Shanxi Province. After he retired from the government, he lived in Puzhou. Thus in present-day Shanxi and Shaanxi Provinces, there are many of his offspring. In the tenth year of the Xianchun Reign (1275), the court called on Shou Sheng to appoint him as the prefect of Jizhou. He knew that the Song's fortune had been reversed. So he did not go. In the third lunar month of the twenty-third year of the Zhiyuan Reign of the Yuan (1287), Cheng Wen Hai, the messenger of Shizu Emperor, called upon capable people in Jiangnan to work for the Yuan's government. Shou Sheng went to take the exam, and his score was the first of the first rank. He was bestowed [with the title of] Zhuangyuan. His wife was from the Jin family, and she gave birth to two sons, Shi Kong and Shi Ri. Shou Geng had two sons who were Shi Wen and Shi Si.

Our eight-generation ancestor Shi Wen married a woman from the Ma family. In the first year of the Dade Reign (1297), he inherited his father's position as the Zhongshu Level Pacifier of the Sea of Fujian.[53]

If the genealogy is truthful, then, several important facts emerge: (1) The Pu family moved quite freely back and forth between north and

---

[53] C.f., Wu, Wen Liang, *Quanzhou Zongjiao Shike* [*Epigraphical Materials of Religions in Quanzhou*] (Beijing 2005 [1957]), p. 266.

south in the Song. (2) Through their exposure to Neo-Confucianism, they became Sinicized. (3) At least during the Yuan, they married only into families with surnames such as Jin and Ma, which were Hanized family names of Muslim households. (4) Pu Shou Geng made a great contribution to the Yuan's conquest of Fujian, and he was appointed by the Yuan court to govern Quanzhou politically, economically, and militarily, and his son Shi Wen inherited his legacy.

In fact, the Pu family was not the only example of Quanzhou's merchant-elite. Local historical records describe Quanzhou in the Yuan Dynasty as a place where "ships from ten thousands of countries were anchored and merchants from ten continents were warmly received" [*gangbo wanguo chuan, shili shizhou ren*]. The Italian traveler Marco Polo, who probably visited Quanzhou at the time, compared the city to the Harbor of Alexandria in Egypt.[54] At the time, Quanzhou prospered as the starting point of the Maritime Silk Road that linked China to South India, the "Southern Ocean" (Nanyang), the Middle East, and Africa. Given its role in trade, Quanzhou hosted a wide variety of "foreign guests" [*fanke*]. The whole southern district, such as Jubaojie (the street where valuable things converge), was a "Foreign Guests' Town" that featured all sorts of exotic goods, enterprises, shops, hotels, restaurants, and brothels.[55] It was in this place that Chinese products, especially silk from Zhejiang and porcelain from Jingdezhen in Jiangxi and inland Fujian, were exchanged with foreign commodities.

By the early fourteenth century, many foreigners had settled in Quanzhou, and a number of local people converted to foreign religions, including Catholicism. In 1326, Andreas, an Italian priest, was sent from Beijing to Quanzhou to serve as a regional bishop. In a letter that he wrote to the head of his monastery in Perugia (still extant), he talked about the difficulties he encountered in the city. According to Andreas, before his arrival, a big church had been built with funds provided by a rich Armenian lady who had settled in Quanzhou. The foreign language that many foreigners and some locals spoke was Persian. It is thus evident that by the arrival of Andreas, Quanzhou was already host to large Catholic and Persian communities.[56]

---

[54] *Quanzhou Haiwai Jiaotong Shiliao Huibian* [*A Collection of Materials of Quanzhou's Overseas Communication History*], p. 14.

[55] Zhuang, Wei Ji, Quanzhou lidai chengzhi tansuo [An investigation of city sites in the historical periods of Quanzhou], *Quanzhou Wenshi* [*Quanzhou Culture and History*], 2(3) (1980): 14–28.

[56] Pierre Corradini, Italians in Quanzhou during the Yuan dynasty, in *Zhongguo yu Haishang Sichou zhi Lu* [*China and the Maritime Silk Route*] 2 Vols. (Fuzhou 1994), Vol. 1, pp. 32–39.

The Culture of Commerce

From the eighth century to the early fourteenth century, several important changes in the dynastic cycle occurred, and they conjoined with the regional cycle of development centered in Quanzhou. During the early Tang, a warlike aristocracy reunited China, which had previously been left in the hands of the Han and "barbarian" aristocracies. Soon it was replaced by a new class of civil servants who had emerged in the previous period. But in later half of the dynasty, military campaigns once again enlisted armies of mercenaries and redivided China into different "states." In the Tang, civilization favored "foreign religions," especially Buddhism, which continued to influence later dynasties. During the Song, the army leaders who reunited China were deprived of their power. A strong administrative apparatus was installed. To foster the "Renaissance" of classical tradition, more emphasis was placed on the "native religion" of Confucianism. In the 1260s and 1270s, the growing power of the Mongols finally took over China and incorporated it into its empire. In this period, cultural pluralism was the norm, as were "race-class" divisions whose contradictions gave rise to popular uprisings, which led to the demise of the Yuan.[57]

Quanzhou, which had been included in the administrative map of the "Central Kingdom" in the third century, was not isolated from the effects of the dynastic cycle. At the same time, however, two factors made this prefecture more "autonomous." First, in spite of the "Renaissance" orientation of the Song, Quanzhou's geographic isolation allowed it to continue to function as a regional economic center. Second, for different politico-economic purposes, the Min State, the South Song, and the Yuan implemented more "liberal" policies toward communication and trade with the outside, which benefited Quanzhou. In the realm of religion, several shifts can also be detected during that period. Buddhism rose to prominence during the Tang, while the extension of official Confucian religion into the city during the Song created conditions under which Buddhism became closely articulated with official cults and, to a lesser extent, with Daoism. In the Yuan, Persian, Arab, and Nestorian influences were prevalent in the city. But if one takes the Song-Yuan as a continuous period of "maritime trade," then it is possible to argue that between the tenth century and the fourteenth century, the city of Quanzhou was characterized above all by its culture of commerce.

Pearson and his associates summarize the "unusual and advanced economy" of Song-Yuan Quanzhou in these terms:

---

[57] Gernet, *A History of Chinese Civilization*, pp. 233–384.

1. the concentration of population and economic strength away from the political center of gravity;

2. the rise of commercially generated wealth that was separable from land;

3. the improvement of a transportation system that facilitated economic integration and overseas navigation;

4. the development of private trade in place of the "tributary system"; and

5. qualitative changes in internal trade and the integration of the city and the countryside.[58]

Along with the these developments, Song-Yuan Quanzhou also featured more local elites engaging in commerce, more foreign enclaves on the coast, more open trade policies, and more technological innovations.[59]

Clark argues that heyday of Quanzhou commerce yielded a "social revolution," which he sees in the rapid increase in Quanzhou's success in the imperial examination system in the tenth and the eleventh centuries.[60] Although cultural refinement may well be treated as the "revolutionary outcome" of commercialization, the reverse is also the case. The relationship between commercial ethics and cultural pursuits in Quanzhou is perhaps best characterized in terms of a "symbiosis" between trade and "cultural success."

In the regional development of Quanzhou, culture—as expressed in cosmology and ritual—played an important role. Its influence manifested in urban spatial patterns. The walled-city of Quanzhou constructed during the Tang Dynasty mainly enclosed an administrative core and adjacent residential neighborhoods.[61] Already by the North Song, an outer wall [luocheng] had been built to expand the city from its administrative core to include the commercial area and its attached religious sites in the south.[62]

---

[58] Richard Pearson, Li, Min, and Li, Guo, Port city and hinterland: Archaeological perspectives on Quanzhou and its overseas trade, in Angela Schottenhammer (ed.), *The Emporium of the World: Maritime Quanzhou 1000–1400* (Leiden 2001), pp. 181–182.

[59] Ibid., pp. 182–284.

[60] Clark, Overseas trade and social change in Quanzhou through the Song.

[61] Zhuang, Quanzhou lidai chengzhi tansuo [An investigation of city sites in the historical periods of Quanzhou]. See also Chen, Yun Dun, Quanzhou Gucheng Takan [Field Research into Quanzhou's Ancient City Sites], *Quanzhou Wenshi* [*Quanzhou Culture and History*], 2-3 (1980): pp. 1–13.

[62] For example, the grand temple for the cult of Tianhou (Heavenly Queen) was at the time respected as the protector of Chinese maritime merchants and their trade.

The government headquarters of the prefecture [*zhou*] and the county [*xian*] were planned on the north-central axis; on either side of the axis were several imperial religious temples, including a literati temple [*wenmiao*], a military temple [*wumiao*], and official Buddhist and Daoist temples.[63] Urban planning in the Song Dynasty represented a local projection of central order, and this projection remained unchanged even after the Mongol take-over.

Co-existent with all the imperial state symbols were many different religions that gave the city a multicultural character during its heyday.[64] In the 1950s, Science Press in Beijing published archaeologist Wu Wen Liang's monograph, *Epigraphic Materials of Religions in Quanzhou*. The book has been reprinted recently with new material. It collects stele inscriptions from imperial Quanzhou representing many different religions. Among them, 342 pieces are Islamic, 76 pieces are Nestorian, 4 are Manichean, 90 are Hindu, and 62 are Buddhist.[65] Most of the inscriptions are dated between the Tang and the Yuan, reflecting religious pluralism in Quanzhou during its heyday.

Between the Tang and Yuan dynasties, Quanzhou's regional system of "world trade" facilitated profound cultural contact between local Chinese cultural forms and the religious traditions brought by foreign merchants, settlers, and religious specialists. Buddhism was the earliest foreign religion accepted by the locals. During the Tang Dynasty, Indian merchants brought Hinduism to Quanzhou. Between the twelfth and the early fourteenth centuries, Nestorians and Franciscans arrived in Quanzhou; and according to thirteenth-century inscriptions, they established three major churches, each with its own graveyard. In the Song and Yuan Dynasties, trade with the Arabic world by the Maritime Silk Road was important to the local economy as well as to the government's tax revenue (in the name of tribute). Many Middle Eastern and possibly Southeast Asian Muslim merchants were allowed to reside there during the Northern Song, Southern Song, and Yuan Dynasties, and they built as many as six mosques in Quanzhou. Even Manichaeism had a place in the suburbs of the city (a Manichean temple dated to the fifteenth century still now exists).[66]

---

[63] So, Kee-Long, *Tang Song Shidai Minnan Quanzhou Shidi Lungao* [*Papers on the Historical Geography of Quanzhou, South Fujian during the Tang and Song Periods*] (Taipei 1991).

[64] It is also interesting to note that as Chuan Han Sheng tells us, night life in the city in the Song was rich and consisted of (1) frequent transportation, with vehicles and people moving around; (2) night markets open until after the midnight; (3) entertainment, music, drinking, prostitution, and dance troupes; (4) religious activities; and (4) charitable activities. See Chuan, Han Sheng, Songdai dushi de ye shenghuo [Urban night life in the Song dynasty], in *Shihuo* [*Economic History*] 1(1) (1934): 23–28.

[65] Wu, Wen Liang, *Quanzhou Zongjiao Shike* [*Epigraphical Materials of Religions in Quanzhou*] (Beijing 2005 [1957]).

[66] Wu, You Xiong, *Quanzhou Zongjiao Wenhua* [*Religious Culture in Quanzhou*].

The prefects not only allowed numerous foreign religious symbols to enter the city alongside foreign goods but also adapted official religion to their regional situations.[67] For example, a local folk cult promoted an immortalized Daoist, the King of Leshan from Yongchun County, to the "King Who Opens Up Distant Lands to Navigation" (Tongyuan Wang).[68] During the Southern Song, while Neo-Confucianism was expanding, in the summer and the winter of every year, in correspondence to the directions of winds, two ceremonies were organized by the prefects to honor the cult. Headed by the prefect, along with officials from the Trade Superintendent Office and the commander of the army (navy), the sacrifice to the King Who Opens Up Distant Lands to Navigation was worshipped by local merchants, who made extensive offerings to the god in expectation of blessings in the form of maritime goods.[69]

The ceremony was known as "Praying for Wind" [*qifeng*]. It was performed annually not only in Quanzhou but also in smaller harbors elsewhere in the prefecture. On the Mountain of Nine Suns (Jiuri Shan), ten pieces of stele inscriptions documenting ten corresponding ceremonies are still present. Among the many prefects who headed the ceremonies, Zhen De Xiu (1178–1235), the renowned Neo-Confucian scholar heavily influenced by Zhu Xi and the Fujian School of Thought, deserves special attention. When serving as the Prefect of Quanzhou in the early half of the thirteenth century, he made the following remarks at a Qifeng ceremony:

> The reason why Quanzhou remains a proper prefecture lies in the fact that it has sufficient finance for both public and private utilities. Sufficient finance in turn relies on foreign ships.
> Whether foreign ships can arrive in time not all depends on winds. And it is only the gods who can make sure that winds come with regularity.
> The state holds its ceremony in order for the subjects (officials) who watch the land for the emperor to make sacrifice in the hope that the god's blessing will descend.
> Alas! The whole government put forth their best effort, and the people have all contributed all their energy. Feeling extreme exhaustion from our tedious work, we now raise our heads and look beyond the south. We are urgently in need of the ships' arrival. Our livelihood urgently requires this.

---

[67] To a great extent, besides the dynamic of the state, as So Kee-long points out: "Neo-Confucian teachings could have had a positive effect on the commercial ethics of these merchants. Their religious beliefs further consolidated ethical constraints and promoted trade." See So, *Prosperity, Region, and Institutions in Maritime China: The South Fukien Pattern, 946–1368*, p. 281.

[68] He, Qiao Yuan, *Min Shu* [*The Book of Fujian*], *juan* 8.

[69] Chen, Si Dong, Quanzhou haiwai jiaotong yu haishen xinyang [Overseas communication and maritime cults in Quanzhou], *Zhongguo yu Haishang Sichou Zhilu* [*China and the Maritime Silk Route*] Vol. 1 (Fuzhou 1991), pp. 360–374.

Please god, make your efficacy revealed, calm the waves, and allow the
ships to move smoothly. Please god, make sure that the ships' are followed
by winds of a thousand miles a day, and all arrive without any delay.
This is for what the officials and the people both pray for.[70]

In addition to the sacrifice to the King Who Opens Up Distant Lands
to Navigation at ceremonies of Praying for Wind each year, the government
organized a "guest ritual" known as "receiving and comforting the foreign
merchants" [*gaoshe fanshang*]. The guest ritual was directly sponsored by
the Southern Song court. The purpose of holding such a ceremony was
said to be "soliciting men from afar" [*zhaolai yuanren*]. The ceremony
consisted of holding a great feast for the foreigners in Quanzhou.[71]

Evidence indicates that both the ceremonies of Praying for Wind and
the Soliciting Men from Afar were mainly Southern Song official rituals.
As to whether they continued to be organized during the Yuan, there
are no first-hand accounts. However, similar kinds of rituals do seem to
have been promoted by the prefects. By 1200, the deity cult of Mazu was
already worshipped by the residents of the southern commercial boroughs.
From the early thirteenth century on, this local cult received the court's
attention, and soon Mazu was transformed into the Heavenly Queen
(Tianhou) by the state. Bestowed with several imperial titles, the goddess
was promoted to the status of protector of maritime order. Her temple in
the south of the city was expanded. The goddess was regarded, like the
King Who Opens Up Distant Lands to Navigation, as a maritime deity
[*haishen*], which, as Chen Si Dong suggests, served mainly to protect the
routes of "Maritime Silk Road." In the imperial ceremonial institution,
the cult was ranked as high as Confucius and was entitled to receive two
formal sacrifices in the spring and autumn.[72]

Notably, during the same periods, interest in "things foreign" also
was evident in the intellectual pursuits of world-gazetteers.[73] In 1225,
Zhao Ru Gua, a customs inspector, based his *Gazette of Foreigners* [*Zhufan
Zhi*] on details supplied by the foreign and Chinese merchants he met at

[70] Cf., Wu, You Xiong, *Quanzhou Zongjiao Wenhua* [*Religious Culture in Quanzhou*], p. 43.
[71] Zhuang, *Haiwai Jiaotong Shiji Yanjiu* [*Archaeological Studies of Overseas Communication History*], pp. 49–50.
[72] *Quanzhou Fuzhi* [*Quanzhou Prefecture Gazetteer*], compiled by Huai Yin, Bu, and Huang, Ren, *juan* 16.
[73] Chinese descriptions of foreigners and foreign produce formed a rich literature of "archaic anthropology." Produced during periods of imperial expansion, the representations of the non-Chinese found in these accounts had a great impact on Chinese conceptions of the Self-Other relationship. A certain sense of diachronic time is observable in such descriptions. But neither was the contrast rendered as an intersubjective retrospection, nor was it serving the purpose of "contrasting to know." Instead, a portrait of the tributary mode as the flow of goods and customs was the primary concern.

the port of Quanzhou. In 1349, Wang Da Yuan, who claimed to have traveled around the Indian Ocean on two merchant voyages in the 1330s, completed his *Brief Gazettes of Island Barbarians* [*Daoyi Zhilue*], in which he describes the geography, local products, and customary practices of a great number of countries. These gazettes were of course different from modern ethnographies in that they were not focused on the analytical descriptions of culture. They were more in the tradition of the Chinese genre of "Gazettes of All Things" [Bowu Zhi]. But they were not simply derived from the extension of tradition. They were closely connected to the quasicosmopolitanism of the world-scale tributary trade at the centralized periphery of China.

By the time these gazettes of foreign places emerged, Chinese representations of the outer zones of the human world had undergone some changes. The earlier descriptions of tributary worlds fused the urban design of the dynastic capital with the design of the whole world. The zones of civilization and its lesser forms were also mapped onto the city of the King or the Emperor. Comparatively, in the gazettes compiled during the Song-Yuan periods, the centers of tributary stations such as maritime trade harbors on the coast were emphasized as the point of reference for measuring distances between China and other countries. Quite like Western Orientalist studies, such gazettes of foreign countries were imperialist in character. They were texts framed by discursive institutions.[74] Jointly they created a structure of center-periphery relationships that culminated in the cosmology of Heaven. In all these works, the subjectivity of other was recognized only as a diversity of local products, mountain monsters, ocean chieftains, and half-humans. In these gazettes, the descriptions of local products were colored by their place within the tributary system. The exchange between China as the center of the world and peripheries of other countries was defined in terms of the Son of Heaven's obligation to pay greater gifts to the tribal chieftains as what he, in turn, as the Father of the people, owned his "sons."

---

[74] Edward Said, *Orientalism* (New York 1978).

CHAPTER 3

Casting the Net: *Pu* and the Foundations of Local Control, 960–1400

In today's Quanzhou, territorial divisions drawn along the boundary lines of *pu* are chiefly involved in the organization of unofficial popular religious festivals that, from the government's perspective, are merely "cultural survivals" of "feudal superstition" (which anthropologists of China abroad have alternatively termed "popular/folk religion"). But a few centuries ago, divisions of *pu* were conspicuously official and politically rational. Archival materials pertaining to the organization of *pu*—contained in the histories compiled under the direct supervision of the ministers and magistrates in between the thirteenth and the nineteenth centuries—are the key documents recording the history of *pu* or, later, the *pujing* system. None of these documents associates *pu* with "superstitious" or "popular religious" celebrations, and all describe *pu* as an imperial state institution.

Local gazetteers trace the origin of *pu* to an archaic time. They suggest that the ideal model of *pu* derived from officials' work in the Zhou court. As legend has it, officials in classical times were sent out to administrate the countryside and wilderness areas. As a means of ordering society, they invented what was known throughout imperial times as *tiguo jingye*. This classical Chinese phrase, *tiguo jingye*, is now translated into Mandarin as "the installation of administrative districts" [*xingzheng quhua*].[1] However, in the *Zhou Li* [*Zhou Scripture of Rites*] it is described as part of the process of installing a fief [*guo*], which is now understood as a form of statehood (in the case of the Warring States). *Zhou Li* says:

> When a king is establishing his state (fief), he first marks out the nodal points of the directions and locations of it. He then installs administrative districts in the demarcated lands [*tiguo jingye*], sets up posts for officials, and allocates them separate responsibilities in order for the state to reach the people.[2]

The characters of *guo* and *ye* consist in a sort of binary opposition and convey the distinction between the city and countryside. *Ti* refers to the practice of intimate understanding and embodiment, whereas *jing* refers to measuring and passing through a span of distance, ordering a place, and configuring and extending the reach of civilization. Philological analysis indicates that in classical China, "installing administrative districts" was a complex performance involving the cosmological ordering of geography and local worlds.[3]

Pu, like all other kinds of place and social group categories, belonged to a hierarchical order that from the beginning of Chinese civilization conveyed the meaning of designated locations of "districts, associations, prefectures, and townships to fulfill the purpose of establishing neighborhood relationships" and "to let the officials know about the interconnections, advantages, and shortcomings of these places and categories."[4]

Charted and governed localities existed for centuries before the emergence of *pu*. Vivienne Shue compares Chinese and European imperial administrative capabilities:

> the centralized Chinese state took shape *very early*, not by making combinations of already acknowledged customary jurisdictions but by territorial conquest using towns as way stations and radiating beacons of its civilizing authority.[5]

[1] Zhou, Zhen He, *Tiguo Jingye Zhidao* [*The Way of Controlling the Country and the Wilderness*] (Hong Kong 1990), pp. 6–12.

[2] Ibid., p. 5.

[3] Much of the symbolic meaning of *tiguo jingye* [embodying the city and ordering the wilderness] was lost in the First Emperor's application of it in 221 B.C.E., in which "administrative district divisions"—prefectures, counties, and other local administrative central places—outweighed the ceremonial divisions. *Pu* could thus be related to the Qing Legalist system of local administration. But curiously, the compilers the 1830 edition of the *Jinjiang County Gazette* believed that it was the Zhou dynasty rather than the Qin dynasty that invented many Chinese institutions including the original type of community model on which the system of *pu* was based.

[4] *Jinjing Xianzhi* [*Jingjing County Gazette*], compiled by Zhou, Xue Zeng (Fuzhou 1990 [1830]), *juan* 21.

[5] Vivienne Shue, *The Reach of the State: Sketches of Chinese Body Politic* (Stanford 1988), p. 94.

Strictly speaking, the kind of *pu* in question was applied to describe local administrative work just a few centuries before local records of it were compiled, and the intended functions of it were not always the same.

In some gazettes, *pu* and their lower-level territorial units were listed in the records of imperial courier-post services [*yipu, pudi*] and in the records of administrative geography [*fengyu*].[6] In other gazettes,[7] *pu* was placed in the range of urban administrative units [*guizhi*] and the records of local wards and precincts [*duli zhi* or *puxiang zhi*], while in some[8] they were, somewhat confusingly for us, recorded in the chapters on *youyi* [postal routes] and local administration. All gazetteers suggested that the *pu* system had come into existence during the Yuan in the thirteenth century. By the Qing Dynasty, the gazette compilers in Quanzhou had become quite certain that *pu* was a system of neighborhood control. But there was no consensus over the issue of whether the system was originally a network of courier-post stations or an archaic form of local administration.

As the compilers of the *Jinjiang County Gazette* argued, "in fact courier-post services and local wards and precincts are indispensable to each other."[9] As to the issue of how postal wards and surveyed places became mutually "indispensable" in the process of *pu*'s authorization, Qing official histories provide some vague clues. If we were to relate these clues to the dynastic histories of the Song, the Yuan, and the Ming, we would become clear that although the word *pu* is now rarely heard in regions outside Quanzhou, a few hundred years ago it existed as a state apparatus and a widely used institution of territorial control and integration. In the Ming and the Qing, *pu* referred to a network of local administrative units in the city of Quanzhou. Before then, the concept of *pu* had been advanced. During the Song and the Yuan dynasties, *pu* had first referred to an extensive network of military wards on imperial communication routes, *pudi*, and then was also used to refer to units of local administration that continued to be in use throughout later periods of imperial China.

Pu as Express Postal Wards, 960–1279

The story of *pu*, and later, *pujing* (a combination *pu* and further divisions of *jing* emerged during the early Ming) began during the heyday of the city's

---

[6] For instance, *Quanzhou Fuzhi* [*Quanzhou Prefecture Gazette*], compiled by Huai Yin, Bu, and Huang, Ren (Quanzhou 1870 [1763]), *juan* 4.

[7] For instance, *Jinjing Xianzhi* [*Jingjing County Gazette*] compiled by Fang, Ding (Quanzhou 1945 [1765]), *juan* 2; *Hui'an Xianzhi* [*Hui'an County Gazette*], compiled Wu, Yu Ren (Fuzhou 1985 [1803]), *juan* 4.

[8] *Hui'an Xianzhi* [*Hui'an County Gazette*], *juan* 4; *Jinjing Xianzhi* [*Jingjing County Gazette*], compiled by Zhou, Xue Zeng, *juan* 20–21.

[9] *Jinjing Xianzhi* [*Jingjing County Gazette*] (ed.), Fang Ding, *juan* 20–21.

prosperity: the florescence of Quanzhou's maritime trade was matched by an extending network of control over the region. If one uses the folklore of the Carp to re-envisage the image of the prosperous Song-Yuan city, then one can also observe, in the installation of *pu*, a simultaneous process of casting a "fishing net." The insertion of administrative centers for control and pacification amounted to the casting of a net over the city, and by the mid-fourteenth century, the administrative net had taken over the urban landscape and replaced the carp shape of the city with a more square cosmological landscape of *tiguo jingye*, or that of an embodied city and ordered wilderness.

Prior to the Northern Song, Quanzhou was loosely administered under eight dispersed cantons named *xiang*.[10] Near the end of the tenth century, rural areas under its direct administration consisted of five *xiang* [townships]. In the prefecture's seat, neighborhoods were managed through divisions of *fangxiang* [streets and lanes].[11]

The character *xiang* in the context of *fangxiang* had several meanings. It could refer to the side rooms of a building, a unit of 25,000 soldiers, or the intermediate level urban blocks. The system of *xiang* began in the early ninth century as an institution of urban district management. As the system developed further in the early Song Dynasty, its designated administrative capabilities increased. The institution was invented to maintain local public security, provide social welfare and medical service, build and maintain local irrigation and drainage systems, protect imperial examinations from disturbances, prevent the sale of low-quality commodities, and conduct population censuses. "Fang" was lower than *xiang* and was further divided into urban districts.[12]

During the Song, the city of Quanzhou had some eighty neighborhoods, which were known as *huafang*.[13] The character *hua* referred in classical Chinese to "maps" or "charts," whereas *fang* usually meant "localities," "neighborhoods," or "workshops." *Huafang* thus referred to urban neighborhoods, which were "mapped localities." "Mapped localities" were a residential ward system regulated and

---

[10] Chen, Si Dong, Qianyan [Preface], to Chen, Chui Cheng, and Lin, Sheng Li (eds.) *Quanzhou Jiu Pujing Jilue* [*An Investigation into the Old Pujing in Quanzhou*] (Quanzhou 1990), pp. 1–2.

[11] Zhuang, Wei Ji, Quanzhou lidai chengzhi tansuo [An investigation of city sites in the historical periods of Quanzhou], *Quanzhou Wenshi* [*Quanzhou Culture and History*], 2-3 (1980): 14–28.

[12] Jia, Hong Hui, Songdai chengshi xiangzhi yanjiu [A study of the *xiang* institution in the Song Dynasty], in The Center for Historical Geography, Peking University (eds.), *Hou Ren Zhi Shi Jiushi Shoucheng Jinian Wenji Jing* [*A Collection of Essays in Honoring the 90th Birthday of Professor Hou Ren Zhi*] (Beijing 2003), pp. 26–48.

[13] Zhuang, Wei Ji, Quanzhou lidai chengzhi tansuo [An investigation of city sites in the historical periods of Quanzhou].

controlled with rigid rules. On the basis of their names, So Kee-long argues that *fang* in Song Quanzhou were designated as residential areas for local elites and merchants who could be grouped into five categories according to their honors: "(1) success in an official career, (2) success in the civil service examination, (3) contribution to local education, (4) moral examples, and (5) commerce."[14] I agree that the names of *fang* were connected with elite residences, but I am doubtful of their perfect correspondence So Kee-long has found between the *fang* names and the social statuses of their inhabitants. In my own view, these *fang* were simply neighborhoods for any of the urban residents of Quanzhou who honored their places with elitist phrases. No evidence is available as to how these "mapped locales" were managed, but it is clear that they were created for local public security purposes.[15]

During the Song, the concept of *pu* was used to refer to armed ward police [*junxun pu*]. These street police had several stations for their own beats within a given *fang*. In Dongjing (Kaifeng), the capital of the North Song, each *fang* contained several such *pu*, and a *pu* was located at a distance of 300 feet [*bu*] from its closest counterpart.[16] But *pu* were not used as a concept for describing territorial units of local administration. Nor was they used in the city of Quanzhou.

In more ordinary contexts, *pu*, which originally referred simply to a span of 10 *li*, began in the early Song to also refer to a level of the pan-dynasty network of information transmission, the system of courier-post stations, whose distance from each other was ideally 1 *pu* or 10 *li*. The *Record of the Armies* (Bing Zhi), official histories of the Song and the Yuan, and modern historical studies of imperial Chinese courier stations, all provide an image of the old form of *pu*.

Zang Rong, who wrote a history of Chinese postal services, shows that in the Song Dynasty each *pu* had a building with an image of a 12-hour circle hanging over its gate as its symbol. A *pu* gate featured a red decorated archway that contained a nameplate. Each *pu* also housed several soldiers who were identified as *pubing*. The soldiers were equipped with bells, weapons, and uniforms and known for their running speed. When an urgent message arrived, the *pu* bells rang. A *pubing*, who stood outside the archway, would take the parcel or document and run to the next *pu*, where he handed over the mail and let another soldier run it over to the next station.[17]

---

[14] So, Kee-long, *Prosperity, Region, and Institutions in Maritime China: The South Fukien Pattern, 946–1368* (Cambridge, MA 2000), p. 175.

[15] Jia, Hong Hui, Songdai chengshi xiangzhi yanjiu [A study of the *xiang* institution in the Song Dynasty].

[16] Ibid., p. 29.

[17] Zang, Rong, *Zhongguo Gudai Yizhan yu Youchuan* [*Courier Stations and Postal Transmission in Ancient China*] (Beijing 1997), pp. 137–140.

Prior to the Northern Song Dynasty, an imperial system of courier-post stations existed, but those who served as messengers were amateur. In the Northern Song, the Ministry of Armies (*Bing Bu*) was for the first time given direct control over the regulation, organization, and management of the postal networks, known as *youyi*. The soldiers involved in both *youyi* and *pudi* then began to be called *pubing*, the lowest ranking soldiers in the imperial army. Some *pubing* positions were filled with *xiangbing*, militia from the rural cantons, but in later periods, they were replaced by army men.

In addition to major courier-post stations, official hostels were also built. They were known as *guanyi* [courier-hostels], and they served to house traveling officials and tribute-paying envoys. The institutions serving to transmit official documents, letters, and the like were generally called *di* [couriers], which in turn were divided into *jijiao di* ["fast-step" couriers], *madi* [horse couriers], and *bu di* [foot couriers].

Pu as part of an armed postal service network was invented during the Song, a period of reunification. During the Song, the administrative apparatus, civil service, and political machinery enjoyed rapid expansion. In some ways, they were not entirely unbeneficial to the development of commerce. As briefly outlined in the previous chapter, in Quanzhou, the direct involvement of the state in maritime trade facilitated the expansion of China's tributary trade system. To welcome foreign "tribute-payers," traders, and envoys, a grand hotel and a whole district for "foreign residents" [*fanfang*] were established near the Trade Superintendent Office and in the south of the city, respectively.[18] But the dynasty as a whole was not quite as welcoming as the Quanzhou region. Constantly faced with external threats from its northern borders, the court established courier-post wards, which were generally related to the character *pu*, in order to ensure speedy responses to frontier emergencies.

In the later periods of the Northern Song, the non-Chinese empires to the north and the southwest borrowed many institutions from the "Central Kingdom" and became what could be called "Sinicized empires." In the North, the Liao and the Jin successively forced the Song into taking refuge south of the Yangtze River and establishing its provisional capital at Hangzhou. By the time of the South Song, postal networks advanced farther, especially on the southeastern, southwestern, and northern frontiers. An institution known as *chihou* emerged. As an institution of postal transmission, *chihou* had existed in the Northern Song, and it referred to the posts of soldiers who were stationed on high points to keep watch over local military situations. In the Southern Song,

---

[18] *Quanzhou Haiwai Jiaotong Shiliao Huibian* [A Collection of Materials of Quanzhou's Overseas Communication History], Quanzhou Museum of Maritime Communication (Quanzhou 1983), pp. 21–28.

chihou changed into a network with multiple functions, serving not only to detect the military movements of the enemies but also to transfer official documents and parcels. In the *chihou* institution, *pubing* were given the task of transferring information, official documents, and parcels, whereas *chihou* were specialized in border watch. During the eleventh century, an advanced system of *didi pu* [express postal wards] came into being.[19]

From Civil Government to Mongol Colonialism

Pu emerged in a period that Jacques Gernet labels "the Chinese Renaissance."[20] In depicting "the Chinese Renaissance," Gernet associates it with the emergence of the "Mandarin state" in the Song. For Gernet, "Mandarin" refers to a Han project of state formation that relied heavily on the civil examination system, competition for status, and bureaucracy. But in his application of "Renaissance," Gernet also points to "a real transformation" taking place around the year 1000. As he believes, this transformation gave the Song and the later dynasties a new character.

Ideologically, this new character had a prototype in Song Neo-Confucianism, which on the one hand drew on what it resisted— Buddhism, which dominated the previous periods of history—but on the other hand sought to revitalize classical traditions. Like the European Renaissance, the return to the classical tradition, to the Zhou philosophy of change (*Zhou Yi*), scriptures of rites, and institutions of government (*Zhou Guan*), dominated much of the academic and political discourse of the Song. In the beginning, these discussions, as in the case of Zhu Xi's, were confined to local academies [*shuyua*]. But soon, benefiting from new information technologies, including advanced paper production and the printing industry, they became available to wider audiences.

The tightening interrelationship between writing and "paper work" yielded a new worldview, which, Gernet argues, was extremely "nationalistic." Within the boundaries of the Song, political culture, society, interclass relations, the military, and the relation between town and country became distinct from the previous periods. Hierarchy was no longer defined by pure force. Bureaucracy relied heavily on written documents. Taking lessons from the late Tang internal conflicts, the Song rulers made many not quite successful efforts to construct their monopoly of the means of force within their realms of rule. Externally, along the northern and northwestern frontiers, the Song began to take advantage of "diplomacy" with the "barbarian kingdoms," whereas along

[19] *Yuan Shi* [*The History of the Yuan Dynasty*], compiled by Song, Lian (Beijing 1983 [1371]), *juan* 49.
[20] Jacques Gernet, *A History of Chinese Civilization* (Cambridge 1982 [1972]), pp. 298–301.

the southeast coast, the expansion of tributary trade with kingdoms on maritime routes was valued as important to the government's tax revenue. As Gernet states: "When all is said and done, the Chinese world, like the West, has its distinctive characteristics."[21] After having made this allusion to European history, Gernet treats the Song innovations as a "very general parallelism of the history of civilizations and the long-term fellowship which had united the Chinese and the European worlds in the course of their development."[22]

Taking China as a whole as the "Chinese world," the line of development that Gernet maps out is valid as an interpretive scheme for post-Tang or, in Gernet's terms, "postmedieval" Chinese history. We can, as Gernet has done, regard the Song as the beginning of the early indigenous modernity of the Orient. *Pu*, the network of "stations" or wards, which came into being in the first dynasty of the "Chinese Renaissance," the Song, and continued to function as an official institution of dynastic integration could be related to the long-term process of Sinicization. Internally, it functioned to link vertically lower offices with higher ones. Externally, it provided an effective channel of information transmission that was vital to the maintenance of the demarcation line between the Song and the non-Chinese barbarians.

The *pu* and *youyi* system of the Song was implemented through military organization. But, as a gradually integrative project, it merged with the protonational consciousness of Neo-Confucianism. During the Song, the installation of *pu* and *youyi*, although initially a State-driven dynamic, was actively participated in by Confucian official-scholars, scholar-gentry, and local nobles. Thus it is not incidental that in a dedication to the establishment of a postal ward in Fengti Yi, situated to the north of Quanzhou, the prefect Cai Xiang said in 1061: "I praise those gentry who contributed to the refurbishment of the postal ward."[23]

The system of courier-post networks was refined during the Song's confrontation with northern "barbarian empires" and expanded along with the expansion of the Song military defense system. In spite of all the attention that the Song paid to boundary maintenance, the northern Sinicized "barbarian regimes" had their own civilizing project: They sought to "unify China" in their own ways. Gradually, their copresence gave way to a unifying larger power, the Mongols. By the thirteenth century, the Mongols eliminated their rivals in the North and conquered the Southwestern kingdom of Dali. Around 1270, it conquered the whole of China, including the Southern Song. A vast empire was inaugurated.

---

[21] Ibid., p. 298.

[22] Ibid.

[23] Cai, Xiang, Xiu yi ji [Inscription of re-amendment of a courier-post station], in *Cai Xiang Ji* [*The Collection of Writings by Cai Xiang*] (Shanghai 1996 [1011]), pp. 497–98.

Like many institutions established in the Song, during the Yuan Dynasty the remaining political properties of *pu* were inherited by the new government. To control the vast empire and bring life to its much-expanded tributary system, the new rulers of the Yuan also extended this system of courier-post stations.[24] In their empire, there were more than one thousand high-level courier-post stations, and the rapid transit wards under them were numerous. These wards continued to serve in their old functions as transit stations for the transfer of official documents and information from inland and the frontier. In addition, they were also combined with a new institution of local administration. In the surrounding rural areas of Quanzhou, several new courier routes were established. There, the highest level *pu* was established in front of the compound of the prefectural government. This *pu* was called *Fuqian Pu* [ward in front of the prefectural government]. Radiating from this ward, which was categorized as a "commanding *pu*" [*zongpu*], were several lines that mapped the country into a centripetal circle. In the suburban county of Jinjiang, there were a total of eighteen larger wards, some following the routes of larger roads, others following the routes of smaller mountain paths. These wards were located to the Northeast, South, and Southeast and linked the major townships, the harbor, and the mountainous areas to the city.[25] Each ward had an office [*pushe*], in which four or five armed servitors, who were commanded by one ward commander [*pusi*], took turns being in charge.

The eighteen larger wards in the countryside were in charge of information transmission among the 135 *tu* [charted areas], which in turn were attached to 47 *du* [rural townships]. Within the city of Quanzhou, the 36 *pu* [local administrative wards equivalent to *li* in rural areas] had co-existed with the higher-level territorial units of 16 *tu* to make up three urban districts or *yu* [urban townships equivalent to *du*]. *Pu*, *tu*, and *yu*, the three levels of Quanzhou's place hierarchy, were placed under the *xian* [county] of Jinjiang, and they had divisions of labor. Whereas the work of *pu* was chiefly concerned with the transmission of information and the maintenance of local public security, *tu* were focused on local household registration and information storage [*huji*]. The Chinese character *tu* conveys the meaning of "map." The *tu* system in Quanzhou was named such, because each *tu* had a book of household registration, the front page of which had a map of the locality under its superintendence. But as the 1763 edition of *Jinjiang County Gazette* indicates, during the Yuan the government's designated functions of *pu* and *tu* were merely "partially fulfilled."[26]

---

[24] *Yuan Shi* [*The History of the Yuan Dynasty*], *juan* 10.
[25] *Jinjing Xianzhi* [*Jingjing County Gazette*], compiled by Fang, Ding, *juan* 21.
[26] Ibid., *juan* 6.

The Yuan's *pu* system was quite different from its counterpart in the Song. During the Northern Song, smaller courier-post stations—including the courier-post wards—were mostly located near rural township level market towns, while larger stations with hostels were built in county seats or regional metropolises. They were both managed by the army and were detached from local communities, with their affairs alternately administered by a well-organized system of *xiangli* and *fangxiang*. By the Yuan, however, the two systems were combined and were subjected to more military control and racial discrimination.

Another source of the Yuan's *pu* system was the Southern Song system of urban armed police stations. Wu Zi Mu, who lived in Hangzhou near the end of the Southern Song, wrote *Meng liang Lu* in the early Yuan, recounting his observations of urban social life in the capital. Volume 10 of his work records most of the government departments and army organization in the city. According to Wu, several *yu* were established within the walled city. In a span of some 200 paces, a *junxun pu* [armed police post] was stationed. Each police-post was attended by three to five armed policemen whose tasks were threefold: (1) preventing theft and fire, (2) transferring local disputes upward to the local government-court, and (3) protecting the wealthier households.

Above the level of *junxun pu*, each urban *yu* had an officers' house [*guanwu*], a tower-like building whose main function was to watch for and control fire. The vacancies of the officers and armed police were filled mainly by *tujun* [local militia]. But they were ready to be dispatched as troops.[27]

Social historian Quan Han Sheng has argued that the *pu* system of the South Song was an administrative response to flourishing night life in Hangzhou, the Southern Song's capital.[28] This nightlife consisted of: (1) streets crowded with vehicles and people; (2) night markets open until after midnight; (3) entertainment, music, drinking, prostitution, and dance; (4) religious activities; and (5) charitable activities. Quan shows that, during late nights, Hangzhou inhabitants spent a lot of time entertaining one another and meeting people in the streets. The public security apparatus, involving *pu* police on patrol, emerged in response to the advancement of night life, primarily to maintain public order and prevent fire.[29]

The system of *Junxun pu* was not put into practice in regional cities such as Quanzhou until the Yuan, although it had already been

---

[27] Wu, Zi Mu, *Meng Liang Lu* [*Records of Mengliang*] (Shanghai 2001 [1270]), pp. 139–140.

[28] Chuan, Han Sheng, Songdai dushi de ye shenghuo [Night Life in the Urbanities of the Song], *Shihuo* [*Economic History*], 1(1) (1934): 23–28.

[29] See also Zhang, Jia Ju, Songshi nandu hou de dushi shenghuo [Urban life after the Song court moved to the South], *Shihuo* [*Economic History*], 1(10) (1935): 36–43.

applied to maintain public order in the capital city of the South Song. Part of the Yuan's *pu* system drew on *junxun pu*, but by no means did it remain the same. In the Yuan, three thousand Persian mercenaries from Yangzhou in Jiangsu were assigned to garrison duty in Quanzhou. In the hierarchy of races officially designated by the Mongol empire, these soldiers belonged to the second-ranking race, the Semu people, higher than both the Han and the Southerners. Some of them were assigned to the offices of *pu*, within which the lowest-ranking Han soldiers performed all the menial tasks. The lowest-ranking soldiers, who were in command of *pu* [neighborhoods], "took from local households clothing and food at will and forced young boys and girls to serve them."[30]

Terms such as *pucun* [ward-villages] and *pu* [warded neighborhoods, precincts] came to refer to the policed Han communities. A *pu* controlled several to dozens of villages in the countryside. In a town, a *pu* stood out from a group of several neighborhoods (precincts) as a superintendent ward [*zongpu*].[31] While the Han and the Southerners were mostly watched within the confines of *pu*, the other ethnic groups had their separate districts in which to reside. The foci of their communal identities were mosques, Hindu temples, Catholic churches, and Buddhist monasteries, which were more multi-ethnic.

Near the end of the Yuan Dynasty, the *pu* system faced a serious crisis. To maintain the large number of *pu*, the imperial state needed sufficient financial resources. In the earlier phases of the dynasty, the imperial state made heavy levies on local households. For each courier-post *pu* or *zhan* [station], ten horses and a sufficiently large amount of grain were needed. The imperial government placed the entire burden of maintaining the wards and feeding the ward soldiers on the local households by assigning one hundred local households to each ward. These special households were named *zhanhu* [station households] or *puhu* [ward-precinct households], and their task was purely to produce what their express postal wards needed. Tensions between these ward households and the ward soldiers and officers developed soon after the wards were established. By the later period of the Yuan, the burden placed on the ward households became unbearable, and many such households left their homes to escape the levies. Gradually, many wards no longer had sufficient food supplies, and ward soldiers likewise ran away to become bandits and thieves.

---

[30] Lin, Hui Xiang, *Zhongguo Minzu Shi* [*History of Nationalities in China*] 2 Vols. (Beijing 1993 [1936]), Vol. 2, pp. 85–86.

[31] Zhuang, Wei Ji, Yuanmo waizu panluan yu Quanzhou gang de shuailuo [The rebellion of foreign ethnic groups at end of the Yuan and the decline of the Quanzhou harbor], *Quanzhou Wenshi* [*Quanzhou Culture and History*], 4 (1980): 19–26.

Pu and *Jing* in the Early Ming, 1375–1520

From 1357 to 1366, the city of Quanzhou suffered through ten years of turmoil. First, rebellion erupted among the Persian mercenaries. They were led by Seif-uddin and Amif-eddin, who sought to establish an independent kingdom of Ispahan, the place name of their hometown near the Persian Gulf. Between 1357 and 1361, their forces gradually merged with one of the factions in the Mongol imperial army who was headquartered in Fuzhou and Putian. Although in the first couple of years, the Persians did gain some control over coastal Fujian, in subsequent years their rebellion gave way to multi-ethic rivalries and factionalist fights. Around 1365, the center of conflict moved northward to the county of Putian.[32]

In the same year, the Pu family, who had surrendered to the Mongols during the late Song, became dissatisfied with the Mongols. They gained support from their Indian allies in the city. The Pu family and the Indians in Quanzhou joined forces at the South Gate of Quanzhou, declaring their sovereignty in a Hindu temple. The independence movement, joined by Persian merchants, Hindu religious followers (which included the Han), and local warlords, influenced a few years of Quanzhou history. In those years, five out of every ten Quanzhou inhabitants were forced to become "citizens" of their state.[33]

The situation did not change until the year of 1366, in which Chen You Ding led his Han army into the city of Quanzhou on behalf of the Yuan emperor. He wiped out the Ispahan rebels, the Pu family, and the Hindu cult activists and ruled the Quanzhou area until the establishment of the Ming. Before Zhu Yuan Zhang sent his imperial army into the area, Quanzhou was dominated by Han warlords. The Mongols, the Semu peoples, and many other foreigners, who had enjoyed high prestige under the Yuan "racial caste" system, were all massacred except for a handful of Hui who escaped deep into countryside and hid their identities.[34]

Before the Ming army took over Quanzhou efforts had already been made in the Ming capital of Nanjing to restore the legacy of the Song "Chinese Renaissance." The native Han Chinese worldview that had been envisaged by Song intellectuals and politicians was revitalized. To maintain

---

[32] Wu, You Xiong, Lun Yuanmo Quanzhou Yisibaxi zhanluan [On the military chaos of Ispahan in uanzhou at the end of the Yuan dynasty], in *Quanzhou Gang yu Haishang Sichou Zhi Lu* [*The Port of Quanzhou and the Maritime Silk Road*] Vol. 1 (Beijing 2002), pp. 311–323.

[33] Zhuang, Wei Ji, Yuanmo waizu panluan yu Quanzhou gang de shuailuo [The rebellions of foreign ethnic groups at end of the Yuan and the decline of the Quanzhou harbor].

[34] Zhu, Wei Gan, Yuanmo roulin Xing Quan de Yisafahanh bingluan [The military chaos of Yisfahang at the end of the Yuan and its harm on Xinghua and Quanzhou], *Quanzhou Wenshi* [*Quanzhou Culture and History*], 1 (1979): 1–10.

the boundaries between the "Central Kingdom" and its others, the Great Wall in the north was reconstructed, expanded, and consolidated.[35] Along the Southeast Coast, a system of garrison-towns was created to fend off the attacks from pirates and other "external threats" [*waihuan*]. Along with these developments, the territorial system connected with the concept of *pu* was refined, transformed, and consolidated.

During his reign, founding emperor Zhu Yuan Zhang (in his reign from 1368 to 1398) reestablished the larger courier-post stations, which had declined in the late years of the Yuan owing to political and financial crises. In the more central provinces of China, to make courier-post system run smoothly "without disturbing the peace of the local communities [*lijia*]," the court cut a great number of smaller courier-post stations, which chiefly included the express courier stations. In some parts of rural Quanzhou, some express postal wards remained in use in local territorial divisions and were gradually merging with popular conceptions of supravillage communities. Within the walled city, the commanding ward in front of the prefectural government compound and its related postal routes were retained. But the urban wards, whose office buildings had been abandoned by the Yuan postmen-soldiers, underwent a transformation. Zhu Yuan Zhang gave new definition to the spaces left behind by the Yuan soldiers, the *yu*, *du*, *tu*, *jia*, and *pu*.

During the Ming, the concept *pu* also continued to be used in the organization of armed police. Zhu Tong, the editor of the *Chongwu Garrison-Town Record*, who commented on the garrison-town constructed in the 1370s, showed that *pu* was used in the early Ming Dynasty in the context of *wopu*, which was a kind of post for military guards within the garrison-town of Chongwu, some 40 kilometers to the north of Quanzhou. *Wopu* were a part of Chongwu town's defense system, and they were constructed in 1387 by Zhou De Xing, the Lord of Jiangxia. In other garrison-towns constructed around the same time, there were also *wopu*.[36]

In the 1765 edition of the *Jinjiang County Gazette*, Fang Ding and his associates inform us that in 1381 the households of Quanzhou were registered according to seven categories (civilians, soldiers, salt producers, handicraftsmen, archers, guards or ward militia members, and doctors). One of the categories is *pubing*, or "soldiers" of *pu* [ward office].[37] These *pubing* were stationed in the forty watch posts located at the high points along the city walls, overlooking the urban neighborhoods. At every interval of

[35] Arthur Waldron, *The Great Wall of China: From History to Myth* (Cambridge 1990), pp. 72–73.

[36] *Chongwn Suocheng Zhi* [*Records of Chongwu Garrison-Town*] (ed.), Zhu, Tong (Fuzhou 1987 [1542]), *juan* 6.

[37] *Jinjing Xianzhi* [*Jingjing County Gazette*], compiled by Fang, Ding, *juan* 3.

10 *zhang* (approximately 3.33 meters), a *wopu* was established. The *wopu* system was under the command of the *Bingma Si* [Office of Soldiers and Horses]. As elsewhere,[38] it was managed by the joint forces of the imperial army [*guanjun*], archers [*gongbing*], and local fire brigades [*huojia*].

From 1375 to the mid-Ming (approximately 1500), the ways in which neighborhoods connected with the concept of *pu* in the city of Quanzhou were managed underwent an important transformation. In terms of its spatial organization, the system of *pu* in the Ming was only slightly changed. The thirty-six divisions of the city under the name of *pu* was accomplished during the Yuan, and the Ming merely inherited these divisions. What was added was the *jing* system, which was placed under *pu* level administration and was equivalent to a *li* in rural local administration. *Pu* and *jing* made up what was later called *pujing* in local territorial cult divisions. In the early Ming, *pujing* consisted of two levels of urban spatial division: *jing* [precincts] and *pu* [wards]. Above the level of *pu*, the *tu* [chartered areas, higher than *pu* and *du* in rural areas] and *yu* [urban districts] continued to be used (Table 3.1). Except for *jing*, all the concepts were familiar to people who had lived in Quanzhou during the Yuan Dynasty. Although the change in the *pu*'s spatial divisions was not as great as one may imagine, the refined system of *pujing* as an administrative organ corresponded to a China-wide administrative institution, which emerged at a political transition point around the late fourteenth century.[39]

The overall goal of the early Ming reform in connection with *pu* was twofold. On the one hand, it was to extend the reach of local government farther down into small communities. On the other hand, local administration also sought to establish what we might call the "units" of the Ming moral community. In rural Quanzhou, these small communities were officially referred to as *lishe* and *lijia*, while in the city they were termed *pu* and *jing*. One of Zhu Yuan Zhang's political ambitions was to realize the cultural ideal developed by Neo-Confucian thinkers such as Zhu Xi. It was to create, below the *xian* level, finer administrative units to render the whole of China an autocratic polity. To change the Song and Yuan express postal wards and "charted areas" into something analogous to the rural *lishe* and *lijia* systems, part of the earlier connotation of *pu* as courier-post wards was removed. Within the city of Quanzhou, the government no longer appointed specialized *pu* soldiers and masters to guard its postal service at the basic neighborhood level. Although *pu* and *tu* remained two distinct levels of locality, their work was redefined as

---

[38] Zhu, Shao Hou (ed.), *Zhongguo Gudai Zhi'an Zhidu Shi* [*The Institutional History of Chinese Public Security Management*] (Zhengzhou 1994), pp. 662–665.

[39] Timothy Brook, The spatial structure of Ming local administration, *Late Imperial China*, 6(1) (1985): 1–55.

Table 3.1 *Yu, pu,* and *jing* in Ming Quanzhou

Name of *yu*	No. of *tu*	No. of *pu*	No. of *jing*
East *Yu*	3	5	13
West *Yu*	4	10	22
South *Yu*	4	15	36

Source: *Jinjing Xianzhi* [*Jingjing County Gazette*], compiled by Fang, Ding (Quanzhou 1945 [1765]), *juan* 21.

serving one common purpose, to register and supervise local households. For the same purpose, each *pu* was further divided into one or more *jing*. The system of *pu* and *jing* thus became a local version of *li* and *she*.

In analyzing forms of modern social control, sociologist Anthony Giddens, following Michel Foucault,[40] refers to "surveillance," by which he means the integration of information and direct supervision of human conduct. He points out that modern social control is based on the regulation and coordination of activities through the manipulation of the setting in which these activities take place. Social control relies on "segmental spaces" where information concerning human activities can be obtained and through which activities can be timed and located[41] If "surveillance" can be understood as Giddens defines it, then it can also be applied to the systems of *tu, pu, jing*, and *jia* in the city and *li, pu, she*, and *jia* in the countryside.

How did this spatial system for surveillance function? In the gazettes of Quanzhou and Jinjiang, little evidence is available that illustrates the early Ming situation of social control. Fortunately, some 40 kilometers to the north of Quanzhou, the rural county of Hui'an, under the control of the same prefecture, had a more detailed account of the spatial system connected with the concept *pu*. Hui'an also had a system of place administration similar to *pu* and *jing*. This system was put into practice at the same time as in Quanzhou city, as an intrinsic part of the prefecture's regional ordering of geographic space. The basic units of this system were also *pu*, even though districts were called *du* [garrisons] instead of *yu*, and neighborhoods were called *jia* instead of *jing*. The *Hui'an County Government Manual* [*Hui'an Zhengshu*], compiled earlier than the Quanzhou and Jinjiang gazettes, provides detailed documentation on the practices of this place administration system.[42] According to this *Manual*, the role of the *pujia* [precinct and tithing] system in Hui'an fulfilled all senses of surveillance.

[40] Michel Foucault, *Discipline and Punish: The Birth of the Prison* (London 1977).

[41] Anthony Giddens, *The Nation-State and Violence* (Cambridge 1985), pp. 44–47.

[42] *Hui'an Zhengshu* [*Hui'an County Political Manual*] (ed.), Ye, Chun Ji (Fuzhou 1987 [1672]).

The original form of *pu* was *xunjing pu*, or "neighborhood police posts," while *jia* [tithing] was transplanted from the imperial *lijia* institution. A *pu* was one of the several subunits of *du*, the more militarily organized territorial units. It consisted of several *jia*.[43]

According to the description of the earliest compiler of the book, Ye Chun Ji, the main governors of a *pu* were the *jia* chiefs [*zongjia*] and their deputies [*xiaojia*]. They were all locally elected and approved by higher-level government units. *Jia* chiefs were responsible for military affairs. They reported directly to the military *du* chief and organized local militia activities. Apart from military functions, *pujia* served four other major purposes. These included (1) organizing meetings and celebrations at local patron temples; (2) registering households; (3) supervising local people's conduct and collecting information on their conduct; and (4) maintaining local public order. The spatial design of a *pu* consisted of a territorial altar or patron temple called a *tan*, arrangements of households according to numerical order, and a group of socially superior governors who served as the "gatekeepers" of the *pu*.

Each *pu* had a altar [*tan*], in which the grain god [*lijia shen*] and the place god [*lishe shen*] as well as a stone that represented the local territorial patron [*shi zhu*] were placed. Within the temple, the northern part was allocated to a representative from the *du* and the governors of the *pu*. Between the deities and the governors was a space for religious specialists. Ordinary members of the *pu* were excluded from the enclosed temple and remained outside the gate of the temple to witness proceedings of meetings and ceremonies organized by the governors.

Several records were kept in the temple. These included lists of households and registration documents of new immigrants who had just moved into the particular *pu*. A temple, or *tan*, was intended as the symbolic center of *pu* as a place. This was where disasters such as floods, fire, theft, disease, and crimes were reported to the governors and gods, publicized to the people, and resolved. It was also where local civil disputes such as those regarding marriage, land ownership, property, and trade were mediated by the governors and elders of the *pu*, and where deviance and criminality were punished in view of the public. On three occasions (the fifteenth day of the fourth and the seventh months and the first day of the tenth month), Universal Salvation Festivals [*pudu*] were officially organized to placate ghosts. The compiler of the manual summarized the temple's functions as "praying when there are recluses [*youqiu bidao*]," "swearing when there are disputes [*youyi bishi*]," "punishing when there is misconduct [*youguo bifa*]," and "exorcising when there are malevolent demons [*youhuan birang*]."[44]

---

[43] Ibid., *juan* 1–2.

[44] Ibid., *juan* 10.

In a given *pu*, each household [*hu*] hung up a placard on their front door [*pai*] distributed by the *pu* officers. This placard not only indicated the registration number of the household and the name of the *jia* and *pu* but also indicated the number of men and women in the household, their social status and occupations, their ownership of land, number of rooms, details of visitors, number of cows, horses, and agricultural equipment, and places of birth. These details were also reported and catalogued in a household registration book [*puce*] kept by the *jia* chief in the *pu* hall.

The governors of the *pu* were appointed as agents of the government, who were responsible for supervising people's conduct and maintaining local public order. But these two tasks were also assigned to the members of a *pu*, who were, ideally speaking, organized as militia. Volume 12 of the *Manual* cites eight model regulations for the community. The regulations were addressed to three audiences: ordinary members of the *pu*, wealthy *pu* households, and *pu* governors. For ordinary *pu* members, it sought to provide a set of guidelines for conduct and unified militia action. For wealthy households, it required a kind of personal sacrifice to public order. For *pu* governors, it warned against the "personalization" of administrative power and against distancing themselves from dynastic concerns by "using the public cause to gain private power." Because of their direct relevance to our understanding of spatial administration, I offer a few excerpts from these regulations:

1. [*Pu* members] should behave according to the regulations put forward in the community compact.

2. Strengthening neighborhood watch: . . . [*pu* members] should conduct a mutual watch. If they find persons who speak different languages and dress strangely, they should report it to the government. The reward for this will be the same as for reporting robberies. Otherwise, if strangers turn out to be responsible for harmful events, those who met them and did not report it to the government should be punished along with the criminals. *Pu* members should also report to the government misconduct such as gambling.

3. Careful place patrol: In the city, each *pu* should assign five people each night to conduct patrols. In rural areas, each *pu* should have ten people on patrol in order to discover unusual events.

4. Networking the local defense system: A drum has been installed in each *pu* at a central position. . . . When faced with an emergencies, a community should send someone to beat the drum. Hearing the sound of drumbeats, all other places should respond and also beat their drums. . . . Drumbeats indicate a military emergency. So all

pu members should find their weapons and await the *pu* chiefs' mobilization.

5. All *pu* members must regularly conduct military exercises.

6. People in each *pu* should equalize their wealth and poverty. Wealthier households are well known to robbers. They would do better to distribute some of their wealth to other people in order to enhance their reputation in the community "and donate some of it to the government for purchasing weapons. By so doing, they then can reduce the risk of robberies."

7. Prohibiting aggression and violence [on the part of the *pu* governors]: Those governors who are weak and unwise are often not able to make decisions and carry out policies. But those who are stronger and cleverer often become treacherous persons. A better way to serve as governor is to exercise self-control, to conduct oneself as a good model for the people, and to refrain from infringing upon the rights of other *pu* members.

8. If *pu* governors think too much of their own families, they often become hesitant in implementing government policies and set obstacles to the implementation of the law. The government will severely punish such governors.[45]

---

[45] Ibid., *juan* 12.

CHAPTER 4

Pujing and the "Civilizing Process" of the Ming, 1368–1520

Obviously, the Song was a special period during which many elements characteristic of later periods appeared.[1] During the Song, Quanzhou prefects relied on the interlinked systems of *fangxiang* and *xiangli* in their efforts to maintain social peace and order, transmit information to and from the bureaucracy and small communities, and collect taxes from the bottom of society.

By the early Ming, several institutions had evolved around the concept of *pu*. In four centuries of historical development, *pu*'s meaning and function changed over time. *Pu* first emerged as fast transit postal wards in the North Song courier-post network. In the Yuan Dynasty, it was turned into a system of territorial divisions, combining the postal wards and local neighborhood watch units into a local system of colonial rule. In the early Ming, *pu* was further divided into some ninety-eight *jing*.[2] It became known as *pujing*, which referred to a local version of a China-wide *lishe* and watch-posts system.

---

[1] Brian K. McKnight, *Village and Bureaucracy in Southern Song China* (Chicago 1971).

[2] In previous times, the size covered by a *xiang* or its urban counterpart *yu*, was larger than what the Ming government saw as useful for local administration. So in the Ming, finer units reaching farther down into local society were charted out and imposed. Timothy Brook, The spatial structure of Ming local administration, *Late Imperial China*, 6(1) (1985): pp. 1–55.

111

The reform of local administration during the early Ming was not a trivial event. In both the Song and the Yuan dynasties, units of territorial division connected with the local administration were relatively larger and more detached from the formal bureaucracy of the government. From the beginning of the Ming on, such units became smaller in geographic scope, drew considerably more attention from the officialdom, and were responsible for a great deal more local affairs. Territorial units in Quanzhou were subdivided into *jing*, which became more efficient units of control. In the earlier reigns of the Ming, *pu* and *jing* residents were so strictly disciplined that they could respond efficiently to emergencies together with the imperial army stationed in the city and the countryside. Hence, in the Ming and the Qing local gazettes, *pu* and *jing* were sometimes associated with posts of military security guards who were on sentry duty in the garrison-towns that Zhou De Xing, the military commander of several large regions to the South of Yangtze, constructed between 1381 and 1387 along the Quanzhou coast, or with militia units responsible for neighborhood security and control.[3]

Compared with the Yuan alone, *pujing* in the Ming also seemed a less severe form of rule. In the Yuan, *pu* were patrolled by specially appointed Mongol and Semu "voluntary soldiers" who ruled the communities in ways similar to direct colonial rule. The rulers and the ruled were divided by different ethnic origins and class into the "consuming" and "producing," the "served" and the "serving." The closely watched households of Han origin were not allowed to keep weapons at home; even kitchen knives were sometimes treated by the *pu* soldiers as potentially lethal weapons and their owners were arrested as Han rebels. In a particular *pu*, guard soldiers often preyed on local households, some taking food, clothing, and women at will. Thus, in the Yuan, local people described these *pu* soldiers, who were actually not wealthy in comparison to the higher ranking soldiers, as local emperors who treated *pu* offices their palaces and local women as their "imperial concubines."[4] Although this system of rule based on race and class segregation seems quite severe, according to Qing gazetteers, the efficiency of *pu* control was very low compared with that of the Ming.[5]

In the Ming, the *pujing* system of control changed greatly. Ethnic discrimination against the Han was brought into an end in the massacre of the non-Han in the last ten years of the Yuan. In this pan-Hanist country, *pu* officers and commoners were Han at least in their outlook.

---

[3] See Chapter 3 of this book.

[4] Zhuang, Weiji, Yuanmo waizu panluan yu Quanzhou gang de shuailuo [The rebellions of foreign ethnic groups at end of the Yuan and the decline of the Quanzhou harbor], *Quanzhou Wenshi* [*Quanzhou Culture and History*], 4 (1980): 19–26.

[5] *Jinjing Xianzhi* [*Jingjing County Gazette*], compiled by Fang, Ding (Quanzhou 1945 [1765]), *juan* 2.

The Ming government no longer felt it necessary to appoint non-Han to control the Han subjects. In the late fourteenth century, the prefects had a new form of control. Instructed by the emperor to let the people rule themselves, they filled *pu* official positions with local men. They allowed local *pu* members to organize themselves into militia units and to defend themselves militarily in times of emergency. Unlike during the Yuan, the household command of weapons was no longer viewed as illegal and dangerous. Instead of the overt discriminative punishment of the Yuan, the Ming emperor devised a new way of governing the people.

The founding emperor of the Ming, Zhu Yuan Zhang, was quick to adopt Confucianism. Soon after he had taken control of the Religion of Brightness (Mingjiao), a sectarian organization tightly connected to Manichaeism, he turned to famous Neo-Confucians such as Liu Ji (1311–1375) for guidance.[6] In compliance with Confucian teachings, Zhu Yuan Zhang divided the population in the "Central Kingdom" into two classes: sage-men [*junzi*] and lesser men [*xiaoren*]. In 1373, an idea occurred to him that during the Yuan "interruption" numerous lesser men emerged and constituted a class of deviant people who did not obey the moral code of the government. Zhu Yuan Zhang attributed the increase in the number of lesser men to the "decline of Chinese customary culture" [*huafeng lunmo*] and to the Mongols' "negation of the ceremonial of Huaxia" [*fei huaxia zhi yi*].

Paradoxically, to the Confucians living during the Song, the copresence of sage-men and interest-seeking lesser men was viewed as not only acceptable but also illustrative of the very essence of urban life. In the geographic work *Fangyu Shenglan* compiled by Zhu Mu during the Song, they quote a long poem praising the convergence of different social groups and cultures:

When the pioneers were sent to guard the prefecture of Clear Source,
They showed their glory of heroism and hard work.
They chose the middle realm of the region,
And they opened up the Southern frontier.
The prefecture that they opened up is the Fountain Town;
And it is known as "the City of Buddha" [Fo Guo];
the town leans back on the fertile land of Wurong;
And it is situated near the coast.
Its glory arises from the horizon of the ocean.
As the renowned prefecture, it is indeed a prosperous town in Fujian.

Here, merchants, ships, and vehicles converge.
Here, account books are numerous and dispute cases are especially complex.

---

[6] Wu, Han, *Zhu Yuanzhang Zhuan* [*The Biography of Zhu Yuanzhang*] (Tianjin 2000 [1963]), pp. 141–142.

Here is the capital of the seven regions of Min [Fujian].
Here ships sail to and from many countries.
Here the royal clan establishes its residence.
Here foreign countries all come to trade.

Inside the enclosed city, more than a hundred thousand households reside.
Outside the city, thousands of stoves [representing households] are installed.
. . .
Warm greetings and humorous smiles welcome thousands of knights from the East.
The prefecture is worthy of the name of "the great residence for the Barons of Southern countries" [*nanguo zhi zhuhou*].[7]. . .

To the locals, this portrait of the city of Quanzhou that Zhu Mu painted was a delightful one. However, to the Ming monarch, it was an object of concern. The convergence of imperial officials, merchants, ships, Buddhism, foreigners, barons, knights, and hospitable locals was the mixture of cultures in which Chinese civilization was merely a part rather than a totality. To rescue Chinese civilization from chaos, the Ming monarch resorted to a new method of class division. He promoted separate treatment for sage-men and lesser men. Zhu Yuan Zhang postulated that the Ming should "treat sage-men with ways of propriety [*li*]" and the minority of lesser men with severe punishment.[8] As he stated:

We can forgive gentlemen who make mistakes. But we should remember that lesser men are treacherous. They will trick and deceive at every possible opportunity. If they commit crimes, we should stop them by the force of law. Otherwise, the people will be harmed. When gentlemen make mistakes, we condemn them with the reasons of propriety and righteousness. They will definitely feel ashamed and conceive of changing themselves. By contrast, lesser men do not know shame. Even if we exhaust our efforts, they will continue their wrong doings. So we ought to take them away [from society].[9]

Obviously, Zhu Yuan Zhang did not regard all the Chinese as lesser men. But he did believe that severe forms of punishment not only could reduce the number of criminals but also could control the expansion of wrongdoing in society. He also regarded performances of ritual and

---

[7] C.f., *Quanzhou Fangyu Jiyao* [*Main Materials of Quanzhou Historical Geography*], Office of Local Gazetteers, Quanzhou (Quanzhou 1985), p. 37.

[8] The number of secret police dramatically increased in the imperial capitals and in the larger metropolises. See Wu, Han, *Zhu Yuanzhang Zhuan* [*The Biography of Zhu Yuanzhang*], pp. 121–124.

[9] *Ming Tai Zu Shi Lu* [*Factual Records of Ming Tai Zu*], Jiangsu Sinology Library (Nanjing 1942 [reprint]), *juan 79*.

control of daily conduct as an effective means of cultivating the disciplined interiority of a subject populace.[10]

In 1371, in order to begin his new way of rule, the first China-wide demographic census was conducted, the outcome of which was applied to the new divisions of territory under local administration.[11] In local communities, surveillance by *pubing* and *huojia* increased. And in the monarch's mind, that was not enough; local communities should also police and supervise themselves. Zhu Yuan Zhang called the mutual watch practice *huxiang zhiding*, or "knowing each other's registered condition."[12] *Lijia* and *pujing* were the basic units within which mutual-watch practices were conducted. The lowest level administrative units reported to police posts established at key points.

The designated goal of the mutual watch was to make sure that all able-bodied men were at work in each of the locations of *lijia* or *pujing*. According to Wu Han, who quotes from the Ming Code, mutual watch consisted of:

1. A method of knowing about the conditions of registered men consists of keeping precise records of the numbers of able-bodied men, farmers, craftsmen, and merchants.

2. A method of confining the distance of the farmers' movement to a span of *li* (away from their homes); that is, it serves to make sure that farmers go out to work in the morning and return home in the evening and know each other's rhythms of work and leisure.

3. A stipulation requiring those engaged in specialized professions such as handiwork to report their work locations to the local government, to let their neighbors know the amount of work in which they are engaged, and to return to their homes before evenings.

4. A standard to differentiate different extents of trade and communication, and a rule which requires the routes and volumes of trade and transportation to be reported to both the government and the neighborhood.[13]

The Ming Code also listed four kinds of deviant conduct, which were *yiwei* [strange behavior], *feiwei* [wrongdoing], *tawei* [secretive conduct], and *tagu* [deceptive performance]. On all these types of conduct and their

---

[10] Luo, Dong Yang, *Ming Taizu Lifa Zhizhi Yanjiu* [*A Study of Taizu Emperor's Rule of Ritual and Law in the Ming*] (Beijing 1998), pp. 6–7.

[11] Luan, Cheng Xian, *Mingdai Huangce Yanjiu* [*A Study of Huangce in the Ming*] (Beijing 1998), pp. 14–91.

[12] Ibid., pp. 347–349.

[13] Wu, Han, *Zhu Yuanzhang Zhuan* [*The Biography of Zhu Yuanzhang*], p. 226.

opposites, negative and positive sanctions were imposed. In front of their own public compact halls, ceremonial performances were conducted as part of punitive practice, except for the rare examples of serious crime.[14]

In the context of Europe, Michel Foucault observes a similar shift of disciplining and punishing, which took place some four centuries later than the Ming transition. To quote from Foucault:"The shift from a criminality of blood to a criminality of fraud forms part of a whole complex mechanism . . . a higher juridical and moral value placed on property relations, stricter methods of surveillance, a tighter partitioning of the population, more efficient techniques of locating and obtaining information."[15] In comparing the Ming's assertion of rule by ritual and Foucault's *Discipline and Punish*, I have found that the dynastic process of local administrative "modernization"—from whose influence the civilians living in Quanzhou could by no means escape—was rather similar to the more recent European experience as described by Foucault. But differences between the two models also existed. The Ming form was more intertwined with a process of anxiously implementing boundary-making and top-down "civilizing" than was the European model to which Norbert Elias pays a lot of attention.[16] It was distinct from "the development of production" and "the increase of wealth" that Foucault saw as embraced by the complex mechanism of the early modern European refinement of "punitive practices" and from the "bourgeois elements" that Elias regards as "mingled" with the "courticizing" force of civilization.

The Assertion of Boundaries

The years during which the *pujing* system was consolidated were also marked by a change in the Chinese body politic. From the broader perspective of the "Chinese Renaissance," the express postal wards emerged as part of the court's quest for a coherent Chinese world, a "national project" of cultural unification. As Qian Mu argues, the Ming transformation in local administration can be seen as an extension of the Song project of social reform.[17] But from the perspective of local history, two inseparable political changes in the Ming should not be underemphasized. First, the Ming state made a forceful move to build up the border along its frontier regions on the coast. Second, the increase in the Chinese empire's concern with internal stability led the rulers to try to reshape Chinese society and culture into a new model.

---

[14] Ibid., pp. 227–228.
[15] Michel Foucault, *Discipline and Punish: The Birth of the Prison* (London 1977), p. 77.
[16] Norbert Elias, *The Court Society* (New York 1983 [1933]).
[17] Qian, Mu, *Guoshi Dagang* [*Outline of National History*] 2 Vols. (Shanghai 1939).

As one of the major commercial centers on the Chinese frontier, Quanzhou had enjoyed a few centuries of regional expansion in the sphere of commerce prior to the Ming Dynasty. As outlined in Chapter 2, between the ninth and the tenth centuries, people in Quanzhou created a relatively autonomous space out of this politically and cosmologically marginal but economically central region. Within this space, important developments occurred and contributed to the expansion of Quanzhou's regional economy. By the late tenth century, Quanzhou had already become a major trading center in East Asia, serving as an intermediary point where the flow of Chinese and foreign products was facilitated. From the Song to the Yuan, the value of the "marginal" position of Quanzhou drew the direct attention of the imperial court. Economically, in the two different dynasties, the city of Quanzhou was continuously given a central place in the imperial tributary-trade system. Government trading offices were established in Quanzhou. These trading offices served as the state's agency of taxation. But their very existence was also an encouraging sign for commercial activities and allowed, within this "marginal region," a space for economic competition. Politically and culturally, the marginal position of Quanzhou in the imperial regional order allowed the city to remove itself, although only to a certain degree, from the moral-ideological control of the court. In brief, during the Song and Yuan dynasties, a "commercial spirit," which was later vividly captured by the legend of the Carp, emerged and prevailed.

Quanzhou was a collection of marginal places linked to the center mainly through the channels of imperial offices and courier-post stations at a time when local social control was comparatively looser. Different religious cultures and social forms were allowed to flourish in the neighborhoods, streets, and suburbs of the city and co-existed with native religious and social forms. In this pluralist cultural environment, place formation and hierarchical organization in the region were effected mainly through economic processes, despite the fact that these places were also controlled by the government.

The development of production and the increase in wealth did not automatically bring about a change in punitive practices. In the legal sphere, contract-like agreements appeared when trading activities became more and more frequent. Zhuang Wei Ji once discovered a contract from the sale of a large estate in the south of the city.[18] Surely, similar examples of transactions governed by contract could be further excavated.

Nonetheless, unlike the European case, this change did not automatically result in an accompanied increase in surveillance. The

---

[18] Zhuang, Wei Ji, *Jinjiang Xinzhi* [*The New Gazette of Jinjiang*] 2 Vols. (Quanzhou 1985) Vol. 2, pp. 129–130.

Northern Song court did attempt to reform the legal system. Its civil policies were complicated by local practices. By the Yuan, although the combination of racial-class divisions and the civil administration of the Song further enhanced the conjuncture of *pu* divisions with colonial rule, at the same time it also led to the decline of the Song's administrative capability. During the Yuan, while the units of surveillance became smaller, their civil administrative functions were reduced to the military method of rule and to the fourfold racial-ethic division of the population.

From the late fourteenth century onward, political changes remolded Quanzhou into a different place. Two factors led to the transformation of the Chinese dynastic polity. Internally, apart from the remaining ethnic tensions, beginning with the early Ming, the Chinese empire was confronted with greater moral crises and social conflicts than ever before.[19] Externally, its encounter with Japanese and European pirates and trader-warriors became a major challenge to the legitimacy of China as the "Central Kingdom" of the world. The Ming court responded to these crises with political, military, and cultural means.

As Farmer shows, the founding and consolidation of the Ming was a prolonged process of political and institutional evolution that took nearly half a century to complete. Prior to the formal inauguration of the Ming, Zhu Yuan Zhang exercised a sequence of military operations to establish his own base areas. Starting with these base areas, he added civil administration to military operations and began to consider questions of the ideological justification, legitimacy, and authority of his emperorship. Once on the throne, Zhu Yuan Zhang started to refine the organization of his government. Between 1368 and 1380, he focused on the reorganization of the central government. Meanwhile, the constitutional problems of the Ming were dealt with in detail. Despite his Manichaeist background, Zhu Yuan Zhang endorsed Neo-Confucianism. Frequently he also favored Buddhist and Daoist rituals in so far as they conformed to the ceremonial tradition that he sought to (re)establish. To give greater legitimacy to his rule, he established a system of hierarchical relationships that permeated social relationships, administration, kinship, communal bonds, and religion.[20]

In the process of constructing orthodoxy and authority, the Ming monarch also took serious measures to make ensure the realms of his rule were safeguarded against crises. Throughout the Hongwu Reign, the notions that foreigners were "barbarians" and trade with them was

---

[19] Frederick Wakeman, *The Great Enterprise: The Manchu Reconstruction of Imperial Order in Seventeenth- Century China*, 2 Vols. (Berkeley 1985).

[20] Edward Farmer, Social regulations of the first Ming emperor: Orthodoxy as a function of authority, in Liu, Kwang Ching (ed.), *Orthodoxy in Late Imperial China* (Berkeley 1990), pp. 103–152.

morally incorrect were advocated. In the official discourse, such a view often became mixed up with the inherited classical view of All Under Heaven. Given this mixed perspective, the emperor organized a sequence of campaigns to keep foreign evils away from the Divine Prefectures (Shenzhou). The regulations "severely punish those who attempt to trade with the barbarians" and "no wood (boat) into the sea" [*pianmu bude xiahai*] replaced the institution of the Trade Superintendent Bureau from the Song and the Yuan.[21]

Along with the implementation of the policy prohibiting maritime contact, a new taxation and labor service institution was imposed. In rural areas, the Ming court established an extensive Liangzhang [chiefs of grain collection] system, which merged with *lijia* control to ensure the fiscal income of the state.[22] The effect of the Liangzhang system was a dramatic increase of the government's income in grain compared to the Yuan. In the Ming, Zhu Yuan Zhang also extended the whole system of taxation, levies, and labor service into the cities. Unlike the farmers, urban residents did not have fields in which to grow grain. However, during the Ming, they were required to pay taxes, part of which were used for the maintenance of courier-post stations and "public properties" such as the official temples. For poorer households, labor service was required. While the *lijia* in rural areas played an important role in collecting grain, *pujing* in the city assisted the government in the imposition of courier-post levies and labor service. As a means of stabilizing local society, the Ming court made efforts to prevent human mobility, setting up strict restrictions on changes of profession and on migration.[23]

Applying the rural model of fiscal management and social control to reform social structure in the city, the Ming emperor was partly implementing a project of moral reform for urban merchants. As in previous times, local Ming society was divided into *shi* [official-scholars], *nong* [peasants], *gong* [industrial workers and managers], and *shang* [merchants]. During the Song and the Yuan, merchants and those who were engaged in industrial production were numerous, but their presence was not troubling to officials, including even the famous Neo-Confucian Zhen De Xiu. By the early Ming, these groups came to be profoundly despised by the monarch.

Zhu Yuan Zhang preferred the countryside and small towns, and he loathed commercial life in the larger cities. He conceived of an idealized

---

[21] Zhuang, Wei Ji, *Jinjiang Xinzhi* [*The New Gazette of Jinjiang,*] 2 Vols., Vol. 1, pp. 226–271.

[22] Liang, Fang Zhong, *Mingdai Liangzhang Zhidu* [*Grain Head System in the Ming Dynasty*] (Shanghai 1956).

[23] Luo, *Ming Taizu Lifa Zhizhi Yanjiu* [*A Study of Taizu Emperor's Rule of Ritual and Law in the Ming*], pp. 82–96.

view of rural gardens. He saw his own capital as perfectly in line with the classical Zhou Dynasty tradition of agrarianism. In the course of making his capital, he expanded his dislike of commercial cities by blaming the "leisure class" living in the metropolises for ruining morals, destroying conventional sorts of human relationships and affection, and creating dishonest ties between people.

Comparing the late Yuan and the early Ming with "ancient times," Zhu Yuan Zhang once sighed that there were too many "wandering and idle people" [*youdou*] in the cities:

> In the archaic times, people who loved leisure [*xian*] and hated work [*gong*] were few. Why? It is because at that time all the fields in the nine prefectures were attached to the government. The fields were divided evenly and distributed to the people. Once fields were given to people with laboring ability, there were no spare men [*kuangfu*] in rural areas. The number of men who produced food was significantly larger than the number of men who lived their lives as men of leisure. In the cities, scholars, farmers, and craftsmen were permitted to exercise their own professional practices only until the time when they received their allotment of fields. They were required to work hard simultaneously on agriculture and their own professions, and the law did not allow them to talk freely. For that reason, the scholars, the farmers, the industrial men, and the technicians all knew the hardship of agriculture; while peasants devoted their lives to agriculture, scholars served politics with a good sense of justice [*ren*]. Men who specialized in different kinds of crafts and techniques dared not deceive one another. In ancient times, merchants developed out of peasants, and they traded only when they had more time than what agriculture required.[24]

The monarch believed that among the four types of professions, the specialized ones were confined to intellectual work, agriculture, and industry. The only profession that was not specialized [*zhuan*] was commerce, which should be pursued only when the demands of agriculture permitted it. He paid tribute to the ancient sage-kings, whose "fine teachings" he believed "could make people work hard without allowing themselves to become idle men." Running contrary to his ideal, according to the emperor, urban merchants had an extensive range of deceptive skills that, under the encouragement of "barbarian regimes" such as the Yuan, had harmed the moral order of the "Central Kingdom." The existence of deceptive merchants and idle city residents also induced imperfection in the people's well-being by generating social contradictions that destroyed men's harmonious relationship with Heaven.

The ideal model of *Huangce* [household registration], taxation, and labor service, deployed by the monarch to reform the people and

---

[24] Ibid., pp. 97–98.

create a strong government, was undoubtedly different in practice. Many unregistered households managed to avoid all these obligations to the state. But ideologically and politically, the burdens levied equally on urban and rural populations seemed to activate certain programs of creating conditions for the demographic and cultural integration of the Chinese.

The Ming court distinguished between *huanei* [inside the *hua*, registered and civilized] and *huawai* [outside the *hua*, unregistered and uncivilized]. The distinction was made chiefly between those who paid taxes and obeyed the rules of labor service and those who did not.[25] Yet, the *huanei* and *huawai* distinction had yet another extended meaning. It referred to the culturally included and excluded, which in turn were associated with an ethnic distinction between the "Central Kingdom" and its others.[26]

To draw a clear-cut line between the "central kingdom" [*huanei*] and the rest of the world [*huawai*], 181 garrison-towns and 1,622 smaller military defense posts were constructed in the early Ming.[27] Along the coastal line from Liaoning in the far north to Guangdong in the south, these garrison-towns formed a new Great Wall.[28] During the Southern Song Dynasty, the Prefect Zhen De Xiu had planned a system of coastal garrison-towns in the Quanzhou area. However, Zhen's plan was not fully implemented, because the court was then more interested in profiting from maritime trade, and Zhen himself authorized a taxation policy on maritime trade previously treated as "tribute-paying" by the court. During the Ming, the military commanders who also ruled the coastal regions constructed twenty-seven garrison-towns between 1381 and 1562.[29] These garrison-towns were located in Xiangzhi, Yongling, Shenhu, Fuchuan, Wuitou, Anhai, and Chongwu, forming a virtual wall along the coast. The city walls of Quanzhou were rebuilt with solid rocks

---

[25] Liu, Zhi Wei, *Zai Guojia yu Shehui Zhijian: Mingqing Guangdong Lijia Fuyi Zhidu Yanjiu* [*Between the State and Society: A Study of Lijia Taxation-Labor Service Institution in Guangdong in the Ming and the Qing*] (Guangzhou 1997).

[26] Arthur Waldron has shown that basic to the process of wall signification through imperial times was the definition of the civilized, Chinese Hua and its negative counterpart, the Yi, or barbarians. As he points out, in the Ming, the question facing the first rulers after the Yuan Dynasty had been overthrown was not how once again to hold the Great Wall but where the Ming Dynasty's own territory should end. See Arthur Waldron, *The Great Wall of China: From History to Myth* (Cambridge 1990), pp. 1–10.

[27] Yang, Guo Zheng, *Min Zai Haizhong* [*Fujian in the Sea*] (Nachang 1998), pp. 155–161.

[28] Gu, Jie Gang, and Shi, Nian Hai, *Zhongguo Jiangyu Yange Shi* [*History of the Changes of China's Borders*] (Beijing 2000 [1939]), pp. 139–200.

[29] Zhuang, Jing Hui, *Haiwai Jiaotong Shiji Yanjiu* [*Archaeological Studies of Overseas Communication History*] (Xiamen 1996), pp. 256–307.

Figure 4.1 Portion of the wall of Chongwu garrison-town constructed in the early Ming (photo by Wang Mingming 2004).

and bricks.[30] They were to protect the Divine Prefectures against the moral harm of piracy and against local outlaws' maritime trade.

To maintain the dignity of the "Central Kingdom," the Ming rulers sometimes also emphasized the importance of restoring its center-to-periphery and top-down tributary relations with the barbarian zones. From time to time, Zhu Yuan Zhang instructed the Minister of Rites (Li Bu) to selectively receive the "barbarian" chiefs from the savage tribes who "came to pay their tributes [*rugong*]." As he saw it, these envoys of tribal chieftains "had traveled as far as tens of thousands of miles and undergone the ordeals of all the mountains and oceans." "So long as they have come with great respect for the empire to show their subservience to us, we should give them as much gifts [*ci*] as possible to show our attitude of cherishing men from afar."[31]

When the Portuguese had just begun to conceive of the plan to explore Africa, Southeast Asia, and Asia, the Ming Dynasty court had already sent

---

[30] *Jinjing Xianzhi* [*Jingjing County Gazette*] (ed.) Zhou, Xue Zeng (Fuzhou 1990 [1830]), *juan* 2.

[31] Chen, Shang Sheng, *Huaiyi yu Yishang: Mingdai Haiyang Liliang Xingshuai Yanjiu* [*Cherishing the Barbarians and Repressing the Merchants: A Study of the Surge and Decline of Maritime Power in the Ming Dynasty*] (Jinan 1997), p. 37. As Havia emphasizes, the idea of "cherishing men from afar" was heightened in the Qing Dynasty by the late eighteenth century in Sino-foreign relations. See James Hevia, *Cherishing Men from Afar: Qing Guest Ritual and the Macartney Embassy of 1793* (Durham 1995).

seven voyages led by Zheng He into the Western Ocean between 1405 and 1433. These fleets included as many as 30,000 officials, soldiers, and sailors and sailed at different times in different directions. They visited many Southeast Asian countries and reached as far as the Persian Gulf and East Africa. The purpose of the voyages was supposedly not to trade but to pursue the nephew of the Yongle Emperor, who according to legend fled into the sea in the hope that he would someday come back to reign as the next emperor. Through the voyages, however, tributary relations with the "barbarian chieftains" were re-established.

Zheng He left behind many legendary accounts of his adventures in foreign lands. The imprisonment on his ships of tribal chiefs who did not follow the dictates of Chinese tributary protocol, the presentation of great presents from the Chinese emperor to obedient chiefs, and the procurement of many images of different barbarian peoples and places form the core contents of these legends. Unlike those of his Portuguese contemporaries, Zheng He's fleets did not emphasize trading relationships and commercial gains. As Needham notes, the Portuguese were from the start more concerned with private enterprise. In contrast, the Chinese expeditions were the well-disciplined naval operations of an "enormous feudal-bureaucratic state" that "gave to China the characteristics of an empire without imperialism."[32]

Civilization during the Ming Transition

As a part of the imperial project to rebuild the Chinese world, the new policies toward the maritime world resulted in important cultural change different from early European modernity in the seventeenth century. As Qian Mu notes, the establishment of the Ming Dynasty signaled a dramatic change in Chinese culture.[33] In somewhat vaguely defined terms, Qian Mu describes the transformation as the change of Confucian philosophical politics from "Kingly Confucianism" [*wangdao zhi ru*] to "Civilizing Confucianism" [*jiaohua zhi ru*].

Qian Mu argues that prior to the Ming Dynasty, the character of Chinese culture and statecraft was centered on the idea of the superior king who ruled his country with the symbolic technology of exclusion. The king or the emperor relied on a cosmological order that was implemented by his advisors for the efficient control of the subject populace. The cosmological order was maintained largely for the purpose of enacting the distinct authority of the king or the emperor.

---

[32] Joseph Needham, *The Shorter Science and Civilization in China,* abridged by C. A. Ronan (Cambridge 1981), Vol. 2, pp. 143–144. For a history of Zheng He's voyages, see Gavin Menzies's controversial book *1421: The Year China Discovered the World* (London 2003).

[33] Qian, Mu, *Guoshi Dagang* [*Outline of National History*] 2 Vols., Vol. 2, pp. 663–703.

The substitution of "Civilizing Confucianism" for "Kingly Confucianism" entailed a new concern with ritual and education [*lijiao*], or with creating dynastic order through what we may call the ritual performance of the politic of ritual performance.[34] This form of Confucianism was primarily a civilizing project that sought to popularize imperial culture into a pervasive form of social order. "Civilizing Confucianism" thus represented a transformation from an ideology of exclusion to one of inclusion. It was also the transformation of imperial cosmology with which the court constantly checked its mandate against the moods of Heaven. In the past, the mandate reflected only the mood of Heaven, but by the Ming, it was supposedly also reflecting the will of the people. This new ideology also rendered "subjects" into "common nobles" of the state.[35]

Civilization had been an important component in the building of the "Central Kingdom" prior to the Ming. Ever since the Qin Dynasty, the quest for a shared writing and communication system [*shu tongwen, che tonggui*] had been an ideal for all emperors. The extension of the center's civilizing presence to the outer zones of "All Under Heaven" had also been desired as that which dignified the "Central Kingdom." However, Qian Mu rightly proposes that from the Ming Dynasty on, the imperial project of breaking down the internal boundaries between the "civilized" and "uncivilized" zones became a prime concern of the court.

The "prehistory" of this change was a Confucian metaphysical one, not a state ideological transformation.[36] It took a few centuries to complete. First, it emerged among the Neo-Confucian scholars of the Northern Song. In the Northern Song, during the phase that Gernet calls "the Chinese Renaissance," more and more Confucian scholars became dissatisfied with earlier dynasties' religious orientations. They regarded the monarchs who ruled China from the Han to the Tang as following *badao*, or the way of the despot. Qian's softened interpretation of *badao* consisted of the argument that emperors prior to the Song cared only about their own realms of power. They did not pay attention to the wills of their subjects. Making a clear conceptual distinction between the public [*gong*] and the private [*si*], they, as "secretively private" despots, did not

---

[34] Angela Zito has provided a detailed discussion of the body politic of Confucianist learning during the Qianlong Reign of the Qing Dynasty. She relates this body politic to the absorption of the Han Chinese literati culture into the Manchurian ruling technology after the pacification of Han ethnicity in the earlier reigns of Qing Dynasty. Her analysis of *li* [rites] is useful also for our consideration of culture in the Ming. See Angela Zito, *Of Body and Brush: Grand Sacrifice as Text/Performance in Eighteenth-Century China* (Chicago 1997).

[35] What made such a project of civilization realizable was a sort of "Chinese nativism" that has basically been ignored by Qian Mu. This has been briefly discussed in Eric Wolf's *Europe and the People without History* (Berkeley 1982), p. 55.

[36] Qian, Mu, *Guoshi Dagang* [*Outline of National History*] 2 Vols., Vol. 2, pp. 794–814.

pay attention to the public. Not until the Song did the idea of the public become widely perceived as significant. The Song Neo-Confucians made great endeavors to change the *badao* philosophy into a kingly metaphysics and then from a kingly metaphysics to a form of civilizing Confucianism. They campaigned through various individual and group efforts to establish a more "public" form of Confucianism.

With regard to post-Song political Confucianism, Qian Mu argues the following:

> [Prior to the Song] Schools of Confucianism all carried with them a narrow sense of aristocracy. . . . Scholars living in post-Song times were radically different. Most of them were not born into aristocratic families. Thus neither did they favor the identity of inherited status, nor did they talk about intellectual achievements and civilization in terms of the narrow identities of elite origins. They pursued a principle that was closer to the commoners, and they sought to deploy this principle in their conceptualizations of human life, government, society, this worldly and other worldly matters, and etc. . . . They called this principle *dao* [the way] or *li* [reason]. Reason was Heavenly Reason [*tianli*], its opposite being *renyu* [human desires]. The distinction between Heavenly Reason and human desires lies in the differentiation between the public and the private, which were further defined in terms of "mutual loyalty" [*yi*] and "interests" [*li*].[37]

A handful of Neo-Confucianists managed to get official positions in the Song and the Yuan governments, but most failed to serve the state and remained outside the capital where they were at pains to campaign for their social ideal. From the Northern Song to the Yuan dynasties, one saw in the government and in the regions penetrated by Neo-Confucians the expansion of several cultural institutions. The first of such institutions were the Confucian academies, which were privately sponsored but open to the public. In these academies, the Neo-Confucians advocated their ideal of the "public." Apart from the academies, there were also new cultural inventions such as communal granaries [*shecang*], lineage-owned charitable organizations [*yizhuang*], [*baojia*] local-watch systems, and communal pacts [*xiangyue*].

By the early Ming, the Neo-Confucian ideal for raising the public was adopted by Zhu Yuan Zhang, with the advice of late Yuan Neo-Confucians. Only by then did the confined programs of the Song Neo-Confucians become available as ideological sources for policy making. It was also by then that "civilizing Confucianism" became the orthodox state ideology.

In my view, what Qian Mu has described is a civilizing process that can be compared with what Norbert Elias has analyzed in the context of

---

[37] Ibid., p. 795.

Western Europe. In his *Court Society*, Elias identifies the aristocracy and the courts that emerged and developed from the Middle Ages onward as a historical form of social organization and civilization with a dual relationship to the bourgeois society that followed it. Elias argued that the royal and princely courts had come to constitute the social nucleus of seventeenth century European societies (with the French as the typical example). These courts evoked a sort of "courtly rationality" that extended not only upward onto the royal families but also downward into the "habitus" of the Protestant bourgeoisie.[38]

In the beginning of the Ming Dynasty, a similar sort of court culture and "rationality" were also apparent. But a major difference exists between Chinese and European patterns of civilization. As Elias argues, the Western European courts played a central role in culturing the upper and new middle classes, the effect of which was a "courticization of society."[39] By contrast, in the Chinese context, as Qian Mu emphasizes, the civilizing project was developed earlier in Neo-Confucian writings and evocations of the Song before the imperial court "discovered" it. Civilization, or *jiaohua* in classical Chinese, was at first realized through Neo-Confucian scholars traveling lecture circuits. The effectiveness of this form of doctrinal dissemination was evident in the extensive spread of Neo-Confucian academies throughout the country. The professors of the academies were either relatively independent scholars, such as Zhu Xi, or regional scholar-officials, such as Zhen De Xiu. From the Song Dynasty onward, these two groups of Neo-Confucian educators were active in different areas of Fujian. They admitted local intellectuals and gentry into their academies as disciples. By the Ming Dynasty, civilization as *jiaohua* had been seen as a critical mechanism for moral and social order by the emperor. It was then absorbed into the court's civilizing project.

Also, unlike the European model that allowed earlier modern bourgeoisie to synthesize courtly rationalities with their own pursuit of wealth and public status, "civilizing" in the Ming context was much more concerned with the question of how to reduce human greed, especially as manifested in the realm of commerce. In both the Ming and the Qing Dynasties, together with anticommercial campaigns, imperial ideological control was re-enforced. Beginning in the period between the late Yuan and the early Ming, the problems of social disorder and moral decay were conceived of as derivatives of overheated commerce. As Brook puts it:

> The proliferation of both domestic and maritime trade was troubling to the scholastic Confucian commitment to social hierarchy resting on settled rural life. Commentators of the mid-Ming remarked on the decreasing

[38] Elias, *The Court Society*.
[39] Ibid., pp. 214–215.

distance between the urban world of markets and traders and the rural world of agricultural production, worrying about the invasive expansion of the former and the corruption of the latter.[40]

The condemnation of greed and desire expressed in the imperial romanticization of rural life made the Ming radically different from Elias's picture of "court society." According to Elias, an important transitional phase in "courticization" was one during which parts of the knightly nobility were transformed into a court-aristocratic nobility. In the process of the nobility's transformation, parts of the knightly nobility were mingled with rising bourgeois elements to remake themselves as a new class. In the course of the process, great changes took place to recreate rural-urban cultural distinctions. "Country life became a symbol of lost innocence." It became "an opposite image of urban court life." Urbanites became centers of civilization, producing more demands on individual self-control" and more hierarchical pressures.[41] Unlike early modern Europe, neither did the Ming "courticization" find its way in the synthesis of the knightly nobility and the emergent "bourgeois elements," nor did it rely on urbanization. On the contrary, the Chinese civilizing process of the Ming consisted in the repression of the "bourgeois elements" hidden in "human desires" [renyu] and the ruralization of the Chinese worlds, in which the rural, "a symbol of innocence" perceived as lost in the chaos of the Yuan barbarianism, became anxiously desired as a symbol of civilization.

Here I should note that to the Ming monarch, the imaginary of the rural garden was also different from the figuration of the early modern European courtiers. Ambiguously, it consisted not only of places where food was produced but also places where the gentlemen read ethical books of Confucianism. In a word, it consisted of places where both geng [ploughing] and du [reading] were practiced as the imperial propriety.

Thus, as early as 1364, when he proclaimed to the King of Wu, Zhu Yuan Zhang had already began to establish a new constitution [gangji]. He attributed the chaos in the late Yuan to lack of constitution. For him, "constitution" was the establishment of li [propriety] and fa [law], which in turn could automatically bring peace to the "above" (the rulers) and the "below" (the ruled). Once the Ming was established, he created two new bureaus in the central government, the Bureau of Li [Ritual] and the Bureau of Yue [Music]. He called on well-known Confucians to "discuss li [yi li]."[42]

---

[40] Timothy Brook, *The Confusions of Pleasure: Commerce and Culture in Ming China* (Berkeley 1998), p. 124.

[41] Elias, *The Court Society*, pp. 214–215.

[42] Luo, *Ming Taizu Lifa Zhizhi Yanjiu* [*A Study of Taizu Emperor's Rule of Ritual and Law in the Ming*], pp. 20–31.

To re-create the moral and cultural order, the court came to view classical tradition re-interpreted in the Song Dynasty via Cheng-Zhu Neo-Confucianism as the preferred mode of culture. This orthodoxy was first a Han tradition that persisted throughout pre-Song times, but during the Song, it was imbued with new support and a quasireligious quality.[43] In classical Confucian discourse, a clear distinction was maintained between rites [li] and customs [su]. There, the notion of li [propriety] was bound up with the reproduction of the imperial polity. Li was organized in such as way that human action [xing], heavenly reason [li], and moral embodiments [ti] were tied to a notion of the aristocracy. Since the conception of Cheng-Zhu Neo-Confucianism, the boundary between the classical sense of li and its popular counterparts (su, or customs) gradually broke down in Neo-Confucian discourse. The leading philosopher of the Neo-Confucian tradition, Zhu Xi, was at pains to simplify elaborate imperial rites into domestic rites [jiali]. To earlier Confucian philosophers, the concept of domestic rites was unthinkable, because to mix the family [jia] and rites was to commit a conceptual crime. But in Zhu Xi's re-interpretation, it became plausible as a good synthesis.[44]

In renewing the moral relationship between rites and customs, the works of Neo-Confucian philosophers had also opened up new horizons for the heteropraxy of customs to flourish in the name of officially propagated propriety. But from the perspective of intentionality, the merging of rites and customs was apparently part of the Ming court's project of engendering a great transformation in civilization that the work of Qian Mu seeks to reconstruct. Specifically, the kind of order that the great transformation was intended to create was a perceived proper hierarchical order for the emperor, ministers, fathers, and sons. Moreover, rites were also defined in terms of a safeguard against "human desires" [yu]. For Zhu Yuan Zhang, the worst harm that humans could inflict on themselves came from indulging in yu. Human desires consisted not only of sexual intercourse, food consumption, and dress. All pursuits related to the private [si] and the self [ji] fell into this category. The only means that could control desires was ritual, which as he assumed, originated from the sage-kings' benign intention to safeguard humans against their own desires.

As civilization was defined in terms of the control of desire (greed), rites helping establish such control often conveyed implications to safeguard against the ritual subjects. During the Ming, a she hall housed an Altar for

---

[43] Liu, Kwang-ching, Introduction, to his edited *Orthodoxy in Late Imperial China* (Berkeley 1990), pp. 6–7.

[44] Patricia B. Ebrey, The early stages in the development of kin group organization, in Patricia B. Ebrey and James L. Watson (eds.), *Kinship Organization in Late Imperial China 1000–1940* (Berkeley 1986), pp. 16–61.

Soil and Grain [*Sheji Tan*], where a series of ceremonies was organized each year. Local disputes within the *she* were resolved after worshipping the *she*'s spiritual master. The two kinds of activities surrounding the institution of *she* were described as *qi* [praying] and *bao* [reporting and thanksgiving].[45] The poetry that was recited during the ceremonies of *qi* and *bao* reads as follows:

> Let us revere filial piety to emphasize human values,
> Let us become loyal to our lineage to enhance harmony,
> Let us be in peace with fellow villagers to calm disputes,
> Let us stress agriculture to satisfy our need for food and clothing,
> Let us refrain from wastefulness to save on expenditures,
> Let us promote education to correct the habits of the scholars, . . .[46]

Ritual as Sanctive Power

"Civilizing Confucianism" was not the only significant cultural trend during the Ming, but it became so pervasive that the official project known as *lizhi*, or "rule by rites," became merged with the rule of Law [*fazhi*] to make up *lifa zhi zhi*, or "rule by rites/laws," which characterized the general pattern of early Ming politics.

The main purpose of "rule by rites and laws"—a Ming concept closely related to the Confucian notion of "governing the people by rites"—was not merely "ethico-moral guidance"[47] but the creation of a correct ceremonial practice that "played by the rules of the dominant culture."[48] Thus moral lessons were taught not only in schools, many of which were built during the Ming, but also in public places where gods and ghosts were worshipped. The civilizing project of the early Ming was targeted at two sorts of *hua*, or transformation: "the transformation of ghosts and gods into law court officers" [*hua hui shen wei fali*] and "the transformation of public rituals into execution grounds" [*hua xiangyin wei xingchang*].[49] These two sorts of *hua* indicate that to the emperors of the Ming rites themselves were laws and means for disciplining subjects.

---

[45] Ye, Chun Ji (ed.), *Hui'an Zhengshu* [*Hui'an County Political Manual*] (Fuzhou 1987 [1672]), *juan* 10.

[46] *Dehua Xianzhi* [*Dehua County Gazette*], compiled by Lu, Ding Mei (Dehua 1987 [1746]), *juan* 9.

[47] Yang, Ching Kun, *Religion in Chinese Society* (Berkeley 1961).

[48] James L. Watson, Rites or beliefs? The construction of a unified culture in late Imperial China, in Lowell Dittmer (ed.), *China's Quest for National Identity* (Ithaca 1993), pp. 80–103.

[49] Luo *Ming Taizu Lifa Zhizhi Yanjiu* [*A Study of Taizu Emperor's Rule of Ritual and Law in the Ming*], pp. 12–15.

As in each *li* or *she* in the countryside, in each *pu* or *jing* in the city, in addition to the communal hall-temple, two pavilions were built, one for making public denunciations against wrongdoings [*shenming ting*] and one for praising good deeds [*jingshan ting*]. This pair of pavilions, which represented both negative and positive sanctions, stood out from the surrounding houses in its location in the public square in front of the local community hall-temple. They were treated as sacred platforms, and even partial destruction of them was regarded as a serious crime punishable with one hundred blows with a stick.[50] These two sorts of pavilions were authorized in the year 1372 as part of *Ming Code*. In the city of Quanzhou, they were constructed immediately after Chen You Ding's regime was terminated.[51]

The establishment of an "official religion" involved the installation of power structure and the evolution of the type of control similar to what Foucault finds in eighteenth-century Europe. Four centuries after the Ming, Europe experienced a historical shift in which punishment tended to become "the most hidden part of the penal process." As Foucault argues, this shift has several consequences, chiefly including that

> it leaves the domain of more or less everyday perception and enters that of abstract consciousness; its effectiveness is seen as resulting from its inevitability, not from its visible intensity; it is the certainty of being punished and not the horrifying spectacle of public punishment that must discourage crime. . . .[52]

As early as the fourteenth century, the Ming monarch had already invented a "civilized way of punishment." However, unlike eighteenth-century Europe, the Ming did not substitute this new way of control and domination for the "horrifying spectacle of public punishment," which in fact continued to be the mechanism for dealing with crime well beyond the nineteenth century. In the Ming context, "power" differs from how Foucault defined it in the European context. Also unlike Europe, the Ming deployed a Chinese concept of power, which as Sangren has suggested, transcended conceptual boundaries of mind/body, subject/object. It relied in its exercise on the invocation of religious efficacy instead of that of modern law.[53]

Perhaps because of the preceding reasons, the Ming mode of disciplinary power retained much of the public aspect of the *ancient*

---

[50] Ibid., pp. 18–19.

[51] *Jinjing Xianzhi* [*Jingjing County Gazette*], compiled by Fang, Ding, *juan* 15.

[52] Foucault, *Discipline and Punish*, p. 9.

[53] P. Steven Sangren, *Chinese Sociologics: An Anthropological Account of the Role of Alienation in Social Reproduction* (London 2000), p. 140.

régime. In this mode of power, a hierarchical structure of relationships in the moral universe was constantly displayed through ceremonial events.

As the Son of Heaven, Zhu Yuan Zhang assumed religious as well as political leadership. To establish an official religion, he adopted the Neo-Confucian ideal model of Zhou rites. Like the Neo-Confucians, he despised the First Emperor (Qin Shi Huang), who dared to declare the five sacred mountains as the media of his monopolized communication with Heaven. Instead, he sought to re-install the entire Zhou Dynasty system of temple and altar worship for the State and the citizenry of the "Central Kingdom." In the capital, platforms were built for sacrifice to Heaven, earth, the sun, the moon, thunder, and rain gods. In the royal domain of the capital and in the prefectural and county seats, he authorized the altars devoted to the Soil and Grain and to ghosts.[54] In these newly constructed temples and altars, the moral value placed on social control was expressed through the medium of ceremonial performance as a subtle means of sanctioning behavior. The structure of Quanzhou city and its neighboring communities was reconstituted in accordance with this campaign.

---

[54] Ling, Shun Sheng, Beiping de fengshan wenhua [The sacred enclosures and stepped pyramidal platforms of Peiping], *Bulletin of Institute of Ethnology, Academia Sinica*, 16 (1963): 1–100.

CHAPTER 5

Heaven on Earth: *Pujing* and the Worlds of Worship Platforms

In 1980, Zhuang Wei Ji, a historian and archaeologist specializing in the study of Quanzhou, wrote an article outlining the shifting locations and spatial patterns of the city.[1] Zhuang told a long story. According to him, when Quanzhou was first established, it was merely a small county seat of only three square *li*. The town was built in a standard rectangular form, a reflection of the traditional Chinese notion of the Earth as square. However, during the time of Quanzhou's commercial boom, the city was reorganized and given a more lively shape. "The urbanite adapted itself to the topography of the region. Its three outer lines formed a non-equilateral triangle. One ran from the northwest to the southwest along the river. The other two curved to the southeast through the plains and the hills."[2] As Zhuang concluded, in its commercial heyday, Quanzhou broke away from the convention of official urban planning and became "a great example of the early industrial and commercial metropolises of the world."[3] During the Ming, the city was "only slightly modified." It

---

[1] Zhuang, Wei Ji, Quanzhou lidai chengzhi tansuo [An investigation of city sites in the historical periods of Quanzhou], *Quanzhou Wenshi* [*Quanzhou Culture and History*], 2-3 (1980): 14–28.

[2] Ibid., p. 27.

[3] Ibid., p. 28.

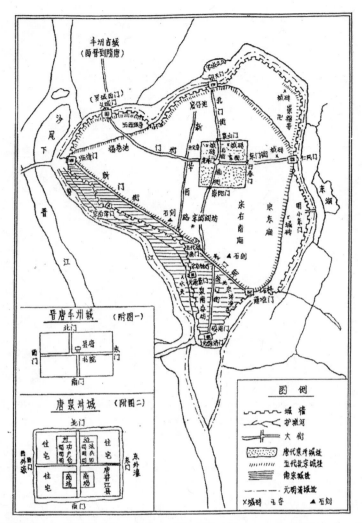

Figure 5.1 Zhuang Wei Ji's interpretation of the historical geography of Quanzhou City. (The two smaller maps in the left corner below the bigger map were, respectively, the map of Fengzhou and the Tang city of Quanzhou.) (Source: Zhuang, Wei Ji, Quanzhou lidai chengzhi tansuo [An investigation of city sites in the historical periods of Quanzhou], *Quanzhou Wenshi* [*Culture and History in Quanzhou*], 2-3 [1980], p. 15.)

ceased to expand, but it was consolidated. Each of its gates was encircled with an additional circle of walls to make the gate look like a jar, and the existing city walls were reinforced with granite. How can we explain the reinforcement of walls during the Ming? Zhuang did not provide an answer.

In terms of urban outlook, the Ming indeed added nothing more than new gates and granite to the city. However, within the confines of the city walls, the Ming did create new cultural forms through its campaign to change the "post-traditional character" of pre-Ming Quanzhou. The increase in walls can be explained in terms of the increase in these "cultural forms."

The overall project was not planned locally. It was conceived by the Ming court, and it was to assert the presence of imperial "civilizing Confucianism." Zhu Yuan Zhang, the Ming monarch, who had adopted Confucian approach, sought to inaugurate an "official religion." He invented a complete sacrificial system for all the prefectures and counties all over the country. In addition to Confucian beliefs, Zhu Yuan Zhang encouraged monastic Buddhist and Daoist cults of immortality and rebirth, which he took as complementary, in a subtle way, to the work of his government. He drew certain elements from popular cults in the belief that once they were rationalized they could harmonize with the classical cosmology of peace and order. He synthesized different religious ideas into a new system with which he began to plan the imperial palaces and worship platforms in Nanjing. He also instructed all prefectures under the mandate of Heaven to adopt his line.[4]

As part of the emperor's program of civilization, Quanzhou absorbed a complex of new bureaucratic and religious-cultural elements. In this process, *pujing* units were reified. As a set of territorial "nexus points," *pujing* not only transmitted information concerning local social, demographic, and political situations to the magistrate but also served to extend the civilizing project of the court into local neighborhoods. As small focal points for the local presence of imperial order, *pujing* were integrated vertically by means of imperial city walls, government buildings, and official religious temples, which stood out from the sketch view of the city to make the outlook of it traditional. By the Ming, Quanzhou's urban structure was transformed by a re-invented image of orthodox hierarchy and an architectural projection of political cosmology. It offered certain imaginaries of unity and cultural integrity, and it helped pattern the segments of urban space into a political body seen as perfectly correspondent with Heaven.

The Project

The remaking of the city was done in line with the traditional forms of construction and thus represented a break from the "post-traditionalism"

---

[4] Tomeyn Taylor, Official and popular religion and the political organization of Chinese society in the Ming, Liu, Kwang-Ching (ed.), *Orthodoxy in Late Imperial China* (Berkeley 1990), pp. 126–157.

of the previous dynasty's notion of urban space. Ideally a proper residence should always strive for a "real" correspondence between the *yin* and *yang* forces on the ground, and the sun and moon in the sky. As one of the oldest Chinese classics, *Zhou Li*, suggests:

> When an architect plans to establish a city (state), he should examine the patterns of water flow and other topographic features and employ natural sights [*jing*] as reference points for measurements. When he tries to shape the forms of the city, he should inspect the sunrise and sunset. This helps him to fix the directional orientations of the city. The architect's city plan should be based on the knowledge derived from the study of the motions of the sun and the changing positions of the stars. Knowledge of the kind serves to set the city in a position consistent with the temporal moods of the universe.[5]

Zhou Li's cosmic city was not mere rhetoric; it was a practiced tradition. Many studies have shown that imperial Chinese town planning was inseparable from a set of cosmological principles whose conception of space influenced the construction of imperial capitals.[6] This system was also implemented in the formation of regional administrative centers including Quanzhou.

Nonetheless, in the dynasties prior to the Ming, owing to the lack of strict central guidelines, Quanzhou "misinterpreted" classical architectural convention, turning its urban spaces into realms of commercial order and cosmological disorder. As the late Ming Quanzhou scholar He Qiao Yuan outlined in his *Min Shu*,[7] after first appearing around 712 in the mid-Tang Dynasty, Quanzhou underwent four phases of expansion between the eighth century and the early fourteenth. The small section that was the oldest part of the city was kept as *zicheng*, or the central part of the city. In the fifty-three years between 904 and 960, Quanzhou became one of the political and economic centers of the Min State. During that period, the city expanded to cover a space of 10 square kilometers and was remodeled. In its inner circle was the *yacheng*, or the government compound, which was surrounded by the old town—namely, *zicheng*. Outside the *zicheng*, the outer circle of the walled city, known as *luocheng*, was constructed. To facilitate transportation and commerce, the government built seven city gates instead of four, which was the standard for a political center. Moreover, some of the gates were directly linked to the sea through the canal

---

[5] *Zhou Li* (Beijing 1985 [reprint]), *juan* 14.

[6] For an example of such studies, see Meyer, Jeffrey F., *Beijing as a Sacred City* (Taipei 1976).

[7] He, Qiao Yuan, *Min Shu* [*The Book of Fujian*] (Fuzhou 1994 [1628–1632]), *juan* 7; 39.

system. Inside the city, there were six major streets, which served as commercial areas. The government buildings were located in the north central area, whereas the commercial center was located in the middle of the city. Adapted to the topography of the Quanzhou basin, the city extended from the northwestern and northeastern corners outward to the suburbs. As He Qiao Yuan confirms, the uneven lines of the city walls made Quanzhou look like the tail of a carp. In the Southern Song and in the Yuan, the city extended southward to the banks of Jin River, which flowed into the Eastern China Sea at the Port of Quanzhou. As an enclosure of built landscapes, the city also consisted of an extensive range of official temples spread in two layers around the government compounds within *zicheng*.[8] But in the pre-Ming periods, the prefects of Quanzhou seemed less concerned with cosmological principles than with practical adaptation to the local topography and the needs of urban commerce. These two factors led the prefects into accepting popular conceptions of the Carp.

Having inaugurated his new dynasty, Zhu Yuan Zhang agreed with the late Yuan Neo-Confucian point of view that all of Huaxia (Han or "Sinic") culture had degenerated during the Tang and the Yuan Dynasties. During this period, economic prosperity was abundant, but ceremonial culture ran off the tracks of orthodoxy [*zheng*].[9] In 1357, the founder of Ming Neo-Confucianism, Liu Ji, in his famous book *Yu Li Zi,* critiqued the Mongol lords as "those who could not command the country without horses [*wuma buneng zhi*]."[10] Accepting the Neo-Confucian critique of the Yuan, the Ming monarch believed that Chinese culture was totally ruined by the Yuan whose "constitution was created in accordance with barbarian/foreign customs [*yi yifeng zhizhi*]."[11]

The "misinterpretation" of landscape in cities such as Quanzhou was perceived as one of the consequences of the pre-Ming "degeneration of culture." One can imagine, had Zhu Yuan Zhang visited Quanzhou, he would have denounced it as the appalling outcome of the preceding monarchs' negligence of "the teachings of classical sage-kings" [*xianwang zhi jiao*]. Zhu Yuan Zhang did not, however, make any trip there, but he did attempt to ensure that a vigorous quest for re-inventing classical tradition was pursued in Quanzhou.

---

[8] Zhuang, Jing Hui, *Haiwai Jiaotong Shiji Yanjiu* [*Archaeological Studies of Overseas Communication History*] (Xiamen 1996), pp. 1–18.

[9] Luo, Dong Yang, *Ming Taizu Lifa Zhizhi Yanjiu* [*A Study of the Taizu Emperor's Rule of Ritual and Law in the Ming*] (Beijing 1998), p. 24.

[10] Feng, Tian Yu, *Mingqing Wenhuashi Sanlun* [*Essays on the Cultural History of the Ming and the Qing* (2nd ed.) (Wuhan 1998), pp. 57–59.

[11] Ibid., p. 28.

During the early Ming, the city of Quanzhou was not rebuilt, but it did undergo a dramatic change in spatial form.[12] In the first decades of the Ming, the city walls were reinforced by strong bricks and rocks. As we mentioned earlier, some forty watch posts were added to the walls as well as a means of improving the city's defenses. In addition to the physical reinforcement of the city walls, seven War God temples were constructed in locations facing outward through the archways of the city gates.[13] Moreover, within the confines of the city walls, a new spatial pattern was envisaged for the ceremonial performances through which the civilizing process was to unfold.

In Nanjing, the emperor supervised in person the compilation of an architectural manual for building the imperial capital.[14] To implement the spatial codes outlined in the imperial manual into local society, the first Ming prefect, Chang Xing,[15] had to systematically reconstruct the symbolic universe for Quanzhou. He insisted that the rebuilding of Quanzhou should be conducted along the following lines:

> The construction of the city must begin with the first important steps and be continued by taking secondary steps. First, a site where the forces of *yin* and *yang* co-exist harmoniously should be chosen. Second, city walls should be built around the site in areas where wind and water converge harmoniously. These walls serve to seal and protect the city and shape the city into a houselike structure. Third, the surrounding areas and the urban areas of the city are to be divided into wards, precincts, markets, and tithings. Finally, temples, government buildings and houses are to be built. Both the urban divisions and buildings should be allocated in such a way that they are consistent with the patterns of movement and locations of waterways.[16]

Not surprisingly, the prefect encountered enormous difficulties reasserting the imperial order of Heaven in a former commercial center. The architectural signs of this order were not as visible in Quanzhou as they were in the imperial capitals of Nanjing or, later, Beijing. In the capital, the symmetries, correspondences, and axial allocations of space

---

[12] According to Fang Ding and his associates, the town was not rebuilt until the mid-Ming, when a serious earthquake demolished most of its walls and buildings. See *Jinjing Xianzhi* [*Jingjing County Gazette*], compiled by Fang, Ding (Quanzhou 1945 [1765]), *juan* 2.

[13] Ibid., *juan* 1; 2.

[14] Ling, Shun Sheng, Beiping de fengshan wenhua [The sacred enclosures and stepped pyramidal platforms of Peiping], *Bulletin of Institute of Ethnology, Academia Sinica*, 16 (1963): 1–100.

[15] Unfortunately, somehow Chang Xing's biography is unrecorded in the books of biography in all the gazettes.

[16] *Jinjing Xianzhi* [*Jingjing County Gazette*], compiled by Zhou, Xue Zeng (Fuzhou 1990 [1830]), *juan* 2.

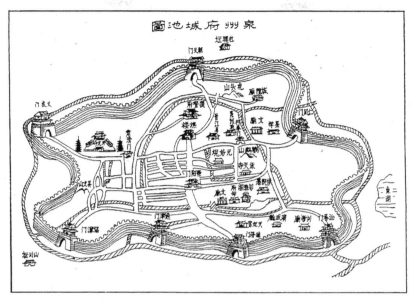

Figure 5.2 Map of late imperial Quanzhou, with city walls, moats, government compounds, and official temples prominent against the background. (Source: *Quanzhou Fuzhi* [*Quanzhou Prefecture Gazette*], compiled by Huai Yin, Bu, and Huang, Ren, [Quanzhou 1763].)

were readily apparent. In Quanzhou, both the existing urban structures and the cultural topography made them much less tangible.

In the orthodox cosmology, places were formatted by a series of concentric squares framed by Heaven, which was round. This ideology was applied in the capitals and was understood as what actually gave life to the elementary networks of spatial relations in the city. However, in Quanzhou, its applicability was limited simply for the reason we already specified: pre-Ming Quanzhou was not shaped according to this model. Furthermore, as all available local official gazetteers admit, prior to the Ming, Quanzhou was not included in *fenye*, the central imperial astrological geography,[17] and, because of the flourishing cultural diversity of the Tang and Yuan Dynasties, buildings in the city contained certain "non-Chinese" features. Large mosques, Hindu monasteries, and Nestorian churches stood side by side with official and popular Buddhist and Daoist temples. The prefects had yet to find a way to compensate for this unorthodox spatial arrangement.

Ideally, as Si Ma Qian said long ago, the city was a composite place and should be a lens through which "people observe the sun and moon

---

[17] Ibid., *juan* 1.

in the sky and envision the forces of *yin* and *yang* on Earth" and the means by which "the sage understands the order of all the cosmic forces and uses it as the basis of his power to rule."[18] For officials working in the Ming government, surveys of local geography and city sites should serve to map the reciprocal relationship between cosmos and city. These surveys, whose results were included in officially compiled gazettes as regional cartographies, applied the standard cosmological terms provided by the Ming court in its descriptions of the topographic features of a city.[19] As I have shown elsewhere,[20] in these cartographic representations, the geography of Quanzhou was outlined in accordance with five levels of space: (1) *xingye* [stars and wilderness], (2) *shanchuan* [mountains and waters], (3) *fengyu* [frontier territories], (4) *chengchi* [city walls and moat], and (5) *puyi/shili* [urban neighborhoods and streets]. The system of place hierarchy and landscape according to the preceding categories served to structure administrative space in the Quanzhou prefecture. "Stars and wilderness" referred to the outer zone of the administrative region; "mountains and waters" designated the rivers and land under the administrative organization of the prefecture. The "sealed territories" were the rural counties [*xian*], villages [*cun*], and tithings [*li*] that were governed by the prefecture [*zhou*]. "The city walls and moat" demarcated the walled capital of the prefecture and its boundaries, and "urban districts" referred to the land within the confines of the city walls.

The five-fold division of Quanzhou was a simplified representation of the ancient institution of the "five zones" [*wufu*]—the royal domains, the lands of the tributary princes and lords, the zone of pacification, the zone of the allied barbarians, and the zone of cultureless savagery.[21] It was concentric and projected an ideal model of the cosmos or, specifically, the harmony between Heaven (stars and wilderness), Earth (mountains and waters as well as the frontier territories), and the world's center, or the State (including rural and urban spaces).

Comparing the outlook of the region with the ancient Chinese cosmic diagram, the Supreme Ultimate Chart (Taiji Tu), one also finds that their basic frameworks are rather similar: the key implication of the Supreme Ultimate Chart lies in its representation of cosmic transformation and genesis. Specifically it is an illustration of the ways in which the cosmic essence (the "supreme ultimate") gives rise to the dual composition

---

[18] Si Ma, Qian, *Shi Ji* [Historians' Records] (Beijing 1959 [reprint]), p. 1342.

[19] *Ming Hui Yao* [*A Collection of Major Event Descriptions of the Ming*], compiled by Long, Wen Bing (Beijing 1956 [1887]), *juan* 1–2.

[20] Wang, Mingming, Quanzhou: The Chinese city as cosmogram, *Cosmos*, 16(1) (1994): 3–25.

[21] Smith, *Fortune-Tellers and Philosophers*, pp. 7–22.

[*yinyang*], which evolves into the four cosmic images [*si xiang*] and produces the hexagrams [*bagua*]. The structure of the city was correlated with the Supreme Ultimate Chart through analogy: the government compound = *Taiji* (Supreme Ultimate) / Oneness of the Universe; the city and its districts = *yinyang*; "frontier territories" = imperial administrative geography = *siyi* [four images]; "stars and wilderness" = *bagua* [hexagrams].

During the early Ming, the prefects began to use the imperial *fenye* system. The *fenye* division was based on three systems: (1) the *Zhou Li* system of the correspondence between the nine divisions of the heaven and the nine administrative regions of China, (2) the system of analogy between the twelve stations in the Jupiter cycle and the earthly branches [*dizhi*], and (3) the assimilation of twenty-eight sectors on earth to the twenty-eight lunar lodges [*ershiba xiu*] in the sky. The *fenye* division served both as a projection of the cosmos and as a map of China as the "Central Kingdom" of the world.[22] These analogies were further cumulated to the ancient threefold model of heaven, earth and man: "stars and wilderness" = heaven; "frontier territories" = earth; and the city = man.

Writing about the Chinese "science" of map-making, Needham notes that the Chinese pictographic character of *tu* possesses a general meaning referring to any kind of diagram, and it indicates the inseparability of cosmic and geographic diagrams in Chinese culture.[23] Furthermore, according to Needham's observation, we find it equally difficult to differentiate between Chinese diagrams or maps and what they represented.

Although this Chinese understanding of projection may be known to people living in different periods of history from the time when it became theorized, in the course of reconstructing the spatial structure of Quanzhou, the Ming prefect must have found it especially useful. In his cosmological representation of the city, the imperial reconstruction of the city was done in a way to facilitate this cosmological projection.

Evidently, the cosmological vision that was reproduced in the city of Quanzhou represented an intended totalizing force, which not only incorporated political and economic reality into its own spheres of influence but also conferred the cosmic order onto social organization and politics. In Bourdieu's words, such a cosmology exemplifies a perfect correspondence between "objective order and subjective principles of organization."[24]

---

[22] Ibid., pp. 66–68.

[23] Joseph Needham, *The Shorter Science and Civilization in China* (Cambridge 1981), pp. 237–238.

[24] Pierre Bourdieu, *Outline of a Theory of Practice* (Cambridge 1977), pp. 164–165.

As a cosmographic system, the city structure was largely a consequence of cultural invention,[25] but it provided a revealing model of politics, ideology, and economy. For example, cosmologically, the north-south axis was consistent with the interrelationship between *yang* and *yin*. In political geography, it reflected the hierarchy of the dominant imperial state (north) and the subjected inhabitants (south). Economically, the south was the most important marketplace, which was inspected by the political north, and, ideologically, the relation between the southern marketplace and the northern government was reaffirmed in the contrast between the commercial Heavenly Queen and the political City God (Chenghuang).

Such correspondences were not accidentally formed but deliberately created to "naturalize the universe of the arbitrary";[26] they were cosmological devices in which, what was classically perceived in the "Chinese Renaissance" or in the Ming version of "civilizing Confucianism," as the "deep relationship" between a physical setting and the nature of its inhabitants" was transformed into a vision of political unity and social harmony.[27] By the Ming, at least to the State, the city of Quanzhou as a type of "cosmogram" was both "ideal" and "real" not so much in the sense that it was an architecturally realized cosmology as in the sense that it reproduced a cultural system that resituated the rulers as well as their subjects and socio-economic formations in their proper cosmological places.

The Locations of Worship Platforms

> In the sky, the lunar lodges [*yuexiu*] govern the compartments of the universe, and in the human world, prefectures and enclosed territories order the people.[28]

The preceding quote comes from Si Ma Qian regarding the role of local administration in the realization of the old Chinese ideal of correspondence between Heaven and Earth. This correspondence could be understood as a dualism, or as a dialectic of relationally constituted

---

[25] It was thus unlikely that the Ming official image of Quanzhou could be displayed purely in terms of its visible spatial structure. Alternatively, it was presented as a "vision" of what the city, as well as the world and the society, *should* be. Like the cosmologies discussed by Edmund Leach, such a vision was "unconstrained" and did not "have to conform to inconvenient limitations," and it consists of "transformation of the real life of those who invent them." Edmund Leach, *Social Anthropology* (London 1982), p. 213.

[26] Ibid., p. 164.

[27] Kristopher Schipper, *The Taoist Body* (Berkeley 1993), pp. 100–101.

[28] Si Ma, Qian, *Shi Ji* [*Historians' Records*], p. 1342.

notions of closure and openness. Specifically, "stars and wilderness" as an "open sphere" existed in contrast to the "sealed territory," which designated enclosure. When related to the space within the confines of "the city walls and its moat," both "stars and wilderness" and "sealed territory" were open spheres, and the only enclosed space was the walled city. The enclosed and the open conveyed the conceptions of the cultured and uncultured and of the center and peripheries: the enclosed space was the cultured zone, which was also the imperial administrative center, whereas the open fields denoted the wild and uncultured areas and the administrative peripheries—that is, the countryside. However, the dialectic of the enclosed and the open created a space for mediation between the two contrasting spheres. A system of communication had to be established between these two spheres. In addition to the reinforced walls and city gates, altars and temples were also built.

Soon after Zhu Yuan Zhang declared himself emperor in 1368, he focused most of his attention on altar and temple construction.[29] First in the capital of Nanjing, altars were established to symbolize the communication channels between Heaven, the Sun, the Moon, Earth, the seas, and the humans. During the Zhengzu Reign (1506–1521), the Ming capital was moved to Beijing together with the Nanjing altar manual. In the imperial capitals, the altars consisted of Huanqiu (the round altar devoted to Heaven) and Fangqiu (the square court devoted to earth), which came to be known as the Celestial Altar (Tian Tan) and the Earthly Altar (Di Tan) in later times. Apart from these two grand platforms for worship, there were also the Sheji Tan, Shanchuan Tan, and Taili Tan. While Huanqiu and Fangqiu, which represented the emperor's power, were confined to the capitals, the emperor instructed his prefects and county magistrates to build up the smaller altars/platforms in their local seats.

In the city of Quanzhou, the first Ming prefect Chang Xing was responsible for the construction of the altars. Among the many buildings that he constructed, imperial altars occupied the prime position. These altars included those that were devoted to Sheji Shen (the God of Soil and Grain) and to Lei Yu Shan Chuan Chenghuang (Thunder, Rain, Mountains, City Gods, and Ghosts). These altars and divinities were equivalents of the emperor's own prerogatives: land under Heaven, grain, mountains, rivers, rain, and to-be-organized civilians (ghosts).[30] They can also be seen as media between the emperor's world and local worlds: the Altar for Soil and Grain represented the State, and the Altar for

---

[29] Ling, Shun Sheng, Beiping de fengshan wenhua [The sacred enclosures and stepped pyramidal platforms of Peiping].

[30] Stephan Feuchtwang, *The Imperial Metaphor: Popular Religion in China* (London 1992), pp. 63–66.

Thunder, Rain, Mountains, Rivers, City Gods, and Ghosts represented the conjunction of imperial authority, the country, and the underworld, which also represented the imperial institutions of justice.

Chang Xing and his associates not only re-invented a whole system of imperial altars in the Quanzhou but also took pains to assert the major topographic features as symbols of sovereignty. In Chinese imperial state symbolism, water [*jiang* or *chuan*] referred to the seas and sacred rivers [*haidu*], including the four seas (the East, West, North, and South Seas) and the four rivers (He, Jiang, Ji, and Huai rivers). Mountains referred to the Five Sacred Mountains [*Wu Yue*]. Water designated two things that played an important part in traditional China's conceptualization of boundary: veins [*xue*] of the land and borders of China as the world center (the seas). Mountains [*shan*] in this symbolic landscape belonged to the category of "land" [*di*]. However, considered to be extremely "high," they were perceived as bridges between heaven and earth or even the combination of the two. Therefore, *Jiangshan* [water and mountains] symbolized China as a living body of politics and ritual: water controls the land and the people, whereas mountains help the rulers to communicate with heaven and legitimate their dominance. In general, the relation between *jiang* and *shan* can be understood as follows: *jiang* = the four seas and the four rivers = borders = veins = political body of the State; *shan* = land = the five sacred mountains = bridge between heaven and earth = ritual.

The image of *jiang* [river or water] in the mapping of Quanzhou was remade through the same kind of imaginaries. According to local historian Chen Yun Dun, *jiang* [water, in this context] outside the city walls did not extend into the sea; it included only one small lake, the Eastern Lake (Donghu) and the moat surrounding the city.[31] The Eastern Lake was an analogue to the seas to the east of China. It was a first layer of the defense line against the outside. The other two parts of river and water in Ming Quanzhou were respectively known as the city moat [*chi*] and the "hexagram channels" [*bagua gou*]. The moat was created along with the city walls prior to the Ming. The hexagram channels were constructed gradually between the Song and the Ming Dynasties as drainage ditches. In spite of their practical use, the moat and the channels were viewed as a series of analogues of the great rivers of China in the Ming. Moreover, like the seas and rivers, each of the Five Sacred Mountains (Wu Yue) found their local counterparts. In the map of China, these Sacred Mountains were the Eastern Mountain (Dongyue), the Western Mountain (Xiyue), the

---

[31] Chen, Yun Dun, Quanzhou Gucheng Takan [Field research into Quanzhou's ancient city sites], *Quanzhou Wenshi* [*Quanzhou Culture and History*], 2-3 (1980): 1–13.

Southern Mountain (Nanyue), the Northern Mountain (Beiyue), and the Central Mountain (Zhongyue).[32] In Ming Quanzhou, five hills were named after the great Sacred Mountains. They had their own gods and temples, and they represented the five directions (each of which was designated in terms of lunar lodges and animal signs) in the same way that the five mountains did.[33]

Cosmic Imperium

In many of Zhu Yuan Zhang's court addresses, he emphasizes that all his efforts were to change the conditions of the Chinese sense of themselves. The emperor regarded the emperors before him as those who ruined this sense. In order to push culture back onto the right track, he called on many Neo-Confucians and astrologists, who assisted him in gaining a correct understanding of cosmology. He placed himself not only on the throne but also in the ritual landscape.

In a way, what Zhu Yuan Zhang did was simply to continue the Chinese emperors' previous techniques for self-legitimation. Many of the altars and temples that he established were seen as perfect reflections of the Zhou cosmic order. Here I should mention that, as Chinese anthropologist Ling Shun Sheng went so far as to argue, Chinese worship of sacred sites (altars or platforms) could be traced back to the *Shan Hai Jing* [Scripture of Mountains and Seas] period. During that period, the king's self-legitimation, known as the ritual of *fengshan,* on the model of which all the Ming altars and temples were based, had already been invented.[34] Before Ling Shun Sheng, in the late 1920s, Gu Jie Gang imposed his folkloric critiques on classical Chinese history. According to

---

[32] Chen, Yun Dun, Quanzhou wuyue [The five great peaks in Quanzhou], *Quanzhou Wenshi Ziliao* [*Cultural and Historical Materials in Quanzhou*], 2 (1983): 145–151.

[33] The numbers four and five, which, respectively, represented the rivers and the mountains not only referred to directions but also symbolized the quarters and the center of the universe. These numerological conceptions were bound up with the ideal of balance and concentration in the cosmos, which in turn played an important role in the formation of imperial control. Not surprisingly, they were repeated in the definition of the imperial temple and administrative areas. See Emily Lyle, Introduction, to her edited *Archaic Cosmos: Polarity, Space and Time* (Edinburgh 1990), pp. 1–5.

[34] Kun Lun, for Ling, represented a culture spreading from the Mesopotamian *ziggurat* [noble places] to Northwestern China. Later, in the Qin and Han Dynasties, that particular cultural complex gave rise to the first systematic institution of the imperial worship of *fengshan*—that is, the authorization of ceremonial centers or altars. Ling did not relate *fengshan* to "pilgrimage"; instead, he presented a diffusionist argument that all these ritual spaces were derivatives of a regional system of the pyramid cult, spreading from Egypt to the Orient. See Ling, Shun Sheng, Zhongguo de fengshan yu lianghe liuyu de kunlun wenhua [A comparative study of the ancient Chinese *fengshan* and the *ziggurat* in Mesopotamia], *Bulletin of the Institute of Ethnology, Academia Sinica,* 19 (1965): pp. 1–51.

Gu Jie Gang, legends in the Han Dynasty stated that all such rituals were invented in the Zhou Dynasty (11 c.b.c. to 256 b.c.). Actually, history is different from legends.[35] In Gu's view, although many of the ideas of ritual can be traced back to *Zhou Li*, the system of imperial altars and temples was initially related to later inventions in the states of Qi and Lü.[36] However, even in Gu's skeptical history, imperial cults had been systematically established by the Spring and Autumn period (Chunqiu) at the latest.

According to Gu, during the Spring and Autumn periods, the rulers of different states had to make sure that they were really fated by Heaven to be kings. They had to ask sorcerers and astronomers [*fangshi*] for advice on the matter. In the Qi and Lü states, the sorcerers and astronomers viewed their own Great Mountain (Taishan) as the ultimate source of authority. They thus led the kings to perform magical rituals toward Heaven on the top of the Great Mountain. These rituals were later adopted by the Qin and Han emperors and became a part of the imperial ceremonial repertoire.[37]

Trying to render earlier ideas of *fengshan* useful for the constitution of his own emperorship, the first emperor Qin Shi Huang redesignated Taishan as a sacred site for his personal communication with Heaven. When he became emperor, he thought that he no longer had to demonstrate to others his mandate to rule. Thus, the legacy of *fengshan*, which once offered a range of transcendental judgments for kingship, became an astrological means through which the emperor's legitimacy was re-affirmed. Along with this change, sorcerers and astronomers, who had been a highly respected stratum in previous periods, were rendered subordinate to the cosmological power of the emperor.[38]

---

[35] In the "Book of *fengshan*" in *Shi Ji*, the historian Si Ma Qian recorded that *feng* was conducted on the Great Mountain (Taishan, also translated as Mount Tai), whereas *shan* was conducted in a hill known as Liangfu Mount by the Great Mountain. Si Ma Qian also claimed that *Fengshan* had been described as an institution in classical cosmological philosophies such as Guan Zi during the Eastern [Late] Zhou Dynasty (770–256 b.c.e.). Gu argued that Guanzi's story was only partially true. According to Si Ma Qian, Guan Zi said that *feng* and *shan* rituals had been performed by 72 great sage-kings who ruled China in ancient times, to convey their gratitude to Heaven for giving them the authority to rule their countries. But the historical truth for Gu was that the oldest notion of *fengshan* was developed no earlier than in the states of Qi and Lü during the Spring and Autumn (beginning in 770 b.c.e.) and the Warring States (ending in 221 b.c.e.) periods.

[36] Gu, Jie Gang, *Qinhan de Fangshi yu Rusheng* [*Necromancers and Confucians in Chin and Han Dynasties*] (Shanghai 1998 [1955]), p. 5.

[37] In most cases, before a *fengshan* ritual was set, the kings had to have already observed 15 kinds of auspicious signs, including the rich grains [*Jia Gu*], the flying phoenix [*Fei Feng*], and so on, which all expressed Heaven's authorization of the ruler's fitness to serve as king.

[38] Gu's point is that they were no longer independent "intellectuals," and their ideas and cosmologies became the ideologies of the ruler.

Gu Jie Gang tried to argue for the Qin and the Han politicization of ritual and cosmology. However, I should point out that politicization itself was merely a temporary practice of an enduring tradition of cosmological action. Throughout the history of Chinese civilization, we observe cycles of dynasties, whereby new leaders emerge to replace old "confused emperors" [*hunjun*] and their disintegrating empires, a pattern in which the growth and decay of politics were depicted as a life cycle. In making the astronomers their advisors, the emperors subjected themselves to the opinions of the astronomers who served in their courts to judge their doings. One of the things the astronomers did was to help regulate the temporal trajectories of the emperors' bodily movements with the rules of sacred almanacs. Another was to advise the emperor how misfortunes in the world could be avoided through ceremonial actions, including correcting the irregular aspects of the emperors' bodily-cum-mental movement and the strategic arrangement of the ceremonial and political propensities of humans and things.[39]

Intriguingly, in contrast with Max Weber's analysis of China,[40] Gu Jie Gang argues that *fengjian* as practiced by the first emperor was evoked within the lordship system known as *fengjian* [feudalism]. *Fengjian* referred to the imperial divisions of the provincial compartments under the Son of Heaven (Tianzi). Originating in the Zhou Dynasty, *fengjian* entailed the political reconstruction of royal descent and area administrative domains. *Fengshan* was the official imperial restoration of the cult of divinities and channels of communication between Heaven and Earth.

In the Han Dynasty, Wu Di (in his reign between 140 to 135 B.C.E.) further envisioned the Chinese world, or what was regarded as All Under Heaven, in terms of the ideal model of the Five Sacred Mountains located in five directions, east, south, west, north, and central. At the same time, Wu Di designed the Palace of Brightness (Mingtang), a microcosm of the whole world represented in terms of seasons and directions, in accordance with which he passed time. He also treated the five sacred mountains far away from the capital, Chang'an, as great altars on which he "paid tribute" to Heaven,[41] paradoxically in the name of *feng*, or authorization.[42]

Clearly, the classical *fengshan* institution emphasized finding a source of authorization from "above," in Heaven, for an order of relations

[39] Wolfram Eberhard, The political function of astronomy and astronomers in Han China, in John King Fairbank (ed.), *Chinese Thought and Institutions* (Chicago 1957), pp. 33–70.

[40] Max Weber, *The Religion of China* (New York 1951).

[41] Gu, Jie Gang, *Qinhan de Fangshi yu Rusheng* [*Necromancers and Confucians in Chin and Han Dynasties*], p. 6.

[42] Concerning the history of *fengshan*, see also Susan Naquin, The Peking pilgrimage to Miaofeng Shan: Religious organizations and sacred site, in Susan Naquin, and Yu, Chun-fang (eds.), *Pilgrims and Sacred Sites in China* (Berkeley 1992), pp. 333–337.

"below," in this world.[43] In the early imperial cosmology of the Qin-Han period, *fengshan* was redefined as part of the ceremonies of *she* and *jiao*. In most of the post-Han dynasties, *she* carried the connotation of "place integrity" and worship at a *she* consisted of paying respect to the Earth God and the Grain God. "Place integrity" was expounded to convey the integrity of the country. Thus, "state" in classical Chinese was also called *sheji*. It is in the legacy of *sheji* cults that *jiaosi* was reproduced. *Jiao*, originally meaning "suburb," referred to sacrifices to Heaven, Earth, and all the powers of nature outside the imperial capital. These sacrifices were also known as *jiaosi*.

As Ling Shun Sheng shows, *she* and *jiao* were derived from the *fengshan* of the Great Mountain. *She* was a derivative of *shan* [worship of an enclosed of earthly deity], whereas *jiao* was a derivative of *feng* [worship of unenclosed heavenly divinities]. But *she* and *jiao* systems had their origins in earlier folkloric traditions. Originally, *she* included *jiao*. It referred to the place where a community made sacrifices to Heaven, Earth, local deities, ancestors, spirits, and other divinities. Later, *she* and *jiao* were separated. *She* became the place where the Earth God and the Grain God were worshipped. *Jiao* was added to the institution of worship and chiefly referred to sacrifices to Heaven and Earth. Over time, *jiao* combined with *she* and became *jiaoshe*, which referred to the altar system located in the outskirts of the capital. Ideally speaking, these suburban altars (some of which were open platforms, some of which were enclosures) included the Heaven Altar (Tian Tan) in the southern suburb, Earth Altar (Di Tan) in the northern suburb, Sun Altar (Ri Tan) in the eastern suburb, and Moon Altar (Yue Tan) in the western suburb.[44]

For the originators of imperial rites (such as *fangshi*, in Gu's definition), the building of altars in the suburbs of the imperial capital was aimed at bringing the distance of the gods nearer, for purpose of fulfilling the same task of *fengshan*. Wang Jing, a highly titled master of ritual who wrote the *Record of Jiaosi of the Great Tang* in the first year of Yongzhen Reign of the Tang Dynasty (805), thus said:

> According to my humble knowledge, in ancient times, the sage-kings (Sheng Wang) sought to command the universe by way of looking up into Heaven and looking down onto Earth. Heaven revealed to them changes; Earth images of the world. The sage-kings thereby invented rites and ceremonial

---

[43] Such ceremonial journeys to the locations of what were in between Heaven and Man shared with Western pilgrimages the sense of the transcendence of local social structure. However, it was obviously an outcome of a process of empire-building and civilization, through which transcendence had gained a different sort of meaning and efficacy.

[44] Ling, Beiping de fengshan wenhua [The sacred enclosures and stepped pyramidal platforms of Peiping].

procedures in accordance with the trajectories of changes and the images of the world. They turned them into a pattern of civilization [*renwen*] and utilized it to enlighten "All Under Heaven" (Tianxia).

Among the patterns of culture, the most important were ceremonies in the suburbs [*jiaosi*]. . . . The core meaning of these ceremonies was the principle of symbolic similarity. The gods in Heaven are far from us; so we make Heaven-like enclosures in the suburbs of the capital to make sacrifices to them. . . .[45]

As part of the totality of the empire, different *jiaosi* were held with different ritual "ranks." The hierarchy of such "ranks" consisted of upper-level worship [*shangsi*], intermediate-level worship [*zhongsi*], and lower-level worship [*xiasi*]. They were devoted to heavenly divinities, earthly deities, and human souls and ghosts, respectively. The worship of earthly deities was chiefly centered on the worship of *she* and *si*, or what we have called "state cults" [*sheji shen*]. *Jiaosi* referred to official worship falling in the other two categories, "upper-" and "lower-level" worship. Within the broad category *jiaosi* itself, there were further divisions, ranging from the more elaborate ceremonies devoted to Heaven at the Heaven Altar, also called the "Round Hill" (Huanqiu), to the simplest offerings to ghosts.

In a sense, *jiaosi* involved worship in the four quarters (the suburban altars in each of the four directions), which surrounded the center of *she* and *ji*, or the Altar of State Worship (Sheji Tan). These ceremonies—or cyclic "pilgrimages" to the suburban altars—defined the center vis à vis the periphery by establishing and renewing the pattern of "quarters round a center." However, the center did not represent the highest level of the cosmos. It was merely understood as the middle realm between Heaven and Earth.

If we may refer to *jiaosi* as an "imperial pilgrimage," then we may also say that the sense of transcendence revealed through it was not purely implicated by the supreme divinity, Heaven [*Tian*]. In fact, *jiaosi* consisted of a large number of ceremonial journeys to the outside of the capital—and in regional contexts the prefectural seats—which conveyed respect to cosmic divinities, including not only Heaven and Earth but also human souls and ghosts, who were perceived as the lower ranking "divinities" of the world.

Each official dynastic history includes a long chapter on *jiaosi*. Throughout the Han, Tang, Song, and Yuan Dynasties, books of rites that received the emperors' direct endorsements were composed, revised, and distributed to different parts of the country, along with official almanacs. In the Liao, Jin, and Yuan Dynasties, the rulers of China were non-Han,

---

[45] Wang, Jing, *Datong Jiaosi Lu* [*The Record of Suburban Ceremonies in the Great Tang Dynasty*] (Beiing 2000 [805]), *juan* 1.

and in the capital, non-Han rituals continued to be practiced by the non-Han court.[46] Yet, the system of *she* and *jiao* was observed as the principal institution of imperial worship.

Throughout the imperial period, the sacred locations of the Five Great Mountains, the Four Great Seas, and the Four Great Rivers played an important role in imperial ceremonial communication between Heaven and All Under Heaven. In different dynasties, the construction of temples and altars to represent these sacred topographic symbols far away from cities was an important task. Even in the coastal city of Quanzhou, so far as we know, by the Song, the Soil and Grain cult system already existed. No doubt, *fengshan* was defined in different ways in different periods of Chinese history, but it constantly served to configure the interrelationship between above and below, a vertical relationship between center and periphery. To honor the imperial mountains, journeys were made from the palace of the Emperor to the outer rings of the world, which was highlighted with visits by the Emperor to the great sacred mountains and to their representative altars set up within the "royal domain" (Di Du) of the capital. Also projected onto the prefectures' capitals, the map of the sacred mountains was represented as the design of the city and its ceremonial spaces. For the Emperor, yearly sacrifices to the mountains and altars rhythmically reconstructed the hierarchical relationship between the court and Heaven. For the prefectural governors, similar kinds of sacrifices were devoted to the purpose of revealing the imperial state's presence in regional worlds.

The official ceremonial performances at the altars and temples conceptualized in this two-way relationship in turn invoked an important synthesis of the Chinese tributary mode of production/representation and the imperial cultural politics of feudal differentiation. The tributary mode was an institution for the hierarchical exchange between the imperial court and its included and partially included subject populations (both Han and non-Han), and the exchange was most manifest in the sphere of luxury products. However, in the exchange of tribute goods, economic values were far less important than symbolic ones. The symbolic outcome of these exchanges most notably involved the respect-tribute from the bottom to the top. It also involved an equally important aspect concerning the imperial cultural politics of the feudal divisions of princely residences in the prefecture. Thus, the picture that we see matches that painted by Max Weber:

[In the religion of China], secular and spiritual authorities were combined, on one hand, with the spiritual strongly predominating. To be sure, the

---

[46] Ling, Zhongguo de fengshan yu lianghe liuyu de kunlun wenhua [A comparative study of the ancient Chinese *fengshan* and the zuggurat in Mesopotamia].

emperor had to prove his magical charisma through military success, or at least he had to avoid striking failures. Above all, he had to secure good weather for harvest and guarantee the peaceful internal order of the realm. However, the personal qualities necessary to the charismatic image of the emperor were turned into ritualism and then into ethics by the ritualists and philosophers.[47]

Reified Deities, Altered Locations

Despite the fact that the Ming reinvention of tradition has struck us as radically traditional, from the perspective of Quanzhou, it had several apparent novel qualities.

First, more specifically, as we can observe in the spatial understanding of Ming Quanzhou, the new official altars were spatially arranged differently from their earlier counterparts. In Zhu Yuan Zhang's understanding, the Sheji Tan for a regional city should be outside the north gate, and the other altars should be placed outside the south gate. His explanation was that a prefectural seat, unlike the imperial capital, could receive the emperor only if it looked down onto the region from the north, whereas the divinities of mountains, rivers, thunder, ghosts, and so on could serve the regional government from "below" or, from the perspective of Chinese geomancy, the south. Yet, for unknown reasons, in both the Song and the Yuan Dynasties, a Sheji Tan, the symbol of imperial state authority, was constructed within the city in the southwestern corner with an altar devoted to mountains, rivers, and other divine nature symbols attached to it.[48] In 1369, Chang Xing removed both the altars and appropriated the land for the government. He then established a new and extended Sheji Tan outside the North Gate. In the same year, a new altar devoted to the divinities of wind, rain, thunder, mountains, rivers, and the City God was constructed near the Southwest Gate of the city.[49]

Second, in previous dynasties, no special altar was devoted to ghosts. In order to "turn ghosts into punitive officers," in 1369, Zhu Yuan Zhang constructed Taili Tan in the city of Nanjing and instructed all the prefectures to build Li Tan in their own cities.[50] In the same year, Chang Xing added a shrine for ghosts at the altar for mountains and rivers (Shanchuan) in accordance with the ceremonial statute of the imperial state.[51]

---

[47] Max Weber, *The Religion of China*, p. 31.

[48] *Quanzhou Fuzhi* [*Quanzhou Prefecture Gazette*], compiled by Huai Yin, Bu, and Huang, Ren (Quanzhou 1870 [1763]), *juan* 5; *Jinjing Xianzhi* [*Jingjing County Gazette*], compiled by Fang, Ding (Quanzhou 1945 [1765]), *juan* 4.

[49] *Jinjing Xianzhi* [*Jingjing County Gazette*], compiled by Zhou, Xue Zeng, *juan* 15.

[50] Ling, Zhongguo de fengshan yu lianghe liuyu de kunlun wenhua [A comparative study of the ancient Chinese *fengshan* and the zuggurat in Mesopotamia].

[51] *Jinjing Xianzhi* [*Jingjing County Gazette*], compiled by Zhou, Xue Zeng, *juan* 15.

Third, following the installation of Li Tan, was the addition of the City God cult to "official religion." Although the name "City God" or the "God of the Walls and Moat" (Chenghuang) appeared as early as the Han Dynasty, it originally referred to the protector-gods of cities worshipped by various regional cults.[52] In 1369, the monarch endorsed the City God in the capital and all cities under Heaven, and one year later, he instructed all the prefects to eliminate the numerous and greatly varied regional titles for the City God and stipulated that the City God should only be called Chenghuang of so and so prefecture or of so and so county.

In Quanzhou, the city's guardian-gods and their temples existed in the Song. One of them was called "Minglie Wang," or "the King Who Brings Heroism to Light," whose temple was located in the Western District of the city. In the Southern Song, prefects such as Zhen De Xiu had paid visits to this temple to pray for rain, for safe maritime transportation, and for the comforting of the orphan souls of those who died in natural disasters. In 1371, Minglie Wang was renamed Chenghuang, and his temple was turned into the prefecture's City God Temple.

Another City God was worshipped as a secondary god in the memorial hall near the government compound for Han Qi, a Tang Dynasty premier. The sagacious man, Han Qi, was born in the city of Quanzhou. During the Song and the Yuan, his memorial hall was situated within the territory of the government compounds near a dynasty-wide "commandment stone" [*jieshi*]. According to He Qiao Yuan, the commandment stone was installed by Taizong (in his reign from 976 to 997) during the Song Dynasty.[53] Taizong personally wrote the calligraphy for the stone whose inscription reads: "Your salary is the flesh and blood of the people. It is easy for you to be tyrannical to the people below, but it is hard to deceive Heaven above [*erfeng erlu, minzhi mingao, xiamin yinue, shangtian nanqi*]." Taizong advised the prefect to place the commandment stone in a prominent site, where the prefect could sit beside it and reflect on his work every morning.

The memorialized effigy of premier Han Qi functioned in the same way as the commandment stone to warn officials away from corruption. By the Yuan, however, Han Qi had become a popular deity, whose statue occupied the central position in his memorial hall. According to Zhu Yuan Zhang's 1369 edict, the cult's effigy of Han Qi should be abandoned and replaced by a wooden tablet symbolizing the depersonified divinity of the

---

[52] For a comprehensive history of Chinese Chenghuang [city god] cults, see Zheng, You Tu, and Wang, Xian Shen, *Zhongguo Chengguang Xinyang* [*Chinese Beliefs in the City God*] (Shanghai 1994).

[53] He, *Min Shu* [*The Book of Fujian*], juan 33.

Figure 5.3 The image of Han Qi (found in a local temple, original carving undated).

City God.[54] Treating Chenghuang as the commander of all ghosts, the emperor found a position for this cult in the imperial hierarchy of gods, as a local commandership of the *yin* counterpart of the city and the region. In order to give Chenghuang a similar status, Chang Xing removed the shrine for Han Qi from the temple and turned the building into part

---

[54] Luo, *Ming Taizu Lifa Zhizhi Yanjiu* [*A Study of Taizu Emperor's Rule of Ritual and Law in the Ming*], pp. 13–14.

of the government compound. He established a brand new City God Temple for Jinjiang County.

Finally, all the reconstitutions of ceremonial space yielded an effect on urban space. During the periods of commercial expansion, Quanzhou city had two centers, which included the government compounds, situated in the center along the axial line of the walled urban space, and a large commercial center with several prosperous streets in the south, east, and west. During the Ming Dynasty, the commercial center in the southern part of the city was closed, and the structure of the city was redesigned so that the city had only one center, which was the government compound.

The creation of a single center was coupled with the extension of ceremonial spaces, which, besides the altars and worship platforms, also involved official religious temples such as the newly built and refurbished City God Temples. Official ceremonies held prior to the Ming were confined to the area surrounding the government compounds. After the establishment of the Ming, they were extended into all areas of the city. Meanwhile, imperial symbols began to spread throughout the city including the southern commercial districts. In the public sacred landscape of Quanzhou, the sections with Chinese government buildings, temples, altars, city gates, and walls were also expanded. Within the city, the *pujing* network of place administration also served to geographically allocate temples and memorial halls [*ci*] of wartime martyrs and model Confucian disciples.

In building or relocating altars and temples and reifying deities, the court absorbed earlier official religious cults and temples into its new tradition. In addition to the temples for civil and military gods, the Tianhou Temple in the south of the city was also legitimated. Nonetheless, by then, the role of the Heavenly Queen had been redefined. According to a stele inscription from the Southern Song written in 1150,[55] the miraculous efficacy of the Heavenly Queen was believed to lie in her ability to conquer floods, droughts, epidemics, and pirates and, more important, in her vision that "the merchants' ships relied on to open the routes of their journeys and make them safe."[56] In the early thirteenth century, Zhen De Xiu organized several ceremonies at the Tianhou Temple to honor Tianhou, then called Tianfei (Heaven's Concubine), to pray for protection against piracy and the blessings of maritime trade.[57] In contrast, during the Ming, Zhu Yuan Zhang himself claimed that this female deity could help realize his ideal of "advocating civilization among

---

[55] Wu, You Xiong, *Quanzhou Zongjiao Wenhua* [*Religious Culture in Quanzhou*] (Xiamen 1993), pp. 25–31.

[56] Ibid., p. 29.

[57] Ibid., p. 30.

West   North

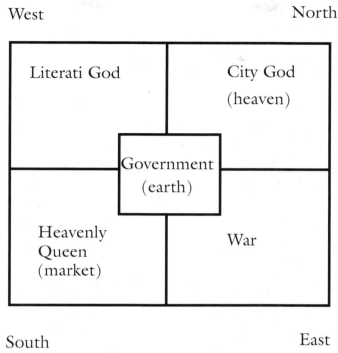

Figure 5.4 The spatial locations of Imperial City temples.

the barbarian states overseas" [*xuan jiaohu yu haiwai zhu fanguo*] and of "changing the barbarians' customs [*bian qi yisu*]."[58]

Each year, at the above-mentioned altars and temples as well as the temples that the Ming government inherited from the preceding dynasties, a number of sacrifices were organized. As Taylor illustrated with the example of Suzhou, official religion as practiced at the prefecture-level included the following:

> (1) "Standard Sacrifices": soil and grain, mountains and rivers, abandoned ghosts, and city gods; (2) "Sacrificial Statutes": the deities formally acknowledged by the imperial government and covered by the "Sacrificial Statutes"; (3) "Former Worthies": cults of notables that apparently had not yet been approved formally; and (4) "The Local People's Private Sacrifices."[59]

---

[58] Wu, *Quanzhou Zongjiao Wenhua* [*Religious Culture in Quanzhou*], p. 67.
[59] Taylor, Official and popular religion and the political organization of Chinese society in the Ming, p. 134.

Gazettes compiled during the Qing provide detailed accounts of official cult ceremonies in Quanzhou. An analysis, which picks out only the Ming practices, indicates that the prefectural and county government financed and directly organized only the first two categories of cults. Table 5.1 provides a list of sacred locations and their sacrifices.

During the spring and the autumn, officials in the city held two ceremonies for each religious temple.[60] At Sheji Tan (located to the north of the city) and Shanchuan Tan (located to the south of the city), two annual ceremonies were also organized. For Li Tan and the City God temples, three ceremonies took place a year in third, seventh, and tenth lunar months.[61] The temples of Confucius, the War God (Guandi), and the Heavenly Queen (Tianhou) were respectively situated in the north (City God), south (Heavenly Queen), east (War God), and west (Literati God). Each of the gods had various official titles and had a distinctive position in official state religion. The City God was emblematic of State power and its responsiveness;[62] the Literati God served to advocate the ideal that knowledge provides the constitution of the state; the War God symbolized the military force that served to maintain dynastic stability and public order; and the Heavenly Queen represented the prosperity of trade and coastal pacification.[63]

The area that they faced was the prefectural and county *yamen* protected by the inner city wall and moat. The temples were placed in the harmonized order of "four clearers," and they presented a version of imperial hierarchy. The differentiation between the City God and the Heavenly Queen temples mirrored the contrast between the controlling (State and politics) and the controlled (economy and the populace). The pairing of the Literati and the War God Temples was arranged according to the analogy of the two arms of the human body, and they were treated as "ministries" of the state. From another perspective, the four temples can also be seen as forming an

---

[60] The gazetteers also list other cult ceremonies, including the sacrifice to Wenchang Dijun, or "God of Literary Prosperity," and seasonal worship of the supernatural insurers of productivity, welfare, and territorial security, such as the spring worship of the agricultural cult (Nong Shen), sacrifices to the water god or the sea-dragon god (Hai Longwang), as well as ceremonies at the Dongyue Miao (the worship at the Eastern Mountain Temple, the burial area of the city). These categories in fact were added to the Ming list, mostly, in the early Qing.

[61] *Jinjing Xianzhi* [*Jingjing County Gazette*], compiled by Zhou, Xue Zeng, *juan* 155.

[62] Stephan Feuchtwang, City temples in Taipei under three regimes, in G. William Skinner and Mark Elvin (eds.), *The Chinese City between Two Worlds* (Stanford 1974), pp. 263–302; Angela Zito, City gods, filiality, and hegemony in late imperial China, *Modern China*, 13(3) (1987): 333–371.

[63] James Watson, Standardizing the gods: The promotion of T'ien Hou ["Empress of Heaven"] along the South China Coast, 960–1960, in David Johnson, Andrew Nathan, and Evelyn Rawski (eds.), *Popular Culture in Late Imperial China* (Berkeley 1985), pp. 292–324.

Table 5.1 The Ming Official Ceremonial of Quanzhou

Altar/Temple Name	Construction Year	Deity	Time of Sacrifice
Sheji Tan	1369	Earth God and Grain Good	Spring, autumn
Leiyu Shanchuan Tan	1369	Thunder, Rain, Mountain, River, Chenghuang, Ghosts	Spring, autumn
Li Tan	1369	Ghosts	15th days of 3rd, 7th, and 10th months
Wenmiao	976 (re-endorsed in 1371)	Confucius	27th of 8th month
Guandi	1373 (?)	Guan Gong War God	Spring, autumn 13th of 5th month
Tianhou	1196 (endorsed in 1368)	Heavenly Queen	Spring, autumn
Chenghuang1 (prefecture)	1369	City God	15th days of 3rd, 7th, and 10th months
Chenghuang2 (county)	1371	City God	as above

Sources: *Jinjing Xianzhi* [*Jingjing County Gazette*], compiled by Fang, Ding, *juan* 5; *Quanzhou Fuzhi* [*Quanzhou Prefecture Gazette*], compiled by Huai Yin, Bu, and Huang, ren, *juan* 4; *Jinjing Xianzhi* [*Jingjing County Gazette*], compiled by Zhou, Xue Zeng, *juan* 14–16.

ideal imperial model of social stratification: City God, Literati God, War God, and Heavenly Queen were symbolic equivalents of officials, scholars, warriors, and merchants, respectively. All the ceremonies were arranged in accordance with the rhythms of the seasons, particularly the ancient binary opposition of spring and autumn that signified regeneration and decline and promotion and punishment. The temples also represented the moral order and played the dual role of praising the good and punishing the bad.

Gods and Ghosts of *Pujing*

During the early Ming, in addition to the above-mentioned alterations in the city's sacred landscape, two more important changes took place in the spaces of *pujing*. At first, the *pujing* system was administered in coordination with the household registration system of Huangce.[64] Soon

---

[64] See a comprehensive survey of Huangce in Luan, Cheng Xian, *Mingdai Huangce Yanjiu* [*A Study of Huangce in the Ming*] (Beijing 1998).

afterward it was merged with the management of garrison-towns as a system of militia units.[65] In the early Ming, however, the most important change was the extension of official religion into local neighborhoods.

Prior to the Ming, the officialdom organized its own religious landscapes and sacrificial practices. Some of the ceremonies—for instance, those that concerned trade and the expulsion of epidemics—were participated in by bureaucrats, army commanders, merchants, and scholar-gentry. For bureaucratic ceremonial spectacle—such as sacrifices to the God of Soil and Grain and to Confucius—extra-official involvement was regarded as unnecessary and, to a large extent, improper. Although the boundary between so-called *li* and *su*, or between "ritual" and "customs," was a difficult line to maintain; the officialdom regarded it as important in the pre-Ming dynasties. In the Ming Dynasty, the restricted bureaucratic 'rituals evidently remained the domain of officialdom. Nevertheless, Ming officialdom held a radically different point of view from earlier dynasties concerning the boundary between ritual and customs. Along with what Qian Mu has defined as the emergence of "civilizing Confucianism,"[66] the distinctions between "public" and "private," popular and courtly, and customs and rites were reduced.

From the bottom up, this was a process of imperial absorption and standardization of "lower places" into the "higher order." Cosmologically, this process was understood in terms of "quarters around a center." Although the 36 *pu* divisions had already existed in the Yuan Dynasty, the numerological aspect of them did not develop until the Ming, when a religious cosmological emphasis on the magic squares that were widely used in geomancy was inserted by the officialdom. Ideally, each quarter was further segmented into nine wards [*pu*] according to the Zhou system of field divisions (Jingtian Zhi). Each *pu* was then divided into two or more *jing*. The administrative divisions of urban space thus took the ideal pattern of 4 x 9 = 36 (wards) and 36 (wards) x 2 = 72 (subwards).[67]

As the cells of the imperial political body, internally *pujing* had the task of maintaining a full degree of "harmony," whereas its outer order served to embody a unified higher dominating order. As the compilers of the 1830 edition of *Jinjiang County Gazette* suggested:

> Through implementing the *pujing* institution, the magistrates can learn about the situations of different places, register households, observe the growth and decline of places, eliminate harmful elements, praise obedient people, and place things and people in right order. *Pujing* can assist the

---

[65] *Jinjing Xianzhi* [*Jingjing County Gazette*], compiled by Fang, Ding, *juan* 7.

[66] Qian, Mu, *Guoshi Dagang* [*Outline of National History*] (Shanghai and Beiping 1939).

[67] This ideal plan was not accomplished until the Qianlong Reign in the early Qing, during which one more *yu* was added to make up four *yu*.

magistrates in implementing imperial policies, supervising people's conduct, and carrying out punishment. Furthermore, it can help the government to predict the potential development of different social tendencies.[68]

Thus *pujing* became an institution of surveillance, but "surveillance" in this context was different from its European counterpart. In the Ming, rule by rites and law, control and observation of human conduct, was only one aspect of the social order. Coupled with it, *pujing* was also integrated into a pan-dynasty system of rule by ritual. As a cosmological principle, *pujing* could be understood as the "realization of harmony in the universe," although as administrative divisions they were charted out by taking into account such factors as pre-Ming population distribution, settlement, and neighborhood formation. In relation to the government compounds, the *pujing* system was consistent with the concept of radiation from the imperial center, and it was quite important as that which linked the organized neighborhoods to the center—that is, to the government. In short, *pujing* served as a means of propagating and enforcing whatever was seen as "good" or "orthodox" by the defenders of universal order.

Unlike before, the altars for the Soil God and the Grain God, which were core to the imperial "state cult," were no longer restricted to use in official ceremonies. In each of the *pu* or *jing*, they were established for civilians to share. The original *pujing* halls were designated as something similar to the halls of *she,* where poems were chanted and rituals of praying and reportage were performed. To further the civilizing process, several memorial halls were established in each *pu* in addition to the communal pact halls. In the late imperial period, the memorial halls that were constructed in the city of Quanzhou involved (1) halls for officials with great fame (Minghuan Ci), (2) halls for local men with virtues (Xiangxian Ci), (3) halls for men with loyalty, morality, filial piety, and obedience (Zhongyi Xiaolian Ci), and (4) halls for those with female merits (Zhenlie Jiexiao Ci).[69] These memorial halls also served as local sites for Confucian moral teaching (Shexue).

In many, if not all, community pact halls [*she*] and official memorial halls [*ci*], two key characters were always inscribed. To those who lived during the Ming and Qing Dynasties, the characters of *he* [harmony] and *tong* [sameness] are most familiar. These two characters had already been propagated since the Han Dynasty formally established its cosmology of the "Central Kingdom." They were inseparable from the notion of *wen* [writing], or culture. Harmony and sameness thus denoted civilization, or the synthesis of the cosmological workings of the universe and the social precepts of order, pattern, and harmony in the processes of life.

[68] *Jinjing Xianzhi* [*Jingjing County Gazette*], compiled by Zhou, Xue Zeng, *juan* 21.
[69] *Jinjing Xianzhi* [*Jingjing County Gazette*], Fang, Ding (ed.), *juan* 5.

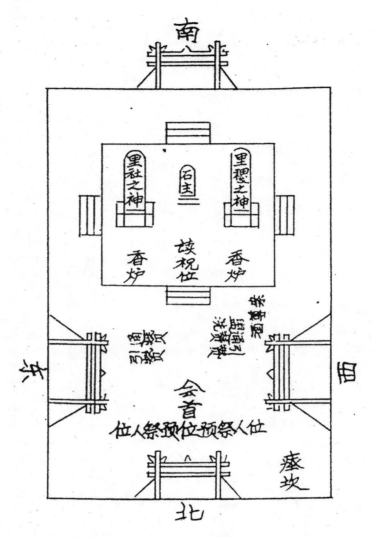

Figure 5.5 The ideal model of the official *Pujia* Temple in Hui'an County (source: Ye, Chun Ji, *Hui'an Zhengshu* [*Hui'an County Political Manual*], Fuzhou 1987 [1672], p. 345).

In spring and autumn each year, ceremonies, sometimes attended by county or prefectural officials, were held within these *pujing* temples to honor all the hero-gods of locality. The three occasions for ghost and City God sacrifices were also organized as official local customary practices. At the prefectural and county level, on fifteenth day of the third, seventh month, and tenth months, the tablet of the City God was carried in procession from the temple to the altar. At the altar, the tablet served as the chief judge of all right- and wrongdoings. All the ghosts—that is, all those souls who had not found descendants to worship them—were called to serve in the City God's temporary court as punitive officers. The prefect or the magistrate was the chief master of ritual. During the ceremony, he read out a standard script in which the City God was said to come join him, together with the ghosts, to punish the wrongdoers and criminals. The same ceremony was also conducted outside the communal temples of the various *pujing*. While the celebrations of the hero-gods were to repetitively recall local memories of good deeds, the sacrifice to the City God and his army of ghosts-turned-punitive-officers was made to resemble the sacrifice at the Li Tan, which involved "the transformation of ghosts and gods into law court officers." The elegiac address for the Altar of the Ghosts reads as follows:

> This ceremony is devoted to the ghosts and the gods who do not receive regular worship from local people from this prefecture (Quanzhou) and county (Jinjiang). . . . Any people in this prefecture and county who are not filial and not harmoniously related, any people who engage in illegal conduct and humiliate the virtuous, and any people who fall into the categories of deviance will be reported by local gods to the City God. Once their ill conduct is convicted, they will be arrested by the government and will be punished to different extents in accordance with their different degrees of criminal offence. . . . If their ill conduct is not yet convicted, they will necessarily be faced with curses from the *yin* world. The ghosts will make their whole families suffer from disasters. Any people who are filial and are harmoniously related, any people who obey the Law and become righteous and virtuous, the gods will also report them to the City God. The force in the *yin* world will protect them and make their families peaceful and complete, their agriculture will develop smoothly, and their wives and children will remain in the hometown.[70]

The elegiac address to ghosts was recited three times a year in front of the tablet of the City God and Li Tan. It was not locally composed but was carefully written and distributed by the court. In *Hongwu Lizhi* [*Ceremonial Statute of the Hongwu Emperor*], the address was provided.[71] In later periods of the Ming and the Qing, the City God cult, as "controller of demons," gradually became "the hierarchy of regulation, the status group of officials and those who aspired to it and joined the hierarchy of demonic command and response usually considered a popular, customary aberration."[72] But in the early Ming, when the cult was first endorsed directly by the court, it was intended to transform the role of ghosts.

---

[70] *Jinjing Xianzhi* [*Jingjing County Gazette*], Zhou, Xue Zeng (ed.), *juan 16*.

[71] *Huangming Zhishu, juan 7*; c.f., Luo, *Ming Taizu Lifa Zhizhi Yanjiu* [*A Study of Taizu Emperor's Rule of Ritual and Law in the Ming*], pp. 14–15.

[72] Feuchtwang, *The Imperial Metaphor*, p. 74.

As we will discuss in more detail later, in the Song, when prefects such as the Neo-Confucian Zhen De Xiu were making sacrifices to ghosts, orphan souls were represented as poor, hungry, and thus harmful. The Song prefects took advantage of Buddhist festivals, such as the Yulanpen Hui, or the Universal Salvation Festival, in which sympathy for the ghosts was expressed most explicitly. As Zhen De Xiu pronounced:

> You, the people [ghosts], who died for no reason, have constantly suffered from manmade disasters. Returning to your old town, you think of the bitterness in the under world. You look for every possibility of transcending your own being and that of being saved. . . . Now, [through this Universal Salvation Ritual], those whose names were registered in the dark book [*heipu*] should all regain your fate in the Red Hill (Zhuling). All the crowds of ghosts no longer need to feel they are drowning in the placeless world. The Pure Land in the West (Buddhist Paradise) has been listed as the destination on your journey of extreme happiness [*jile zhi you*].[73]

Teiser dwells on the cosmology of the ghost festival in the Tang and the Song Dynasties. He points to a transformation in the Song around the tenth century in which the festival was given new contents in a social milieu, among the majority of the illiterate Chinese. Through this transformation, the concept of ghosts was merged with an altered cosmology of the hell, which was somewhat an underworld reflection of court bureaucracy that sanctioned the right and the wrong of the uncared-for ancestors.[74]

In the city of Quanzhou, a similar transformation also took place, but officialdom was not particularly concerned with the punitive functions of ghosts. As Zhen De Xiu's statement shows, ghosts could impinge on local society and exert harm on the living for "good reasons." As uncared-for souls, their poverty, hunger, and homelessness entitled them to induce catastrophe and disorder. Making offerings to them was to comfort them and make them less harmful. By the early Ming, this sense of mercy was completely replaced by the imperial appointment of ghosts as punitive officers in the City God's court. The new status for ghosts was endorsed as *li*. *Li*, as Feuchtwang interprets it, is "the more classical rendering of what in common speech were and are called 'orphan souls' [*guhun*]." *Li*, however, also carries the meaning of "severely disciplining." Thus, *li* can be summarized as "the equivalent in the *yin* world of spirits to the imperial magistrate in the visible, living *yang* world."[75]

---

[73] C.f., Wu, You Xiong, Quantai "pudu" fengsu kao [An investigation into the Pudu festival in Quanzhou and Taiwan], *Quanzhou Daojiao Wenhua* [Daoist Culture in Quanzhou], 1 (1994): 21.

[74] Stephan Teiser, *The Ghost Festival in Medieval China* (Princeton 1988), pp. 168–195.

[75] Feuchtwang, *The Imperial Metaphor*, p. 64.

CHAPTER 6

Local Worlds on the Margin, 1400–1644

In the period between 1375 and 1400, an important shift brought with it many changes to Chinese history. Central to this shift was the transition from a tributary empire to a bounded monarchy. From the point of view of culture and ideology, this change was manifested in the turn from "Kingly Confucianism" to "Civilizing Confucianism." But this transition had more to it: the Ming's synthetic approach to orthodoxy characterized by its pursuit of perfect order and harmony and its quest for the "national" consciousness of the Chinese yielded a political and symbolic outcome.

Pujing in the Ming definition emerged from the politico-economic, bureaucratic, and cultural changes in which it became—though only ideally—a microcosm for the perfecting of the political and moral order. Each *pu* or each *jing* had several local headmen or captains to command its own territory. A *pu*'s or a *jing*'s office created out of the urban neighborhood under its command a communal space in which a variety of things became visible. As an office, it kept household records [*Huangce*], accommodated local official meetings, set up community pact regulations, and sent out officials to collect taxes and guard the community. But the office was also a temple in which the Lord of the Community was worshipped as the God of Soil and Grain, a divinity that the Ming monarch saw as the localized symbol of his sovereignty. "Public spaces" within the territory were marked out as locations of divinities and punishing ghosts/spirits. Outside the office-temple, memorial halls for the virtuous, the heroic, the loyal, the filial, and essentially, for all those who performed good deeds before death were established. The tablets within the halls recorded the names, the good deeds, and the imperial titles bestowed on the virtuous dead, and they formed a moral force that was policed not only by gods but also by ghosts who were released from the underworld three times each year to catch the vicious, the deceptive, the criminal, the offensive, and the greedy. The sanctioning divinities paired as the praising versus the condemning and the positive versus the negative, perfectly corresponded with the secular pair of sanctioning pavilions, the declaring boards in the Shenming Pavilion and the Jingshan Pavilion.

Inefficiency

Economic historians have treated Ming territorial units as irrationally planned channels of financial income. According to them, the construction of local public buildings, pavilions, and platforms resulted in greater amounts of expenditure, and it ended up creating financial problems for the court. These sacred spaces can thus be perceived as contradicting the financial policy of the Ming.[1] However, the monarch was neither "irrational" nor ignorant of the fiscal affairs of the state. He merely viewed problems from a perspective different from that of modern economics. He cherished the archaic ideal that harmony between the cosmos and men outweighed perfecting the efficiency of economy and administration. Thus, he paid most of his attention to the making of an "official religion" and drained more resources than his government and civilians could afford.[2]

Ideally, a *pu* or a *jing* office should serve to collect taxes. The taxes were then to be transferred bottom-up from the community to the state through courier-post routes, which had been merged with grain transportation networks.[3] Then, the concentrated resources were redistributed

---

[1] Liang, Fang Zhong, *Mingdai Liangzhang Zhidu* [*The Grain Head System in the Ming Dynasty*] (Shanghai 1956).

[2] As Ray Huang shows, the monarch and his government were "too idealistic" about how an economy and polity should be run properly to know how an efficient state economy should be managed. Huang, Ray, *Taxation and Government Finance in Sixteenth-Century China* (Cambridge 1974).

[3] In *Volume* 99 of *Dushi Fangyu Jiyao*, Gu Zu Yu mentioned that in the ninth year of the Hongwu Reign (1377), the headquarters of Quanzhou's courier-post wards was reconstructed as a station that combined the functions of postal service and transportation. See *Quanzhou Fangyu Jiyao* [*Main Materials of Quanzhou Historical Geography*], Office of Local Gazetteers, Quanzhou (Quanzhou 1985), p. 257.

through different levels of government back into the local community. For a *pu* or a *jing*, the redistributed resources were particularly useful for the sponsoring of the extensive range of ceremonies in which local public affairs, security issues, and social relationships were dealt with in a holistic manner.

The emperor was known to have placed a heavy emphasis on "assiduous political work [*qinzheng*]." However, as one can imagine, even a most tedious official could not deal with the fine details of state-to-community resource flow.

Gu Yan Wu (1619–1692), the economic geographer and historian who wrote *Tianxia Junguo Libing Shu*, provides a treatment of the changes in taxes and corvée in Quanzhou during the Ming.[4] According to Gu, from the first years of the Hongwu Reign to the beginning of the Zhengde Reign (1506), the tax burdens placed on Quanzhou were unbearable. A commoner in a *pu* or a *jing* (which Gu Yan Wu, who adopted the central official terminology, called *li* or *she*) in the city, or in a *li* or *she* in the countryside, was required to pay a state tax in grain and/or an equivalent amount in silver currency. Besides that, he was obliged by Ming Code to support the livelihood and activity of the soldiers and armed police. Local ceremonies within a *pu* or a *jing* were in turn financed with the tax income. The centralized taxation policy was a great burden for the *pu* or the *jing* civilians, and it was equally a burden for the government. Tax collection was a hard job, but the government officials and the *pujing* officers had yet to redistribute their limited resources. Especially when performing local official ceremonies, several levels of government had to bear the burden of carefully calculating and allocating their financial expenditures.

Not only was taxation felt to be a burden by the citizens of the Ming in the fifteenth century, but these citizens were also exasperated by the channeling of resources by state agents for their own "private" [*si*] purposes.[5] As a result, throughout the fifteenth century, much of the local administration as well as ceremonial organization at *pujing* level was left in the hands of local activists who both complained about corruption at higher levels and took advantage of their local influence to extend their own interpretations of power and social order. Not long after Zhu Yuan Zhang distributed his *Ceremonial Statute*, the high "Civilizing Confucianism" fell into "low worlds" of the divided realms of gentry dominated communities.

The situation became troubling to officials. Having worked on it, they decided to rationalize fiscal management. In accordance with their

---

[4] *Juan 92–96, Tianxia Junguo Libing Shu*, c.f., *Quanzhou Fangyu Jiyao* [*Main Materials of Quanzhou Historical Geography*], Office of Local Gazetteers, Quanzhou (Quanzhou 1985), pp. 191–248.

[5] Ibid., pp. 193–194.

proposal, in the fifth year (1510) of the Zhengde Reign, taxes were re-ordered into *guanmi* [government grains] and *minmi* [civilians' grains]. According to Gu Yan Wu, 70% of the tax was designated as *minmi* and kept at the level of local government, while only 30% was transferred to the capital. In response to the remaining problems, in 1521 and 1537, taxation was reformed twice more. Although these three attempts at tax reform solved some minor problems, they did not resolve some of the bigger problems, such as corruption.[6] Evidently, corruption at the regional level turned out to be even more serious. In the first year of the Wanli Reign, the single whip tax method (Yitiaobian Fa) was imposed to integrate the previous large range of taxes and corvée into one. Taxes were collected in the summer, while grains were collected in the autumn. In addition, a certain amount of tax was levied on a particularly specified occasion for labor service and army conscription. Together, these were called *yaoyi*. The rest of tax and corvée system consisted of the following: (1) *gangyin* or silver payment for the administrative functions of the government and for the expenditures of government administrative functions as well as prefectural and county ceremonies, (2) travel expenses for scholars taking exams, and (3) *junyao yin* for payment for all sorts of local administrative services, post-courier services, altar maintenance, and so forth.[7]

In Fujian in the sixteenth century, this series of tax reforms was targeted at ensuring the central monopolization of financial income. They stemmed from the State's need to accumulate redistributable capital owing to the increase in defense expenditures incurred by the wars against piracy in the first half of the sixteenth century. The consequences of the reforms were various, but from the point of view of the prefects and the county magistrates in Fujian province, they simply reduced local capability to respond to emergencies and to adjust to local circumstances.[8] In terms of *pujing* or rural *lishe*'s work in the fields of culture and religion, the decrease in regional tax income and financial resources also brought about the decline of imperial control over local communities.

With the implementation of these reforms, financial support for local community work was reduced. Meanwhile, during the same period, the *pujing* and *lishe* headmen had become local tyrants. They placed old imperial taxes and levies on local households as autocratically as the emperor. When a celebration was being organized, they went from household to household to collect "tax." In order to maintain all the

---

[6] Ibid., pp. 194–195.

[7] Ibid., pp. 195–196.

[8] Zheng, Zhen Man, Minghouqi Fujian difang xingzheng de yanbian: jianlun Ming zhongye de caizheng gaige [The transformation of local administration in late Ming Fujian, also commenting on the financial reform in mid-Ming], *Zhongguo Shi Yanjiu* [*Chinese History Research*], 1 (1998): 147–157.

altars, temples, pavilions, and the postal service and to make neighborhood policing effective, they needed to employ altar keepers, temple and pavilion caretakers, postmen, and watchmen. But the salaries were low, and volunteers could do some of the work. Furthermore, as Zheng adds, the long-term result was that most local organizations and local public affairs returned to the hands of community members under the leadership of gentry groups [xiangzu jituan].[9]

Piracy, Trade, and Emigration

In the late fourteenth century, Quanzhou was upgraded into one of the three "upper prefectures" [shangzhou] in Fujian (the other two being the provincial capital Fuzhou and the regional center of Jianyang in the hinterland). From then until the 1520s, the court inserted more administrative, financial, and educational functionaries in Quanzhou. But at the same time, Quanzhou's position as the center of trade inspection was removed. Fuzhou was selected as the official station of tributary trade. In the decades prior to the beginning of the fifteenth century, the Ming received the envoys from nearby "barbarian kingdoms" directly in the provincial capital. Smaller envoys from abroad were allowed also in Zhangzhou and Mingzhou (Ningbo) but not in Quanzhou. Quanzhou's role in maritime trade was thereby marginalized.

During the Wanli Reign (1573–1620), Guo Zao Qing reflected on this change and critiqued the State policies from the earlier reigns in a treatise on coastal defense.[10] He argued that to allow foreign envoys directly into the provincial capital was to create a condition under which the bandits of "island barbarian kingdoms" [daoyi] could directly challenge one of the centers of the empire. In addition, to raise the economic statuses of Zhangzhou and Mingzhou was to make it possible for these bandits to develop into potentially threatening forces. Guo Zao Qing traced the history of Fujian's "maritime communication" back to the Song and the Yuan. He said that prior to the Ming, Quanzhou was designated as the center of both tribute-transfer and trade. Because this prefecture differed at the same time from more central Fuzhou and more marginal Zhangzhou, it did not suffer from the problems that Fuzhou and Zhangzhou was to have. Because of the change in regional planning, during the Ming foreigners brought more calamities for the government in coastal Fujian and Zhejiang, while Guangdong merchants were more freely doing business

---

[9] Ibid., p. 156.
[10] Guo, Zao Qing, Minzhong bingshi yi [A treatise on the feeding of the army in Fujian], selected in Gu Yan Wu's Tianxia Junguo Libing Shu, juan 92–96, c.f., Quanzhou Fangyu Jiyao [Main Materials of Quanzhou Historical Geography], Gazetteer Office of Quanzhou (Quanzhou 1985), pp. 229–236.

with the tribute-paying chiefdoms [*tuqiu*]. As a means of reform, Guo Zao Qing proposed that the emperor should return Quanzhou to its old status, moving both the Trade Superintendent Bureau in Fujian and the Border-Pacifying Office (Anbian Guan, the lower level foreign envoy reception bureau and trade office) in Zhangzhou back to the city of Quanzhou.

Guo Zao Qing, to whom Gu Yan Wu held a sympathetic attitude, might have been biased against Fuzhou and Zhangzhou, but he was quite sensitive to the complex difficulties that the Ming government faced in the period prior to the Wanli Reign. In spite of all the efforts to create a state of "more [or only] culture, less [or no] commerce" in the first half of the Ming Dynasty, there was a gradual resurgence of regional trade in the Jiangnan and Fujian regions.[11] As Guo Zaoqing observed, had the government imposed taxes on maritime trade in Quanzhou, instead of prohibiting the trade, the financial resources drawn from the taxes would have been sufficient for the consolidation of the coastal defense system and for the maintenance of the army. Yet at the beginning of the Ming Dynasty, the emperor and his government were not at all interested in the fiscal benefits of trade. The consequence was that local civilians who could not do business felt greatly burdened by the increasing taxes and levies. Gradually, some of them turned to illegal trade, escaped from the household registration system, or joined those who were defined by the Ming orthodoxy as *dao* [robbers].[12]

Guo Zao Qing also recounted that in the middle of the Zhengtong Reign (1436–1449), many Quanzhou groups joined Deng Mao Qi's uprising. In the Zhangzhou prefecture, a sectarian religious leader, Jiang Fu Cheng, also called for a resistant movement. Later Deng and Jiang joined forces, moving in-between the north and the south of the province and besieging many towns. After the rebellion was put down, Quanzhou was under siege from 1488 to 1548 by several "robber-bandit groups" from rural Zhangzhou and Guangdong. All these so-called bandits were part of or closely related to the Guangdong-Zhangzhou pirate groups gradually expanding in the East and South China Seas.[13]

In the first four decades of the sixteenth century, many Fujianese laborers and merchants concentrated around the Moon Harbor (Yuegang) in Zhangzhou, taking part in the private manufacture of large ships and in the trade with Southeast Asia and South Asia. Because of all these local commercial activities, another macro-regional cycle emerged in the southern Fujian area as a substitute for the declining Quanzhou-centered cycle of development. Centered in the Moon Harbor (Yuegang)

[11] Fu, Yi Ling, *Fuyiling Zhishi Wushi Nian* [*Fu Yiling's Papers on the Study of History, 50 Years of Efforts*] (Shanghai 1989), pp. 45–49.
[12] Ibid., pp. 233–234.
[13] Ibid., pp. 243–246.

of Zhangzhou (some 150 kilometers to the south of Quanzhou), this region's development was stimulated by the coming of the Portuguese, who had been expelled from Guangzhou in the years 1521–1522. They came to offshore islands near Zhangzhou and increased their position through frequent contact with the Spaniards in the Philippines.[14] The Moon Harbor of Zhangzhou first emerged not as a licensed trading port but as an illegal smuggling and pirate bay. Thus, in 1506, when an official on a visit home to Zhangzhou learned that his kinsmen were involved in unlicensed transportation and maritime trade, he was shocked and said that he would report them to the authorities.[15]

To the government, the overseas trade occurring in Zhangzhou demonstrated why it was so difficult to pacify pirates on the sea [daohai bujing]. In 1548, a cross-provincial office was established to impose another maritime prohibition policy in Zhangzhou. Within this region, over 90 civilians who were involved in maritime trade were convicted and decapitated. The decapitation of traders was intended as a demonstration of the determination of the government to ban maritime trade. The unintended consequence, however, was that many traders and their associates had to flee Fujian. Some coastal households escaped into mountainous areas, but in most cases, they joined the pirate groups know as wo [the Japanese]. By the mid-sixteenth century, some 40% of the so-called "Japanese pirates" were from Fujian. These pirate groups expanded along with the implementation of more aggressive policies toward maritime trade.[16]

In official dynastic histories and local gazettes, the year 1557 has long been treated as a turning point in which the threats of robbers gave way to incidences of wohuan [troubles induced by the Japanese pirates]. As shown in a comprehensive history of Chinese piracy,[17] in the Jiajing Reign of the Ming, Fujian piracy entered a period of great prosperity and splendor. The small bandit groups from Guangdong and Zhangzhou were integrated into larger regimes of pirates [haidao]. Dressed in Japanese warrior-merchant costumes, the pirates became highly organized and

---

[14] G. William Skinner, Presidential address: The structure of Chinese history, Journal of Asian Studies, 44(2): 271–292.

[15] Timothy Brook, The Confusions of Pleasure: Commerce and Culture in Ming China (Berkeley 1998), p. 120.

[16] Xie, Fang, 16–17 shiji zhongguo haidao yu haishang sichou zhi lu [Chinese pirates and the maritime silk route in the sixteenth aend seventeenth centuries), in Zhongguo yu Haishang Sichou Zhilu [China and the Maritime Silk Route] 2 Vols. (Fuzhou 1991), Vol. 1, pp. 46–54.

[17] Zheng, Guang Nan, Zhongguo Haidao Shi (History of Chinese Piracy) (Shanghai, 1998), pp. 163–274.

were extremely well armed.[18] Gu Yan Wu listed 11 instances of *wohuan* in Quanzhou. For example, in 1557, the *wo* killed the top commander of the Quanzhou garrison-towns. Having taken the garrison-town Chongwu, they besieged the prefectural city of Quanzhou, and from where they moved further north into the inland counties of Yongchun and Anxi. Between 1559 and 1571, they successively invaded most of the counties in the prefecture and plundered the coastal garrison-towns of Tong'an, Anhai, and Yongning. Several magistrates were killed. From 1563 to 1571, the armies commanded by Qi Ji Guang in Fujian and Yu Da You in Guangdong successfully defended the prefectural seats, but the coastal garrison-towns remained constantly endangered.[19]

The tribulations brought by the *wo* in local history induced "disasters" or "sufferings" [*nan*] that ironically helped make for a heroic history. Throughout the late Ming, long lists of those who died in the action against the *wo* were placed in the official city temples and *pujing* memorial halls. As a moral force, the tablets of these named heroes honored the virtuous deaths of war heroes. At the same time, they also narrated an epic history for the city walls on the coast, which marked the boundary between the "Central Kingdom" and its fearsome enemies. Intended as a moral lesson for the local civilians who might potentially join the *wo*, the enemy of civilization, these honorific tablets became numerous in late Ming Quanzhou.

These battles, however, did not bring an end to piracy. It continued to challenge imperial attempts at coastal pacification. Transregional trade that was officially denounced and prohibited continued to develop quietly. By the Wanli Reign, pirate traders had communicated with the Portuguese. Known as "turtle dragons" [*guilong*] of the sea, these pirate trader groups were viewed by officialdom as one of the three major "harms" [*hai*] for the Chinese (the other two being the "black tigers" [*heihu*, or bandits] in the mountains and the Portuguese).[20] Between the 1560s and the 1590s, great pirates such as Lin Dao Qian and Lin Feng developed extensive organizational networks. Near the end of the sixteenth century a more elaborate organization was developed under the pirate chieftain of Zheng Zhi Long. Zheng Zhi Long, the father of Zheng Cheng Gong (also known as Koxinga), who called himself Nicholas when meeting with the Portuguese, was from a rural fishermen's village near the garrison-town

---

[18] Xie, Fang, 16-17 shiji zhongguo haidao yu haishang sichou zhi lu [Chinese pirates and the maritime silk route in the sixteenth and seventeenth centuries).

[19] C.f., *Quanzhou Fangyu Jiyao* [*Main Materials of Quanzhou Historical Geography*], pp. 196–197.

[20] Chen, Si Dong, Luelun Mingdai Fujian yanhai de fan zousi cuoshi [A brief treatise on the anti-smuggling policies along the Fujian Coast during the Ming Dynasty, in *Quanzhou Wenshi* [*Quanzhou Culture and History*], 6-7 (1982), pp. 125–127.

of Anping (Anhai). At first, he traded with the Portuguese, and then he established his own maritime trade network, which covered a vast area from South China to Japan. In the first half of the seventeenth century, taking advantage of the Ming's campaigns to eliminate pirates, Zheng Zhilong conquered most of the small pirate-traders' organizations. He became so powerful that be became a constant threat to Dutch power in Taiwan.[21]

Meanwhile, owing to financial shortages, the imperial state gradually lost its ability to maintain the coastal garrison-towns. These widely dispersed towns were thus left in the hands of the descendants of the military households [*junhu*], which had originally been assigned to the positions of the gatekeepers of the "building of Hua [China]" [Huaxia]. In such towns as Anping—mostly the formal garrison-towns in the early Ming—merchants became ever more active. A Confucian scholar from Quanzhou in the late Ming Dynasty, Li Guang Jin, commented:

> In Quanzhou, in the neighborhoods, we listen to the sounds of music and recitals. People here prefer Confucian scholarship [*ru*] to commerce [*gu*]. Yet, in the market town of Anping, people are solely interested in commerce. These people are not confined to its local markets. When their children grow up, the husbands just leave their families. They trade all over the country—in the northern provinces, such as Yan [Hebei]; in the southern provinces, such as Wu [Jiangsu]; in the eastern provinces, such as Yue [Guangdong]; and in the western provinces, such as Bashu [Sichuan]. Some of them combat the winds and waves of the sea to compete for profits [*zhengli*] in the islands where only barbarians reside.[22]

While the pirate chieftains and the half-authorized merchant-smugglers in the formal garrison-towns quietly revitalized "the Maritime Silk Road," the "ungrounded empire" of emigrants expanded to Southeast Asia.[23] Between the eleventh and the fourteenth centuries or even later, local traders transported local products abroad and brought back foreign goods. Their homeland was not a place they wanted to leave. But from the Ming onward, a lot of merchants and migrant laborers decided to leave their homes to struggle in foreign countries, not because of their

---

[21] Zheng, *Zhongguo Haidao Shi* [*History of Chinese Piracy*], pp. 238–274; see also Tonie Andrade, The company's Chinese pirates: How the Dutch Each India Company tried to lead a coalition of pirates to war against China, 1621–1662, *Journal of World History*, 15(4) (2004): 415–444.

[22] C.f., Fu, Yi Ling, *Fuyiling Zhishi Wushi Nian* [*Fu Yiling's Papers on the Study of History, 50 Years of Efforts*], pp. 87–89. A similar phenomenon was also described in several records available in Hanjiang, Chongwu, and many other ex-garrison-towns.

[23] Zhang, Xi Lun, Mingdai hukou taiwang yu tiantu huangfei juli [Some examples of escaping households and deserted fields in the Ming], *Shihuo* [*Economic History*], 3(2) (1935): 50–53.

commercial needs but because of the fact that a self-sufficient mode of production—the agriculture and small handicraft industries promoted by the government—could not sufficiently support the economic life of the region. Most emigrants expected to struggle in the foreign countries for the sake of better fortunes for their families back at home. Otherwise, they went abroad for the sake of reducing pressure on oversized families. To seek better fortunes abroad was related to the existence of "worse fortunes"—such as commercial degeneration induced by agrarianism—at home.

Disasters and Politics

Two schools of thought emerged in officialdom as to how to deal with all the complex problems of governing local society. Several local-born officials proposed that the government should take advantage of trade with foreigners and even the pirates. Others, however, including many officials and generals, insisted that the political line of the Ming orthodoxy should be maintained.[24] In the early seventeenth century, the second line of thought gained dominance. Consequentially, the walls of the garrison-towns were once again consolidated. To fight against piracy and trade, more soldiers from other provinces were transferred to Quanzhou. Furthermore, in the *pujing* neighborhoods the government also prepared a new project to once again extend moral education and surveillance.

By the early seventeenth century, the administrative efficiency of *pujing* control was urgently needed. However, by the late Ming to reinforce local administration was to be faced with a serious problem. Much of the problem of piracy stemmed from the lack of effective household registration. Simply put, it was a problem of more people becoming unregistered and fewer people paying taxes. Commerce, which as the prefects knew was traditional to the people of Quanzhou who, as Gu Yan Wu vivid described, "perceived the oceans as agricultural fields [*yi hai wei tian*]," was another aspect of the problem. Whereas in the Ming orthodoxy "desire" or "greed" was the enemy of culture, the livelihood of the people of Quanzhou relied so heavily on it that even such scholar-officials as Guo Zao Qing considered it to be a solution to the government's financial crises. Yet, the government was obviously not giving in, and the prefects were required to stick to the Ming Code.

What then can at the same time help increase administrative efficiency and prevent more financial expenditures from being incurred? Forceful imposition of taxes would still have been regarded as viable, had numerous

---

[24] Chen, Si Dong, Luelun Mingdai Fujian yanhai de fan zousi cuoshi [A brief treatise on the antismuggling policies along the Fujian Coast in the Ming Dynasty], p. 126.

natural disasters not occurred. During the Jiajing and the Wanli Reigns, in addition to the *wo* tribulations, serious floods, droughts, hunger, earthquakes, and epidemics arrived one after another in Quanzhou. In 1533, heavy snow coupled with rain created a flood. The next year, a famine killed many and made numerous people homeless. In 1545, most of the houses in the Southern Yu of the city burned down in a large fire. In the same year, several earthquakes wrought serious damage. Besides several more earthquakes and floods, in 1563, a pestilence killed 60% to 70% of Quanzhou residents. Later in the Wan Li and Chongzheng Reigns, there were one or more natural disasters each year.[25]

In a plea submitted to the prefect, a local scholar said that all the disasters were manifestations of the imbalance between *yin* and *yang*, which in turn showed that Heaven demanded the government's mercy toward the people.[26] Meanwhile, several stories of a sorcery scare circulated. In 1551, a story was spread among the civilians that a horse spirit [*majing*] was intruding on the city of Quanzhou. When it arrived, some stars would fall from the sky. If women saw these falling stars, they would fall into coma and die unless they were whipped with willow twigs. To prevent harm from sorcery, each night women would sit in open spaces, surrounded by groups of men on guard. To scare off the harmful spirits, they continuously beat drums and gongs, despite the government's effort to stop them. The sorcery scare did not end until the police arrested a wandering Daoist who was supposedly the fire star. Several other instances of sorcery scare also occurred when large birds from the sea were said to be standing on the tops of the pagodas in the Buddhist monastery of Kaiyuan Si. The birds, supposedly, were as large as huge wheels. White in color, they smelled badly and brought misfortune.[27]

In response to all the disasters besieging the city, the local government changed their methods of neighborhood control. Central to the new method was the system of *xiangyue*, a re-invented form of the *pujing* community pact.

A 1589 stele inscription found in Jinjiang presents a brief history of *xiangyue* in Quanzhou.[28] According to the inscription, until the time of Wang Shi Jun, Quanzhou did not appoint *yuezheng* or *yue* chiefs. Wang was a Jinshi (a high imperial degree holder) of 1526 and served for a period in

---

[25] He, Qiao Yuan, *Min Shu* [*The Book of Fujian*] (Fuzhou 1994 [1628–1632]), *juan* 67–71.

[26] *Jinjing Xianzhi* [*Jingjing County Gazette*], compiled by Zhou, Xue Zeng (Fuzhou 1999 [1830]), *juan* 74.

[27] Ibid.

[28] The stele inscription was discovered in the Xiangxia Ci of the Cai Lineage in Qingyang. The author is named Hong Fu, and the stele was first dedicated in 1546 and rededicated in 1589. See Nian, Liang Tu (ed.), *Jinjiang Beike Xuan* [*Selected Stele Inscriptions in Jinjiang*] (Xaimen 2002), pp. 52–56.

Quanzhou as prefect. He was famous for organizing Confucian lectures and regarded *xiangyue* as important. During his service, Quanzhou saw the expansion of commerce and "decadent customs" [*mosu*]. Many disputes also developed. He expected the gentry [*shifu*] to lead local customs away from chaos. Thus he adopted the institution of *xiangyue* developed in the Song. Yet, soon after Wang Shi Jun left Quanzhou it was abandoned. In Qingyang, Zhuang Yongbin (1504–1588), a *jinshi*, who was straightforward and sharp in his determination [*ruizhi*], lost his job in the government and returned to his hometown, where he called together a group of local scholar-gentry to revitalize *xiangyue*. During the Jiajing Reign, a collective meeting was held. It was announced that Qingyang was full of social inequality. There were stronger families that dominated weaker families. There were households that conducted more rituals than were stipulated by the government (in the Ming Code). The participants of the meeting all elected Zhuang Yong Bin to lead the reform of local customs. Zhuang rebuilt a local temple called "Shigu Miao" (Stone Drum Temple), which had been in ruins. He moved the images of local cults to the two side halls of the temple. In the middle hall of the temple, he created a space for the "congregation of the masses" [*zhonghui zhisuo*]. A piece of *yue* [community pact] was hung up in this hall. He led forty members of his lineage to declare their deeds [*shenming*]. The lineage was divided into ten *jia*. Each year, the two largest branches chose two men to be in charge of the hall. Their services consisted of (1) promoting mutual persuasion and mutual regulation [*xiangquan xianggui*], (2) encouraging mutual friendship and mutual charitability [*xiangyou xiangxu*], (3) organizing congregations to praise the virtuous [*youshanzhe yuzhong yangzhi*], (4) organizing congregations to punish the bad [*youfanzhe yu zhong fazhi*], (5) repressing the strong and supporting the weak [*yiqiang furuo*], (6) clearing away immoral elements and preventing theft and robbery in the community [*chujian yidao*], and (7) resolving disputes and reducing competition [*jiefen xizheng*].

The origin of *xiangyue* can be traced back to Zhu Yuan Zhang's *xiang yinjiu*—the communal drinking ceremony in which members of a neighborhood congregated to make an oath while drinking wine. But strictly speaking, the model that was adopted in Quanzhou was what Wang Yang Ming had initiated in rural south Jiangxi together with Baojia.

There was a significant difference between Zhu Yuan Zhang's *xiang yinjiu* and Wang Yang Ming's *xiangyue*. In a *xiang yinjiu* ceremony, two things were emphasized. The first was the oath made to declare local loyalty to the state and its constitution. The second was the emphasis on local acceptance of the orthodox pattern of social hierarchy. Thus, during a *xiang yinjiu* ceremony, lining groups, whose locations in the ceremony were carefully arranged in accordance with sex, age, and social status hierarchies, recited the most important chapters in the Ming Code. In Wang Yang Ming's version of *xiangyue*, the notions of loyalty and hierarchy were retained. However, a sense of mutual belonging among local residents was more heavily emphasized. In addition, *xiangyue* ceremonial recitations also included sentences such as "refraining from harboring escaped criminals and refugees [*jie huo tao*]" and "congregating into Baojia [*lian* Baojia]."[29]

As a local historian shows, *xiangyue* was referred to as the *xiangyue* recitation ritual [*jiangdu*], drawing on a Song Neo-Confucian model.[30] The ceremony was held in the community pact hall that was situated nearby the old Jingshan Ting, the pavilion for praising the virtuous. Owing to lack of maintenance, by the Jiajing Reign (1522–1566), the pavilion system in the local communities was in ruins. A new community pact hall was established. The ceremony took place on the platform in front of the hall and was attended by county-level officials, who stood on the east side of the platform, joined by the local gentry [*xiangshen*], who stood on the west side. The two groups of superiors faced the orderly lines of local elders, students, civilians, and soldiers. An elected elder was in charge of leading the recitation. The recited sentences were composed in the genre of classical poetry, but the elder-in-charge also had to explain them using local examples and stories.

As an organization, *xiangyue* consisted of a self-governed group of local men. The heads were known as *yuezheng* [pact head], *yuefu* [vice pact head], *yuezan* [pact pronouncing officer], and *zhiyue* [pact holder], whose positions replaced those of the *pujing* or *lishe* officials. During the early Ming, *pujing* or *lishe* officials had already been locally appointed, but terms such as "pact heads" had the connotation of more local autonomy. Their work was no longer paid for by the redistributive system, which was the case for the earlier officers of *pujing* and *lishe*. These locally elected pact officers were "agreed on" locally, and they were in charge of local ceremonies, dispute resolution and moral education. They also formed a committee for organizing the building and maintenance of public properties such as bridges and community pact hall-temples.

Xiangyue had one other aspect, which was militia organization. In Qi Ji Guang's time, local brave men [*xiangyong*] had already been mobilized to defend the city from the invasion of pirates, the *wokou*. As I discuss further in Chapter 9, after the *xiangyue* system was established, militia groups were recognized as an efficient form of local defense. To the prefects, one benefit of the militia groups was that they did not incur

---

[29] Wang Yang Ming, Nangan Xiangyue, in his *Wang Yang Ming Quanji* [*The Collection of Writings by Wang Yang Ming*] (Shanghai 1992 [1572]), Vol. 1, pp. 599–603.

[30] Li, Yu Kun, Mingqing shiqi Quanzhou tuixing xiangyue ruogan wenti, in *Mintai Minsu* [*Folklore in Fujian and Taiwan*], 2 (1998): 5–17.

financial expenditures. Most of the time they were farmers, becoming temporary soldiers only during emergencies. Militia groups, whose function was local defense, were under the leadership of Baojia.

From the late Ming to the mid-Qing, a project of boundary creation developed out of an era of profound social change. Philip Kuhn reconstructs a portrait of the "soul-stealing crisis" of 1768, when the imperial government sought to hunt down people accused of sorcery. The crisis originated at a time of long slow inflation and regional economic expansion that resulted in flourishing commerce and led to the rise of "free labor." A competitive and crowded society grew on the scant margin to encourage the constant movement of people that in turn resulted in the breakdown of the ideal social bonds designated by rulers and the elite. This population of "out-of-place" people then became a major source of social unrest. The *yamen* [government] thus plunged itself into campaigns against the rootless as sorcery suspects and the enemies of the imperial moral order.[31]

The example of the "soul-stealing crisis" is also representative of what was happening in Quanzhou during this particular period of time. By the time the *xiangyue* system was fully established in Quanzhou, local civil, religious, political, and military affairs were mostly left in the hands of local elites. In the ideal design of officialdom, the new local administration system continued to function in the same way as it had in the early Ming. But in practice, left in the hands of local elites, it immediately became subject to localization. Intended as a means of loosening up the tension between the government's need for more efficient local administration and its shortage of financial sources, the *xiangyue* system had many designated functions. To some extent, it did help the prefects govern local society according to local interests and helped reduce the heavy financial and manpower burdens that the officialdom faced in the crisis of the late Ming. However, neither could *xiangyue* control the expanding pirate regimes such as the Zheng's nor could it solve the problems of poverty and economic depression. It also failed to stop Heaven from unleashing more misfortunes on the marginal regions of the Celestial Empire. *Xiangyue* did bring about a great transformation, but the transformation did not progress in the direction that was designated by the prefects. Running contrary to the intentions of the state, the change consisted in the alternating and sensationalizing of popular cults and festivals, to which we now turn.

---

[31] Philip A. Kuhn, *Soulstealers: The Chinese Sorcery Scare of 1768* (Cambridge, MA 1990).

CHAPTER 7

Unorthodox Cults and the Expulsion of Demons, 1500–1644

In the early seventeenth century, officials in Fujian were working their way through an evocative approach to *xiangyue*, whereby civilization continued to be promoted as what would bring together officialdom and local society. Huang Cheng Xuan, the provincial governor, one of the officials who first launched the project of *xiangyue*, called for local elites to fulfill their roles as servants of the state. He advised *yue* chiefs to "share a period of spiritual communication with the local people [*jingshen yu xiangren xiangtong*]" in order for "civilization to be achieved effectively [*huacheng zhi xiao*]." He also issued a warning, asking: "Would a community pact exist without the accompanying conferences [*hui*] of dialogue? They would lose their significance." As he supposed, the worst consequence of it was that "each place would build its own pact hall [*geli yuesuo*] for its own purpose and convenience without obeying the regulations of the official *xiangyue*."[1]

There is no evidence showing how many *yue* chiefs had actually followed Huang's advice, but Huang's instruction itself proves to be a good demonstration. Had most *yue* chiefs obeyed the rules of the

---

[1] Li, Yu Kun, Mingqing shiqi Quanzhou tuixing xiangyue ruogan wenti, in *Mintai Minsu* [*Folklore in Fujian and Taiwan*], 2 (1998): 5–17.

provincial *yue* regulations, Huang would not have felt it so urgent to place such a strong emphasis on their roles and practices.

Intersected by local gentry and townsfolk, the civilizational project launched by the Ming court was far from an unhindered process. In the late sixteenth century, this project began to be questioned by a new generation of philosophers. Li Zhi (1527–1601), the great liberal thinker of Quanzhou origin, wrote many critical essays on Confucianism, and he collected them in works titled *Book for Burning* [*Fen Shu*] and *Book for Hiding* [*Cang Shu*].[2] In these essays, Li Zhi sought to establish alternative principles of being human. The core concept of person that he developed was that of *ren qi*, or "human energy," which implicated free exercise of individual capabilities. In several places, Li Zhi also praised the pirates, who, as he argued, were a byproduct of maritime trade. For him, there was no reason to despise maritime trade, which had been forbidden by the Ming monarchs. Toward love affairs, Li Zhi also held a rather anti-Confucian attitude.[3]

While the Ming court was faced with intellectual challenges from such thinkers as Li Zhi, its civilizing program also ran into some obstacles. A big problem stemmed from the self-contradictory character of civilizing Confucianism itself. It could be argued that the Ming civilizing mission was a late imperial Chinese project of creating a "national culture."[4] In promoting *jiaohua*, the court deployed a two-pronged method. In order to extend "national culture" into local worlds, the State constructed temples, altars, and institutions expressing and realizing the monarch's sovereignty and hierarchy. The court utilized the segmenting mechanism of territorial divisions to make its own presence a condition of existence in which local people lived their lives. What began to bother the late Ming prefects was the observation that while the making of "official religion" created a China-wide "national" consciousness of culture, many local administrative techniques had the unintended consequence of strengthening local identities. Along with the development of *pujing* and *lishe* systems in Quanzhou, territorial bonds were reinforced, depriving *jiaohua* of its official connotations.

During the Song and the Yuan Dynasties, the prefects' tolerance or, even, encouragement of a higher degree of demographic and social economic mobility made it easier for the people of Quanzhou to move from place to place. The civilizing project of the Ming intended to place the mobile population "back" in place. Zhu Yuan Zhang's goal "was to immobilize the

---

[2] Li Zhi was imprisoned and died in his cell in Tongzhou, Hebei province.

[3] Fu, Yi Ling, *Fuyiling Zhishi Wushi Nian* [*Fu Yiling's Papers on the Study of History, 50 Years of Efforts*] (Shanghai 1989), pp. 313–315.

[4] James Watson, Rites or beliefs? The construction of a unified culture in late imperial China, in Lowell Dittmer (ed.), *China's Quest for National Identity* (Ithaca 1993), pp. 80–103.

realm."[5] In his image of the country, people "were to stay put and could move only with the permission of the State."[6] As components of *jiaohua*, the differentiation between *huanei* and *huawai*, the construction of garrison-towns, the ban on maritime trade, and the moralistic denunciations of commerce were all targeted at making a stable polity in which households were fully registered, carefully surveyed, and firmly situated.

The emperor did succeed in demarcating and labeling many localities on the maps of his domain. But ironically, in so doing, he also created new contexts for the formation of local identities. Gradually, the territorially segmented social groups became confined to the places they lived. The confinement of local communities such as *pujing* in Quanzhou led to two somewhat conflicting outcomes. Although for the court and its regional officialdom, territorial confinement was good for the pacification of the coast, it was experienced and perceived differently by local inhabitants. It meant not only a break from pre-existing trade connections but also an exclusionist understanding of locality in which local places were conceptualized as distinct both from one another *and* from what James Watson calls the late imperial "national culture."[7]

Unofficial senses of place advanced under this arrangement. Previous territorial boundaries set up by the prefects transformed into fertile sites for the growth of folk cultural traditions. Prior to the turn of the mid-Ming, all the official altars, temple halls, and pavilions were designated as routes through which "court society" penetrated local worlds. During those decades, local people were required by the Ming Code—but not spontaneously congregated—to perform ceremonies fitting into the official code. The Altar for the God of Soil and Grain, the Altar for Ghosts, and memorial halls for the virtuous in a *pu* or a *jing* formulated a ceremonial system in which passively located people were inspected and disciplined by gods and ghosts. Yet, when the *xiangyue* system was developed in the 1610s, many officials became seriously worried about the changing nature of some of these ceremonies, and they began to see them as part of local "licentious cults" [*yinci*]. In the late Ming, particularly during the Longqing and the Wanli Reign (1567–1620), the prefect's government initiated several campaigns against these "licentious cults."

What were the "licentious cults"? In his *Miscellaneous Notes on Fujian* [*Min Zaji*], Shi Hong Bao, the Ming scholar from Quanzhou, described a sort of cult temple that was the epitome of the word "licentious" [*yin*], the opposite of moral integrity. He said that in Fujian, there were temples devoted to deities known as Hu Tian Bao and Hu Tian Mei. The deity

---

[5] Timothy Brook, *The Confusions of Pleasure: Commerce and Culture in Ming China* (Berkeley 1998), p. 19.

[6] Ibid.

[7] Watson, Rites or beliefs.

Hu Tian Bao had two images, one slightly older looking, and the other younger looking. The two statues were usually placed as if they were seated side by side, supporting each other. The female deity, Hu Tian Mei, was in the form of a beautiful woman, with one hand loosening her clothes and the other waving in an ambiguous manner toward the worshippers. These two deities were meant as patrons of illicit love (likely also including homosexuality). As the perfect example of a "licentious cult," they offered blessings for those who desired to make love with their chosen mates. Shi Hong Bao said that the government saw these temples as places of "customs harmful to civilization" [*you shang fenghua*] and as "inducing "illicit affairs" [*daoyin*].[8]

It seems true that the term "licentious cults" derived, first, from the official condemnation of the cult-temples of love deities. When Ye Chun Ji came to govern Hui'an County in the Quanzhou prefecture, he witnessed a similar problem. According to him, in Hui'an, a large number of temples were involved in providing spaces for "men and women to commit adultery" [*tongjiao nannu*]. But, for the imperial magistrates, temples for "illicit affairs" seemed to involve only one category out of the several kinds of improper religious sites. In the single county of Hui'an, Ye Chun Ji located 551 "licentious cult-temples." These temples held rituals that were connected to heterodox magic [*xieshu*], contradicting the Ceremonial Statute of the Ming. Some temples even worshiped the county magistrates as protectors of gambling. Most temples caused disputes instead of harmony among local people. Next to the temples, he often saw shops that sold alcohol, which made worshippers drunk and even more prone to misconduct, especially "licentious practices." He arranged all the temples into the following categories: (1) those that were not clearly stipulated in the "ceremonial code" [*sidian buzai*], (2) those that set obstacles to the extension of orthodox culture [*youfang zhengjiao*], (3) those that ruined good local customs [*shangfeng baisu*], and (4) those that in a hidden way impaired the wealth of the people [*ansun mincai*]. According to Ye, he "cleaned" 220 temples by re-installing official Sheji Shen cult tablets and local schools. He destroyed all the rest.[9]

The campaigns against "licentious cults" and their temples resulted in the destruction of many local temples in Quanzhou, but they did not stop the rapid diffusion of unofficial regional cults. These cults and temples held more ceremonies than stipulated by the government, and they honored more gods than the "standardized" cults of Earth, Heaven, and sagacious men. Running contrary to *jiaohua* unity, they seemed "licentious," or

---

[8] Shi, Hong Bao, *Min Zaji* [*Miscellaneous Notes on Fujian*] (Fuzhou 1985 [1857]), *juan 7*.
[9] Ye, Chun Ji, *Hui'an Zhengshu* [*Hui'an County Political Manual*] (Fuzhou 1987 [1672]), *juan 9*.

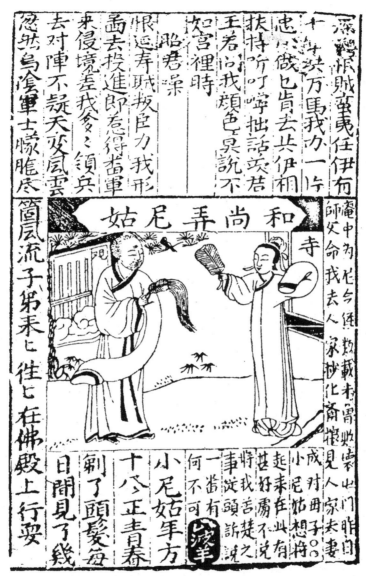

Figure 7.1 Portrait of *A Monk Flirting with a Nanny* in the script of a Ming local opera (source: *Ming Kan Minnan Xiqu Xuanguan Xuben Sanzhong* [*The Ming Editions of Three Play Scripts of Minnan Regional Operas*], compiled by Peter van der Loon, Beijing 2003, p. 32).

heterodox, to the officialdom. The campaigns against them encountered many difficulties. They could clear away some obviously unofficial sectarian cults, but they could not wipe out the popular religious activities that usually took place at the intersection of the dynastic and the local, in the State-established but locally appropriated temples, open altars, and pavilions.

Local Cult Temples

More than a hundred years before Huang Cheng Xuan implemented the *xiangyue* policy, many of the communal hall-temples, altars, and pavilions were in ruin. These local public places were constructed in the Hongwu Reign under the state's sponsorship and in accordance with the state's blueprints for ceremonial building. Had they been civilians' houses, they would have been well-maintained or renovated, but these public buildings designated by the government for the civilizational and administrative functionaries of local communities gradually became neglected. For a long period, they remained "relics" to local residents.

In the early sixteenth century, the situation began to change. The decaying symbols of imperial state cults received more attention. Stories circulated that the deities and spirits in those public places were performing miracles. Without good temples to reside in and good offerings to consume, the deities and spirits were becoming angry. Gradually, they not only had lost efficacy but also had lost their willingness to protect the communities. Thus more and more demons and epidemics attacked local society.

To address the situation, petitions were put forward to request the government to expel demons. For example, in 1535, Yu Da You, the general assigned to combat piracy in coastal Fujian, was pressed by local gentry representatives to hold an exorcism ceremony on Jinmen Island. The ceremony was organized to expel the epidemic causing demons (*yigui*, who supposedly haunted Quanzhou prefecture along with the *wokou*). With the participation of local gentry delegations, Yu Da You called for several sacrifices to the City God, the Earth God, and all the divinities in different localities, who were petitioned to catch the epidemic-demons and neutralize them.[10] A decade later, Qi Ji Guang also organized several Universal Salvation ceremonies for his soldiers who had died in action against the *wokou*. According to Qi's own description, many soldiers from the Quanzhou area sacrificed their lives for the dignity of the empire, but their souls found no places to reside. The ceremonies were intended to bring them comfort. Qi Jiguang also

---

[10] Wu, You Xiong, Quantai "pudu" fengsu kao [An investigation into the Pudu festival in Quanzhou and Taiwan], *Quanzhou Daojiao Wenhua* [*Daoist Culture in Quanzhou*], 1 (1994): 19–24.

Figure 7.2 Interiors of a recently rebuilt community pact hall (territorial temple) (photography by Mingming Wang 2004).

petitioned the emperor to establish memorial halls or shrines for these war heroes.[11]

Around the same time, many *pujing* temples began to be constructed or reconstructed to house the old Soil and Grain God and the images of great sage-gods. Added to the list of official cults were also some regional cults that had gained popularity in the Quanzhou region. These temples were mostly located on the old sites of *pujing* community pact halls. Still useful, pact halls were reorganized according to local conceptions of temple arrangement in which all the divinities in the local communities were allocated altar space. The dilapidated pact halls were rebuilt with local sponsorship. In the early seventeenth century, many of these restored pact hall-temples were treated once again as official pact halls in which *xiangyue* were established. However, these pact halls quickly returned to their old ways, functioning as "licentious cults."

In 1996, a stele inscription was discovered in Quanzhou. The inscription was written in 1827 and entitled "Inscription of the Reconstruction of the Xiting Compact Hall." This valuable text offers a

---

[11] Qi, Ji Guang, Shang yingzhao chenyan yipuenshang shugao [A treatise handed over to his majesty on broadly delivering bestowals and awards] and Jibie min zhang yici zhenwang jiangshi [A eulogy read in a farewell ceremony held at the memorial halls for martyred commanders and officers], both in his *Qi Jiguang Wenji* (*The Collection of Essays by Qi Jiguang*) (Beijing 2001 [1567]), pp. 23–33; 189–190.

direct testimony of the historical transformation of pact halls into popular temples. The stele inscription, jointly written and carved by the hall's management board, gentry, elders, reads as follows:

In ancient times, each community had its own officials to manage local affairs. Each had its own hall for regulating the conduct of *shi* [scholars] and civilians [*min*]. The purpose of setting up communal halls was to facilitate and foster filial piety and mutual attachment, to transmit the culture of harmonious marriage and merciful government, and to uproot bad customs of quarrelling, deception, and humiliation. [In the ancient times], each community had also a gate. The young went out through the neighborhood gate every morning to study and work, while the elders remained seated beside it to supervise the activities of the young. After the Tang and the Song period, local customs became less refined. But throughout history, the establishment of pact halls has been intended as what was just said— revitalizing the old tradition originating in classical times.

The earliest pact hall in Xiting Pu was established during the Yongle Reign of the Ming Dynasty. In its later form, the hall consisted of one compound of two halls. In the left part of the front hall, the Holy Mother in Heaven (Tianshang Shengmu, that is, Tianhou) was worshipped. The Holy Mother was born as a water divinity. Our forefathers placed the statue of the Holy Mother here because they regarded this place as situated in the south and therefore prone to fire. They conceived of the Holy Mother as a water divinity that could defeat fire. The cult did not emerge out of an accident.

In the right section of the hall, General Tiandu (Tiandu Yuanshuai) was worshipped. General Tiandu was the god on whom local people relied to guard their communities. He was the lord of locality. Elders say that this god was a person who lived during the Tang Dynasty. His surname was Tian. In the *Manuscript of Min Shu* [*Min Shu Chao*], it is said, however, that the name of the god is unknown. The god was, during his life, a military commander of the Wurong Prefecture [the first prefecture established during the Quanzhou region]. He died in the mountains in the Luoxi Township [to the Northeast of Quanzhou city]. He was known for his efficacy [*ling*] and was bestowed with title of Revealed Benefactor (Zhaohui). Today, elders tell us that in the old days a territory was carved out from [two characters referring to a place are missing] to Pengshan hill. A garrisoned canton was established there, and the general was assigned to its commandership. These three kinds of explanation have co-existed until now, and we have no basis to judge which is correct.

People of [two characters missing, possibly Xiting] needed the heroism of the gods. Since the time when General Tiandu was given his title, they have regularly paid tribute to the god in this place. The temple was repaired several times; but it was not expanded. In the years of [three characters missing] *Hai*, the forerunners of this *pu* joined force and rebuilt the temple. The compound was not much changed. This year is counted as the third year of an auspicious cycle. Thus the management board of the temple bought a piece of land [beside the temple] and planned to expand the temple. Now, the future of the newly built temple is splendid.

A gate hall and a flight of steps have been added. A courtyard and several rooms for residing monks have been expanded as well. The money spent on the rebuilding of temple amounts to one thousand and several hundreds in silver coins. In the year of Dinghai, the completion ceremony was held to inform the god of his honor. This inscription is written now to keep a record of the past event and to reveal history to later generations. The regulations of this temple might be inadequate. We hope that in the future those who have wisdom will revise them in a proper way. . . .[12]

Reading the inscription, it is apparent that the pact hall of Xiting was established as an office in the beginning of the fifteenth century. Later, it transformed into a local temple, in which the territorial guardian-god General Tiandu was worshipped together with the Holy Mother (also known as the Heavenly Queen). The local patron cult, Tiandu Yuanshuai, which was also worshipped as the Opera God, was a later invention that absorbed two other sorts of divinities—the cult of the founding magistrate of Quanzhou city and the cult of a military commander who controlled several cantons between Luoxi and Pengshan situated to the East of Quanzhou. The temple, which was first built on the site of the pact hall of the Xiting ward, thus was a synthesis of local reconceptualizations of *minghuan ci* [memorial halls for famous officials] and *zhonglie ci* [memorial halls for officials who died heroically]. The temple was, however, named after the *xiangyue* system. It was called a *yuesuo*, which indicates that in the late Ming, the temple was used also as an official pact hall.

There are, in today's Quanzhou, at least two other temples also called pact halls, one located in Qingyuan Pu in the north, the other in Sanjiao Pu in the east. Their main local patron cults are the God of War and the Supreme Emperor (Shangdi) of Daoism, respectively. Although these two pack hall temples do not have stele inscriptions to chronicling their histories of change, similar lines of historical development can be inferred.

Most other territorial temples in the city of Quanzhou are known as Jingzhu Gong, palaces of the Lord of Jing. In a couple of *pu* that are not divided into *jing*, local temples are instead called Puzhu Gong, palaces of the Lords of Pu. Like Xiting Pu, all the Jingzhu Gong and Puzhu Gong have their own histories of cult formation.

In 1928, two pieces of stele inscription were made available by Gu Jie Gang, who made a brief research trip to Quanzhou a couple of years earlier. In one of the inscriptions written near the end of the nineteenth century, the history of a Jingzhu Gong is clearly recorded. Like Xiting Pu, the cult region described in the stele was a local administrative

---

[12] C.f., Chen, Jian Ying, Dubei santi [Three discussions on three stele inscriptions], *Mintai Minsu* [*Fujian and Taiwan Folklore*], 1 (1997): 65–73.

territory in the early Ming. The foundation for the territorial temple was the old ward office, which also served as a police post and site for the altar devoted to the God of Soil and Grain. The local patron deity, Taizi (Crowned Prince), was inserted into the office, which was later turned into a "palace" by locals in an effort to respond to mythic miracles. As the stele inscription describes:

> In the old place of Puquan, a statue of Crowned Prince was placed on the central altar of the temple. This is done in the old way.
>
> Residents in the community pray to this god when they have problems. During floods and droughts, they conduct divination rituals in the temple. Yearly, the god receives sacrifices from the local people.
>
> The place has been under the protection of the god for nearly two hundred years. But many local people know little about the origin of this cult. Recently, we [the gentry who collectively composed the text] visited some elders and were informed that the palace used to be where the armed police were stationed. An Earth God Temple was added to this old police station. Later, Quanzhou suffered from a serious flood. The temple for Earth God was moved to across the street from the police station. To its left, there was a well known as "Puquan Well." One day, water surged up and a statue of a god floated up to the surface of the water. Local residents picked it up and placed it in the Earth God Temple.
>
> In the beginning, people did not make sacrifice to the statue. But the god several times performed miracles for local people and cured many sick. Local people thus donated money and renovated the statue. The god has since become more honored and more efficacious. Many worshippers have gathered and made petitions to the god. The god has responded to all requests with great efficacy. Therefore, local residents built a palace for it where they worship the god with sincerity.[13]

There were also examples in which territorial temples grew within the official public buildings. For example, Wenxiang Miao of Xiting Pu had been a memorial pavilion built in memory of the Song patriot Wen Tian Xiang. The location of the pavilion was said to be the place where Wen Tian Xiang hired to accommodate the Song emperor who was pursued by the Mongol army. Concerning how the pavilion was turned into a temple, there is no record. But a short paragraph in *Jinjiang County Gazette* clearly indicates that a local named Tao Shaoxi first built a temple on the base of the pavilion. Later, the temple was regarded as the "palace" of local guardian-gods.[14]

---

[13] Gu, Jie Gang, Quanzhou de Tudi shen [Locality gods in Quanzhou], *Minsu Zhoukan* [*Folklore Weekling*] (Guangzhou, March 28 and April 4, 1928).

[14] *Jinjing Xianzhi* [*Jingjing County Gazette*], compiled by Zhou, Xue Zeng (Fuzhou 1990 [1830]), *juan* 69.

Local Heavens: Temples of Guardian-Gods

Visiting one of the rebuilt old *pujing* temples in today's Quanzhou, we can gain a perspective on its pattern of spatial organization. In each temple, the enclosed space is divided into several sections. The central shrine or altar is devoted to one or several local guardian-gods (Puzhu or Jingzhu). Next to the local guardian deities one usually finds the Earth God on the right and a female deity on the left. In front of each of these three shrines are a desk for offerings and an incense burner. Further out toward the gate, is an open, unroofed space, which is locally known as a "Heavenly Well" (Tianjing) and serves as the place where offerings to Heaven are made. Next to it there are two minor shines. These two minor shines accommodate several small, fierce-looking statues. The category of beings that they represent are described as *bantou ye*. *Bantou ye* are in-between gods and men. They are a team of armed police who also appear in the imperial government and City God temples. In imperial times, when suspects were brought forward to face the magistrate in court, these armed police would stand on either side and exercise their punitive functions. *Bantou ye* are also like the low-ranking police in the City God Temples, who are sent out by the City God to arrest the convicted.

For the officials working for the Ming government, the local guardians, their associates, and their armed police were considered "licentious cults." But these cults were organized in a way similar to the imperial bureaucracy within which the officials worked.

Emily Ahern argues that the Chinese worship of gods resembled the petitions addressed to imperial magistrates. In popular ritual, a god was treated as the foremost authority of a given place. It provided clues to local people's destinies, resolved their mental uncertainties, provided "solutions" to their practical problems, and, for doing so, it received respect and offerings. Like an official, this imagined authority was seated in a chair, facing his subjects, and from this seat he received pleas and took care of legal cases, civil disputes, and moral problems. Created in the popular search for a religious means of managing local affairs, this authority was distinguished from the real political authority of the imperial magistrate, even though it was modeled on imperial prescriptions. It represented a popular effort to turn distant but real power into an intimate symbolic authority.[15]

In my own view, what Ahern only generally speaks about has a more particular historical background. This background is a historical process in which a local system of symbolic authority was created through the appropriation of imperial infrastructure and ideology.

---

[15] Emily Martin Ahern, *Chinese Ritual and Politics* (Cambridge 1981).

As Paul Katz suggests: "Temples were usually built after a deity had gained a large or diverse enough following for sufficient funds to be raised for such a project."[16] A cult creating process beginning in the mid-Ming either made metaphorical reference to real officials or, more often, constituted a historical linkage with historical persons. Deities suitable for creating a temple or a congregation were various. They could involve ready-made popular cults or officially promoted and/or recognized divinities. But for cult-followers, the difference between "real" or "metaphorical" and "official" or "popular" was trivial.[17] What was important for them was that it could bring peace and order to the local community, could defend the locality from outside attacks including epidemics, and could give expression to the local pursuit for strength.

Official gazettes compiled from the late Ming and the Qing provide much rich material on local history. But these gazettes are biased against the "licentious cults," and for that reason they have only extremely limited information on territorial temples and sacrifices. Fortunately, in the past twenty years, studies of local religious history have flourished in Quanzhou. One such study done by Chen Chui Cheng and Lin Sheng Li of the Society of Daoist Culture Research in Quanzhou systematically surveys the remaining and reconstructed territorial temples and their cults.[18] Chen and Lin do not bother to reconstruct a historical genealogy the temples, but they have produced a general survey that, read from our own perspective, can shed light on the general historical condition of *pujing* between the late Ming and the end of the Republican era.

Taking into account only Daoism and "feudal superstition" (popular religion), there were in late imperial times more than 130 temples in *pujing* local society. A quarter of these temples were constructed as official temples and formal Daoist monasteries. The rest were sites of local popular religious worship. The number of deities worshipped in Quanzhou was equally large. Among the one hundred odd deities worshipped in the temples, some were Daoist cults, but many were local guardian-gods. My own analysis has indicated that most *pujing* temples feature local territorial guardian-gods in the central shrines. These local guardian-gods can be divided into the following categories: (1) Xianggong Ye (Great Men); (2) Wang Ye (Marshal Lords); (3)

---

[16] Paul Katz, *Demon Hordes and Burning Boats: The Cult of Marshal Wen in Late Imperial Chekiang* (New York 1995), p. 118.

[17] In each of the *pu* or *jing* temples in Quanzhou, a synthesis is always apparent.

[18] Chen, Chui Cheng and Lin, Sheng Li, *Quanzhou Jiu Pujing Jilue* [*A Brief Survey of Old Pujing in Quanzhou*] (Quanzhou 1990).

loyal generals, heroes, and heroines; and (4) life-protecting (including medical) deities.[19]

As the stele inscription of Xiting Pu indicates, Xianggong Ye, who has been studied by contemporary local historians as an Opera God,[20] was a mixture of several legendary figures, the most important among them, I believe, was the local commander of several cantons to the east of the city.

In his historical study of Marshal Wen, Katz has argued that the cult of Wang Ye emerged in Southern Song Zhejiang as Marshal Wen, an anti-epidemic god. In the late imperial dynasties of the Ming and the Qing, the cult gradually spread all over the Southeast Coast.[21] In Quanzhou, the role of Wang Ye in epidemic expulsion rituals was also important. It is evident that this category of cults derived from the same sort of deity of which Katz has offered a history. But Quanzhou's Wang Ye, which is also locally called "A-Ye Gong" (Benign Old Man) or "Wang Ye Gong" (Benign Marshal), has many different surnames.

Folklore suggests that in historical Quanzhou there were 360 Wang Ye surnames. Many of the Wang Ye were real historical figures who were famous officials and generals of the Han ethnicity from the Tang to the Ming. Most Wang Ye were fierce looking, resembling severe magistrates and military commanders, despite the fact that they were sometimes called "the Benign Marshals." Some of them were said to be locals who in ancient times served the emperor or died of an injustice. Others were not local and were inscribed in both local legends and dynastic histories.

The loyal generals, heroes, and heroines worshipped in *pujing* temples in late imperial times were equally diverse. Notably, the three brothers of the Yang Family who were worshipped in several ward temples were heroic defenders of the Song Dynasty. In several other ward temples, local guardian-gods were said to be two generals who resisted An Lu Shan in defending the integrity of the Tang Dynasty. There were also heroines such as Wanshi Ma (Motherly Goddess of Wan), a woman who lived near the Eastern Lake of Quanzhou in the Tang, who legendarily saved the city of Quanzhou from an impending military catastrophe. In the category of loyal heroes, there were also deities known as Yinglie Hou (Heroic and Martyred Barons) and two little babies who miraculously saved the life of the emperor.

---

[19] Wang, Ming Ming, *Shiqu de Fanrong: Yizuo Laocheng de Lishi Renleixue Kaocha* [*The Bygone Prosperity: A Historical Anthropology of an Old City, Quanzhou*] (Hangzhou 1999), pp. 201–215.

[20] For instance, see Liu, Hao Ran, Xishen Xianggong Ye zai Quanzhou de fengsi [Local Worship of the Opera God Xianggong Ye in Quanzhou], *Mintai Minsu* [*Fujian and Taiwan Folklore*], 1 (1997): 145–164.

[21] Katz, *Demon Hordes and Burning Boats*.

The most notable life-protective cult was the "Great Emperor Who Protects Life" (Baosheng Dadi).[22] Originating in Tong'an County, this Medicine God began to receive the prefects' tributes in the Song. In local communities such as Huaqiao, the cult was also a territorial guardian-god who offered medical advice through divination.

In any case, the making of local guardian-gods involved popular re-appropriations of local and imperial symbols. When some pact halls were first turned into popular temples, the remaining altars were still those that were devoted to the God of Soil and Grain. In many wards, there were also memorial halls for heroes, famous Confucians, and officials that were newly constructed or renovated in the early Ming. By the mid-Ming, these memorial halls had fallen into disrepair owing to lack of care. Although a handful of local elders could still remember of the names of those commemorated, most locals had forgotten them. Whether remembered or forgotten, the remaining statues of the named historical figures ceased to convey any sense of imperial *jiaohua*. As I noted earlier, what attracted local people's attention in the mid-Ming was simply the fact that in their own communities certain divinities existed and were still performing miracles. Out of fear of offending these divinities and in the hope of gaining protection from them, local inhabitants moved the statues into the pact halls.

Among the four categories of local guardian-gods, most cults that fell into categories one to three originated from such movements of statues. The most obvious was category three in which the entitlements of gods assimilated much of the commemorated heroes and Confucians in the official memorial halls. In category two, the regional cult origin of Marshal Wen seems apparent, but there were many historical heroes also named Wang Ye in the region.

Of course, the "confusion" of territorial cults with officially recognized virtuous men and women was not the whole story of cult creation. In the mid-Ming, a process of diffusion of several regional cults was also in progress. For instance, the Great Emperor Who Protects Life first originated in the rural county of Tong'an. Prior to the Ming, a temple for this cult had already been built. In the mid-Ming, several more branch temples were established on the old foundations of community pact halls. Likewise, once established, temples that drew on the sources of official memorial halls also had the tendency to regionalize. For instance, from the mid-Ming onward, Xianggong Ye and Wang Ye began to serve as centers of a regional system of branch temples that gradually extended from South Fujian into Taiwan and Southeast Asia, following the emigration routes of locals.

---

[22] For a history of this cult, see Kenneth Dean, *Taoist Ritual and Popular Cults in Southeast China* (Princeton 1993), pp. 61–98.

In accordance with their different personified characters, the character of territorial cults could be divided into two broader categories: those that were more fearsome and militant (Wang Ye and the Loyal Generals) and those that were more benign and protective (Baosheng Dadi). However, the distinction was merely relative, and in practice each local guardian-god combined both personalities in one body. For instance, a Wang Ye was often portrayed as a fearsome general, but he was also treated as a "Benign Old Man." Although the Great Emperor Who Protects Life was a Medicine Man, his statue was often dressed as a serious official and was legendarily said to share Wang Ye's military capability of expulsing devils and epidemics.

What is important is thus not the differentiation between different personified deities but the fact that all the deities had become territorial guardians by the late Ming. Equally important, the emergence and spread of territorial guardians came about together with a spatial transformation in the gods' hierarchy, which took place within the temples. In the early Ming, the God of Soil and Grain was treated as the official divinity speaking the voice of the state in local communities. In the early Ming pact hall plan, the god was located in the center of a temple. By contrast, starting in the mid-Ming, this deity had been turned into the Earth God and placed on the side of the main god, who was the local guardian deity.[23] The marginalization of the Earth God corresponded to the rise of the territorial cults. By the late Ming, all the locally made guardian-gods, who would have been outranked by the God of Soil and Grain, the symbol of the imperial state, became the supreme kings who commanded different territories. Moreover, in the imperial plan of the city, boundaries between *pujing* had only relative significance (especially because they were vertically integrated through *yu* and *tu* and through the imperial city temples). Along with the ascendance of the status of the territorial cults, a new ritual that enacted the army's protection of the local kings' sovereignty emerged. In this new ritual, boundaries, local autonomy, and solidarity were strongly emphasized.

Each year, a ritual called *zhenjing*, or "guarding the territory," was conducted in each *pu* and *jing*, which reconfirmed the boundaries of the *pujing*. The ritual was performed in two phases: one part in the spring and the other in the winter. In the spring, a date was chosen by divination within the territorial temple for a ceremony that was known as *fangbing* [sending the guards to stand sentry]. On this day, all households within the same *pu* or *jing* placed offerings at the main entrances to their homes in order to placate the guards [*bing*] and generals [*jiang*]. Near evening, an image of the *pu* or *jing* patron god was carried in a procession to survey

---

[23] Gu, Jie Gang, Quanzhou de Tudi shen [Locality gods in Quanzhou].

the territory [*xunjing*]. The route of the procession was the borderline of the *jing* and *pu*. During the procession, a talisman was attached to each dividing point between different *jing* and *pu*. In the winter, the same series of ceremonies was repeated, though this time they were called *shoubing* [calling back the guards].[24]

The rituals of "sending the guards to stand sentry" and "calling back the guards" formed an annual cycle. In this ritual cycle, a year had a beginning and an end. It began with the task of guarding the territory and ended in the accomplishment of this task. Repeated annually, the ritual cycle constantly created a local time-space that differentiated one *pu* or *jing* from another.

Besides the "guarding the territory ritual," each year a community held two birthday celebrations for each territorial patron deity. The two birthdays for one god usually occurred in the spring and in the summer or autumn. One of the birthdays was supposedly the birthday of the god as a living person; the other was regarded as the birthday of the dead man born again as a god. During the god's birthday anniversary, all residential households gathered in the front courtyard of their local temple. The temple space was shaped into a world of sacrifice altars and pantheons. Daoists were invited to arrange local festivals and to perform liturgical rituals. This festival was known as *fo shengri* [the god's birthday festival], but it was treated chiefly as an occasion for the neighborhood to hold a banquet for the general (territorial guardian-god) and his soldiers [*jiangshi*]. This feast was a reward [*bao*] for his role in the "guarding the territory ritual" and the efforts made by the general and his army in defending the community against potential intrusions from the outside.

Dealing with Ghosts

In the early Ming, a long walled boundary was constructed along the frontier of the southeast coast. It defined the "Central Kingdom" as a totality within which all local communities became the interior. External to it was a large world termed *huawai*, or outside civilization. In the interior totality, each local place was dealt with as a microcosm of civilization. Although in the orthodox cosmology *huawai* was conceived as where the evil of greed could rise, Zhu Yuan Zhang and his followers paid more attention to the internal roots of moral decay. To make sure "desires" do not upsurge from within, fearsome ghosts, which had, for centuries, been construed as unplaced outsiders, were incorporated into the punitive practices inside *huanei*. As "disciplinary officers" under the

---

[24] Wang, Ming Ming, Place, administration, and territorial cults in late imperial China: A case study from South Fujian, *Late Imperial China*, 16(2) (1995): 33–78.

command of the City God, lonely souls or ghosts received three honorific sacrifices at the Altar for Ghosts. In each community, three events were arranged by the officers of the pact hall. In each of the sacrifices, the City God and these ghosts-turned-officers were summoned to presence while the criminals and wrongdoers who escaped conviction and punishment were threatened with demonic horror.

Beginning in the mid-Ming, the relationship between the territorial inside and outside was repatterned. Along the southeast coast, more crises were induced by external forces such as pirates, emigrants, and transregional traders. In combating pirates, numerous generals and soldiers sacrificed their lives. Outbreaks of disease in Quanzhou came one after another and aroused not only sorcery scares but also widespread fear of foreign devils and the returned souls of the dead generals and soldiers. During this time, the ideology of demonic horror gave way to a guardian-god-centered religion. From the Jiajing Reign (1522–1566) onward, the prefects and military commanders in Quanzhou stopped forcing local people to deal with ghosts in their own home communities. Sacrifices to ghosts ceased to convey the message that ghosts were punitive officers. The altars for ghosts degenerated. Ghosts were ambiguously treated as both the lonely souls of the dead soldiers and as demonic sources of epidemics, earthquakes, and war.

As we briefly mentioned earlier, in organizing the sacrifice to ghosts in the 1550s, Yu Da You, the great general who led many anti-*wokou* battles, was advised by several local elders and members of the gentry who knew the "public opinions" of Quanzhou's citizens. In such "public opinions," ghosts had become a disturbing "external factor," ceasing to be vertically imposed internal punitive officers. The opinions were likewise ambivalent. On the one hand, they treated ghosts in the same way as they treated epidemics. To them, ghosts came from placeless worlds, water routes, and drainages to haunt local places, bringing illness and death without cause. On the other hand, they believed that ghosts, as lonely souls having no place to reside, also deserved mercy. Their fates were like—if not worse than—pirates and emigrants who knew where their homes were but could not return.[25]

How to deal with the combined forces of the frightening and the poor? The question must have been posed more than just a few times to religious specialists and officials alike. Although no evidence is available to show how the question was answered, we know through historical records that the question made its mark on history. Territorial cults surely had other roles to play in local society, but the local guardian-gods were

---

[25] Wu, You Xiong, Quantai "pudu" fengsu kao [An investigation into the Pudu festival in Quanzhou and Taiwan], pp. 22–23.

made into benign forces that could combat the ghostly forces impinging
on local communities. As generals who led their army, they conducted
yearly surveys of local households. Sending their soldiers to "guard the
territory" in *zhenjing* rituals, they protected the territories against invasion
by the placeless souls. Ghosts, in such ceremonies, were the enemies to be
expelled from the community. As Feuchtwang suggests:

> Homes, neighborhoods, and larger localities are favored (or not) by
> gods, and they are also protected (or not) by gods against *kuei* [*gui*]. The
> image of gods controlling *kuei* is a religious metaphor of a heavenly court
> hierarchy, of purgatorial judges and their court, of physicians, magicians,
> and of generals and their troops . . . . heaven or the god of heaven, through
> lower orders of localities control *kuei* and favor and protect the central
> places, neighborhoods, homes, and individuals of the social world.[26]

Thus in the mid-Ming, a transformation of the annual cycle of sacrifices
to ghosts proved extremely important. According to Zhu Yuan Zhang's
instruction, three sacrifices were made at the open alters for ghosts each
year. By the late Ming, although the compilers of official history still kept
records of how these sacrifices should be properly done, when they wrote
about "local customs" [*fengsu*], they intentionally or unintentionally left
some traces of their transformation. From the late Ming, the third lunar
month sacrifice was no longer treated as a ghost festival. At the same time,
the ancient Clear and Bright Festival (Qingming) occurring during the third
lunar month was continued as a tradition. During the festival, the worship
of ancestors was the core observance. "People decorate their houses with
azalea and offer a rice noodles, bean cakes, and so forth to their ancestors.
The next day or a few days later, they unearth the graves of their ancestors
and decorate them with spirit money."[27] During the seventh lunar month
sacrifice, people stopped inviting the City God to lead ghosts-turned
officers. In the Buddhist monasteries, the Tang era Universal Salvation
festival was renewed. In the streets, "all households prepared vegetarian
food and offered it outside the doors or in the streets to pay respect to
[*zhu*] those killed in action [*shangwang*] and wild ghosts [*yegui*]. The
tenth lunar month sacrifice ceased to be a proper sacrifice; it was simply an
old Han Dynasty style Winter Solstice festival during which people made
simple offerings to their ancestors and ate small sweet dumplings.[28]
While ghost sacrifices were turning into a sequence of observances
of ancestor and ghost worship, two other public festivals connected to

[26] Stephan Feuchtwang, Investigating religion in Maurice Bloch (ed.), *Marxist, Analyses of Social Anthropology* (London 1975), p. 78.
[27] *Quanzhou Fuzhi* [*Quanzhou Prefecture Gazetteer*], compiled by Huai Yin, Bu, and Huang, Ren (Quanzhou 1870 [1763]), *juan* 20.
[28] Ibid.

ghosts were also developing. Sacrifices to ghosts gradually merged with the Daoist annual cycle of Upper Yuan, Middle Yuan, and Lower Yuan celebrations. In the Daoist Temple of Pingshui Miao, these three time periods were marked with sacrifices to three Daoist cults who were in charge of the upper (Heaven), middle (Earth), and lower (Water) levels of demonic existence. There is little evidence concerning who organized the Upper Yuan celebrations for the whole city of Quanzhou, but it is clear that in the late Ming, the Upper Yuan festival was treated as an occasion for a "conference of gods" [*yingshen saihui*]. It was modeled on the third day of the fifth lunar month exorcism festival from Hangzhou and Suzhou in the South Song. The festival involved all the territorial cults converging in public spaces of the city where they displayed their different efficacies and by so doing expelled ghosts.

In the *Gazette of Quanzhou Prefecture* from the Wanli Reign, "conferences of gods" that involved the coming together of different neighborhoods in ceremonial contests are vividly described.[29] As the *Gazette* tells us:

> Annual festivals, such as Lantern festivals during the Upper Yuan, boat racing festivals during the fifth month [*duanwu jie*], moon festivals during mid-Autumn and so on, should originally be domestic celebrations of time's harmony [*shihe*] and seasonal harvests and should originally be mutual amusements among families who are satisfied in their daily life. Yet, [in recent years], people sculpt images of their deity cults and decorate them with luxurious items. They carry the gods' images in sedan chairs and parade in the streets, showing off. Conflicts thus occur.[30]

In the Qianlong Reign edition of the *Gazette of Quanzhou Prefecture*, the compiler quoted from *Wenling Jiushi* [*Old Things in Wenling (Quanzhou)*] written earlier to provide a detailed description of *shehui* in the city:

> In Sanwu [the broad region developed under the Wu of the three warring states, surrounding the Suzhou and Hangzhou areas], people call such festivals *she* and *hui*. There, they are held in the period in-between spring and summer, or in the fifth [lunar] month. . . . In our city Wenling [Quanzhou], people treat the first [lunar] month as a period for pilgrimage festivals [*chaobai*]. Festivals of the kind are also known as *hui*. These festivals bring all the highly valued things in different neighborhoods together to pray for the bestowal of blessings. They also inherit the old connotation of *nuo* [mask dance] and have a long history. So they have nothing to condemn.

---

[29] Fengsu Zhi [Record of Local Customs], *juan* 3, *Quanzhou Fuzhi* [*Gazette of Quanzhou Prefecture*], compiled by Yang Ming, Qian (1612), c.f., *Quanzhou Jiufengsu Ziliao Huibian* (*Collection of Materials on Old Customs in Quanzhou*), Office of Local Gazetteers, Quanzhou (Quanzhou 1985), pp. 6–24.

[30] Ibid., p. 8.

For purpose of organizing the festivals, during the first [lunar] month, each ward [*jing*, or neighborhood] elects the most respected and wealthiest members to lead. These men then mobilize all the possible funds, decide the particular dates of celebration, and prepare for the establishment of exposition stage. When a festival occurs, people in each neighborhood practice the ritual of welcoming the gods [*yingshen*]. They carry the images of their local patron gods on parade along the boundaries of their neighborhood.

During the gods' procession, each household sets up a worship desk in front of its house. Incense sticks are burnt to show the household's respect toward the gods. Wealthier households that have made earlier requests to gods shape images of the gods to show their respect. Such practices are known as "competitive thanksgiving acts" [*saida*].

These faces of gods in processions are luxuriously decorated. They are seated higher than the beams over the front door of a house. The main deities are placed in sedan chairs, and they sit in them in good style. Those who carry the processional deities at the front are called so and so generals and so and so admirals. They are known as the "eight carriers" [*batai*] and are selected from the strongest looking men in the neighborhood. When they stand up straight, they look no weaker than the gods. Some of the performers who play the roles of deities hold nothing in their hands. They keep their hands together and bow their bodies. They look just like clay statues in the temples. They [walk] with stilts high above the others. Even when the streets twist and turn, they stand so still without any movement. They have great skill.

In the processions, there are musical sections. Some musicians play instruments on horses. Some play while walking. A certain kind of drum is played known as the "five ton bronze drum" [*wuyin tonggu*]. According to Huang Chuan, those who win the musical competition are awarded with these drums, which are called also "Drums of Zhuge Liang" (Zhuge Gu).

There are also banner sections. Banners carried in processions involve numerous categories—the high waving banners [*gaozhao qi*], the five direction banners [*wufang qi*], commanders' banners [*shuai qi*], commanders of three armies' banners [*sanjun siling qi*], path-purifying banners [*qingdao qi*], flying tiger banners [*feihu qi*], and surveying banners [*xunshi qi*].

In addition, many kinds of weaponry are brought on display. They include the dagger-ax, fast spears, pikes, winged spears, shelves of arrows, swords and shields, dragon heads, hook-sickles, and so on. The kinds of daggers are numerous. More than a hundred men play the roles of talented officials, knights, umbrella-holders, horsemen, servitors, army men, small army trainers, and banner-holders. Some, who really enjoy getting involved in the proceedings, select some poems or legends. They write them on the sides of the movable little houses that the little actresses dressed in the maids' uniforms. Such performances are known as "holding the rooms" [*taige*]. Some build a kind of stage with nice cloth and decorate it with attractive colors. They carry them and walk in the streets. These are known as "soft stages" [*ruanpeng*]. All these are prepared with tiring labor, and they occupy all the energy of the local men. But they are prepared just for momentary visual satisfaction.

A god's statue is usually carried by four men. But those of the God of War from Tonghuai Temple (Tonghuai Guandi), the True Immortal Wu from Huaqiao Temple (Huaqiao Wu Zhenren), the Heavenly Queen at the South Gate (Nanmen Tianhou), Master Wang from Hushan (Hushan Wang Xianggong), and the Original Altar Commander from Gurong Precinct (Gurong Jing Yuantan Yuanshuai) are carried by eight men. All of them move very fast. With great foot speed and coordinated action, they fly like the wind and cannot be caught up to even with running horses. In the processions, they paint their faces with strange patterns and look extremely ugly. Some make noise with gongs and their voices. They do so to induce laughter.

Daoist priests walk in front of the gods' sedan chairs. In front of them, there are in turn teams of drum and organ plays headed by masked dancers, which may be a local expression for the ancient *zhuyi* [drive away pestilence] rite. These masked dancers wear the masks of fierce ghosts [*ligui*], and they dance in the same manner as ghosts. They hold metal weapons and peach wood when performing the ancient ritual of *nuo* [exorcism].

The procession of the True Immortal Wu, the most massive, involves hundreds of people. Some other processions involve half the number or less. This procession takes a long time to pass by the crowds. After Heaven and Earth are both shaken by the noise of drums and gongs, the images of gods gradually emerge among the crowds. The daytime celebrations end mostly in this manner.

In the evening, the leaders of the festivals beat gongs to mark the start of a lantern-raising ceremony. Each household head then lights the lanterns. Near midnight, all the households are called out to join the parades of lanterns and torches. All the adults and children hold lanterns and incense sticks in their hands, and they walk in the streets. The lantern cover is inscribed with two phrases: the winds are tuned and the rains smooth [*fengtiao yushun*], peace and security are prayed for [*qiqiu ping'an*] . . .[31]

The second grand sacrifice ritual occurred during the Lower Yuan. In Daoism, during the Lower Yuan, ghosts and epidemics took water routes to arrive in the human world. The commander of water [*shuiguan*] had to be called on to expel them. Obviously, the Daoist message was widely received during the late Ming. During the tenth lunar month, along the water routes in and out of the city, the Universal Salvation of Water Ghosts [*shuipu*] ceremony was held. The salvation ceremonies were held in the territorial cult temples of Wang Ye, which were chiefly located along the water routes in the South of the city. These Wang Ye temples formed a line of coastal protection, which began in the Northwestern part of the city, on the bank of Jinjiang River, and reached the seashore near the old harbor to the Southeast. The headquarters of the sacrifice was Fumei Gong, a territorial temple in the Southern Yu of the city. The temple

[31] C.f., *Quanzhou Fuzhi* [*Quanzhou Prefecture Gazette*], compiled by Huai Yin, Bu, and Huang, Ren, *juan 20*.

was established in the early sixteenth century in the process of pact hall transformation. The main patron deity was Xiao Wangzhi, a Han Dynasty adviser to the emperor. Secondary patron deities consisted of Wenwu Zunwang and twenty-four Wang Ye. Wenwu Zunwang were Zhang Xun and Xu Yuan, who were two heroic generals loyal to the Tang Dynasty. They legendarily became military commanders of the underworld after death and they were determined to be enemies of ghosts. By the late Ming, the Fumei Gong Temple was regarded as "The Office of All Wang Ye's in the City of Quanzhou" (Quanjun Wang Ye Guan, although usually it was just a normal territorial temple).[32]

The annual tenth month sacrifice to water ghosts was held in a manner similar to the Universal Salvation festival during the seventh lunar month. But some of the offerings, which were first displayed outside the gates of households and in the streets, were dumped into the river and the sea. In those years when serious epidemics invaded the city, special ceremonies of "releasing the Kings' boats" [fang wangchuan] were organized. As Katz shows, the boats, which were sent off into the sea, carried with them statues of Wang Ye and their army as well as food offerings, which were intended as what could took with them plague-demons. In Wenzhou and Hangzhou, where Katz conducts his excellent study, "sending off the boat" festivals always involved extensive processions in which Marshal Wen patrolled the roads to catch sinners and demons.[33] Similar rituals can be reconstructed in Quanzhou. But as Zeng Jingmin indicates, although "releasing the Kings' boats" festivals were, like their counterparts in Zhejiang, plague-expulsion rites, local people saw them as religious efforts to "give the floating souls [youhun sanpo] places to belong and, by so doing, turn them into ghosts who do not harm people."[34]

During a "sending off the boat" ceremony, all the Daoist and local deities were brought forth to the temporary worship altars. These local deities, by the late Ming, included the City God. As Yang Guozheng notes, some of these ceremonies were held also to send off boat men who would travel a long distance from home. During a ceremony of the sort, the registered list of boat men were read out in front of the tablets of the City God and local deities. The worshippers prayed for gods and demons' protection for the maritime travelers.[35]

---

[32] Wu, You Xiong, Quanzhou Zongjiao Wenhua [Religious Culture in Quanzhou] (Xiamen 1993), pp. 69–60.

[33] Katz, Demon Hordes and Burning Boats, pp. 143–174.

[34] Zeng, Jing Min, Qiantan Quantai "wangye" xinyang [An informal discussion on the cults of Wang Ye in Quanzhou and Taiwan], Quanzhou Daojiao Wenhua [Daoist Culture in Quanzhou], 1 (1994): 46–49.

[35] Yang, Guo Zheng, Min Zai Haizhong [Fujian in the Sea] (Nanchang 1998), pp. 150–155.

Ritual as "Moral Decay"

In the last fifty years of the Ming Dynasty, *pujing* halls in the city of Quanzhou occasionally served as *yuesuo*, public places for *xiangyue* rituals. But official religious activities were not at all characteristic of them. In these decades, neighborhood festivals dominated the ceremonial landscape of Quanzhou, and they had in common three features. First, they were extremely "noisy" [*nao*], "chaotic" [*luan*], and "ecstatic"[*kuang*]. Second, they often led to dramatic intercommunity conflicts. Third, wealthier households in each *pujing* were active in the organization of these festivals.

Official histories invariably depicted these festivals in terms of "chaos." The editor of the late Ming edition of the *Prefectural Gazetteer* mentioned that during local festivals people in Quanzhou "got drunk day and night" and "still did not want to stop drinking."[36] In a vernacular history cited in the later edition of the gazette,[37] the late Ming popular "craze" for neighborhood temple festivals in Quanzhou was vividly described. Temple festivals occurring on the dates of the local deities' birthdays were known as *hui* [communal celebrations], a term that was also applied to describe the ritual of *xiangyue*. On such occasions, each *pu* or *jing* collected donations from its member households. In addition, some households contributed specially shaped images of gods [*foxiang*]. Processions of masked dancers, operatic troupes, musicians, people holding flags and weapons, and people dressed as soldiers or in costumes from classical dramas marched in the streets. The cacophonous "noise" of music and human voices as well as firecrackers continued late into the night. The editor of the gazette concluded that those who celebrated such festivals looked as if they were "mad."

Attempts to ban what Robert Weller has aptly called "hot and noisy religion"[38] were made from time to time. However, the efforts of the imperial government were obviously unsuccessful. The "chaos" of the festivals was repeated annually. When the "conferences of the gods" took place, different *pujing* territorial temples carried their own gods' statues and offerings to show off their local wealth and strength. The idea was that more offerings and more respect for gods meant more blessings for local communities. The conferences provided opportunities for local communities to compete for more gods' blessings. Such festivals became more and more extravagant. During the contests, wealthier

---

[36] *Quanzhou Fuzhi* [Gazette of Quanzhou Prefecture], compiled by Yang Ming, Qian (1985 [1612]), *juan* 3.

[37] *Quanzhou Fuzhi* [*Quanzhou Prefecture Gazette*], compiled by Huai Yin, Bu, and Huang, Ren, *juan* 20.

[38] Robert Weller, *Resistance, Chaos, and Control in China* (Seattle 1994), pp. 113–128.

households also did their part to gain more respect for themselves and for their neighborhoods. When the competitive offerings and performances escalated to an extent that some neighborhoods could not bear them, plots to stop others' performances began to appear.[39] Conflicts became even more likely to emerge during rituals of boundary maintenance. In *zhenjing* ceremonies, images of territorial patron deities were carried along the major boundaries of the *pu* or *jing* in question. Sometimes, processions that were meant to patrol the territory of a particular *pu* or *jing* transgressed neighboring *pu* or *jing* boundaries. People in the invaded *pu* or *jing* envied their rival communities for their great celebrations as well. Members of a *given pujing* would then organize to cause trouble for their rivals. Under such conditions, intercommunal conflicts occurred.

To the imperial magistrates, *pujing* served the purposes of administration and civilization and played a role in the local re-enactment of the imperial cosmos. In contrast, as rituals of territorial solidarity and community status competitions, popular *pujing* festivals created a sense of local autonomy and competence, which in turn were merged with local conceptions of entrepreneurship.[40] Entrepreneurship grew out of the development of commerce in the heyday of the Quanzhou harbor (960–1368), and contributed to the expansion of local economic power. While the Ming court had treated the decline of Quanzhou commerce as a sign of the growth of civilization, local folk tales regarded the decline as a misfortune.

As we have retold from the outset, the message is conveyed most explicitly in one local folk tale. The tale, which was popular as a part of Quanzhou's oral tradition before and during the 1930s, when it was documented by the folklorist Wu Zao Ting,[41] is an indirect folkloric refraction of imperial *pujing*. Whatever its origin, the tale makes

---

[39] Perceived as an overall pattern, the territorial festivals were characterized by economic hierarchy, a logic of reciprocal exchange between the wealthy people and the community (and between people and gods), and a heated competition. Gates has suggested that Chinese rituals express a popular petty-capitalist economic culture that offers a counterpoint to the ideal state model of society. She has analyzed this petty-capitalist economic culture from the perspective of the reciprocity between gods and people, and a symbolic medium (spirit money) that articulates this relationship. Her concept of "petty-capitalist economic culture" could easily be applied to the territorial festival. The popular craze for celebrations in Quanzhou was encouraged by the quest for "good fortune." Contests between households to make the most lavish offerings to the gods reflected the "irrational idea" that the more offerings, the better the fortune. It was on this ideological basis that economic hierarchy was recognized and was explicitly acted out in ritual performance. See Hill Gates, *China's Motor: A Thousand Years of Petty Capitalism* (Ithaca 1996).

[40] Steven Harrell, The concept of fate in Chinese folk ideology, in *Modern China*, 13(1) (1987): 90–110.

[41] Wu, Zao Ting, *Quanzhou Minjian Chuansuo Ji* [*A Collection of Folk Tales and Legends in Quanzhou*] 4 Vols. (Fuzhou 1957 [1940].

unwavering commentaries on the imperial ideal model. This is a history of the conflicts between the imposed imperial order and the local order. The central argument in the story refers to the intrusion of supralocal political domination on the local universe.

Unlike the storytellers who told us the legend of Carp City, the authors of official histories perceived the Ming transition as a *jiaohua* movement that failed only when all the forms of "moral decay" came to dominate the customary culture of Quanzhou. Yang Ming Qian, the compiler of the Ming edition of the Quanzhou Prefecture Gazette, argued that extravagant festivals should be held only in "harmonious times and in good harvest years [*shihe nianfeng*], during which households had more than sufficient income [*jiaji renzu*]." He wondered why during these times local people still could bear the burden of spending so much money and energy on public festivals. He said that "in these years, the population has grown larger, and the mountains cannot grow enough trees for people to fell. The fish in the ponds are fewer than the fishing nets, and hardly any merchants' ships can be relied on." Yet, wasteful expenditures increased. The conferences of gods involving "sculpting gods' statues, decorating temples and theater stages, and processions rituals" incurred more costs than the local economy could support. "Words cannot exhaust the harms and evils" of such wasteful customs, and yet "it is already too late to prevent what has occurred from occurring."[42]

What Yang Ming Qian did not see was the gradual return of merchant forces in late Ming Quanzhou. In many stele inscriptions, it is indicated that *pujing* temples were constructed through the joint efforts of local temple committees, elders, gentry, merchants, and household donors. In the late Ming, the category of social group known as *Shenshang* [gentry-merchants] became outstanding sponsors of both local territorial and larger Buddhist and Daoist temples. Names of many Shenshang also appeared on the stele inscriptions of several official temples. The so-called Shenshang were, as the Ming famous scholar Li Guang Jin described, merchants who exchanged wealth for a promotion in social status. Or, in Brook's words, the category Shenshang was a combination that stemmed from a change in the Ming society:

> The strictest Confucian model of Chinese society placed the gentry on the top rung and the merchants at the bottom, but the distance between the rungs lessened in the mid-Ming as some merchants gained entry into gentry circles and some gentry accepted them and searched the scholarly tradition for precedents to justify commerce.[43]

---

[42] *Quanzhou Fuzhi* [*Gazette of Quanzhou Prefecture*], compiled by Yang Ming, Qian, *juan* 3.

[43] Brook, *The Confusion of Pleasures*, p. 135.

In the late Ming, Quanzhou's social units diversified into several types. The smallest were still the households, loosely organized for mutual help and public works in neighborhoods. Merchants, scholar-gentry, and gentry-merchants also lived in the neighborhoods. The two groups interacted in public life at a higher level. The imperial bureaucracy organized monopolies over taxation, military defense and control, and administration. In addition, in the late Imperial City, there were also migrants from other provinces or prefectures who forged their own foci of identity through building guilds and native-place temples.[44] In the city of Quanzhou, the Tianhou Temple allowed Ningbo Merchants to set up an native-place compatriots' association on its grounds. Pingshui Miao, the Daoist temple for *sanguan* and a territorial temple for local *pu* also accommodated the Anhui beggars' camp. Moreover, as Yang Ming Qian himself observed, the conferences of gods offered opportunities for the wealthier households to show off their ownership of status goods. The merchants, who sometimes dressed in costumes that were called "noxious fashions" [*yaofu*] often wandered with pride along the streets to the serious disgust of the Confucians.

During the "conferences of the gods," local operas were performed in front of the cult temples. In the late Ming, these theatrical performances mainly consisted of Liyuan opera and Jiali puppet theater. The former, transmitted from the Southern Song Hangzhou to Quanzhou in the tenth century and surviving the Yuan and the early Ming, presented two sorts of dramas—the dramas of "illicit love affairs" and the dramas of ghost stories.[45] The most common puppet theater was that of Mulian Rescues His Mother, a Sinicized Buddhist salvation story.

Plays of romance, such as the well-known *Xixiang Ji*,[46] were performed mostly during the territorial guardian-gods' birthday anniversaries. A renowned local play that was widely received was the *Kapok Story* [*Banzhi Ji*]. It was a story of the birth of the sage, Han Qi. As we noted earlier, the memorial hall devoted to Han Qi was turned into the City God Temple by the early Ming prefect Chang Xing. Later, in the mid-Ming, the hall was turned into a territorial temple with Han Qi as the guardian deity. The drama of the *Kapok Story* was "licentious" in its quality and

---

[44] Stephan Feuchtwang, City temples in Taipei under three regimes, in G. William Skinner and Mark Elvin (eds.), *The Chinese City between Two Worlds* (Stanford 1974), pp. 263–302.

[45] Peter Van der Loon, *Mingkan Minnan Xiqu Xuanguan Xuanben Sanzhong* [*Three Selected Plays of the Ming Editions of Minnan Local Opera*] (Beijing 1995).

[46] In the late Ming, local opera performances became so popular that even some scholar-officials loved to see them. A Ming witness of a dramatic incident in the city of Quanzhou tells us that, to many people's surprise, in the late Ming a professor invited a troupe to perform the play *Stories of the West Chamber* (a popular "licentious play") that he enjoyed within the Hall of Brightened Morality (Minglun Tang, the hall for worship of Confucius). See *Fujian Xishi Lu* [*Historical Materials of Fujian Operas*], Fujian Institute of Arts Research (Fuzhou 1983), pp. 62–63.

contents. According to the story, one day, in the prefectural government compound, a banyan produced a flower of kapok. The maid who served the father of Han Qi brought the flower to Han Guo Hua, the father of Han Qi. Han Guo Hua fell in love and made love with the maid who later gave birth to Han Qi.[47]

By way of enhancing on the adultery-birth of the sagacious man, the *Kapok Story* offered a reverse interpretation of the sagacious. It was performed during the gods' birthdays in various temples (not just in the temple of Shenghan Jing, the precinct where Han Qi was born), portraying the gods as more humane than the sagacious.[48]

· While extramarital orgies in the operas rendered the local temples the meaning of fertility during the birthdays of gods, the ghost story dramas were mostly devoted to the ghosts themselves during the Universal Salvation festivals of the seventh month (they were also performed for mourning rites). But the ghostly dramas did not simply draw on the concept of death. Instead, they emphasized the notion of filial piety, which was in turn defined in terms of the "blood relation" between Mu Lian and his mother. In a metaphoric manner, ghosts were thus turned into female ancestors who were, as the play *Mulian Rescues His Mother* [*Mulian Jiu Mu*] describes, lonely souls falling into the underworld, waiting to be saved by living men.[49]

In an ironic way, all the festivals, processions, opera performances, and puppet shows turned what was officially defined in the early Ming as the unorthodox and immoral into a part of Quanzhou's human worlds. Along with this change, the demon expulsion ceremonies also succeed in incorporating the expelled, the subjects who had been categorized as wrongdoers and the enemies of ghosts in the early Ming: the "hooligans" who were activists in territorial processions and conferences of gods, the merchants who harmed Confucian orthodoxy, and the family members of pirates. In short, all those who could easily slip into the zones of *huawai* now became the reformers of culture within the realm of civilization.

Along with all these changes, the imperial symbolic landscape was also altered. By the late Ming, the popular understanding and meaning of the War God (Guandi), who was worshipped at the seven city gates, had changed. He was no longer simply the War God; he was re-appropriated

---

[47] *Fujian Xishi Lu* [*Historical Materials of Fujian Operas*], p. 152.

[48] According to a note inscribed beside the carved image of Han Qi, during the Wanli Reign of the Ming, Han Qi had been worshipped by locals who had admired him. His original carved image was discovered in the east side room of the City God Temple. See Kenneth Dean and Zheng, Zhen Man (eds.), *Fujian Zongjiao Beiming Huibian: Quanzhoufu Fence* [*Epigraphic Materials on the History of Religion in Fujian: Quanzhou Region*] 3 Vols. (Fuzhou 2003), p. 349.

[49] Also see Stephan Teiser, *The Ghost Festival in Medieval China* (Princeton 1988).

as the God of Righteousness who could bring wealth to local households. Sometimes, the statue of the god was carried in epidemic expulsion processions through the streets of the city.[50] Guandi by then had become a normal territorial patron deity who combined the personages of the Wealth God and Marshal Lord.

The five sacred peaks—the Eastern, Western, Southern, Northern, and Central Mountains, which symbolized the sovereignty of the monarchy—that Chang Xing pointed out in his cosmography of Quanzhou had changed into five popular Daoist temples, where different "kings of hells" resided. The Daoist cults of Liu Xingjun and Zhang Tianshi, the historical figure Chen Hong Jin, and the locally invented River God were respectively allocated to the commanding posts for the western, central, southern, and northern peak-temples of the city. Each year, these hell kings and commanders of ghosts were entertained twice with great puppet performances of the play *Mulian Rescues His Mother*. Afterward, the commanders of ghosts were brought out to patrol the city in procession.[51]

The transformation of the five peaks in Quanzhou was not an isolated phenomenon. As early as the Zhengde Reign (1502–1521), a similar process had taken place in Beijing. The overall model of a worship platform system, which was brought to Beijing in the early fifteenth century, was re-appropriated in the popular festivals of "peaks" [*ding*]. The system of "peaks" was said to be, like official altars, a derivative of *fengshan*, although legends trace it directly back to the Great Mountain, Taishan. Thus, there were five *Dings* in suburban Beijing, four of which were located outside the four great gates of the city in the directions of the east, south, west, and north, and one of which located in the "middle," inside the city.

In Beijing, these "tops" were connected to the cult of Bixia Yuanjun (Prime Monarch of Azure Clouds), which was also known as "Mother Mount Tai" (Taishan Nainai).[52] They all claimed their own historical linkages to the official Dongyue Miao (Eastern Peak Temple). Ceremonies devoted to Her Majesty the Prime Monarch of Azure Clouds chiefly involved "incense congregations" [*xianghui*], also known as *Dingxiang* [incense-burning at the five tops]. During the first ten days of the fourth

[50] See *Quanzhou Tonghuai Guanyue Miao Zhi* [*The Gazette of the Temple of Guandi and Yue Fei at Tonghuai in Quanzhou*], Zeng, Huan Zhi, and Fu, Jin Xing (eds.) (Quanzhou 1986).

[51] Chen, Yun Dun, Quanzhou wuyue [The five great peaks in Quanzhou], *Quanzhou Wenshi Ziliao* [*Cultural and Historical Materials in Quanzhou*], 3 (1983):145–151.

[52] Liu, Shou Hua, Lun Bixian Yuanjun xingxiang de yanhua jiqi wenhua neihan [On the evolution and cultural significance of the cult of the Prime Monarch of Azure Clouds], in Liu, Xi Cheng (ed.), *Miao fengshan: Shiji Zhijiao de Zhongguo Minsu Liubian* [*Miaofeng Shan: The Changes of Chinese Folk Customs at the Transition of the Century*] (Beijing 1996), pp. 60–68.

lunar month in the Chinese calendar, different neighborhoods and sectarian religious groups came to the "five peaks" to pay tribute to the goddess. The groups of what we may call "pilgrims" performed either martial arts [*wuyi*] or "literary techniques" [*wenyi*]. The goddess—a feminine figure representing a folkloric reversal of the male figure, the God of the Great Mountain (Taishan Shen)[53]—became the center of the world during these "incense congregations." The tribute-paying groups had different titles and cult organizations, but during the "incense congregations," they described themselves as part of the "incense" of the Prime Monarch of Azure. The tribute-paying rituals at these "peaks" gained their meanings by virtue of a differentiated connection with imperial *fengshan*. They emerged in the cultural diffusion of the folk cults of Taishan, in which the regional cult associations and local neighborhoods—the collective donors and tribute payers of the peaks—played a critical role.[54]

From Local Administration to Territorial Cults

Following the work of Freedman and Skinner, several scholars have stressed the importance of place in studies of Chinese social structure. Among these studies, two approaches can be identified. In "administrative space theories," discussions of Chinese place institutions emphasize the politico-economic and bureaucratic roles of place. One aspect, to which Skinner had previously drawn our attention, has been the role of place is the state's institutions of local administration and social control.[55] Influenced by Foucault's theory of power, Michael Dutton has alternatively analyzed place from the perspective of state policing of the household and the neighborhood.[56] Although not explicitly emphasized, ordinary inhabitants are portrayed as having a passive role in the making of place in both of these approaches.

Unlike "administrative place" historians, several anthropologists have examined Chinese places in terms of ideological and symbolic models. First, Feuchtwang[57] and deGlopper[58] showed how a temple in a place, be

---

[53] See Gu, Jie Gang, *Miaofeng Shan* [*The Miaofeng Mountain*] (Guangzhou 1928).

[54] Zhao, Shi Yu, Guojia zhengsiyu minjian xinyang de hudong: yi jingshi deDing yu dongyuemiao wei ge'an [The interaction between orthodox rituals and folk beliefs: A case study of the dings in Beijing], *Beijing Shifan Daxeu Xuebao* [Beijing Normal University Bulletin], 6 (1996):1–15.

[55] For an example of this approach, see Timothy Brook, The spatial structure of Ming local administration, *Late Imperial China,* 6(1) (1985): 1–55.

[56] Michael Dutton, Policing the Chinese household, *Economy and Society* 17(2) (1988): 195–224.

[57] Feuchtwang, City temples in Taipei under three regimes.

[58] Donald deGlopper, Religion and ritual in Lukang, in Arthur Wolf (ed.), *Religion and Ritual in Chinese Society* (Stanford 1974), pp. 43–71.

it a neighborhood in a city or a much smaller place, acts as a "religious" representation of community. Allowing an adequate degree of "self-determination" to the ordinary inhabitants, Feuchtwang regards Chinese places as communities whose boundaries are marked out and maintained by a local annual cycle of ritual. By way of emphasizing the importance of grassroots "demonic order," in his *Imperial Metaphor*, Feuchtwang further argues that grass-roots place-identities are removed from central imperial ideological and social domination.[59]

Another anthropologist, Steven Sangren, conceptualizes place in terms of local cults as well as regional pilgrimages and hegemonic cosmology.[60] Sangren agrees with Feuchtwang in his definition of Chinese places as inhabitants' self-representations of communal identity and solidarity. But he soon turns to a synthesis of Levi-Strauss's cosmological structure and Bourdieu's practice theory, by way of which he suggests two alternative linkages between local places and their cults. The first is the pilgrimage ritual, a kind of collective and "sacred" tour transcending local confines and giving local solidarity a higher sense of historical identification.[61] The second is the domination of the centers over peripheral places in a cosmological structure based on the hierarchical ordering of *yin* [darkness, femininity, subversion] and *yang* [brightness, masculinity, domination].[62] Central to Sangren's argument about place, paradoxically, are certain "non-place" symbols and values. As he suggests, "the universalistic emphasis of core symbols in pilgrimage cults resonates with widely shared values that transcend local particularities."[63]

Data on *pujing* during the Ming suggest that local places indeed were involved deeply in the imperial project of surveillance. Later evolutions of *pujing* into territorial cult areas also validate Feuchtwang's argument concerning the role of bureaucratic metaphor in popular religion. Further, the ties that seemingly bound together popular religious cults and the officially promoted worship of sagacious men, heroic figures, and punishing spirits appears to prove Sangren's thesis of "transcendence." Thus, it seems that all the changes occurring in *pujing* places were highly complex. They were not simply a one-way dynamic in which the imperial influenced the popular or the other way around. Instead, they can be characterized as several interrelated processes through which different senses of place came to draw on and, in turn, bear on one another. And

[59] Stephan Feuchtwang, *The Imperial Metaphor: Popular Religion in China* (London 1992).

[60] P. Steven Sangren, *History and Magical Power in a Chinese Community* (Stanford 1987).

[61] Ibid., pp. 61–92.

[62] Ibid., pp. 132–140.

[63] P. Steven Sangren, *Chinese Sociologics: An Anthropological Account of the Role of Alienation in Social Reproduction* (London 2000), p. 117.

in the historically specific setting of Quanzhou, these interplays involved one more important performance—the interaction between different conceptions of morality and vitality, which defined the city in different terms during different periods of time.

CHAPTER 8

"Congregations of the Gods," Rule of Division, 1644–1720

Public life in the city of Quanzhou during the first half of the seventeenth century continued to display colorful new developments. The temples of guardian-gods locally created within the territorial spaces of *pujing* became the foci of communal festivals. Participating in these popular ritual activities, residential groups in urban neighborhoods became more mobile as they neared the dynastic turn of the Qing. As the conditions of their existence changed, these groups brought the rationalized imperial cults closer to their everyday practices. *Pujing* was still used in official discourse, but it became increasingly intertwined with popular ritual and separate from local administration.

The Dynastic Turn

In 1644, the Qing Dynasty was inaugurated in Beijing. By then, the Manchu troops had won great victories in the north, but in the south, they met much greater difficulties. The South Ming (1644–1663) migrated along the coast from Nanjing, to Zhejiang, and then to Fujian, Guangdong, and Yunnan.[1] It organized considerable resistance against

---

[1] Liu, Ya Zi, *Nanming Shigang* [*An Outline of the History of the South Ming*] (Shanghai 1994), pp. 3–25.

the Qing. Desperately fighting for survival, it depended on powerful locals and other available supporters. In conquering the southern parts of the country, the Manchus relied on the collaboration of some surrendered Han generals and scholar-officials, among whom Hong Cheng Chou was an outstanding example. Born in a *xiang* of Nan'an County attached to Quanzhou in 1593, Hong Cheng Chou succeeded in the imperial examinations at the age of 23. At the age of 24, he earned the high imperial title of Jinshi. By the fourth year of the Chongzheng Reign (1631), he was appointed as the chief general commanding the frontiers of the empire. During the Ming-Qing transition, he was in charge of military affairs for the court.[2] In 1642, during a decisive battle to defend the Ming in Songshan in the northeast, his army suffered from a great defeat. After a few failed attempts to break out of the Manchu Army's encirclement, Hong Cheng Chou was captured and later surrendered to the Qing. Soon he was entrusted with great power by the Qing emperor. In the early Qing, Hong Cheng Chou was one of the most important Han elites who made great contributions to the Qing pacification of the south.[3]

For a period of time, the prince of the Southern Ming was harbored by Zheng Zhi Long, the powerful pirate of Quanzhou origin. Zheng Zhi Long held the prince who had earlier bestowed him with the title "Earl of Nan'an" (Nan'an Bo). He took advantage of his Ming imperial title in integrating most of his rival pirate groups into his own kingdom. He turned himself into a kingly hero of the maritime world, including the coastal prefectures of Fujian and Guangdong. In consideration of his importance, the Qing generals, advised by their Han colleagues, offered him amnesty. Pressed to accept the offer, Zheng Zhi Long was then taken to Beijing, where he supposedly died of illness in 1646. Upon Zheng Zhi Long's surrender, his son Zheng Cheng Gong declared war against the Manchus. Having accepted an imperial title from the Ming court, Guoxing Ye (also transliterated as Koxinga), Lord with a Royal Surname, Zheng Cheng Gong supported the remaining Ming royal descendents and continued to resist the Manchus for two decades.[4]

For much of the late seventeenth century, the Zheng's kingdom in fact ruled much of coastal Fujian. Their activities were not quite different from the *wokou* in the sixteenth century. The kingdom was a mixture

---

[2] The life of Hong Cheng Chou is outlined in various official histories and gazettes. See Yang, Qing Jiang, Hong Cheng Chou zhuanji liuzhong bikan [A comparative analysis of six biographies of Hong Cheng Chou], in Su, Shuang Bi (ed.), *Hong Cheng Chou Yanjiu* [*Studies of Hong Cheng Chou*] (Beijing 1996), pp. 238–254.

[3] Wang, Hong Zhi, *Hong Cheng Chou Zhuan* [*Biography of Hong Cheng Chou*] (Beijing 1991).

[4] Liu, *Nanming Shiliao* [*Historical Materials of the Southern Ming*], pp. 24–26.

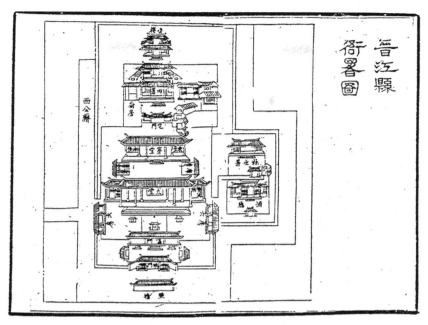

Figure 8.1 The Qing government compound (source: maps, *Jinjing Xianzhi* [*Jingjing County Gazette*], compiled by Fang, Ding, Quanzhou 1765).

of piracy, commerce, and military operations, which the earlier Ming court had condemned. However, by the late seventeenth century, all this mattered nothing to the Southern Ming. What counted more was Zheng's recognition of his Han identity (despite that fact that he was half Japanese). In those years, the Manchus, who had yet to conquer South China, were perceived as invaders by the local people in Fujian. Between 1647 and 1649, on the mainland side of the Taiwan Strait, some Quanzhou secret societies, brotherhoods, and communities joined Zheng Cheng Gong's resistance against the Qing. After Zheng Cheng Gong's death, in 1674, Geng Jing Zhong, who had earlier repressed several peasant rebellions against the Manchus, declared independence in Fuzhou and established a separatist regime. In the beginning, he formed an alliance with Zheng Jing, the son of Zheng Cheng Gong ,who ruled Taiwan after his father's death. Later on, he became a rival of Zheng Jing in their contests to control coastal Fujian.[5]

The interrelationships between the neighborhood associations in Quanzhou and the Zheng and Geng separatist regimes remain

---

[5] Zhou, Gui Zu (ed.), *Fujian Haifang Shi* [*History of Coastal Defense in Fujian*] (Xiamen 1990), pp. 158–167.

212   CHAPTER 8

unclear. However, it is evident that some of the neighborhood feuds that territorial temples became involved in developed during this period of political unrest. Territorial organizations sometimes took part in the resistance against the expanding empire of the Qing. Local protests were often conveyed through rituals and popular deity-cult symbols in local neighborhood temples. For example, the cults of Wen Wu Zun Wang (Respected Literary and Military Kings) began to appear in the neighborhoods in the early Qing. When Hong Cheng Chou surrendered to the Qing, his brother Hong Cheng Jun took the opposite track. He denounced the Manchus and called his own brother a shameful "Han traitor." He established a shrine nearby the Hongs' house, in which he worshipped Zhang Xun and Xu Yuan, two loyal officers of the Tang Dynasty. He called the shrine the "Temple for the Loyal and Heroic of the Tang" (Tang Zhonglie Ci). Later, the shrine was accepted in his neighborhood as a *pu* temple, and the two loyal and heroic figures were renamed "Wen Wu Zun Wang."[6]

To prevent locals from involving themselves in the Zhengs's anti-Manchu movements, the Qing imposed a "boundary-removing policy" [*qianjie*] on the coast in 1656.[7] The policy continued to be effective for twenty-four years, overlapping with the period of Geng Jing Zhong's short reign. It was forcefully imposed by the Qing army and was targeted at dividing the neighborhood communities in the city of Quanzhou into mutually unrelated individuals and families. During this period, many urban dwellers were forced to move into the mountains. Meanwhile, thousands of rural households in Guangdong were moved into Quanzhou. Obviously, the Qing's intention was to weaken the kinship and communal ties of the urban communities that linked local ethnic Han Chinese into groups with great social solidarity.

Prior to the nineteenth year of the Kangxi Reign (1680), the Manchus took every measure to pacify Quanzhou. In 1680, the Qing troops defeated Zheng Jing, and in 1683, Taiwan was finally taken over under the military leadership of the famous Quanzhou Admiral Shi Lang, a traitor of the Zhengs's kingdom.[8] When the island became part of Fujian province, it also became possible for the Qing court to accept local officials' recommendations that the "boundary-removing policy" should be abandoned. Thus, a new political strategy was needed to restructure local society. Shi Lang and all his underlings (generals) from the South Fujian

---

[6] Gu, Jie Gang, *Quanzhou de Tudi shen* [Locality gods in Quanzhou], *Minsu Zhoukan* [*Folklore Weekly*], March 28 and April 4, 1928.

[7] Zhuang, Wei Ji, *Jinjiang Xinzhi* [*The New Jinjiang County Gazette*] 2 Vols. (Quanzhou 1985), Vol. 1, pp. 288–289.

[8] Lian, Heng, *Taiwan Tongzhi* [*The Comprehensive Gazette of Taiwan*] 3 Vols. (Beijing 1983 [1920–1921]), Vol. 2, pp. 532–538.

area who fought against their own compatriots in Taiwan were bestowed with many imperial titles. The green banner army [*luying*] commanded by Manchu generals finally established its headquarters in Quanzhou. Many of the generals who went to war with Shi Lang were assigned to civil offices. Appointed by the Kangxi emperor as regional governors in Fujian and Taiwan, they began to exercise their power as regional leaders.

Changing Political Culture

The two first emperors of the Qing, Shunzhi (1644–1661) and Kangxi (1662–1722) spent much of their energy on the conquest of South China. To complete their military campaigns, they imposed repressive policies on the Han and their former tributaries. When most of the remaining defiant regimes were wiped out, Kangxi began to modify his way of rule. Kangxi and the other rulers of the Qing were Manchus who had their own language, culture, and political system. They were originally chiefs of some of the allied nomadic tribes. Having conquered a vast country populated mainly by the Han and their tributary chieftains, the monarch and his underlings were faced with a great challenge: how to fit themselves into a civilization established long before they came to power.

Beginning with the Kangxi, the three great emperors of the Qing—the other two being Yongzheng (1723–1736) and Qianlong (1736–1796)—showed their way of adapting, which was, as Gernet puts it, "an openness of mind, and . . . a degree of intelligence which makes them deserve the description 'enlightened despots.'"[9] As Laura Hostetler describes in her excellent work on empire building in the early Qing:

> In order to successfully claim the "Mandate of Heaven," which according to Chinese cosmology legitimized the emperor's rule, the new rulers had to successfully meet a number of challenges. Not least was to gain a thorough familiarity with the classical Chinese language, the dictates of Chinese custom, and particularly the values and practices prized by the elite in order to convince this crucial segment of the population that, even as foreigners, they could legitimately fill the requirements demanded of the imperial house.[10]

The early Qing inherited many of the Ming's cultural and religious inventions, but it adopted them in a new context of "imperial openness." Between 1680 and 1796, a new project of empire-building was launched. During Kangxi's Reign, the Qing court began to apply advanced technologies of mapping and ethnographic description to envisage their

---

[9] Jacques Gernet, *A History of Chinese Civilization* (Cambridge 1982), p. 474.
[10] Laura Hostetler, *Qing Colonial Enterprise: Ethnography and Cartography in Early Modern China* (Chicago 2001), pp. 34–35.

empire. Particular attention was given to the old tributary states and tribes on the peripheral zones existing as important components of the Qing notion of "unity in diversity." The Qing colonial enterprise actively involved itself in incorporating these groups into its elaborate cultural system.[11] Meanwhile, within the "subcelestial worlds," the early monarchy of the Qing also "drew its power from its participation in categories significant in everyday life, embodying such morally charged imperatives as filiality [*xiao*] through use of a shared repertoire of gesture, architecture, and language."[12] The symbolic outcome of ritual landscape was the rebuilding of temples and open worship altars and the further refinement of imperial rituals re-invented during the Ming Dynasty. Toward the outside world, despite the fact that Western and Japanese maritime empires were expanding into the China Sea, the monarchy further advanced its "world constituting practices" by way of reinstituting guest rituals that served to include the new powers in its world system of tributaries.[13]

On the southeast coast, having succeeded in its pacification campaigns, the Qing changed its attitude toward local society. The frontier, situated on the mainland along the line of garrison-towns installed in the Ming, now moved farther out to Taiwan. Between 1682 and 1750, emigration to Taiwan was allowed—and, to some extent, encouraged—and the strict prohibition of commercial contacts with the maritime world, which the Shunzhi emperor had imposed, was loosened.[14] Within the prefecture of Quanzhou, all the local administrative institutions were restored. Upon the pacification of the coast, in 1682, local households moved inland by force were allowed to move back to the city. The system of *pujing* was re-established along the Ming model, and one more district [*yu*] was added to the previous system of three *yu*. Within *pu* and *jing*, households were further classified into local residents and those who had moved from other places. All the imperial official temples and altars of sacrifice were renovated. *Xiangyue*, which was invented in the late Ming, was repromoted to "advance the enterprise of civilization [*shang jiaohua*]." A new worship platform, the Altar for the God of Agriculture (Xiannong Tan), was added, together with a number of new rituals such as the "sacrifice to the Dragon and the generals and soldiers who died in the battles against the Zhengs's kingdom."[15]

[11] Ibid., pp. 33–50.

[12] Angela Zito, *Of Body and Brush: Grand Sacrifice as Text/Performance in Eighteenth-Century China* (Chicago 1997), p. 6.

[13] James Hevia, *Cherishing Men from Afar: Qing Guest Ritual and the Macartney Embassy of 1793* (Durham 1995).

[14] Chen, Shang Sheng, *Huaiyi yu Yishang: Mingdai Haiyang Liliang Xingshuai Yanjiu* [*Cherishing the Barbarians and Repressing the Merchants: A Study of the Surge and Decline of Maritime Power in the Ming Dynasty*] (Jinan 1997), pp. 198–221.

[15] *Jinjing Xianzhi* [*Jingjing County Gazette*], compiled by Zhou, Xue Zeng (Fuzhou 1990 [1830]), *juan* 15–16.

Figure 8.2 The Qing's map of Quanzhou (source: maps, *Jinjing Xianzhi* [*Jinjing County Gazette*], compiled by Fang, Ding, Quanzhou 1765).

The three great emperors of the early Qing continued the Ming tradition of treating the Neo-Confucian way of rule and civilization as orthodox. However, in implementing their policies, they made an important change in their political rationale. They pursued a more "tolerant and merciful" [*kuanyu renci*] model for ruling the empire. To create a new government, the court adopted a policy in support of ethnic and regional diversity. Unlike Zhu Yuan Zhang whose prime politic was targeted at repressing "human desires" and creating a single culture, Kangxi, Yongzheng, and Qianlong showed an open mind toward "human nature" [*xing*] and cultural difference. Quite in line with the thinking of Li Zhi, in the minds of the "enlightened despots," "a desire to unify different customs of different characters inevitably induces chaos" and "the intention to erase human nature (*fu renzhixing*) is bound to fail."[16]

In the early Qing political climate of "tolerance and mercy," much greater regional autonomy was permitted. Shi Lang and other generals who fought for the Manchu monarchy against the Zhengs in the previous decades were entrusted with greater regional power. Several local scholars were promoted to work in the court directly for the monarch. These two groups of senior officials who had risen up the military [*wu*] and scholarly [*wen*] ranks, respectively, enjoyed considerable growth in the early Qing. The family of Shi Lang not only controlled the Fujian Navy but also created a network of local elite and merchant associations.[17] The family of Fu Hong Ji, an early Qing senior academician who worked for the court, created the conditions for his ascendance to local dominance. Both groups were capable of applying their comprehensive knowledge of their home regions for their own political purposes. Permitted by the emperor, they put such knowledge into their political practices. Together with newly appointed prefects and officials, they jointly started a new project of revitalizing regional culture.

Dong Xi Fo

An important part of the project was the invention of what was later known as "Dong Xi Fo," a sort of pan-city ritual contest of two opposing alliances. The two parties in the competition were called "Eastern Buddha" (Dong Fo) and "Western Buddha" (Xi Fo). The contest involved a hundred or so temple areas within the city and in the suburbs (especially those belonging to Nan'an and Jinjiang Counties). These areas were divided in accordance with the old Ming *pujing* system. The goal of the project was to integrate these basic units of local society into larger, competing alliances in order to foster more spectacular "congregations of gods" rituals. Contests were encouraged in so far as they displayed their spectacles of regional vitality.

---

[16] Gao, Xiang, *Kang Yong Qian Sandi Tongzhi Sixiang Yanjiu* [*A Study of Kangxi, Yongzheng, and Qianlong Emperors' Ideas of Political Rule*] (Beijing 1995), p. 92.

[17] Zhou (ed.), *Fujian Haifang Shi* [*History of Coastal Defense in Fujian*], pp. 168–182.

Chen Bu Chan, a Nan'an native with the imperial title of Fengzhi Daifu serving in the prefecture as a Zhongshu, wrote two papers in 1839 discussing the Qing invention of "congregations of gods." Although only three thousand characters in total length, the two essays explained how the Dong Xi Fo divisions and competitions originated and how they changed over time.[18]

As we can see through the eyes of this scholar-official, who observed many such events in the late Qing, a Dong Xi Fo competition often occurred around the time of the Upper Yuan festival. The timing of the contests was based on a popular festival during the spring. But in the early Qing, this festival was treated as the annual pilgrimage festival for some temple-neighborhoods in Quanzhou.

The festival was led by five neighborhood temple associations located in the eastern part of the city and their seven counterparts located in the west. Both the associations (locally called *fo*, or "Buddhas") worshipped the same cult, Xianggong Ye. As Chen Bu Chan describes, during the festival it was "customary" for the east association to conduct a "begging fire (efficacy)" [*qihuo*] ceremony. On that day, the five temple districts located in the eastern part of the city carried their statues of gods and conducted a procession ritual from east to west. Bypassing the streets in the Western part of the city, their well-organized formations marched toward the larger Xianggong Ye Temple in Kengkou Township in Nan'an County.

According to an agreement, when the five temple associations from the east passed through the streets under the command of the Western Buddha (Alliance), they were to politely "borrow the roads" [*jielu*] from the seven temple districts. Yet, it was also customary to break this convention and deliberately trespass on their neighbor's territory in order to display the fierceness of their local community. As they had done before, the Eastern Buddha Alliance's processions invaded the Western Buddha's territory. To respond to the organized territorial transgression, the seven temple districts sent teams of warriors to stop the procession. Feuds broke out and quickly spread all over the city. The five Eastern Buddha neighborhoods in the east mobilized and were joined by other neighborhoods belonging to the same cult network to attack the Western Buddha brigades led by the seven temple districts.

When all the neighborhoods of Quanzhou became involved in feuds, the city was soon engulfed in chaos and violence. Soon after the

---

[18] Chen, Bu Chan, Shang daguancha Quanzhou Dong Xi Fo ce [A formula presented upward to his superior observer concerning the problem of Dong Xi Fo in Quanzhou] (1839) and Cewen xiedou luqiang shi [A formula- response to the question of feuds, kidnaps, and robbery] (1839), both in Chen, Guo Shi (ed.), *Fengzhou Jigao* [*Collection of Manuscripts from Fengzhou*] 2 Vols. (Nan'an 1992), Vol. 2, pp. 466–467; 467–469.

Dong Xi Fo divisions and competitions emerged, the city's blood feuds escalated and soon were beyond the control of the government. As Chen Bu Chan described:

> As the fights occurred, all the lethal weapons converged like bees. Among them, fowling pieces and big guns were the most harmful. Most people were killed by gunshot. The relatives of those who were killed in the battle never resort to [reporting their deaths] to the magistrate. Instead they kidnap people from the opposing faction [*pai*] and demand great amounts of compensation. If the kidnapped are relatively wealthy, their families will pay for their return. If they are poor, then they have no option but death. When the feuding factions decide to kidnap each other's men, they thus first make a careful plan of which families and individuals deserve kidnapping. Late at night, they organize dozens of warriors into groups who break through the walls and doors of the houses of those who they plan to capture. Once they get their men, they wrap them in cloth. These acts are known as "night captures" [*heiye zhilu*]. . . .[19]

Dong Xi Fo contests and their ensuing feuds seemed excessively "unofficial" in their social and symbolic qualities. However, Chen Bu Chan argued strongly that these contests and the chaos they generated were purposefully devised by the provincial governor Lan Li who took office in Fujian in 1706:

> The governor-commissioner [*tishuai*] Lan Li began to make the distinction between Eastern and Western Buddhas. At the time, the distinction referred merely to different topographic features [*dishi*] of the city. The governor-general was most skilled in the arts of geomantic magic [*qing wu zhi shu*]. He perceived Quanzhou as the City of Carp [*Liguo*] and regarded it as more suitable for motion than for stability. So he organized competitions between deity-cult congregations [*saihui yingshen*]. He endorsed these festivals as expressions of the [gods'] blessings for the prosperity of the country and the peace of the people [*guo tai min an*].[20]

Lan Li (1648–1720), the governor-general, was one of the key figures in Shi Lang's military leadership. Throughout the Qing wars against the Zhengs in Taiwan, he followed Shi Lang and fought in many battles to take Taiwan. He was first described in historical accounts as a Zhangpu guerrilla [*Zhangpu youji*]. In 1684, he fought bravely in Shi Lang's push to take the Penghu Islands, during which he was shot in the stomach. He wrapped the wound with his own clothes and fought on. After Taiwan was taken over by Shi Lang, he was called into the court, where the Kangxi

---

[19] Chen, Shang daguancha Quanzhou Dong Xi Fo ce [A formula presented upward to his superior observer concerning the problem of Dong Xi Fo in Quanzhou], p. 468.
[20] Ibid., p. 467.

emperor bestowed him with the name of Pofu Jiangjun (General with a Broken Stomach). In the forty-fifth year of the Kangxi Reign (1706), he was appointed as governor of Fujian province.[21]

Accounts of Lan Li's life are widely available in various local writings and oral history.[22] According to one of his descendants, Lan Ding Yuan, a late Qing magistrate of Chaozhou in Guangdong, Lan Li was a colorful figure. He was illiterate and spoke nothing of the Mandarins' tongue. He was extremely rough. Although he had a very high position, he paid respects to low-ranking men. He laughed loudly and dared to express anger in any situation. When he became governor, he wanted to do some good for the local people, but at the time the provincial government suffered from revenue shortfalls. Thus he conceived of a plan that involved using the wealth of the unrighteous [buyi zhicai] to benefit the masses [wanmin zhili]. He encouraged the poor to take from the fortunes of the wealthy households. During the years of his service in Fujian, secret societies and brotherhoods enjoyed a great boom. They became those who judged right and wrong. Gradually, the stronger wealthy households grew intolerant and decided to fight back. Joined by many Manchus, they submitted an accusation to the court against Lan Li. Just five years after his appointment as provincial governor, the Kangxi emperor removed him from office and sent him to Tibet, where he was placed in military action for the second time and re-established his reputation on the battlefield. In recognition of his military service he was called into the capital city Beijing, where he lived until his death in 1720.[23]

Chen Bu Chan's writings depict a change in the broader context of early Qing that we can also detect in local oral tradition. Folklore suggests that the local deity cult festivals [hui] and their related feuds were closely related to a Qing political strategy of fen er zhi zhi or "ruling by division."[24] Despite the fact that Lan Li was illiterate, his "geomantic arts" were obviously part of the cultural heritage of the Chinese. They contained a strategic dialectic of differentiation and integration. Their binary classification of temple-neighborhoods was meant to divide the city into two competing factions. By pushing all the neighborhoods into struggles against each other, he tried to advance a transcendental order in

[21] Lian, *Taiwan Tongzhi* [*The Comprehensive Gazette of Taiwan*] 3 Vols., Vol. 1, p. 537.

[22] The biography of Lan Li is often included in that of Shi Lang or Li Guang Di, but not independently.

[23] Lan, Ding Yuan, Shuzu Fujian tidu Yishan Gong jiazhuan [A family biography of Yishan Gong (Lan Li), the governor of Fujian], in his *Luzhou Quanji* [*A Collection of Works by Mr. Luzhou*] 2 Vols. (Xiamen 1995 [1732]), Vol. 1, *juan 7.*

[24] "Ruling by division" [*fen er zhi zhi*] as a strategy of unification was adopted in the early Qing to control Han Chinese society. It was also adopted by Lan Li in his scheme to transform local neighborhoods, which was meant to bring mutually feuding groups and places into lively ceremonial competition.

which the "prosperity of the state and the peace of the people" [*guo tai min an*] were both celebrated as an annually reoccurring festival.[25]

Regionalism and Court Politics

Chen Bu Chan's writings offer an accurate portrayal of the history of Dong Xi Fo. Lan Li was the one who was directly responsible for the creation of opposing Dong Xi Fo alliances and "congregations of gods." Nonetheless, in inventing Dong Xi Fo, Lan Li was bound to draw his project on existing patterns of regional culture that he sought to re-order in accordance with the court's policy of cultural openness.

By the South Song at latest, rituals of the same sort were practiced in Southeast China. In southern Song Hangzhou, which became the capital of the country in 1138, Zhou Mi recorded the same "custom." Zhou Mi, an imperial bureaucrat and scholar from Shandong province lived on Kuixin Street in Hangzhou, observed local annual festivals, customary practices, and imperial rituals. He wrote *Wulin Jiushi* [*Old Things in Wulin*] as an account of what he saw. In volume three of his book, he devoted a paragraph of three hundred characters to *shehui* in Hangzhou. In the 1920s, the term *shehui* was used by Chinese sociologists (notably Wu Wenzao and Fei Xiao Tong) to translate the English concept "society."[26] Yet, in Zhou Mi's time, *she* and *hui* had separate meanings. *She* referred to neighborhood associations in Hangzhou in which deity cults, musical performances, and martial arts were the core elements of organization. *Hui* referred to the gods' birthday celebrations during which such neighborhood associations came together in ceremonial competitions in the demonstrations of the gods' efficacy and displays of local luxury objects.[27]

As we have indicated, available historical sources also indicate that by the mid-Ming Dynasty at the latest, *shehui* already pervaded local society and had attracted the attention of the imperial state. In the dynastic transition between the Ming and the Qing, territorial rivalries and their related feuds further developed when State control was temporarily lacking. These feuds frequently occurred on the southeast frontier, and they can be divided into different types. First, in Taiwan, they emerged when migrants from different prefectures competed over landholding rights in the newly settled areas, and they often resulted in the redrawing

---

[25] Ruan, Dao Ting, He, Jian Hun, and You, Guo Wei, Luetan Quanzhou Dong Xi Fo xiedou [A brief comment on Dong Xi Fo feuds in Quanzhou], *Quanzhou Wenshi Ziliao* [*Cultural and Historical Materials in Quanzhou*], 7 (1962): 41–51.

[26] Wang, Ming Ming, *Renleixue shi Shenma* [*What Is Anthropology*] (Beijing 2002), pp. 135–177.

[27] Zhou, Mi, *Wulin Jiushi* [*Old Things in Wulin*] (Jinan 2001 [1242–1252]), *juan* 3.

of territorial divisions between the two groups. Known as *fenlei xiedou* [classificatory feuds], these struggles were closely related to the rivalry between Quanzhou and Zhangzhou migrants to Taiwan.[28] Second, in the Fujian countryside, minor feuds erupted over the problems of marriage and interfamily disputes between lineage-villages, but major ones broke out among the lineage-villages or lineage settlements that had different levels of access to resources such as water, roads, and fields.[29] During the whole of the Qing, people from Quanzhou and Zhangzhou prefectures were widely known as violent fighters who frequently organized themselves into competing factions. In Taiwan and Southeast Asia, migrants from this area were engaged in feuds of the first type, organizing along native-place lines against other migrants.

In Quanzhou during the early Qing, competing territorial communities were undoubtedly characterized by their own divisions, and they easily became involved in secret society movements and developed into ungovernable alliances. These alliances did not always oppose the imperial state, but they were by themselves unifying forces that could organize local people into potentially rebellious larger movements. Why then did Lan Li still insist on deploying a system of division that was so conducive to feuds and chaos? Part of the answer lies in the specifics of the provincial governor's appropriation of cultural tradition and court policy.

To solve the problem of chaos, there were two strategies available to Lan Li. The usual one was the repromotion of Confucianism that was legendarily said to be what characterized the coastal region. As some officials saw it, the problem of feuds simply stemmed from the decay of "good customs" of the Confucian sort, which were the ceremonial dispositions of harmonious human relationships in line with orthodox hierarchical cosmology.[30] Feuds, however, proved to be the very opposite; they were not harmonious but chaotic. To reduce their harmful influence, Confucianism once again became important. Nonetheless, Lan Li also had the *Art of War* [*bingfa*] at his disposal, which seemed to him to be more effective than Confucianism (at least in his military actions to pacify the Taiwan frontier). The art of war involved an element that was lacking in Confucianism, which was its refusal to take civilization as the goal of governance. Placing the prime emphasis on utility, the *Art of*

---

[28] Chen, Chi Nan, *Taiwan de Zhongguo Chuantong Shehui* [*Traditional Chinese Society in Taiwan*] (Taipei 1994 [1987]), pp. 250–270; Lin, Mei Rong, *Taiwan Ren de Shehui yu Xinyang* [*Taiwanese Society and Beliefs*] (Taipei 1993), pp. 7–28.

[29] Harry J. Lamley, Lineage feuding in Southern Fujian and Eastern Guangdong under Qing rule, in Jonathan Lipman and Steven Harrell (eds.), *Violence in China: Essays in Culture and Counterculture* (Albany 1990), pp. 27–64.

[30] *Quanzhou Jiufengsu Ziliao Huibian* [*Collection of Materials on Old Customs in Quanzhou*], Office of Local Gazetteers, Quanzhou (Quanzhou 1985), pp. 6–24.

War suggested that an effective strategy of war or social control could be deployed only if it was effective. For instance, if one wanted to really turn chaos into order, one should not limit one's thinking to the promotion of moral order. Instead, one should always consider all possible strategies for creating order, including those applied by the "enemy." In the case of suppressing feuds, one strategy was thus to use feuds themselves, so long as they were arranged by the *yamen*. In addition, as an amateur geomancer, Lan Li obviously knew something about Daoist philosophy as well. Long ago, Laozi had said: "The softest thing under Heaven is able to run in and out of the hardest. The invisible force is able to penetrate that in which there is no crevice" (Chapter 43, *The Book of Laozi*). Lan Li did not end up with a politic of "doing nothing" [*wuwei*] like the Han Dynasty emperors, but he clearly had in mind the efficacy of refraining from forceful intervention.

When Lan Li came across the doctrine of *wuwei*, a political and cultural change was also underway in the court in Beijing. In the Qing Code from the previous reign, which Lan Li was vaguely aware of, it clearly stated that all the leaders of the "congregations of gods" should be punished. The "statute [*luwen*] concerning the prohibition of practicing witchcraft and heterodox methods" in the chapter on ritual law included a quotation that the lawmakers from the Shunzhi Reign had copied from the Ming Code:

> Soldiers and commoners who make statues of gods and beat gongs and drums in welcoming the gods to compete in congregations of gods will be flogged one hundred times as punishment. The leaders of these rituals will be imprisoned. Those neighborhoods chiefs who know about the matter but do not lead such gatherings will be flogged forty times each. The spring and autumn festivals organized for the purpose of communal adjustments, seeking gods' blessings, and giving thanks [*qibao*] are exempted from this law.[31]

From the legal perspective of the Shunzhi Reign, Lan Li had thus violated the laws governing ritual. He was the one who used his power to organize the "congregations of gods" and thus deserved one hundred floggings. Fortunately, as Wu Tan, the compiler of Qing laws and regulations, stated, during both the Kangxi and Qianlong Reigns, the tough measures against organized "congregations of gods" were temporarily loosened.[32] Lan Li was a military commander and provincial governor during the Kangxi Reign. Thus his actions did not evoke the ire of the emperor or lead to legal sanctions.

[31] Wu, Tan, *Daqing Luli Tongkao* [*The Comprehensive Survey of Laws and Regulations in the Great Qing*] (Beijing 1992 [1779]), p. 543.
[32] Ibid., p. 544.

The Manchu emperors' tolerance of local ritual stemmed from a new pattern of lordship that the Manchurian rulers had envisaged with the assistance of some Han scholar-officials. In those years, in ruling such a vast country, the Manchu emperors and their advisors had to deal with the problem of the "great unity" [*datong*]. One cultural strategy that they implemented was the re-invention of all the orthodox rituals that legitimated the emperors as the true rulers of All Under Heaven. These finely arranged ceremonies honored the Son of Heaven and enacted a perfect union of the emperors' bodies, the cosmos, ritual performances, and textual inscriptions.[33] Fitted into a cycle of royal seasons of ritual, they brought to the emperor his own greatness. To prevent the subject population from unifying into an unconquerable whole, as in earlier dynasties, the new empire needed a method for governing local society.

How could the emperor truly conquer the diverse social groupings of the Han? Many Manchu commanders in the earliest years of the Qing simply regarded repression as the most effective measure. But in the south Fujian area, they had obviously failed and become politically unreliable in Kangxi's eyes. During his reign, Kangxi adopted a different line of strategic thinking. Throughout the long years of colonial war against the Zheng and Geng regimes, he frequently consulted Neo-Confucian scholars in the court. He adopted the view that "[Neo-Confucian] lectures and diligent politics are both important," and he was the first emperor in the Qing to start systematically learning "the difference between Heaven and men through consultation and debates with Confucian scholar-officials."[34] These senior scholar-officials were mostly Han who had learned not only from the classical writings of Confucius, Mencius, Zhu Xi, and so on but also from the great thinkers of the previous Qing Reign.

When the Kangxi emperor was still small, Wang Fu Zhi, Huang Zong Xi, and Gu Yan Wu, the three greatest Han Chinese master thinkers, were engaged in an analysis of the decline of the Ming monarchy.[35] Joining different anti-Manchu movements, they had been denounced by the court of the Shunzhi emperor as intellectual rebels who conspired to re-establish the Ming. Yet, by Kangxi's time, the ideas that they developed under the repressive atmosphere of the early Qing were seen as enlightening by the new reign. Wang Fu Zhi (1619–1692), who spent many years in the southwest with a separatist prince, understood a lot about the weakness of Wang Yang Ming's theory of the "inner sage." He adopted the perspective of the "way of the ruler" [*Wangdao*], which emphasized the importance

---

[33] Zito, *Of Body and Brush.*

[34] Gao, *Kang Yong Qian Sandi Tongzhi Sixiang Yanjiu* [*Study of Kangxi, Yongzheng, and Qianlong Emperors' Ideas of Political Rule*], p. 21.

[35] Hou, Wai Lu, *Zhongguo Zaoqi Qimeng Sixiang Shi* [*History of Early Enlightenment Ideas in China*] (Beijing 1956).

of reshaping the "propensity of the empire" [*guoshi*]. In order to change local customs and mold the country into a strong empire, he saw it as necessary to use State intervention to release the great potential of the empire rather than limiting it because of a constant anxiety over order. The harnessing of traditional local social energies into effective patterns involved the transformation of the customs [*fengsu*] of many far-flung and diverse groups. It was central to the formation of the new imperial worldview. Huang Zong Xi (1610–1695) had been an active follower of the Donglin Faction during the Ming Dynasty. After having failed to slow down the southward advance of the Manchu troops, he wrote books examining the over-centralization of the empire. On the one hand, he insisted that the emperor's power should be limited. On the other hand, he advocated the old Chinese ideal of moral governance by scholars in local communities. In a slightly different way, Gu Yan Wu (1619–1692), who also dwelt on the issue of locality, provided a similar line of thought. For Gu, by the time he wrote, the customs of the country had degenerated into chaos similar to what had emerged during past periods of barbarian invasion. Thus what was needed was to re-assert the Confucian order of *li* and *she*, the communal spirits of morality and order that could change people's customs into proper forms of ritual and, in the end, lead to the formation of a perfect civilization [*jiaohua*].[36]

The writings of Wang Fu Zhi, Huang Zong Xi, and Gu Yan Wu had become widely read. In the eleventh year of the Kangxi Reign (1673), Li Guang Di from Anxi County in the Quanzhou prefecture achieved the highest score in the first All-Qing imperial exams. By then, he had read Zhu Xi and the Ming Neo-Confucians. Gradually, he was also reading some works by other great thinkers such as Wang Fu Zhi, Huang Zong Xi, and Gu Yan Wu who were roughly twenty years older than he was. After gaining his imperial title, Li Guang Di was soon appointed to the Hanli Yuan, or the Imperial Academy, where he served as premier advisor to the Kangxi Emperor for forty-eight years. During the Qing, the court relied on the scholar-officials in the Imperial Academy to directly advise the emperor. For many years, Li Guang Di in fact was the premier of state affairs. He not only wrote extensively on Neo-Confucian ideas, politics, and history but also advised the Kangxi emperor on specific political and military matters. In particular, it was he who advised Kangxi to utilize local Han Chinese generals such as Shi Lang, Lan Li, and many others to fight against the Han Chinese separatist regimes in Taiwan and Fujian in the later part of the seventeenth century.

Probably for political survival, Li Guang Di formed native-place alliances with several other members [*Hanlin*] of the Academy from

---

[36] Ibid., pp. 37–52.

Quanzhou, including the renowned Quanzhou scholar Fu Hong Ji, who was admitted into the Academy eight years earlier than was Li Guang Di. It was Li Guang Di and Fu Hong Ji who recommended the services of both Shi Lang and Lan Li to the Kangxi emperor, who was anxious to take Taiwan. In an episode from his own record of historical events, Li Guang Di recorded a conversation between him and the Kangxi emperor concerning the appointments of Shi Lang and Lan Li. This episode in his life history vividly demonstrated his preference for his hometown associates:

> Lan Li is a fighting general, whereas Shi Lang is a general with honor and fame. When I recommended Shi Lang to pacify the sea [Penghu and Taiwan], His Majesty [Kangxi] asked: "Can you ensure that he does not have disloyal plans?" I respectfully replied: "If we consider his talent, then no one can compare with him. As to the issue of the time after his successes [in the battle against Zheng Cheng Gong], it entirely depends on how His Majesty arranges his career." His Majesty asked: "How?" I said: "Shi Lang is extremely proud. If he can control himself after his success and pay attention to the harmonious relationship between the army and the people, then His Majesty will automatically have a good way to cope with him."
>
> When I recommended Lan Li,[37] His Majesty asked: "Didn't Yao Qiwang just make an accusation against him?" I said: "He accused him of corruption. What I am talking about is merely his courage." His Majesty asked: "Is Lan Li really corrupt?" I said: "Since ancient times, there have been few pure and morally conscientious military generals. Today, even the civil officials cannot maintain their purity and moral virtue. How can we expect the military generals to do so?"[38]

Although Han ministers such as Li Guang Di trusted his own people, the Kangxi emperor obviously held a ambiguous attitude. In Qing history, this particular emperor was famous for his two-sidedness. He sometimes used Han officials as advisors, and other times imprisoned or killed them. Li Guang Di, who boasted a friendship [yi] with Kangxi, sometimes also suffered from the emperor's suspicion.[39]

Not long after Shi Lang and Lan Li conquered the Zhengs in Taiwan, Li Guang Di's fellow Quanzhou *Hanlin* [academy member] Fu Hong Ji retired. Shi Lang made a petition to establish formal government control in Taiwan and to place the local counties under his rule. Upon Li Guang Di's

---

[37] Lan Li tried to lessen the gap between the rich and the poor in Fujian and for that he offended many wealthy families, who in turn accused him of corruption.

[38] Li, Guang Di, *Rongcun Yulu, Rongcun Xu Yulu* [*Quotations of Mr. Rongcun, Continued Quotations of Mr. Rongcun*] 3 Vols. (Beijing 1995 [1690–1719]), Vol. 2, pp. 688–689.

[39] Xu, Su Min, *Li Guangdi Zhuanlun* [*The Biography with Comments of Li Guangdi*] (Xiamen 1992), pp. 222–237.

advice, the Taiwan prefecture, along with three counties, was established. Shi Lang also proposed that his army should serve in Taiwan as a defensive force. He was rejected because of Kangxi's fear of potential complications that might develop in the army and make the situation uncontrollable.[40] In 1684, Shi Lang was bestowed with the imperial title of the "Lord General Who Pacified the Oceans" [*Jinghai Jiangjun Jingha i Hou*] that served as his award for his contribution to the conquest of Taiwan.

The Kangxi emperor sometimes suspected that Li Guang Di and his "Quanzhou gang" might share the political intentions of the late Ming Neo-Confucian master Wang Yang Ming and conspire to revive their Han culture.

Nonetheless, Kangxi was often moved by the political conscience and diligence of this group. Moreover, Li Guang Di was not simply a follower of the Neo-Confucian tradition. He was deeply innovative. In particular his stance on local religious festivals marked a departure from orthodoxy. He often said to Kangxi that the worship of deity cults [*shenming*] was not a bad thing. The deity cults in areas such as Fujian had emerged out of real historical figures' good deeds. They attracted many local followers owing to their moral power. For instance, as Li Guang Di once said to the emperor, a corrupt Fuzhou official became quite attached to deity cults in the later phases of his life, and he became so virtuous that after his death the locals established a temple commemorating his birth.[41]

With regard to local administration, Li Guang Di also had a rather different view from that of Wang Yang Ming, whose ideas of social order mostly derived from his experience in South Jiangxi, where gangsters often challenged the local government, tended to over-emphasize forceful control through the *baojia* household registration and policing system. Li Guang Di felt that people in their native-places could be reformed in a milder way. For instance, lineages that were considered divisive forces in local society were indeed good things for the promotion of orthodox order. By forming into lineages and yielding power to local educated elders, the settlements bonded together in natural relationships based on kinship, ancestral cults, and temple congregations and could therefore be managed more efficiently.[42]

There is no direct testimony of the way in which Li Guang Di helped Lan Li to experiment with a new strategic philosophy of regional government. But Li Guang Di's own description of his intermediary position between provincial elites and the emperor tells us that the invention of Dong Xi Fo was inseparable from the relationship between provincial elites and

---

[40] Ibid., pp. 235–236.
[41] Li, *Rongcun Yulu, Rongcun Xu Yulu* [*Quotations of Mr. Rongcun, Continued Quotations of Mr. Rongcun*] 3 Vols, Vol. 2, pp. 474–475.
[42] Ibid., Vol. 3., pp. 823–825.

the court. Evidently, the reason why Kangxi's loosened control over local festivals could be partly attributed to Li Guang Di's synthesis of Neo-Confucianism and regionalism, which became effective when combined with his regional factionalist attachment to Shi Lang and Fu Hong Ji, who were both closely allied to him in court politics. Li Guang Di, Shi Lang, and Fu Hong Ji were all ambitious politicians who shared the ideal of drawing the emperor's attention to their own home region, the "Southeast Half of the Rivers and Mountains [Empire]" [*Banbi Jiangshan*], as they called it.

The Truth of Folkloric "Biography"

In a report published in 1962, entitled, "A Brief Commentary on Dong Xi Fo Feuds," Ruan Daoting and his associates recorded a legend about the origin of Dong Xi Fo:

> During the Kangxi Reign of the Qing Dynasty, to suppress popular "anti-Qing and revitalizing Ming" [*fanqing fuming*] movements, under the pretense of maintaining public security, the *yamen* divided Quanzhou into two sections, one in the east, another in the west. The real purpose was to diffuse the power of the masses. The *yamen* gave the retired officials Shi Lang and Fu Hong Ji each the command of a section of the city. Shi Lang and Fu Hong Ji thus controlled the two factions [*pai*], and each had sixty soldiers as their "public security officers" [*zhi'an*] and gave each a banner. In the west, Shi Lang had a triangle-shape banner. In the east, Fu Hong Ji had a square-shape banner.
>
> Following this, the *yamen* also took control of the deity cult congregations/contests [hui]. It encouraged the factions to carry their statues of deity cults in processions all over the city. For the eastern section, the processing deity cults most often involved the Heavenly Deity Zhao (Zhao Tianjun) from Tongyuan Temple and the King of Broad Pacification (Guangping Wang) from Xingchun Temple. In the western section, the Supreme God (Shangdi Gong) from the Sanchao wards and the Heavenly Deity Zhao (Zhao Tianjun) were also often carried on the streets in processions. During the procession rituals, the eastern and western factions (sections) frequently got into serious disputes. Gradually, such disputes gave rise to feuds. Progressively, the feuds known as "Dong Xi Fo" became a tradition.[43]

Ruan, He, and You's materials may have been re-organized into a cultural politic of polemic against "feudalism,"[44] but they provide a piece

---

[43] Ruan, Dao Ting, He, Jian Hun, and You, Guo Wei, Luetan Quanzhou Dong Xi Fo xiedou [A brief commentary on Dong Xi Fo feuds in Quanzhou], p. 41.

[44] In 1962, when "Mao Ze Dong Thought" was beginning to be promoted, an investigation into Dong Xi Fo feuds became once again necessary. According to oral tradition, in the 1950s, the new government did not entirely extinguish "superstitious practices" and feuds in Quanzhou. How could the problems be solved? A number of local historians and officials were assigned to the task of investigating them historically. This report was the outcome of their joint work.

of supporting evidence for Chen Bu Chan's history of Lan Li's politics. Lan Li came to be the governor-general of Fujian a decade after the conquest of Taiwan. During the decade between when Shi Lang took Taiwan and Lan Li's appointment in Fujian, the coastal province was to be reconstructed as a set of "upper prefectures" in the Qing empire. "Upper prefectures" entailed more prosperity, less destruction, and sufficient imperial examination successes. To return Quanzhou to its previous age of economic prosperity, peace, and educational success, Lan Li sought first to reconstruct an image of the "energetic Carp" that local people regarded as essential to the name and fortune of their city. Festivals that demonstrated the local ethos of competition became what were readily there to be deployed. As Lan Li saw it, these local ceremonial forms were beneficial to the imperial state as well. They invoked pan-city reunions that could direct local energies away from rebellious activities.

However, the story also has another side. In Lan Li's plan to revitalize local festivals as elements of a strategy to conquer chaos with more chaos and to penetrate local society using local means, he first had to divide the whole city into two mutually antagonistic Dong Xi Fo factions, as in a game of Chinese chess. As the preceding paragraphs indicate, Shi Lang and Fu Hong Ji, the two retired senior officials, took charge of the game. Each led his "troops" to bring the divided territorial communities into the play of combat. While Lan Li expected the old chaotic feuds to be reformed into relatively more organized "congregations of gods," the mutually opposed alliances were not so easily led into what he saw as fierce competitions without violent consequences.

Before Lan Li took office of Fujian in 1706, both Fu Hong Ji and Shi Lang had passed away. Nonetheless, their families (lineages) still had considerable influence in south Fujian. Fu Hong Ji's family was accorded a lot of prestige among the locals. According to the Qianlong Reign's *Gazette of Quanzhou Prefecture*,[45] Fu Hong Ji, who was well versed in classical Confucian philosophy of ritual, was treated by the locals in Quanzhou as the author of customs. In addition, his family seemed to be widely recognized as an authoritative group who helped locals resolve their disputes. Shi Lang, whose military and social influence continued growing in the decade after his conquest of Taiwan, rebuilt the garrison-town of Xiamen and trained a large navy brigade on the island. At home in Quanzhou, he was a great philanthropist who contributed a great deal to the construction of bridges, temples, and schools. After his death in 1697, his son inherited his title and position in the navy, and the Shi family continued to be one of the most powerful lineages in Fujian.

---

[45] *Quanzhou Fuzhi* [*Quanzhou Prefecture Gazette*], compiled by Huai Yin, Bu, and Huang, Ren (Quanzhou 1870 [1763]), *juan* 45.

Although it is evident that Lan Li was the man who divided the city into two factions and provoked territorial feuds, during the Qing (by Chen Bu Chan's time at the latest) two other explanations also became available. One suggests that the Dong Xi Fo division was a derivative of interfamilial conflict between Shi Lang and Fu Hong Ji.[46] It is said that after a lengthy consideration Shi Lang decided to allow one of his daughters to marry the son of Fu Hong Ji. Three days after the wedding ceremony, Shi Lang's family was supposed to visit the son-in-law's house to pay respect. At the time, Shi Lang was excessively proud of his imperial title. As a way of showing off, he asked Fu Hong Ji whether he should perform an official ceremony, but Fu Hong Ji knew of his intention. To make him lose face, he agreed to the ceremony.

On the day of his visit, Shi Lang dressed up in his official costume. Accompanied by a formation of seventy-two guards of honor, he marched toward Fu Hong Ji's house. To his surprise, to receive Shi Lang, Fu Hong Ji simply hung on the wall of the sitting room the "iron nose" [*tiebi*] directly bestowed to him by the emperor. When Shi Lang saw the royal item, he had to perform the tributary rite as would an official paying respects to the emperor in person. But Fu Hong Ji was seated under the "iron nose," and made it seem like he was the emperor who was receiving the honor. Shi Lang was disgraced. To get revenge on Fu Hong Ji, he organized some residents of the neighborhoods in the eastern part of the city to help him humiliate Fu Hong Ji, who lived in the western part of the city. Fu Hong Ji did the same. Their personal conflict was thus the source of the Dong Xi Fo feuds.

The second story is also related to Shi Lang, but this time he is said to be only indirectly responsible for feuds. Instead of the interfamilial ritual rivalry between him and Fu Hong Ji, this second story associates the formation of Dong Xi Fo with the conflict between a small local official and a minister. It is said that the low-ranking official Zhu was once very ill. He went to consult the regional medicine god, the True Master Who Protects Life (Wu Zhenren), whose temple was located in Baijiao (Tong'an, Xiamen). He was cured after his visit. To express his gratitude to the god, he established a temple for the god in his own neighborhood and called it "Miao'en Temple." Later, the temple was moved to Zengjing Lane (a small street in the western part of the city). At the time, Minister Lin was trying to forcefully occupy the public land of the Fengsheng Ward Temple (Fengsheng Gong). He removed the temple from its original location and moved it across from the Miaoyin Temple.

---

[46] Wu, Zao Ting, Quanzhou Dongxi Fo [The Eastern and Western cult factions in Quanzhou], in *Quanzhou Jiu Fengsu Ziliao Huibian* [*Collection of Materials of Old Customs in Quanzhou*], Office of Local Gazetteers, Quanzhou (Quanzhou 1985), pp. 165–171.

When the building of Fengsheng Temple, whose cult was the Opera God (Xianggong Ye) was completed, Minister Lin was in charge of the opening ceremony. He arranged a procession ritual in which his neighborhood locals conducted a "begging fire" ceremony (pilgrimage) to Kengkou of Nan'an. As a display of his power, Minister Lin borrowed seventy-two guards of honor from Admiral Shi Lang who was a relative of Minister Lin's. At first, Shi Lang loaned him the guards, but soon he went back on his word. He organized dozens of strong young men from his neighborhood Fengchi ward. Hiding themselves in the middle of lanes, they planned to take back the guards with force. Meanwhile, Minister Lin was informed of Shi Lang's plan. He immediately organized a similar number of thugs to fight against the Shi Lang's men. The men from the Fengchi ward failed to stop Minister Lin's procession.

To take revenge on Fengsheng ward, they mobilized more strong men, who sneaked into Fengsheng territory to tear down its temple. However, the people of Fengsheng were prepared. Under Minister Lin's leadership, they arrived in great numbers to fight against the intruders. The Fengchi gang, who were losing the battle, retreated into the temple. By chance, a man known as "Qing the Lame" passed by the front gate of the temple. The Fengchi gang mistook him as a warrior from the Fengsheng ward. They ran out the temple, and on the way, knocked down one of the temple walls. Qing the Lame was killed in the accident. Fengchi was located in the east section of the city, whereas Fengsheng was in the west. Their mutual enmity continued to fester, and they soon led eastern and western Buddha congregations to fight against each other.[47]

Both stories give legendary accounts of the origins of Dong Xi Fo. Both suggest that Dong Xi Fo had originated when Shi Lang was still alive and had seventy-two guards of honor. The first story refers to two of the great officials in Quanzhou as rivals who, for the sake of "face" [*mianzi*], drew the whole city into violent fights. The second story instead traces the origin of Dong Xi Fo to inter-neighborhood enmity between Fengchi and Fengsheng, which were symbolized by the Master who Protects Life and the Opera God, respectively. Admiral Shi Lang was only indirectly involved in the cause of the feuds.

According to oral tradition, the division and feuds associated with Dong Xi Fo had existed well before Lan Li arrived in Fujian, and Lan Li only formally authorized the division. In other words, if the magistrate was really the one who "invented" this customary conflict, he did not do it without the intervention of the families and symbols of Shi Lang and/or Fu Hong Ji, whose extensive estates were, respectively, located in

---

[47] Ruan, Dao Ting, He, Jian Hun, and You, Guo Wei, Luetan Quanzhou Dong Xi Fo Xiedou [A brief commentary on Dong Xi Fo feuds in Quanzhou], pp. 42–43.

the Fengchi ward in the eastern half of the city and near Fengsheng in the western half.[48] Imaginably, although the outcome of their joint efforts to reform local rituals was the same, Lan Li's authorization of the Dong Xi Fo feuds was intertwined with several different political considerations. Both Shi Lang and Fu Hong Ji might have had different interests in the feud. After their deaths, their families needed to maintain their influence and manage their legacies. Their ancestors were undoubtedly both highly regarded for their power and success in the imperial bureaucracy; but many Quanzhou residents secretly resented their surrender and subordination to the colonialist Manchus. Using traditional Quanzhou festivals to revitalize the city could not only display their continued legacy but also serve as subtle expressions of belonging to their hometown.

For Lan Li to demonstrate that he came to rule Quanzhou with his own political skills, he needed to "to set three fires upon coming into office" [*xinguan shangren sanba huo*]. That was necessary especially for a man who was well known as an illiterate and uncultured person. In military actions, he did not need to show that he was powerful, because he possessed effective skills of ritual work. However, now he was the magistrate, but he lacked the good education and imperial title that was normally required not only by the court but also by the urban residents. His proficiency in geomantic arts thus served to fill the gaps in his résumé. Moreover, he also needed to face both the families of Shi Lang and Fu Hong Ji. These two men were admittedly more successful in both the art of war and scholarship and were both senior to him (in terms of their age and titles). One can imagine that before Dong Xi Fo was put into practice, there must have been many behind-the-door discussions between Lan Li and the two great families of the Quanzhou "tribe." Moreover, one thing that we can be sure of is that the authorization of an institution such as Dong Xi Fo was not simply a product of the imperial State or the prefectural *yamen*. It was complicated by the intricate personal and political relations that characterized regional politics in early Qing Quanzhou.

There was a cultural aspect to these processes as well. In late imperial Quanzhou, Shi Lang and Fu Hong Ji were perceived locally as personified symbols of the military and literati, respectively, which in turn symbolized the powerful but unintelligent and the bodily weak but wise. The marriage

---

[48] In August of 1688, Shi Lang met with the Kangxi emperor in the Forbidden City. By then, he had been accused of arrogance in his own accomplishments. Yet the Kangxi emperor did not listen to the reports. He encouraged Shi Lang to "establish peaceful relationships between the army and the people [*heji bingmin*]" and to "make local society a quite place [*shi difang anjing*]." It is thus evident that in his later years Shi Lang was one of the most powerful persons in Fujian, and he was given the task of recreating local social order. See *Qing Shilu Taiwan Shi Ziliao Zhuanji* [*Special Collection of Materials on Taiwan History in the Factual Record of the Qing*], compiled by Zhang, Ben Zheng (Fuzhou 1993), p. 65.

alliance between these two symbolic persons was coupled with the legend of their mutually contradictory characters. These were in turn re-asserted in the rival cults of the fierce Xianggong Ye and the knowledgeable Great Emperor Who Protects Life, which formulated a complementary pair of *Wu* [the Martial] and *Wen* [the Literary]. The same symbolic logic was also found in imperial state cults of the God of War and Confucius, who were envisioned as part of a much more peaceful pattern of relationship.

The preceding analysis also lends credence to the second story, which treats Admiral Shi Lang as merely one of the puppets that neighborhood associations manipulated to assert their own power. In this story, Shi Lang is represented as a promise-breaking man whose power resided only in his seventy-two guards of honor. The real players of the drama were the sincere believers, the low-ranking official Zhu and Minister Lin, who were both unknown in official history. What they in turn represented were two neighborhoods that led feuds throughout later periods, Fengchi and Fengsheng. The importance of Shi Lang and Fu Hong Ji in the neighborhoods' struggles for their own senses of dignity and honor simply consisted in the two men's utility as symbols of "local face."

Whatever happened behind closed doors among Lan Li and the two great Quanzhou families, Lan Li's intentions seem to be rather consistent. Using local forms of "congregations of gods," he intended not only to lend power to his fellow officials' families but also to make the city a lively place. In both efforts, Lan Li did not try to let matters get out of hand. By mobilizing the neighborhood communities and their associations, or what in those days were known as *she* and *hui*, into officially arranged "congregations of gods," he was determined to create a new image for the prefecture. The people of Quanzhou, who had suffered seriously from the conflicts between Qing colonizing forces and local separatists, were hoping for a long period of peace. Nonetheless, the popular hope for peace was coupled with a sense of scorn for the prominent men who had surrendered to the Manchus in the name of remaking a complete empire.

CHAPTER 9

Pujing Feuds, 1720–1839

In spite of the lack of data on his state of mind, one may well imagine that Lan Li was quite proud of his proficiency in geomantic magic. Channeling the energy flows of local political power into ceremonial competition, his method "killed two birds with one stone," entertaining both the local divinities and his superiors. During this time, Lan Li's superiors were anxious to mobilize local people, whose social life, as he sensed, depended ever more heavily on festivals in the aftermath of war. The local patron deities became ever more respected during this expansion of festivals.

However, a century later, Chen Bu Chan brought forth evidence blaming the violent feuds on him. Chen said, soon after Lan Li invented this new form of ceremony, Dong Xi Fo feuds moved beyond government control:

> Since then [the time when Lan Li invented Dong Xi Fo], when some ward temples sculpted their statues of gods, they also inscribed on them the characters *guo tai min an* [prosperity for the state, peace for the people]. Meanwhile, other temple neighborhoods became jealous and caused a lot of trouble.[1]

---

[1] Chen, Bu Chan, Cewen Xiedou Luqiang Shi [Questions and answers concerning feuding, kidnapping, and robbery], in Chen, Guo Shi (ed.), *Fengzhou Jigao* [*A Collection of Manuscripts from Fengzhou*], 2 Vols. (Nan'an 1992), Vol. 2, p. 468.

In December of 1711, Lan Li was dismissed by the Kangxi emperor, who believed the story that he was "full of ferociousness and evil" [*xiong'e manying*].[2] One of his "evils" was his promotion of local violence.

Escalating Feuds

After Lan Li's death, the brotherhoods and secret societies that based themselves on local territorial communities but often transgressed neighborhood boundaries became the real power holders in the region. Probably, Shi Lang and Fu Hong Ji used these organizations as local political props. However, by the time of the death of both men, they had gained independence and become independent organizations that enjoyed charismatic authority among the local neighborhoods. Feuds became occasions in which they demonstrated their own greatness.

Chen Bu Chan gave the following account of the new divisions of feuding alliances in the city:

> In the eastern part, the city is divided into five brotherhood-zones [*wu lun*], which are in turn symbolized with seven bloods [*qi xue*]. In the western part, it is divided into seven humble-men cult areas [*qi she*] that also worship three deity cults [*san xianggong*]. The so-called "five brotherhood-zones" are neighborhoods that are mutually related through alliances of sworn brothers. The so-called "seven bloods" were alliances formed out of blood oaths. They swore to "be always good to one another and never break their promises." So, the Shuixian precinct [*jing*] belonging to the alliance is also known as "long friendship" [*yichang*], and the Shuangzhong precinct is also known as the "palace of the allies" [*mengfu*]. The so-called seven *she* are those neighborhoods that worship the cult of Humble Men [*Sheren*] or the "Great Guards of the Sun and the Moon" [*riyue taibao zhishen*]. The so-called three deity cults [*san shen*] refer to three neighborhoods worshipping the same cult of Tiandu Yuanshuai.[3]

Evidently, Eastern Buddha referred to the alliance of the "five brotherhood-zones" in the eastern part of the city, whereas Western Buddha referred to the faction of the "seven humble-men cult areas" located in the western part of the city. Given that during the whole of the Qing Dynasty, Quanzhou had some thirty-six wards and seventy-eight precincts, each of which as a temple area had a local cult temple,

---

[2] Zhang, Ben Zheng (ed.), *Qing Shilu Taiwan Shi Ziliao Zhuanji* [*A Special Collection of Materials on Taiwanese History in the Factual Record of the Qing*] (Fuzhou 1993), pp. 77–78.

[3] Chen, Bu Chan, Shang daguancha Quanzhou Dong Xi Fo ce [A formula presented upward to his superior observer concerning the problem of Dong Xi Fo in Quanzhou], in Chen, Guo Shi (ed.), *Fengzhou Jigao* [*A Collections of Manuscripts from Fengzhou*] (Nan'an 1992), p. 466.

in the Eastern and Western Buddha divisions, not all neighborhoods were members of this alliance. The "five brotherhood-zones" and the "seven bloods" were thus the two most notorious alliances—not that all the other neighborhoods were merely passive participants in the feuds. In fact, as Chen Bu Chan argued, they were involved in the feuds in the alternating sociologics of "mutual attachment" [*xiangfu*] and "mutual opposition" [*xiangbei*]. That is to say, as alliances spread, unallied neighborhood brotherhoods faced much greater threats to their security than did the allied ones. Thus, alliances gradually spread throughout the city.

Starting in 1763, the time of the compilation of the Qianlong edition of *Quanzhou Prefecture Gazette*, this urban chaos began to concern many officials. Huai Yin Bu, the Manchu prefect who compiled the gazette along with his Han associates, obviously viewed these feuds differently than did Lan Li. Huai Yin Bu was astonished at how local festivals had differed from the stereotypical Confucian view of civilization:

> People's mentalities [*renxin*] are developed after civilization [*jiaohua*] has succeeded in changing them. Customs stem from people's mentalities. From the Tang Dynasty onward, Xi Xiang, Chang Gun, and others had promoted civilization long before Cai Xiang, Wang Shi Peng, and other virtuous men continued striving to pave the way for civilization. Furthermore, Quanzhou is a place where many prominent Confucian scholars visited and lectured. Its Confucian heritage has never been abandoned. The remnants of local scholarly writings from previous periods are sufficient for the cultivation of many later generations. Thus, Quanzhou has a reputation as "Confucius's home on the coast" [*haibin zhoulu*].
>
> However, popular customs now have changed. Surprisingly, they have changed in just over ten years. A careful examination suggests that measures must be taken to prevent these developing bad tendencies from expanding. [In contemporary Quanzhou], the dearth of great civilizational culture coincides with the flourishing of these inferior customs. Some [bad customs] are becoming into social trends. They have merged with the unconstrained expression of emotion. When inspired, local people respond actively, like the responding gods. Is current Quanzhou so different from the old days? Has it been pushed onto a strange track [of history]?[4]

In the same volume, many such "bad tendencies" are listed and described. Among them, ceremonial competitions such as those also described in *Wenling Jiushi* [*Old Matters in the Warm Hill* (Quanzhou)] were included. The compiler continued to describe these phenomena as follows:

---

[4] *Quanzhou Fuzhi* [*Quanzhou Prefecture Gazette*], compiled by Huai Yin, Bu, and Huang, Ren (Quanzhou 1870 [1763]), Vol. 20.

Within the prefectural city, there are an excessive number of pantheon halls [*yinsi*, or popular neighborhood temples]. The city is divided into precincts [*jing*]. Each precinct has a number of daring hooligans [*chuanggun*]. When a congregation of gods [*yingshen*] occurs, they fight with their counterparts in the neighboring precincts.

In the rural areas, large lineages [*daxing*] congregate and live in the same settlements. They gradually form hostile relationships with their neighbors and lead entire lineages [against each other] and arm them with weapons. They dare to offend the law.[5]

Between 1763 and 1839, most outbreaks of feuding occurred during pilgrimage seasons. In Quanzhou, each territorial cult temple had a patron god whose root temple was located outside the city. The linkage between the local (branch) temple and root temple was treated as a vertical relationship. In addition to the branch-to-root vertical linkage, an urban neighborhood cult organization also recognized several other official state cults and Daoist cult temples as higher in the spiritual hierarchy. Each year, to renew the efficacy of local gods, territorial cult temples organized pilgrimage rituals in which the gods' statues were carried to either the root temples or the official and Daoist temples, which primarily included the Eastern Peak Temple to the east of the city and the Yuanmiao Guan Temple on the Eastern Street.

Such pilgrimages were known as "fetching incense rituals" [*jinxiang*]. They were in general characterized by processions that transgressed other neighborhoods' territories. Through territorial transgression, a place—a neighborhood as defined as a ward or precinct—demonstrated its own greatness. However, a display of this sort was by necessity conducted at the expense and degradation of the honor of the encroached neighborhood. Thus feuds erupted most often during these symbolic invasions.

Feuds brought about by fetching incense rituals might have been simply ritualistic. But historical sources have indicated that they involved serious violence that not only affected local neighborhoods but also spread into the *yamen*. Starting in the Kangxi Reign, officials who worked in the *yamen* were mainly selected locally. As local elites they were different from local commoners, but they could not avoid getting involved in local affairs of such a large scale. Thus, they could not help but judge the cases of violence from their own territorial biases. Chen Bu Chan states:

In the past, even intelligent officials were not sure how to judge cases of feud. They thus judged only the more egregious offenses and rejected the smaller cases. The punishments meted out were slight. They sentenced the convicted only to punishment with chains and sticks [*jiazhang*]. They had few additional means of dealing with them. During the feuds, the Eastern Buddha or Western

---

[5] Ibid.

Buddha would form alliances, and they both sought to influence the officials in charge. The officials were confused. They had to allow them to go up and down in the government (give bribes) without any knowledge of what the outcome would be. During the fights, some scholars and military officers took action and instructed the involved parties to stop fighting. But low ranking *corvées*, the runners in the *yamen*, would inform the criminals in advance of how to escape. Now, the wards of Fengsheng and Ciji are the sites of lots of trouble. The magistrate comes personally to cope with the problem. He was astonished by the ways in which good civilians in the neighborhoods and households have now become those that prey on the weak. The most serious problems exist at the borders of neighborhoods. There, women's hair is cut and their personal ornaments are stolen by the offenders [from the opposite faction]. Many civilians' houses have been destroyed to such an extent that we cannot find the proper words to describe their current state of ruin.[6]

In the city, the connections to the *yamen* complicated things and made the resolution of feuds more difficult. In the countryside, however, the tensions between larger and stronger lineages and smaller and weaker ones were the key problem. Chen Bu Chan stated in his second piece on the same issue:

> Feuds most often occur when the bigger surnames (larger lineages) try to provoke conflicts. Most of the kidnapping is done by the bigger surnames. When the misery of robbery arises, there are bigger surnames behind it. Given this state of affairs, some lesser surnames (smaller lineages) whose members feel powerless thus subordinate themselves to and align with the bigger surnames. Although it is true that many lesser surnames also involve themselves in feuds, robbery, and kidnapping, they do those simply to get revenge on the bigger surnames.[7]

The social ties that characterized feuds in the city and countryside were structured differently. But the violent events observed by Chen Bu Chan were similar in that they linked different localities and social groups into larger totalities encompassing the whole Quanzhou region and the rural counties of Nan'an and Jinjiang. Small incidents frequently escalated into large feuds, because even the smallest of incidents affected the pride of an entire neighborhood, which were organized as a lineage-village or a multisurname community.

For example, in 1800 (the fifth year of the Jiaqing Reign), a feud broke over a slight reason.[8] On the tenth day of the second lunar month,

---

[6] Chen, Cewen xiedou luqiang shi [Questions and answers concerning feuding, kidnapping, and robbery] p. 467.

[7] Ibid., p. 468.

[8] Ruan, Dao Ting, He, Jian Hun, and You, Guo Wei, Luetan Quanzhou Dongxi Fu Xiedou [A Brief Treatise on Dongxi Fu and Feuds in Quanzhou], *Quanzhou Wenshi Ziliao* [*Cultural and Historical Materials on Quanzhou*], 1 (1962): 40–51.

Taoyuan Xiang of Nan'an County (to the west of Quanzhou city) was holding a ceremony celebrating the placing of the upper beam in its territorial cult temple. On such occasions, it was customary for all the neighborhoods belonging to the same western faction to come to join in the happiness of their neighbors. When delegations from the leading Western Buddha neighborhood Fengsheng ward passed by Fengle Xiang, belonging to the Eastern Buddha alliance, residents there insulted the procession. They said that these delegations were the wives' brothers of the small community Taoyuan. Two men from the procession came out and cursed the Fengle Xiang people in response. The others did not want the situation to escalate so they quickly left the Western Buddha alliance's territory.

A few months later, on the first day of the fifth lunar month, a gentry man from Fengle Xiang carried his "ward patron deity" [*puzhu*] Xuantian Shangdi on a procession ritual to Xuanmiao Guan Temple on Eastern Street in Quanzhou city to gain blessings for his family. Passing the territories of the Eastern Buddha alliance, his procession was soon joined by fellow alliance formations. The parades peacefully entered the Western Gate of the city and reached Xuanmiao Guan Temple. However, when the pilgrims from Fengle Xiang were making their journey home, they encountered some problems. To avenge what the Fengsheng ward did to them a couple of months earlier, they cursed the whole of Fengsheng ward as "sons of bitches." Upon hearing these insults, some brick factory workers who belonged to Fengsheng ran out from their workshops and threw broken bricks on the neatly organized formations. They tore the banners of the parading pilgrims into pieces, and one man from Fengle was serious wounded. The other members of their community joined the fight. They lost in the end.

The next day, the wounded man from Fengle made a petition to the magistrate of Nan'an County. He made a list of men from Jinjiang who he said organized the attack on the Nan'an County pilgrims. The Jinjiang men on his list then also handed over an accusation against the whole Su lineage, to which the wounded man belonged. They said that the Nan'an men had conspired with the *yamen* of their county to insult and bully good people [*qiya liangshan*]. Feuds between Fengle and Fengsheng immediately broke out and brought Nan'an and Jinjiang Counties into conflict. To resolve the dispute, two members of the gentry from the Western Buddha alliance made peace with Eastern Buddha alliance. Both sides kept quiet for a few months.

However, during the third lunar month of 1801, the wounded man died of illness. His brother took advantage of his death, telling the magistrate of Nan'an County that his brother was killed by the people of Fengsheng. The magistrate ruled that the accusation did not contain sufficient evidence, but he detained the accused on the grounds that it was necessary to the investigation of the incident. Soon, the accused from Fengsheng also made a petition to the magistrate of Jinjiang county. They said that the accuser committed the crime of false accusation and deserved a serious punishment. The Nan'an and Jingjiang magistrates could not resolve the dispute. Both parties then made further petitions upward to the prefectural and provincial governments. In fact, neither the county magistrates nor the prefect governor found a solution to the problem. This small incident became the root cause of mutual hatred between the Eastern and Western Buddha alliances, which continued to make accusations and engage in violent clashes against each other.[9]

In the whole of the eighteenth century and in the early decades of the nineteenth century, feuds were not limited to the territorial transgression festivals. They expanded into all spheres of local celebrations. When a neighborhood was holding its local god's birthday celebrations, neighboring communities would send over young thugs to destroy the theater stages where operas were to be performed for the god. During the seventh lunar month festival, different territories competed to buy as many offerings for ghosts as possible. Around the fifteenth of the seventh lunar month, they converged at local food markets located in the east, south, and west of the city. There they often sought to buy up all the remaining goods so that other territories would get nothing. Fights thus also took place at these markets.

Control and Loss of Control

To solve the problem of chaos, the prefects conceived of several measures. One of these was to create an official pilgrimage center for all territorial cult regions. In the middle of the eighteenth century, within the official Tianhou temple, two long corridors were built on the two sides in front of Tianhou's main hall.[10] In these two corridors, dozens of shrines for territorial guardian deities worshipped by different *pujing* communities were established. The corridors and their shrines were intended to serve as the "official capital" of all territorial cults receiving tributes and pilgrimages from local communities. During catastrophes, the prefects also authorized the Tianhou temple to organize exorcism rituals in which all the territories were incorporated.

---

[9] Ibid., pp. 49–51. As I should add, as late 147 years later, in 1945, the governors in both counties put their heads together. After lengthy discussions, the Fengsheng ward agreed to compensate Fengle Xiang for the loss of all the banners and drums in 1800. A small sum of money was also paid to Su Xiang's descendants. The case was finally closed.

[10] *Quanzhou Tianhou Gong Jianjie* [*A Brief Introduction to the Tianhou Temple of Quanzhou*], Tianhou Temple of Quanzhou (Quanzhou 1990), pp. 2–3.

However, the prefects' attempts were largely unsuccessful. During the same period, two temples became pilgrimage centers. In the southern part of the city, Fumei Gong was turned into a hall for all Wang Ye cults, where communities worshipping Wang Ye conducted pilgrimages during the fifth lunar month. In the eastern part of the city, the Daoist temple of Yuanmiao Guan was recognized as the top pilgrimage location where the efficacy of different local guardian-gods was recharged every year during the first lunar month. Followers of territorial temples that housed regional cults, such as the Great Emperor Who Protects Life, also paid visits to the root temples of their cults in the several rural counties around Quanzhou.[11]

In the late eighteenth century, in order to prevent the chaos associated with the Universal Salvation festival in the seventh lunar month, the government devised a new form of local ritual practice. The one-day ghost festival was turned into a thirty-day cycle of rotational appeasement of ghosts.[12] In this cycle, the ninety-eight urban and suburban wards [*jing*] were re-organized into thirty units, each of which was assigned a day for making offerings to ghosts. Soon the official rotational cycle was extended into a ninety-day cycle in local practice. The cycle was divided into three phases, each of which took a month. The first phase (during the sixth lunar month) was renamed "hanging up the local banner" [*shuqi*]. The second phase (during the seventh lunar month) was renamed "universal salvation" [*pudu*]), and the third phase was renamed "lowering the banner" [*luofan*]. Much like the *zhenjing* ceremonies, the *pudu* festival displayed a ritual reconstruction of the divisions of the imperial *pujing*

---

[11] The territorial units were integrated into one or more higher orders, but they were not integrated into the imperial regional hierarchies. Sangren has argued, on the basis of Taiwanese materials, how lower-level territorial cults were vertically integrated into regional networks culminating in certain regional central places. Sangren related the map of popular territorial cult areas to Skinner's regional place model through the conceptualization of "root temples." The data from Quanzhou, however, does not support this argument. (P. Steven Sangren, *History and Magical Power in a Chinese Community* [Stanford 1987], pp. 105–126). Territorial cults in late imperial Quanzhou traced their origins to certain "root temples" in a manner similar to Sangren's Taiwanese temples, but the regional network of cults did not quite fit into the pattern of imperial place hierarchies. If Sangren's argument were applicable, then territorial temples in the city of Quanzhou would have all become the root temples of small temples and shrines in the prefecture's subject counties. But this was not the case. In the city of Quanzhou, only a limited number of *wangye* [kings or lords] temples were regional root temples. Most other territorial temples had their root temples in the countryside. These were mainly the Baosheng Dadi (God who Protects Life) temple in Tongan, the Linshui Furen (Goddess Lin) temple in Gutian, and the Qingshui Zushi (the Zushi God in Mount Qingshui) temple in Anxi. It seems that the lower-level places (in the subject counties of the prefecture) in the ideal imperial model were treated as higher-level places (those in the prefectural capital) in the popular territorial cults.

[12] The *pudu* festival was an occasion in which the *pujing* rotational divisions became the defining feature of social activities.

system. The rotational expulsion of ghosts was a series of ritual occasions in which different *pujing* sought to "purify" their territories. They were also occasions for them to mark the uniqueness of their own territorial identities. During the rotational celebrations, each *pu* or *jing* had its own territorial banner. In the first month, each territory had a special date for hanging its own banner in front of the territorial temples. The banner remained there until the end of the festival and symbolized the locality's territorial identity. The series of occasions in which it was raised and lowered were times for a *pujing* to sanctify its unity.[13]

In addition to *pudu*, in the middle of the Qing Dynasty, each *pu* or *jing* temple celebrated the birth and death (rebirth) anniversaries of one or more "lords" as they had in the past. These anniversaries served as neighborhood public festivals. At these events, offerings to gods were made in front of *pu* or *jing* temples, the gods' images were carried out from the temple to "survey" the neighborhood territories, and operas were sung day and night on the temple's stage. During the annual celebrations at the major Daoist or regional cult temples, *pu* or *jing* neighborhoods would go on collective pilgrimages to these great temples. They did this in order for their local cults to return to their root temples or to be recharged with new efficacy in larger temples. The key ritual of pilgrimage was procession, whereby selected local young men carried the images of local gods on the streets and marched together with all the household representatives toward the great regional temples.[14]

The Chaos of 1839

The fight between Fengle and Fengsheng was brought before the *yamen* to be treated as criminal offense. It was only one of numerous incidents during the nineteenth century. Although incidents like this were usual to many locals living at the time, they began to concern officialdom.

By the end of 1838, the degree-holding elites had developed among them an anxious hope for villages, urban districts and neighborhoods,

---

[13] Ke, Jian Rui, *Quanzhou Pudu Fengsu Kao* [An Investigation of Pudu Customs in Quanzhou], in *Quanzhou Jiu Fengsu Ziliao Huibian* [*A Collection of Materials of Old Customs in Quanzhou*], Office of Local Gazetteers, Quanzhou (Quanzhou 1985), pp. 143–150.

[14] Stephan Feuchtwang, who has worked in the same cultural area, has provided a useful conceptual framework in which Chinese gods and ghosts can be analyzed as two mutually constructive cosmologies of community. Gods define the public face of community from the inside, whereas offerings to ghosts serve to shape the same imagery of community from the outside (Stephan Feuchtwang, Domestic and communal worship, in Arthur Wolf [ed.], *Religion and Ritual in Chinese Society* [Stanford 1974], pp. 103–130). Popular religious practices surrounding the *pujing* system could be analyzed with this same framework as deity-ritual definitions of social space and communal identity.

and rural townships [*xiang*] to organize themselves into militias as parts of a joint force readily available to be mobilized in the empire's action against the foreigners. In the fourth lunar month of 1838, Huang Jue Zi pleaded not only for the prohibition of opium consumption but also for the promotion of the "mutually related *baojia* serial punishment system" [*baojia lianzuo fa*]. Concerning *baojia*, Huang Jue Zi wrote to Daoguang emperor:

> Please Your Majesty do urge all the governors in different regions to inquire into *baojia* registration. The governors should instruct the residents of their regions to organize together into multiple household units. If someone commits a crime, the residents should be allowed to report him. Those who report others should be awarded. Those who help hide or associate with criminals should be punished along with the latter.[15]

In the court, when Huang Jue Zi's propositions were endorsed as policy, Admiral Lin Ze Xu and his comrades in Fujian also began to gain more and more confidence in local *baojia* support for their campaigns. Apart from using *tuanlian*, local militia associations headed by gentry-scholars and captains, they also sought to exploit the less organized militia warriors, whom they called *xiangyong*. They hoped to develop a new source of power for the empire's self-defense by placing these usually unorganized *baojia* members in the midst of well-disciplined teams of warriors.[16]

Pujing territorial feuds had become ever more troubling to officials. The villages and urban neighborhoods used to have local administrative system. However, by 1839, the system seemed to be effective only when territorial festivals occurred. Certainly, in rural settings, these festivals went hand in hand with more substantial local political struggles for land, status, and power, but frequently these struggles degenerated into a form of chaos, which to some of the scholar-officials was far removed from these more "rational" considerations. What was worse, the feuds and chaos, accompanied by inner-factional protection and harboring, hindered the implementation of the "mutually related *baojia* punishment" policy, allowing opium smugglers to escape the *yamen*'s punishment. As "loosely dispersed" and mutually fighting groups, they turned out to be nothing like what was expected by the scholar-officials in the court.

In 1839, a few months after several senior advisors of the Daoguang emperor had submitted their memorial on the opium issue, Liu Yao Chun, a Shandong native with an imperial title, was sent to the city of

---

[15] Wang, Zhi Chun, *Qingchao Rouyuan Ji* [*A Record of the Qing Dynasty's History of Cherishing Those from Afar*] (Beijing 1989 [1879]), pp. 185–186.

[16] Philip A. Kuhn, *Rebellion and Its Enemies in Late Imperial China: Militarization and Social Structure, 1796–1864* (Cambridge 1980 [1970]).

Quanzhou.[17] This was also just a couple of months before Lin Ze Xu was appointed as Admiral to End the Practice of Opium Trade. Liu Yao Chun was assigned to a new position, the General Commissioner of the Military Regions under the old prefecture of Quanzhou.[18]

As a senior official siding with the anti-opium faction in the imperial court, Liu had in mind a Neo-Confucian model of order and control. He believed in the enterprise of organizing loosely dispersed local groups into well-organized local militia warriors [*xiangyong*] who could combat the challenge from the outside. However, in the first few days of his stay in Quanzhou, the situation there proved to be a lot worse than he imagined. When the ships of foreign merchant-military invaders[19] anchored in the harbor of Xiamen, a garrison-town and navy base under the Quanzhou prefecture, small-scale confrontations between the Qing army and the British broke out. Locals disappointed Liu Yao Chun. They did not join the Qing army to fight the foreigners. In the very prefecture, the presence of outsiders' challenge did not automatically yield his expected outcome, the spontaneous gathering of insiders' self-defending forces.

Quanzhou, a city renowned for its maritime trade for many centuries, had been one of the homes of opium smugglers since the eighteenth century. By the early nineteenth century, smugglers, secret societies, and corrupt officials had grown in numbers and notoriety. Now, while Lin Ze Xu and many patriotic officials were struggling against their rival political factions in the court for the sake of the anti-opium movement, many of these groups were enjoying the profits that they continued to accrue from the opium trade.[20] To make matters worse, just one day after Liu Yong Chun's arrival, internal rivalries connected with the old territorial *pujing* divisions once again broke out. During the first few days of his stay (in the fifth lunar month), the territorial communities of the city grouped themselves into the two rival factions of Eastern and Western Buddha. The feuds, or *xiedou*, which involved a hundred or so temple regions within the city and in the suburbs (especially in Nan'an and Jinjiang Counties), drew on social linkages that implicated different urban neighborhoods and rural villages into factional conflicts.[21]

---

[17] Fu, Jin Xing, *Quanshan Caipu* [*Picking Up Jades in the Mountains of Quanzhou*] (Quanzhou 1992), pp. 149–155.

[18] Including Xinghua, Quanzhou, and Yongchun (several newly designated South Fujian regions) and Jinxia (Jinmen and Xiamen).

[19] They demanded that the Qing court receive them as "free traders" instead of "tribute-givers."

[20] Zhuang, Wei Ji, *Jinjiang Xinzhi* [*The New Jinjiang County Gazette*] 2 Vols. (Quanzhou 1985), Vol. 2, pp. 294–303.

[21] Fu, Jin Xing, *Quanshan Caipu* [*Picking Up Jades in the Mountains of Quanzhou*], pp. 149–150.

Anti-opium campaigners rather optimistically viewed such neighborhood entities as potential sources for trained *xiangyong,* or local militia warriors, which could be channeled into a force defending the "inside" (*nei,* China) against the "outside" (*wai,* in this case, Britain). However, the alliances formed in feuds were not the sort of solidarity that Liu and his superiors would have desired. Instead of banding together against an external threat, they formed intracity divisions in which brotherhood associations brought the neighborhoods and their territorial cult organizations together to fight against their own kind.[22]

Eagerness to reduce internal divisions and enhance public order existed among the officials and scholars long before Liu Yao Chun promoted it. However, in the years around 1839, the "shape and propensity" [*xingshi*] of the celestial dynasty was different. Just a few decades before, a British delegation had been received in the empire's capital. At that time, the monarch and his court were still able to impose the ceremonial civilization of his Mandate on the foreigners.[23] By contrast, what was then known as "All Under Heaven" now became merely one of the many states [*wanguo*] in the world. After all the defeats at the hands of foreign barbarians, a late imperial academician wrote in 1892 reflecting on the two hundred years of the contact between the Qing and countries from afar. He could still beautify history in the name of "cherishing men from afar" [*rouyuan*]. However, long before him, many had been at pains to explain the loss of China's dignity in the face of those "little countries of dogs and sheep" [*quanyang xiaoguo*]. How to "be unified into one to face the foreigners" [*yizhi duiwai*] had been an issue for the scholar-officials, who began to realize the strengths of the "ocean (Western and Japanese) barbarians" [*yangyi*].

A few years later, China's defeat in the Opium War pressed such thinkers as Wei Yuan, the author of *Haiguo Tuzhi* [*Cartographic Gazette of Ocean States*], into the remapping of the world according to the new perspectives of military and political geography. As merely one of the many provincial governors who served the court during that difficult period of transition, Liu Yao Chun did not possess this sort of far-reaching and comprehensive of knowledge. He had heard from Lin Ze Xu about his

---

[22] As a mature scholar-official, Liu Yao Chun was aware of what historians now attempt to reconstruct. He grew up in Shandong where boat-gangs [*chuanbang*] coming northward from South Fujian had long organized along a mixture of kinship and territorial bonds of a Fujian type. In Shandong, in a rather patriotic manner (although also in consideration of profit), they competed against the incoming foreign religious, commercial, and military forces and impressed Liu Yao Chun as a courageous force. What confused Liu Yao Chun was that the same South Fujianese men who in those years were brave fighters combating the foreigners in Shandong were roots of the tree of internal chaos [*neiluan*] in their own homeland.

[23] James Hevia, *Cherishing Men from Afar: Qing Guest Ritual and the Macartney Embassy of 1793* (Durham 1995).

idea of cultural revitalization, but he was more interested in simply doing his job. Wondering how he could bring the feuds to an end quickly, he summoned all the local intellectuals to address to the problem:

> Feuds, illegal captures, and robberies are the most serious in Quanzhou. How can we solve the problem when it has been like this for quite some time? How can we prevent them from happening when they have developed into something like this? Should we bring the troops together and make extensive arrests? You all should put forth your opinions without disguise.[24]

Quanzhou's gentry-scholars had long been quite good at bureaucratic discursive exercises and political essay writing. Upon Liu Yao Chun's call, many of them presented their own opinions in the form of papers. These papers were combinations of historical-cum-social explanations and policy propositions. They were conventionally entitled as *ce* (usually translated as strategy, plan, or scheme, or more properly as strategic formula).[25] Somewhat disappointing to Lin Yaochun, none of these local gentry-scholars thought that extensive arrests should be made. Moreover, many presented strong evidence to show that the entire system of *pujing*, on of basis of which the feuds had developed, was the earlier prefects' invention.[26]

---

[24] Cf., Chen, Guo Shi (ed.), *Fengzhou Jigao* [*A Collection of Manuscripts from Fengzhou*] (Nan'an 1992), p. 469.

[25] It did not mean that Liu was fully supported by the whole scholar-official class of Quanzhou. However, it did mean that a widely shared attitude toward the social conditions in Quanzhou had evolved among the scholar-officials in the city. The attitude, or a state of intellectual and discursive mood, was developed not simply to fit into the court's call for the restoration of order. It was prevalent as a sort of response to the historically particular situations of change that were going in the direction of a culturally undesirable pattern.

[26] After more than 150 years of turmoil, the prefecture's file office [*dang'an guan*] in Quanzhou contains nothing about Liu Yao Chun's call and Chen Bu Chan's responses. Fortunately, a copy of a book called *Fengzhou Jigao* [*A Collection of Writings on Fengzhou*] compiled in 1904 by Chen Bu Chan's son, Chen Guo Shi, was rediscovered in the Library of Xiamen University. In 1992, in consideration of the significance of the book for local historical and cultural studies, it was reprinted with the support of overseas Chinese from the Fengzhou township and the Nan'an County Gazette Office. The reprinted version that is now available as an internal publication has two volumes, and it includes a great variety of writings by local officials and scholars from not only Fengzhou but also other parts of the Quanzhou prefecture from the Tang to the Qing Dynasties. In this book, Chen Bu Chan's two papers are included in full. Should the other corresponding papers become available, together with these two, they would make up an excellent reservoir of data with which the history, practices, and representations of *pujing* feuds could be more fully reconstructed. At this stage, Chen Bu Chan'a papers, although only two among many, provide sufficient information on the history and representations of territorial feuds.

As the scholars all wrote, the prefects in the old days, with the Kangxi emperor's permission, directly authorized the "congregations of gods," which later became the basis for feuds. Chen Bu Chan, whom we have quoted extensively on the matter of feuds, was among the scholars present. Chen and others were clearly aware of the fact that the problem of chaos on the southeast coast was not so easy to solve, because not all the people in this prefecture were "wise" [*zhi*] in the Confucian sense. In the *Analects* [*Lun Yu*], Confucius once said: "It is goodness [*ren*] that gives to a neighborhood its beauty. One who is free to choose, yet does not prefer to dwell among the good—how can he be accorded the name of wise" (Book Four: 1)? At that time, many people in Quanzhou did not qualify to be wise men in this sense; they were free to choose but did not choose to dwell among the good. They fought against one another out of a stubborn disregard for moral order, turning their neighborhoods into travesties of the good. While senior officials were eager to get rid of the feuding over night, to a local scholar-official such as Chen Bu Chan, who knew more about the temperament of the local people, a long process of reconstructing local administration lay ahead:

> The great constitution is as bright as the sun and the moon. So apart from resolving the disputes between a couple of wards, the magistrate should make a plan to rescue [local society] from a hundred years of bad customs [*loufeng*]. He should dig into the roots of the plan. Before feuds occur, he should call for all the chiefs of wards [*pu*] and militia trainers of *bao* and ask them to provide a list of the names of the hoodlums in the neighborhoods. In larger wards, ten names should be required; in a smaller one, five or six is enough. The magistrate then should keep a good record of the names of these troublemakers. He should display some of the name lists and instruct the residents to check on them. He should urge them to refrain from false accusations. He should levy heavy punishment on those who allow his kinsmen and neighbors to form alliances and join the feuds between the Eastern and Western Buddhas, if he can locate neighborhood members in his files. Surely, those who stir up trouble are the ward thugs [*pufei*], but there are also individuals who benefit from helping the gangsters to extort money from ward households and corrupt the *yamen*. They should also be punished like ward gangsters. The most effective measure is to pull the problem out by its roots and resolve it all at once. However, I am afraid that these wrongdoings have become deeply rooted in the hearts and minds of locals. They cannot be reversed just over night.[27]

Furthermore, Chen Bu Chan suggested that the magistrate should rely more on local lineage chiefs and *baojia* organizations. According to him, in the past, when the two factions began to fight, officials from

---

[27] Chen, Bu Chan, Shang daguancha Quanzhou Dong Xi Fo ce [A formula presented upward to his superior observer concerning the problem of Dong Xi Fo in Quanzhou], p. 467.

the *yamen* would immediately be sent to the spot. "They imposed light penalties those who stopped fighting first and harshly punished those who did not heed their advice and continued to fight." They did not know who were the real hooligans [*wulai*]. Now, to really solve the problem, in Chen Bu Chan's opinion, the *yamen* should transfer power to the neighborhood chiefs and rural villages who could deal with the matter better. He writes:

> I hear that in the ancient times there were officially recognized xiang governors [*xiangzhang*] and lineage chiefs [*zuzheng*]. The recognition of them constituted a classical method [for the resolution of local conflicts]. Thus, the magistrate should instruct the *xiang* and lineages to elect their own righteous and properly dressed. He should recognize their authority as governors and chiefs. He should allow these local doers of good to cultivate those who live close to them from time to time.[28]

However, what Chen Bu Chan proposed was not much different from what Wang Yang Ming did in South Jiangxi in the late Ming Dynasty. Policy formulas similar to this one became widely accepted in the decades of the late nineteenth century.[29] Available as conventional but newly implemented methods of local control, such formulas gained their popularity as ways of governing areas in which imperial state control had demonstrated to be ineffective.

Yet, scholar-officials such as Chen Bu Chan missed one important point that came to historians' attention only much later. Gentry rule as he proposed had from the late eighteenth century onward united with the militarized alliances of local communities in Fujian.[30] Throughout the decades of Shi Lang's wars against separatist regimes, they had grown into a regional force that was not only impervious to the imperial state but also conspicuously beyond the control of regional magistrates. Partly,

---

[28] Chen, Bu Chan, Cewen xiedou luqiang shi [Questions and answers concerning feuding, kidnapping, and robbery], p. 468.

[29] As a genre of writing, Chen Bu Chan's strategic formulas certainly drew heavily on Confucian discursive techniques. They were not structured in the form of modern scientific historiography, that is, written as policy propositions for the control of chaos in a period in which the position of China in the modern world was becoming a serious issue. In the two formulas (proposals), the author tried to answer the question of how the problem of feuds can be resolved. In so doing, he stressed the importance of reconstructing neighborhood control and public security work, which had been understood as critical to the making of an orthodox order since the emergence of Neo-Confucianism in the Song Dynasty. Thus, through an intellectual historical linkage, the proposal was well in line with Lin Ze Xu's project of revitalizing classical Chinese morality.

[30] Zheng, Zhen Man, Minghouqi Fujian difang xingzheng de yanbian: jianlun Ming zhongye de caizheng gaige [The transformation of local administration in late Ming Fujian: Also commenting on financial reform in mid-Ming], *Zhongguo Shi Yanjiu* [*Chinese History Research*], 1 (1998):147–157.

Dong Xi Fo was devised as a strategy to at once recognize these well-militarized secret societies and brotherhood associations and to neutralize them through involvement in religious festivals. The dilemma that Chen Bu Chan sensed mainly consisted of the unintended consequences of governor-general Lan Li's "geomantic arts." The formula of governing local worlds through local elites, however, did not generate good results for the imperial government or officialdom.

From the 1840s to the 1860s, local elite activism developed to such an extent that it came to constitute a large part of dynastic defense. The irony was that "it was primarily the local militarization" that "tipped the balance of power away from bureaucratically organized, centrally controlled imperial forces and toward personalistic, locally recruited irregular forces."[31] In addition, in places like the neighborhoods of Quanzhou City, feuds continued to have a heavy impact on local society. They did not stop when local elites gained control over local communities. On the contrary, in the later half of the nineteenth century, it was feuds that shaped the image of the region. Sometimes they emerged when localities were involved in controversies over land ownership, but more often they occurred when different localities fought to win honor for their native-places. In these examples, land ownership controversies were merely the expressions of local concerns over the symbolic patterns of their respective settlements. In the city, fights for such honors occurred mostly during the seasons of pilgrimage to central official state cults, Daoist, and regional temples.

Quite confused by local gentry scholars and, paradoxically, encouraged by their mentioning of Lin Ze Xu's formula, Liu Yao Chun accepted Chen Bu Chan's points. But before he seriously implemented a positive policy, the situation dramatically changed.[32]

In the same month that he made his call for local participation in his campaign again foreigners, Lin Ze Xu blockaded the section of Guangzhou city, where the British and Americans were based. He forced them to surrender opium that they had in hand and publicly destroyed it in entirety. A couple of months later, British troops landed on the island of Xiamen. Under Deng Yanzheng's leadership, Liu Yao Chun successfully

---

[31] Kuhn, *Rebellion and Its Enemies in Late Imperial China*, p .1.

[32] *Chongzheng Jing Shijin Bei* [*A Stele Inscription of the Pronounced Prohibition*] found in the ward of Shengde indicates that the government's prohibition of feuds was imposed. The document of prohibition was written on the sidewalls of the *pujing* temples. The stele inscription was carved in 1859. Prior to that, chaos had re-emerged, and a group of scholar-officials were approached by their related local elites to petition to the county government for a solution. In response, the county governor provided a pact of prohibition. See Kenneth Dean and Zheng, Zhen Man (eds.), *Fujian Zongjiao Beiming Huibian: Quanzhoufu Fence* [*Epigraphic Materials on the History of Religion in Fujian: Quanzhou Region*] 3 Vols. (Fuzhou 2003), Vol. 1, p. 385.

defended the town twice. But in a later battle, he escaped from the battlefield after a serious defeat and left no trace his later whereabouts. While Liu Yao Chun disappeared, celebrations and feuds in the wards and precincts of Quanzhou city continued to extend their horizons.

CHAPTER 10

The Ceremonial Redemption, 1840–1896

During the Ming, the local residents of Quanzhou suffered a great deal from the court's prohibition of maritime trade. But between then and the mid-Qing, offshore or disguised forms of trade prospered to help some recover from the loss. Despite all the political turmoil, maritime trade continued quietly at sea. Centered in Guangzhou and organized partly by the pirate kingdoms and partly by the government, trade in Chinese silks, nankeens, and porcelain for European silver advanced between the seventeenth century and the early nineteenth century. In the eighteenth century, the amount of tea exported from the southeast coast also increased to such an extent that more and more silver flowed to China.[1]

Historians in Quanzhou mostly date the beginning of their town's misfortune to the late Yuan catastrophe, but many of them also know that the year of 1839 brought even more dramatic misfortune. In the same year that witnessed Liu Yao Chun's campaign to eliminate feuds,

---

[1] Marshall Sahlins, Cosmologies of capitalism: The Trans-Pacific sector of the "World System," in *Proceedings of the British Academy*, lxxiv (1988): 1–51.

history began to unfold in a pattern different from the past.[2] The heroic struggles and defeat of the first generation of China's "modern patriots" were inscribed in the newly written national history of the "Central Kingdom." In this history, Liu Yao Chun's conscience, ambition, and tragic defeat are included as a tragic story belonging to the great legends of Lin Ze Xu and Deng Yan Zheng. It is precisely this sense of tragedy that also characterized the mood of cultural awareness in the city in the period following Liu Yao Chun's defeat.

The Shift in Regional Centers

To protect the interests of its own "national wealth," the British launched the Opium War from 1839 to 1841 and succeeded in making the Qing Court sign the first treaty. This treaty, along with several unequal trading agreements signed in later years, stipulated the opening of several coastal seaports in East China, in which the European nations, the United States, and Japan were entitled to substantial commercial advantages. The city of Amoy, the foreign name for Xiamen (literally, "gate of China"), one of the several small harbors in the Quanzhou prefecture, and the Mawei Harbor in Fuzhou—the provincial capital of Fujian—were selected as two of the first five treaty ports along the China Coast.

Paradoxically, it seemed that from around 1840 to the Republican era (ending in 1949), the southeast coast was presented with a new opportunity to re-create its ancient commercial glory and "multiculturalism."[3] When the treaty ports of Xiamen and Fuzhou "inspired the return of overseas trade and the reconstruction of urban systems,"[4] many Quanzhou merchants, smugglers, and transporters became actively involved in trade with the foreigners.[5] Nevertheless, the treaty port, once established, began to intervene in the old order of Chinese place hierarchy. The economic fortune bestowed on Fuzhou and Xiamen, where the treaty ports were located, bypassed the old abandoned harbor of Quanzhou. For

---

[2] Between the 1840s and 1895, the "Central kingdom" was defeated in several major battles against foreigners. The result was that not only did the foreign imperial powers have an important impact on the territories within their spheres of influence, but they also gained a high degree of control over regional transportation systems in China. Previously, transportation and communication were both under central State control. Now, foreign forces converted the ancient roads and courier postal routes into modern rail and communication systems. Furthermore, foreign delegations politically influenced even the highest level of decision making of the Qing.

[3] G. William Skinner, Presidential address: The structure of Chinese history, *Journal of Asian Studies*, 44(2) (1985): 271–292.

[4] Ibid., p. 279.

[5] Zhuang, Wei Ji, *Jinjiang Xinzhi* [*The New Jinjiang County Gazette*] 2 Vols. (Quanzhou 1985), Vol. 1, pp. 294–303.

Quanzhou, this geographic shift in regional "central place" diminished its former economic and political positions.

Xiamen, some 90 kilometers from Quanzhou, was only one of the many garrison-towns built in the late fourteenth century under Zhou De Xing. Prior to that time, it was merely a deserted island under the administration of Tong'an County, one of the several rural counties in Quanzhou.[6] Xiamen's earliest promotion to a metropolis was made possible by the pirate kingdom of the Zhengs, who resided there. Zheng Zhi Long and Zheng Cheng Gong based their power in Xiamen, where they maintained a military and commercial network between Fujian and Taiwan during the late Ming and the early Qing. Zheng Cheng Gong's "activities, like those of the Wokou in the sixteenth century, were a mixture of piracy and commerce. . . . He pillaged the rich maritime cities of the coast, extending his raids as far as southern Chekiang [Zhejiang] and northeastern Kwangtung [Guangdong]."[7] At about the same time, the "Red Hair" (Hongmao), a local name for the Dutch, sought also to establish themselves on this island. The Zhengs' pirate kingdom guarded the mainland from the Dutch invasion; the Dutch had to stay in Taiwan. But in 1665, they gained the opportunity to join the Qing troops. In a successful battle, they took Xiamen from the Zhengs. Although bestowed with honors for their assistance, they were still allowed to conduct only offshore trade. Xiamen was, even by the early reign of Kangxi, little more than garrison-town. Not until the Qing conquest of Fujian and Taiwan was Xiamen turned into one of Fujian's major coastal defense outposts (while it also secretly served as one of the many smuggling harbors in the region).

Established as a treaty port, Xiamen grew into one of the most open metropolises in China. Although the Quanzhou prefecture retained its high administrative rank, the rise of Xiamen's position as a peripheral center of the world system led to a great change in the regional hierarchy of centers and peripheries. The relative importance of Xiamen to Quanzhou grew out of a newly systemized spatial relationship between the region, the dynasty, and the outside world, which favored the new port and contributed to further the decline of the old port of Quanzhou.[8]

The co-presence of treaty ports and the remaining old prefectures in the late nineteenth century led to a state of affairs that was later characterized by Chinese patriots as "semicolonialization" [*ban zhimin hua*]. This peculiar form of colonialism had particular economic and

---

[6] *Xiamen Zhi* [*The Gazette of Xiamen*], compiled by Zhou, Kai (Xiamen 1996 [1840]), *juan* 8.

[7] Jacques Gernet, *A History of Chinese Civilization* (Cambridge 1982), p. 470.

[8] Such an transformation of spatial relations was further affirmed and to an extent reinforced in the Republican era (1911–1949), when Xiamen was formally separated from Quanzhou to become a separate administrative region (municipality).

cultural effects on the region. The new central places where Western footing was strongest acted like magnets, attracting capital and Chinese migrants. In contrast, in the old regional metropolises such as Quanzhou, industry and commerce were less advanced, and local economic and demographic resources flowed outward toward the new centers. The imbalance became even more pronounced when the development of foreign commerce gradually pushed the local economy into a kind of semicolonial dependence on the local segments of the world market.

The privileged position that the Christian missionaries enjoyed after the Treaty of Tianjin in 1858 created a more particular kind of friction. The people of Quanzhou were not at all ignorant of the existence of "other religions" in the world. In the Song and the Yuan Dynasties, they lived quite comfortably with the influx of foreign priests and religious followers, while maintaining their own deity cults. The Christian missionaries who came in the late nineteenth century, however, saw their doctrine as the *only* path of righteousness. Mutual intolerance broke out as a result of local resistance to such an imperialist view. Meanwhile, foreign cultural values and the industrial capitalism closely linked with these new ethics were appropriated into local political discourses, which in turn contributed to a new synthesis of the natives' view of history, in which the foreign was seen as the new and the powerful, the local as the traditional and the ideal, and mixtures of both began to appear in the national political debates.

Local economic and cultural responses to this change were, to be sure, diverse, and we should not pretend that all the local people consciously hated foreign imperialism. To those with a well-established tradition of commerce in Xiamen, and to those small fishing villages and harbors in Quanzhou, the coming of foreign imperialism brought new opportunities. Some of the local "opportunists" began to even engage in illegal opium trafficking. Some gentry enjoyed playing the role of compradors [*maiban*] in relations with foreigners, while hatred toward foreigners and their images advanced apace among other social groups. Although the existence of such more or less "relaxed" cultural attitudes was apparent, a kind of cultural self-awareness developed, and its self-contradiction became the central dilemma for later intellectual and political imaginations of identity.

Gernet characterizes this self-contradiction as follows:

> The desperate quest of certain intellectuals for a saving ideology in the Confucian tradition and the touchy conservatism of numerous patriots illustrate this reaction of national pride, which was so good in principle but so harmful in its effect. It was China torn apart—incapable of recognizing her own countenance, and soon led to deny herself—that foreign nations quarreled over from the last few years of the nineteenth century onward.[9]

---

[9] Gernet, *A History of Chinese Civilization*, p. 587.

Soon after the Qing defeat in the Opium War, several important intellectual attempts were made to reform the late imperial Chinese worldview. In the late 1840s, in Guangdong, Wei Yuan published his *Map-Gazette of the Maritime States* [*Haiguo Tuzhi*]. His work devoted forty-three chapters to the "six oceans" of the world. Wei already knew a great deal about Western geography and cartography. In the late seventeenth century, Matteo Ricci, an Italian Jesuit missionary, who ironically served as a Confucian scholar and advisor in China, had produced a world map in Chinese, and Wei had read it. He also read and translated many other maps in Western languages. However, although he was fully aware of the geographic divisions of the continents, he thought that the Western maps of the world were useless, because, as barbarians' products, they did not share the Chinese spirituality of Heaven. To fit the maps into the "Heaven-scape of China," Wei Yuan, influenced by the ancient Buddhist theory of four continents, rearranged the continents of the world into "prefectures surrounded by oceans" [*zhou*]. Relocating China in the middle of the world, he produced extensive descriptions of world geography. He intended to use them to enlighten the Qing emperor and to reorient China and revitalize its centrality. Although Wei Yuan took Western powers seriously, the strategic composition of his book argued for a regional world system that could benefit China. His view of the Chinese maritime empire included Southeast Asia, but Europe, Russia, and America were still regarded as the outer zones of civilization.[10]

Similar visions of the "Central Kingdom" in a new world order dominated most of the intellectual and political discussions of China's fate throughout the nineteenth century. In the 1880s, Kang You Wei first sought to revive Confucian ideas of the "turn of civilization" [*liyun*] and the "great unity" [*datong*] into a native theory of progress. The renewal of the Zhou ideal of civilization and cultural integrity was combined with Hegel's conception of history. In the last three decades of the nineteenth century, Kang You Wei, Yan Fu, Liang Qi Chao, and many other Chinese intellectuals began to undertake their attempts to synthesize Western evolutionist doctrines and Chinese cosmological concepts. Social Darwinism became one of their foci of attention, and Yan Fu became a creative proponent of Darwinist and evolutionary theory. Kang You Wei was both China's first prophet of progress and a critic of Darwin. Liang Qi Chao was a Chinese Huxley, insisting on a new kind of history of advancement. Each departing from a different perspective, they all attempted to translate Western evolutionism into a Chinese worldview. However, the concerns that first made them turn to

---

[10] Jane Kate Leonard, *Wei Yuan and China's Rediscovery of the Maritime World* (Massachusetts 1984).

Darwin and evolutionism was not particularly complex. It was simply China's weakness and turmoil that drove them to look for the evolutionist way out.[11] The questions that they struggled in common to answer were simply: "How can we be strong?" "How can we survive?"

The Salvation

To reconstruct the "structure of history" of the pre-twentieth-century southeast coast of China, Skinner presents an elegant model of a macro-regional development cycle in which Quanzhou played a central role.[12] Focusing his narrative on the temporal shifts and turns of economic central places, Skinner shows from his etic perspective how Quanzhou emerged and declined as a regional economic metropolis.

Anyone who has been drawn to Skinner's economic and geographic modeling might overlook his negligence of the natives' own sensational views of history. However, we should not forget that the "natives" of Quanzhou have not viewed the shifts in economic centers simply as changes in the objective regularities of economic loci. Over the past two decades, the Historians' Association of Quanzhou has published volumes of historical works analyzing the same regional processes of the city. In these local historical studies one can sense a sentiment that is lacking in Skinner's modeling. These narratives have also defined the period (from approximately the third to the fourteenth century) prior to the imposition of the ban on maritime trade in the early Ming Dynasty as a "golden age" [*huangjin shidai*]. But unlike Skinner, these local historians do not simply conceive of this period in terms of a history of economic development. The idea of "golden age" in their writings expresses a sentiment of mixed pride and sadness about the past.

Local historians in Quanzhou are aware of the fact that the Quanzhou-center cycle was replaced first by Zhangzhou and then by the Fuzhou-Xiamen cycles. However, they insist that the Quanzhou cycle of growth not only predated but also inspired the two later cycles of regional development. Many of these local historical studies have thus been so single-mindedly focused on the presentation of the "golden age" that it seems as if it is still "here." Other studies that have focused on the later stages of regional development have paid attention to foreign imperialism, but they have drawn conclusions quite different from Skinner's. This is due to the fact that while most local historians view it as a catastrophe, Skinner regards the coming of foreign imperialism as what "inspired" the new phase in the regional economy.

---

[11] James Pusey, *China and Charles Darwin* (Cambridge, MA 1983).
[12] Skinner, Presidential address.

In Quanzhou, local historical studies contain certain elements of regionalism, but this sort of regionalism is embedded in a larger-scale history. The larger-scale history incorporates a sense of regional pride and sadness and transforms it into a bigger complex of feeling about the fate of the "Central Kingdom," which several generations of Chinese intellectuals have sought to change. To Skinner, the emergence, expansion, and decline of Quanzhou as a center of "world trade" are nothing more than certain "cold" historical facts used to illustrate and validate his macroregional model. In local historical narratives, such processes are instead associated with the question of the "Central Kingdom's modern fate" as the key issue in Chinese civilization. They are regional illustrations of how the worldliness of China was replaced by a combination of late imperial "backwardness" and semicolonialism. This complex of feeling, which admittedly has induced certain "objective" treatments of local history, is as an expression of lament over late imperial decline and is deeply rooted in the perceived loss of the "Chinese Heaven" in the nineteenth century.

Closely related to the preceding discussion, more than a century ago, in late 1896, one year after the Qing's defeat in the Sino-Japanese War (1894–1895), a grand ritual of Universal Salvation was held in the City of Quanzhou at the Chengtian Buddhist Temple. Organized through the joint efforts of the local gentry, elders, religious specialists, and government officials, all households and neighborhoods in the city and its outskirts participated. The ritual was named exactly the same as an annual festival of *pudu*. or Universal Salvation, and was devoted to neglected ghosts. The special ceremony of 1896, however, was organized around the ninth and tenth lunar months as a special event instead of during the seventh lunar month, when the festival of *pudu* normally occurred. It was part of a religious campaign launched to overcome some of the catastrophes affecting local life. Created to mobilize urban households and neighborhoods into an integral whole, it also was meant to regenerate the power of the old empire in the aftermath of several defeats at the hands of foreigners. The Bureau of Prolonged Happiness (Yanxi Ju) in the Buddhist Monastery of Chengtian issued a proclamation specifying the purpose of holding this special ritual:

A few years ago, a great number of incidents took place in the coastal frontiers. The virtuous city [Quanzhou] suffered from disasters. Catastrophic fires left the city in ruins, and the remains of soldiers killed in action piled up in the wilderness. Small jokers [foreigners] performed the roles of great heroes. Their armies showed their capability in military campaigns. When the flags of war appeared, the sun and the moon lost their colors. When lethal weapons were drawn, the winds and clouds began to change. People felt great sadness for the turmoil of the city, just like animals crying for the death of their own kind; they cried for the coldness of the deserted country like hordes of dragons and tigers.

Later on, our army was able to demonstrate its strength. To the great
fortune of the people, we defeated our enemies and returned to praises of
our triumph. All the birds sang the merit of our generals and soldiers who
captured the enemies. People began to sweep away the signs of war and to
pave new roads penetrating the thorny wilderness. They came together to
plant new trees and grow new grain. The spring was to arrive on our great
country, and all people under Heaven were to celebrate victory. Nobody
expected our sudden defeat in the Eastern Sea.

Last year, the army went to war and returned without any victories. As a
consequence of the defeat, the southern frontiers had to defend themselves
against the encroaching enemies. The three islands of Taiwan had to be
erased from the map. The accomplishments of our officials and generals
were reduced to the necessity of letting the foreigners share our territory.
The will of Heaven had been so veiled so as to have not seen the devolution
of our military morale, and the small states of dogs and goats [*quanyang
xiaoguo*] were able to act with the force of wolves and tigers.

The people in Taiwan have long benefited from our country. They
have long lived in their home country, and so came to care for the beauty
of the rivers and mountains and feel ashamed of our allowing the savages
to put on human clothes. They thus opened their loyal hearts and joined
forces to fight for the country. They shaved their beards, realizing that the
empty words of Confucius had lost their effect. However, they lost control
of the situation, and the enemies took advantage of the opportunity and
invaded Taiwan. Although many tried to fight the savages, they were
swept up in a thousand tides of horror and found no rescuing poles for
their drowning lives. Their weapons lost their effectiveness, and their
drums lost their sound. Their troops were dispersed, and their lives came
to an end.

The mood of bitterness has now developed into a deadly epidemic. . . .
The atmosphere of war has nurtured catastrophic diseases. . . . In and
around the city of Quanzhou, the sky is full of poisonous air. All forms
of life die from breathing this wind. . . . People thus sigh like wild swans
to express sympathy for all the antlike lives. A wish has sprung up to
reintroduce auspicious clouds to the famous mountains of the five counties
and to turn the water in the two rivers into sweet droplets. The gentry and
elders have thus come together to pay their respects to gods. They propose
to imitate the ritual masters of the Zhou Dynasty in their exorcism of devils
and witches and to perform the Chu tradition of deity processions in the
hope of purifying the world. . . .[13]

Beginning on the twenty-fifth day of the ninth month with the issuing
of passes [*tongguan wendie*], which the roaming souls could use to enter
hell, the ritual itself began on the sixth day of the tenth month. The forty-
nine days and nights of the salvation ritual was performed in the Buddhist

[13] *Chengtian Wangyuan Pudu* [*Pamphlet Soliciting Contributions to the Great Universal
Salvation Ceremony at the Chengtian Temple*], Bureau of Prolonged Happiness (Quanzhou
1896), *juan* 1.

Temple of Chengtian and was divided into seven phases. During each phase, "all the men and women [from the city] were divided into rows and lines in front of altars where monks recited Books of Sutras." They were "instructed to refrain from making noise and to obey all instructions given by the ritual masters."[14] The seven phases of the ritual were intended to guide the lonely souls of the soldiers who died in action into the governed realms of hell, where all their sins [zui] were to be forgiven and all their misfortunes [jie] were to be transcended.

The 1896 ritual of salvation was a special ceremonial event that resembled a "revitalization movement."[15] As a dramatic moment in the cultural history of popular religious transformation in Quanzhou, it rose from the depths of historical experience as a "special kind of culture change phenomenon."[16] Organized with old or newly rehabilitated images, it was bound up with a sense of crisis, and it was to transcend the old millennium together with its mood of bitterness. The ritual was meant to reintegrate the disintegrated World Under Heaven by synthesizing collective mourning and religious demonstration of the native cosmological order. It was to bring about the sense of cultural integrity that paved the way for modern nationalism in China.[17]

Scholars are not certain whether or not the same kind of salvation ritual was held in other parts of China, but we are certain that the spiritual message it conveyed was widely shared by the Chinese. In the mood of sadness and the feeling of humiliation that dominated late nineteenth century Quanzhou there was seen on the one hand extreme cultural conservatism, clothed in the ceremonies like that of salvation, and on the other hand extreme modernism that viewed tradition as a "dish of loose sand" [yipan sansha] waiting to be integrated into a nation. The acceptance of modern social theories that originated in Europe as the medicine to cure China's ills paradoxically contributed to the resurgence of a tributary conception of other world cultures in the modern age. As Myron Cohen puts its, on the one hand, in order to create a new society and to justify its creation, "it also required that the 'old' society be defined in such a way as to provide the basis for its thorough rejection."[18] On the

---

[14] Ibid., juan 2.

[15] Anthony Wallace, Revitalization movements, *American Anthropologists*, 58(1) (1956): 264-281.

[16] Ibid., p. 264.

[17] Wang, Ming Ming, *Shiqu de Fanrong: Yizuo Laocheng de Lishi Renleixue Kaocha* [*The Bygone Prosperity: A Historical Anthropology of an Old City, Quanzhou*] (Hangzhou 1999), pp. 279-324.

[18] Myron Cohen, Cultural and political inventions in modern China: The case of the Chinese "peasant," in Tu, Weiming (ed.), *China in Transformation* (Cambridge, MA 1993), p. 151.

other hand, a sense of Chinese cultural essence was re-envisaged as the opposite of foreign imperialism.

On the national level, this ideological imbalance gradually evolved into a demand for extra-local solutions, which was in turn satisfied by the return of overseas Chinese sojourners who in the first decade of the twentieth century came to be formally identified as *huaqiao* [overseas Chinese] by the "constitutional monarchists" led by Kang You Wei and the Republican nationalists led by Sun Yat-sen. In a recent work, Prasenjit Duara observes that the concept of *huaqiao*, or the overseas Chinese, emerged in modern China's national politics as a desperately needed solution to the central problem in modern territorial nationalism, namely that "while it [territorial nationalism] is the only acceptable form of sovereignty in the modern world, it is an inadequate basis of affective identification within the nation-state."[19] To find a solution to the problem, nationalists turned to "the deracinated transnational communities" of the overseas Chinese for new energy.

Aftermath: The City without Walls

In the decades after the 1842 Treaty of Nanjing, Shanghai, previously a fortified town much smaller than imperial Chinese regional metropolises such as Quanzhou, expanded, together with the European settlements defined as "extraterritorial concessions," into one of the largest modern European-style cities in Asia. The provincial city Fuzhou, along with other four coastal towns, had also been established as one of the five treaty ports. By the end of the nineteenth century, it had grown into a large harbor-city. In the process, the city lost some of its own old city walls. Closer to Quanzhou, in the treaty port of Xiamen, and in small towns such as Anhai, similar kinds of development were seen. There, along with the expansion of imperious spaces, the partially destroyed city walls lost some of their old functions.

In the so-called semicolonized cities, the modern model of the city began to have an impact much earlier than in Quanzhou, which continued to be an imperial city until the second decade of the early twentieth century. In 1922, a local mapmaker still marveled at the greatness of the city walls in Quanzhou,[20] which were over nine *li* in length. Soldiers could still ride their horses on the tops of the walls when patrolling the city and its outskirts. The protecting walls formed a barrier much like the Great Wall

---

[19] Prasenjit Duara, Nationalists among transnationals: Overseas Chinese and the idea of China, in Aihuwa Ong and Donold Nonini (eds.), *Ungrounded Empires: The Cultural Politics of Modern Chinese Transnationalism* (London 1997), p. 19.

[20] Wang, Yu, Quanzhou Gu Chengzhi Pingmian Tu [Map of the old city of Quanzhou] (1922), *Quanzhou Wenshi* [*Culture and History in Quanzhou*], 2 (1980): 2.

in northern China, but they also had various openings that linked the city to the countryside. Seven grand gates were situated along the wall facing out in different directions from the city, each having its own name and own temple of the God of War (Guan Di Miao). Within the city, temples and government compounds stood out from their surroundings as imperial structures that signified the heavenly power of the government. In the streets, there were stone poles on which the good deeds of honored men and women were inscribed. Even in the small lanes, territorial temples generated their own symbols of greatness.[21]

However, during the same period when the city continued to be treated as a great symbol of the Chinese empire, the cultural attitudes of the intellectuals began to change.[22]

Near the end of the late nineteenth century, the Dutch ethnologist J. J. M de Groot was in Xiamen for eight years working for the Dutch East Indies Company, while also spending a great deal of time on his ethnographic investigation of "Chinese religion." Despite all "the hardships he endured on Chinese soil in collecting data during the best years of his life,"[23] de Groot was not only intrigued by local religious practices and cosmology as manifested in death rituals and temple festivals but also deeply involved in efforts to uncover the mysteries of local practices of the classical ceremonial tradition.[24] As he states in his book, he intended to compare the classical Chinese tradition and what he observed on the ground in order to gain a complete view of the religious system of China. For that purpose, he was selective in his choice of research subjects. As he said,

The customs described in this book as observed by the Chinese of the present day are by no means conformed to by all classes of society. As has been remarked already by the ancient Li-ki (Chapter 4, leaf 40), "the rites and ceremonies do not go down to the common people," whose means are small and manners rude. As a basis for our description we have selected the well-to-do classes and families of fashionable standing, amongst whom, in China, we chiefly moved, and these may be said best to maintain the whole system of the rites and ceremonies prescribed by the laws of custom.[25]

---

[21] Until the early twentieth century, Quanzhou did not cease to be proudly conservative. In imperial administrative maps, new cities such as Xiamen and Anhai were still designated as small garrison-towns subordinated to the rule of the superior officials headquartered in the prefectural city; and to the officialdom, their expansion was nothing more than a derivative of the new foreign-related heterodoxy. However, outside officialdom, political perceptions of culture had begun to change dramatically.

[22] Prasenjit Duara, *Rescuing History from the Nation: Questioning Narratives of Modern China* (Chicago 1995).

[23] J. J. M. de Groot, *The Religious System of China*, Vol. 1 (Leiden 1892), p. xv.

[24] Maurice Freedman, On the sociological study of Chinese religion, Arthur Wolf (ed.), *Religion and Ritual in Chinese Society* (Stanford 1974), pp. 19–41.

[25] De Groot, *The Religious System of China*, p. 2.

At approximately the same time in Quanzhou, Wu Zeng, a scholar with an imperial Juren title, who had absorbed some Occidental ideas of science, hygiene, and rationality, was also writing about local customs. Being from a "well-to-do" class, Wu Zeng himself suited de Groot's criteria for ideal research subjects: local elites who supposedly obeyed classical Chinese "Laws of Custom." However, from his perspective, unlike de Groot's, what he observed in local funerary rituals, temple festivals, and divination practices did not constitute an enduring manifestation of the classical tradition. It was, instead, a conglomeration of "present chaos" resulting from local people's confusion, irrationality, lack of hygiene consciousness, and feudalism, much like the Ming monarch's understanding of "licentious cults."[26]

The different attitudes of de Groot and Wu Zeng toward "superstition" deserve a further comparative analysis that can be pursued elsewhere. Here it suffices to say that along with the intensification of intellectual critiques of "superstition" and "feudalism" in the early twentieth century, the prior official view of the city encountered a challenge.[27] In the officially organized "universal salvation ceremony" held in 1896 intended to rescue those who died during the Jiawu Sino-Japanese War, the walled city was still praised in the eulogies recited during the ritual processes as what made Quanzhou great. Not long later, desires for change derived their power from the assumption that the premodern city, whose walls formed a self-contained world, represented a shameful "feudal history."[28] Critiques of Chinese city walls had been made between the 1850s and the beginning of the twentieth century together with critiques of geomancy. Near the end of the Qing, critiques of Chinese geomancy emerged among several

---

[26] Wang, *Shiqu de Fanrong* [*The Bygone Prosperity*], pp. 382–393.

[27] Prior to the publication of Wu Zeng's criticism of local tradition, the ancient ideal of Tianxia (All Under Heaven) had given way to a view of the degenerated Chinese cosmos. Many Chinese scholars and politicians believed that faced with the expanding Occidental empires, the only possible way out of imperial degeneration in China was to rebuild their country as a nation that could safeguard its territorial and cultural integrity against the "other" as enemy or rival. Struggles for "survival" in the world of the nations in which the Occident had already consolidated its hegemony became the most important supporting narratives for many outstanding scholars and politicians, whether they were constitutional monarchists, republicans, or communists. To first-generation Chinese nationalists, China urgently needed to complete a double-sided task: It should immediately resist external imperialism and reject internal "backwardness." For these reasons, "old China" [*Jiu Zhongguo*] was deemed out of date. It had been the "plate of loose sand" that had made China weak in the face of foreign incursion. The political foundation for such a "plate of loose sand" had been "feudalism," which radically differed from national unity, a precondition for modernization.

[28] A decade earlier, such an assumption had made an impact in Guangdong Province. Within ten years, as part of a new conception of a city, it was transmitted into Quanzhou and gained a certain degree of popularity among local officials, merchants, and scholars.

camps, principally including the missionaries and the Chinese technocratic Westernizers (Yangwu Pai). While the missionaries (both Western and Chinese) denounced geomancy for its "faulty beliefs" in order to spread Christianity in China, the earlier technocratic Westernizers saw geomancy as an obstacle to the construction of railways, roads, and electric works and to exploring for mines.[29] Gradually, the technocrats' critiques of geomancy were combined with critiques of traditional Chinese culture and the promotion of Western scientific and biomedical knowledge, as found in Wu Zeng's assault on "superstition," The city walls became core symbols of "feudalism," which the new generation of Chinese modernizers and revolutionaries felt needed to be done away with.

In the city of Quanzhou, the first generation of Republican revolutionaries were physicians, schoolteachers, and students trained in modern disciplines. In 1911, the Republican Revolution began in Guangdong, and these revolutionaries formed a "united front" [*tongyi zhanxian*] with one of the factions of late Qing military commanders to attack the prefectural government compound. In former garrison-towns such as Anhai, the Republican alliance organized into militias and established a new local government. However, such actions did not work for long. There actions were soon followed by the rise of feudalist warlords who preferred constitutional monarchism of the Yuan Shikai type. From then until 1922, the Republicans in Quanzhou engaged mainly in underground activities. In 1922, the Eastern Expeditionary Regiment of the Republican Army took Quanzhou and helped the local Republicans to establish a regional regime. Unfortunately, it lasted only a few months. For the next ten years, Quanzhou deteriorated into an area where competing Republicans, communists, and provincial warlords fought for political and military dominance.

Despite the fact that the major political and military groups in the Republican era did not actually agree on who should rule the country, they obviously shared a common concern for the creation of what we may call a "saving ideology."[30] This was a cultural vision that ironically fed on the destruction of "backwardness" [*luohou*] as manifested in the "superstition" of the people.[31]

Huaqiao, or overseas Chinese, as one other important political force were active in pushing the province toward forming a peaceful coalition. On the southeast coast, *huaqiao* were those who left their homelands in the Ming and Qing dynasties as a consequence of what Skinner called the "dramatic centrifugal effects" of the clash between economic decline and

---

[29] Guo, Shuang Lin, *Xichao Jidang Xia de Wanqing Dilixue* [*Late Qing Geography under Western Tides*] (Beijing 2000), pp. 267–288.

[30] See Duara, *Rescuing History from the Nation*.

[31] Wang, *Shiqu de Fanrong* [*The Bygone Prosperity*], pp. 361–362.

population growth.[32] As expected by the nationalist projects of identity politics, these partial-locals, as they were locally perceived, were to link the old and the new, the foreign and the Chinese. In Quanzhou, it was the *huaqiao* who led the Republican Revolution. They were the first generation to invest in the destruction of the imperial city walls, and the first to invest in the remaking of the city as something modern, industrial, and commercial.

Interviews with living elders who were actively involved in the politics of urban reconstruction,[33] coupled with miscellaneous documents kept by the Files Office of the current Urban Planning Department of the Municipality of Quanzhou, indicate that the imperial city walls of Quanzhou were mostly gone by the mid-1930s. The strong granite walls built in the Ming were torn down in the campaigns launched by different regimes to remake the city. The most destructive phases included the periods from 1921 to 1926 and between 1930 and 1932.

From 1913 to 1922, Quanzhou was controlled by a regional government aligned with the Northern Warlords (1912–1927). In 1921, the regime established a Bureau of Construction Affairs (Gong Wu Ju), appointing Zhou Xing Nan as its director. Zhou Xing Nan, a Cantonese, who had followed the KMT Army into South Fujian, was responsible for the radical reconstruction of Zhangzhou in 1920. Under him, Huang Zhong Xun, a wealthy *huaqiao* who had returned from Vietnam, prepared the first project of urban planning for the city of Quanzhou. The main objective of the project was to tear down the southern parts of the city walls and build a south-to-north thoroughfare, traveling across the bridge (Xin Qiao) over the Jinjiang River into the heart of the city. Zhou and Huang succeeded in knocking down many parts of the city walls and older buildings in the southern part of the city, but their plan to construct the roadway failed, owing to local residents' and merchants' resistance. His successor completed only 200 meters of road and encountered great obstacles moving forward. Soon afterward, in the winter of 1922, the regional government was overturned by the Eastern Expeditionary Regiment of the Republican Army from Guangdong, and the directors, engineers, and investors of Bureau of Construction Affairs mostly fled.

In the spring of 1923, several wealthy *huaqiao* visited Quanzhou and advised Huang Zhan Yun, the commander of the Eastern Expeditionary

---

[32] Wang, Gungwu, *China and the Chinese Overseas* (Singapore 1991), pp. 3–21.

[33] Wang, Lian Mao, Quanzhou chaicheng pilu yu shizheng gaikuan [The destruction of city walls and the paving of new roads in Quanzhou's urban planning], in *Quanzhou Wenshi* [*History and Culture in Quanzhou*], 2-3, 1980: pp. 33–39. See also Cai, Ruoshui, Quanzhou shizheng xingban chuqi qingkuang huigu (A look-back at the beginning of Quanzhou's urban planning), *Quanzhou Licheng Wenshi Ziliao* [*Historical and Cultural Materials in Licheng, Quanzhou*], 3 (1988): 20–24.

Regiment of the Republican Army, to change the "backward conditions" of Quanzhou. They pointed out that the Xinhai Revolution (1911) had taken place more than ten years ago. Many new things had emerged in other parts of the country. Even in the nearby towns of Xiamen and Anhai, considerable new construction had occurred. In contrast, Quanzhou, their hometown, still seemed relatively "backward." They suggested that a new Bureau of Urban Construction Affairs (Shi Zheng Ju) should be established to remedy this state of affairs. Following their advice, Huang Zhan Yun invited Ye Qing Yan, a Quanzhou native *huaqiao* living in the Philippines, to return home and serve as the director of the Bureau. Ye was the leader of Xinhai Revolution in South Fujian. In 1913, when Yuan Shi Kai inaugurated his Monarchist regime, Ye was assigned by the KMT Army based in Guangzhou to lead the Fujianese rebellion against Yuan Shi Kai. After having failing to accomplish his tasks, he moved to the Philippines to teach in a school. In early 1923, Ye accepted Commander Huang's invitation.

As the director of the Bureau of Urban Construction Affairs, Ye Qing Yan appointed Lei Wen Quan, a local young intellectual, who had just earned his Master's Degree in Architecture from the University of Edinburgh, as chief engineer. Lei was born in Nan'an County in Quanzhou. He also had a Philippine *huaqiao* background. He and his brothers had been educated in the British-Chinese School (Yinghua Zhongxue) located on Gulangyu Island in Xiamen before he went to Scotland. Prior to his appointment in the Bureau, he had worked as chief engineer at the Quanzhou-Anhai Motor Transportation Company, where he trained Quanzhou's first generation of modern architects.[34] Under Lei's direction, the Bureau prepared a design for the new city.

The ultimate aim of Lei's project was to make Quanzhou into a medium-sized modern city. In the plan, the new city of Quanzhou was to be based mostly on the new Zhangzhou with a small bit of Edinburgh thrown in. According to Ye Qingyan's memory, the key points of this urban construction plan were the following: (1) destroying all the city walls that hindered urban transportation, excluding a few temples and gate-buildings that did not influence the advancement of transportation, (2) constructing one north-to-south thoroughfare and four east-to-west streets that intersected the center of the city, and (3) constructing two-story buildings combining commercial and residential functions on both sides of the new roadways.[35]

---

[34] Cai, Quanzhou shizheng xingban chuqi qingkuang huigu [A look back at the beginning of Quanzhou's urban planning], pp. 17–23.

[35] Wang, Quanzhou chaicheng pilu yu shizheng gaikuan [The destruction of city walls and the paving of new roads in Quanzhou's urban planning], pp. 34–35.

Most aspects of the newly planned city looked more like those of the new towns in Guangdong and nearby towns such as Zhangzhou, whose streets had been "modernized" by lining them with newly built shop-houses that resembled medieval buildings from Mediterranean Europe. Curiously, Lei did not mention Edinburgh Castle. Excluding a great example of Occidental "feudal" architecture with which he was familiar when was in Scotland, he presented to Quanzhou a "progressive" image of Europe. He emphasized that streets should be more than 10 meters broad, sufficiently commercialized, and spacious enough for buses and trolleys to run smoothly. To finance the project, Ye and Lei gained some support from local merchants and *huaqiao*. To add to the budget, they also set up the stipulation that the granite from the city walls and the spaces previously occupied by the city walls could be treated as government property that could be sold to private owners. In addition, after the streets were paved or broadened, the spaces alongside them could be sold to those who would build their own shop-houses.

In the first couple of months of Ye Qing Yan's directorship, this project began to be implemented. Most the southern city walls were knocked down. Starting from northern end of the bridge across the Jinjiang River and moving northward, an 800-meter-long new street was built and was named the "Southern New Road" (Nan Xin Lu).

Unfortunately, soon after the street was completed, commander Huang led his regiment back to Guangdong, and Ye and Lei lost their support. Soon regional military leaders Gao Yi and Kong Zhao Tong successively took control of Quanzhou. They appointed new directors and chief engineers for the Bureau, but the new regime did not change the KMT government's plan. Under Gao Yi's rule, in late 1923 and 1924, New South Road was extended toward the north, making it 2,400 meters in length. In the process of construction, more old buildings and walls were torn down. In 1925, Shi Ze Cun, a local strongman, was appointed the director of the Bureau of Urban Construction. The four east-to-west streets designed by Lei started to be built. By 1926, the city walls and gate-buildings in the east, west, and north ends of the city were sold as construction material (granite) to local merchants and *huaqiao* for more funds to support road construction.

Between the winter of 1930 and the summer of 1932, the local gangster Chen Guo Hui came into power in Quanzhou. Soon he reappointed Lei Wen Quan as chief engineer. Under his office, the Bureau of Urban Construction continued to create more and more new streets and tear down more and more city walls. During this period, the trade in granite taken from the city walls became a popular business in Quanzhou. A group of merchants locally described as the "granite tigers" emerged. By the mid-1930s, some 60% of city walls were gone, and the remaining

40% were all torn down during the first year of the Anti-Japanese War (1937) under the instruction of the municipal military commander, who had just received the order from the Central Government in Nanjing to "evacuate the noncombatants" [*jianbi qingye*], that is, to tear down the city walls, which were seen as no longer being able to help defend the city in a modern war. The city walls reinforced during the Ming to protect the city against Japanese pirate-traders [*wokou*] now were weakened for their protection from a new threat.[36]

Many historical and sociological studies that examine the Chinese city in relation to the question of modernity have emerged in recent years. Especially deserving some attention here is the new collection, *Becoming Chinese: Passages to Modernity and Beyond*.[37] Editor Yeh Wen-hsin's introduction "highlights the city and the nation as the twin foci for the construction of Chinese modernity."[38]

In this book, different contributors consider different factors in the making of a culture—print culture, medical expertise, technologically powered forms of material culture, nationalism, individualism, new elitism, and so on, but they all seek to map the trajectories of Chinese modernity onto the traces of cultural novelty in the cities.[39]

> Cities in the first half of the twentieth century were high in that they held the commanding heights of most technological, cultural, and political change and low in their apparent inability to translate this advantage into a stable, urban based economic, political, and social system capable of governing China.[40]

This sentence from David Strand elegantly sums up one of the volume's key points about urban China's road to modernity. In the modern history of Quanzhou, one finds evidences to support this point. Indeed the central issue of the "modern" has been the "inability" of the rapidly rising "commanding heights" of the city to become a stabilizing factor. However, we can also see in all this a different reality. The so-called inability has an aspect of being a deliberately devised "destabilizing

---

[36] Wang, Quanzhou chaicheng pilu yu shizheng gaikuan [The destruction of city walls and the paving of new roads in Quanzhou's urban planning].

[37] Yeh, Wen-hsin (ed.), *Becoming Chinese: Passages to Modernity and Beyond* (Berkeley 2000).

[38] Yeh, Wen-hsin, Introduction, to his edited *Becoming Chinese: Passages to Modernity and Beyond* (Berkeley 2000), p. 3.

[39] For me, their approach is "accumulational" in the sense that they all search for the many new things that piled up in Chinese cities in the early 20th century, making up "Chinese modernity."

[40] David Strand, "A high place is better than a low place": The city in the making of modern China, in Yeh, Wenhsin (ed.), *Becoming Chinese: Passages to Modernity and Beyond* (Berkeley 2000), p. 99.

mechanism." The pursuit of modernity in Chinese cities was oriented radically against tradition.[41]

Represented as "noncombatants" that hindered communication, during the 1920s and 30s, the city walls of Quanzhou changed from imperial icons of protection and cosmography into a perceived manifestation of Chinese weakness. The walled city became a target of the sensational struggles against Chinese history. The destruction of imperial city walls was imagined as a revolution against the "confinements" of feudalism, which was, in turn, conceived as a necessary step toward the opening up and the self-strengthening of the region and nation.

In the process, the new social forces in Quanzhou, those of *huaqiao* revolutionaries, engineers, the Republican Army from Guangdong, and students in the new schools became locally active. These groups not only sought to break from the past by tearing down city walls but also actively participated in several campaigns to wipe out popular religious cults or what they deemed "superstition" [*mixin*].[42]

The destruction of the "feudal" derived its calling and ideological power from an ethos of historical optimism, which took technology as a precondition of economic growth and engineered communication as the prime characteristic of a modern state. Ironically, as Kirby has noted in a wider context, in economic terms, this was not rational. "The planned

---

[41] To restrict ourselves to a consideration of the accumulating new "heights" is to push aside things and patterns also excluded by the modernizing projects. A large part of what Strand calls "inability" derives from the discrimination and destructiveness of the urban "heights" themselves. In addition, I should emphasize that the destructiveness of the modern urban "heights" can be observed in other parts of Asia. In modern Asia, many great stories of social transformation can be told surrounding the concept of the city borrowed from the Occident. As a translated version, the concept of the modern city has its Asian expressions. On this issue, in his discussion of the global impact of the European city, Leonardo Benevolo offers a valuable comment. As he notes, in many parts of Asia, urban transformations stemmed from a stronger intention to make a break with local (national) pasts than those in Europe: in Europe, the modern city was regarded as "a state of mind, a body of customs and traditions" "based on an idealized conception of the creative medieval period." By contrast, in Asia, the model of the modern city has created a more definite discontinuity with its "premodern history," whether it was "tribal" or "Asiatic" (Leonardo Benevolo, *The European City* [Oxford 1993]), pp. 73–74.

[42] In 1923, 1926, and 1932, these new social forces organized three major campaigns against superstition. The first campaign was organized by the Eastern Expeditionary Regiment from Guangdong to revolutionize the city. The second was organized by students in *huaqiao*-related Liming College to destroy religion [*fan zongjiao*]. The third was organized by anti-Japanese military organizations to stop a religious parade organized by several popular religious temples aimed at eliminating deadly epidemics. See Su, Tao, Dageming hou Quanzhou sanci pomi yundong [Three antisuperstitious movements in Quanzhou after the Xinhai Revolution], *Quanzhou Wenshi Ziliao* [*Cultural and Historial Materials in Quanzhou*], 13, 1982: 172–180.

application of international technology under the leadership of hometown scientific and technical talent" was "gospel and ritual."[43]

As in many other civic endeavors, urban reconstruction projects relied on boosterism. The rebuilding of Quanzhou was imposed under the guise of the commercialization of the town. In fact, commercialization was nothing new to Quanzhou. Between the tenth and the early fourteenth centuries, Quanzhou served as a way station on the ancient Maritime Silk Road and gained a lot economically from this role. Those who advocated the new projects publicized their complaints against the old streets of Quanzhou, claiming that they were too few and too narrow. In fact, all the new streets they "planned" had already existed by the thirteenth century at the latest, and they were crowded, because commerce in the city was too busy.

The idealism behind the projects was hard to realize under the frequently shifting regimes. None of these regimes gained the legitimacy sufficient to put a new property law into practice. After the downfall of the Qing, the state was confronted with the issue of how to manage the old imperial spaces, including the city walls. It was also faced with the new mixture of old and new conceptions of property. Regional thugs took advantage of the ambiguity of property ownership to develop real estate or to facilitate trade with the other powerful groups. As Ye Qing Yan recalled in the early 1960s during an interview, in 1923 the Bureau of Urban Construction established the "Rules for the Management of Urban Construction Affairs" (Shizheng Guanli Guize). These rules turned the area of 15 meters along the sides of the city walls into so-called governmental property [*guanchan*]. To broaden the streets, the Bureau also tore down many private houses that stood in the way. In return, the owners of the private houses were given some compensation, but it was much less than what they expected.[44] There were many instances in which bureaucrats, local big merchants, and *huaqiao* practiced their own "rationality" by turning public projects into their private businesses. Thus, during this period, many accusations against "corruption" led to collective demonstrations. As Ye admitted, "without the military presence of the Eastern Expeditionary Regiment, the project would have been overthrown."[45]

In defining the targets of campaign, the new urban designers and politicians drew a sharp line between "feudalist culture" and the rest of the

---

[43] William C. Kirby, Engineering China: Birth of the developmental state, 1928–1937, in Yeh, Wen-hsin (ed.), *Becoming Chinese: Passages to Modernity and Beyond* (Berkeley 2000), p. 152.

[44] Wang, Quanzhou chaicheng pilu yu shizheng gaikuan [The destruction of city walls and the paving of new roads in Quanzhou's urban planning], p. 34.

[45] Ibid., p. 35.

Chinese tradition. Both the imperial city walls and "feudal superstition" were treated as "cultural survivals" of feudalism that prevented China from modernization. However, the new social forces maintained a conservationist attitude toward well-organized "institutional religions" such as Buddhism, Christianity, Confucianism, and Taoism. In the new urban plans, both imperial city walls and popular religious temples were treated as the targets of elimination, but these plans always stipulated that the magnificent old temples belonging to the great religions should be protected as symbols of tradition. While the division between "feudal superstition" and "religion" was taken for granted by the intellectuals and new politicians, it was harder to make among the people. The ambiguity of this distinction was also felt among the dominant groups, who often fought against one another over their own definitions of "religion" versus "superstition."

CHAPTER 11

Conclusion

In 1989, I returned to the city of Quanzhou, where I was born and grew up. But this time, I was here to study it as an anthropologist. Prior to my fieldwork, I had studied anthropological theories and ethnographic methodology in London. I was told by my teachers that conducting an ethnography of one's own society was unlike doing ethnographies of other places where the researcher naturally views the local society through the perceptive eyes of a stranger. In the case of anthropology at home, one should try to distance oneself from one's own familiar houses, relatives, friends, streets, and so on in order to gain the perspective of an anthropologist. I was not entirely convinced (I thought that the schools I attended had already detached me from home and created too wide a gap between me and my home community). But I saw no harm in experimenting with it in the earlier stage of my research. I looked for things unfamiliar to me. I acquired two maps, with the help of which I tried to gain a bird's-eye view of my city.

The first map was from a Qing Dynasty local gazette compiled in 1763. Strictly speaking, it was a cityscape. The second map was drawn by the newly established Office of Place Names in 1985, one year after the Maoist place names—such as "The East Is Red Road" [*Dongfanghong*

Lu]—were abandoned. Drawn in two very different time periods, the two maps of the same city looked quite different.

The imperial cityscape highlights the city's walls, temples, and government offices. Depicted like a walled kingdom, my home town, the prefecture's capital, is divided into several well-defined layers. These layers are patterned in a "heavenly" manner. Even if we just glance at it, we are able to capture some of the distinctive features of the prefectural residence of the empire. The inner or central layer is made up of the government compound. The middle layer is composed of a number of official temples symmetrically arranged along an axial line and in the quarters of the walled kingdom. The outer layer includes some unnamed spaces (urban wards and precincts) and is represented by the circular zone outside the city walls, on the outskirts.

The new map is equally "centralistic." In it, the headquarters of the current municipal government is located at the middle point (to the south of the late imperial government's location). However, the other layers of the city are not as clearly arranged as in the imperial map. Temples are indicated by small characters as "traces of the ancient times" [*guji*]. Having been torn down by the combined efforts of new elites—modern bureaucrats, architects, the Republican Army, returned overseas Chinese, and students—during the 1920s and 1930s, the extensive city walls and gates in imperial Quanzhou disappear on the new map. The names of gates are given as terms of direction and as place names. The new urban planning project has not yet been realized, but some zones of residential blocks and commercial areas extending far outside the confines of the old town have already been designated. Many street and neighborhood names that do not appear on the imperial map are now given significant positions. Even the large department stores have their locations marked on the small map. Visitors would find it useful as a practical navigational tool. However, with too many place names written on it, the new map looks so confusing that some locals complain that it is a mess.

The two maps contain representational symbols that hardly include any details about the "biographies" of places, with which most ethnographers are concerned. To one who had lived for years in the small neighborhoods of the city, what they provided was radically strange. Before I had attempted to do ethnography, I felt no need to wander around the back streets of Quanzhou. They became useful only now, as that which could make my hometown seem new and unfamiliar.

Sitting in my chair and trying to envisage what had shaped the patterns of Quanzhou's past, I took the maps to be important indexes of the processes of urban change.

Long before the Qing map was drawn, Quanzhou had already been charted by the imperial institutions of field administration, and between the tenth and the early fourteenth centuries, it developed into one of the world's major trading harbors. The question as to whether Qing cartography was a late imperial invention is debatable, but one thing seems to be certain: it embodied the late imperial official understanding of the place and its local worlds. Placing a heavy emphasis on the walls and the sacred layers of government and religious sites, the map was neatly in line with the political cosmology that incorporated the city into a system of rule. In this model of order, hardly any space is allowed for the neighborhoods and marketplaces that had contributed to the establishment of Quanzhou as a metropolis.

By the early twentieth century, Quanzhou had changed from a late imperial city into a modern town. Acknowledging a series of urban reform projects, the new map celebrates the triumphs of the twentieth-century regimes and their efforts to turn the city into a "garden" of modern culture. Despite its own status as a product of the postreform denunciation of the Cultural Revolution (1966–1976), it has continued the modernist line of "urban revolution." Beginning in the first thirty years of the twentieth century, through the combined efforts of several actors, the new designs of the city were inspired by "local knowledge" of the outside world. Transplanted from the West via the treaty ports, returned overseas students, and overseas Chinese [huaqiao] communities, these designs highlight the city as certain arenas in which the ancient glorious city fights to regain its prestige through the revitalization brought by modernity, understood as the creation of "open places."

The two maps that I acquired had not emerged out of nothing, and I was not unaware of the fact that the maps themselves contributed to the making of spatial worlds. What caught my attention, however, was the asymmetry between the maps and "reality." The imperial map seems to be a model of "feudal enclosure." Closed to the outside world, it structures the inside as an ordered space. One of its most outstanding features is the city wall, which seems so restrictive. Yet, it is within the same confines of the wall that the city advanced into its heyday of trade and "openness" during the Song-Yuan period. The new map illustrates a post-wall period in which the pursuit of an "open city" became a political calling. Nonetheless, as W. J. F. Jenner has observed: "Though most city walls have been torn down, the walled compound is still the standard way in which to organize a group of buildings."[1] "The openings in walls were never supposed to be many. For all the changes of the last half century, the state has wanted its subjects kept in boxes."[2]

---

[1] W. J. F. Jenner, *The Tyranny of History: The Roots of China's Crisis* (London 1992), p. 83.
[2] Ibid., p. 101.

During my year of fieldwork, I concentrated on the co-presence of the "cultures" of the nation, the region, and the neighborhoods of the city, but since then I have also spent a great deal of time studying archival and archaeological materials that I began to research in the mid-1980s as an archaeology student. I imagined that the trajectories of history, in particular, the transformation of a site of empire into a modern town have left deep marks not only on the geography but also on the social worlds of contemporary Quanzhou. I felt that a study of these trajectories could shed important light on the interrelationships between the past and the present.

In Quanzhou, historical materials have proved to be "too rich." After reading through some of Quanzhou's abundant archives, I have come to believe that Quanzhou was not a slowly moving "cold society." After one sifts through the history of the "city of archives," a portrait of a constantly changing "hot society" gradually emerges.

I have not been insensitive to the "holes" in the archives. "Archives are cultural artifacts which encompass the past and the present."[3] That is to say, the authors of these files are historical actors. As such actors, they both write and make history. Read in the present, they are not merely "facts" but also meaningful expressions.[4] However, encouraged by the new definition of ethnography as "a historically situated mode of understanding historically situated contexts,"[5] I have gained a new understanding and appreciation of these historical materials. As I have found in the city of Quanzhou, different portions of different books portray the history of the prefecture from different perspectives. They are undoubtedly incomplete, and they are not free from official State or local elite biases and distortions. But they offer a wide range of accounts of people, politics, government, economy, official ritual, and popular culture, and, for my purposes, these "interviews with the dead," as Maurice Freedman called them, can be used to revise, enrich, complicate, and deepen interviews with the living.[6] In an attempt to develop my own form of historiography, I have worked with both kinds of "interviews."

In using these materials as the basis for a historical anthropological study, I have decided to focus on an institution of spatial organization, that of *pujing*. This institution has certain similarities to what anthropologists

---

[3] Bernard Cohen, *The Bernard Cohen Omnibus: An Anthropologist among the Historian and Other Essays* (New Delhi 2004), p. 48.

[4] Emiko Ohnuki-Tierney, Introduction, to her edited *Culture through Time: Anthropological Approaches* (Stanford 1990), pp. 1–25.

[5] John and Jean Comaroff, *Ethnography and the Historical Imagination* (Boulder 1992), p. 9.

[6] Maurice Freedman, The politics of an old state: A view from the Chinese lineage, in G. William Skinner (ed.), *The Study of Chinese Society: Essays by Maurice Freedman* (Stanford 1979 [1974]), pp. 334–350.

of China have called "territorial cult communities." Having survived many historical twists and turns, it has continued to survive locally in "popular religion." Its historical figures have not receded, and in the social life of present-day Quanzhou, they are still observable. Having witnessed all the important events in local history, *pujing* contain a great deal more than the ethnography of the place can reveal. These contents are both historical and cultural. In order to "decode" what has been "encoded" in them, I have organized historical and ethnographic materials around the long genealogy of *pujing* and attempted to reconstruct the interactive drama of imperial cosmologies and local worlds. But where have I arrived after having taken such a long trip back to history?

The City in History

The "premodern" Chinese city is not a new topic for research; on the contrary, it has attracted much attention in recent years. In sociology, anthropology, and history, it has been analyzed from a variety of perspectives—the locations of imperial political structure,[7] the "princely residences" where the aristocracy of imperial China was situated,[8] the nexus points in regional networks where rational economic choices were made that influenced the surrounding periphery,[9] and as "public spheres" in which political viewpoints were expressed and commercial regulations were formulated.[10]

Each of these phenomena finds its own trace in the relics of Quanzhou—a former way station along the tributary trade route, a prefectural capital during imperial times, a center of the "great tradition" of the urban elites, and the site of many temples bridging official and local notions of the "public" [*gong*]. Likewise, the relics of small temples on street corners and in narrow lanes of the city also display an equally complex history. After one inquires into the history of *pu* and *pujing*, one sees that the full significance of the urban forms of Quanzhou emerge only when analyzed in relation to each other. For lack of a better phrase, the complex of processes can be tentatively described in terms of the "structure of conjuncture."

This model comes from the work of Sahlins, who has equipped the concept with an interpretive power. It refers to what goes beyond the

[7] Yang, Kuan, *Zhongguo Gudai Ducheng Zhidu Shi Yanjiu* [*A Study of the Institutional History of Capital Cities in Ancient China*] (Shanghai 1993).
[8] Max Weber, *The Religion of China* (New York 1951).
[9] G. William Skinner, Cities and the hierarchy of local systems, in his edited *The City in Late Imperial China* (Stanford 1977), pp. 275–353.
[10] William Rowe, *Hankow: Conflict and Community in a Chinese City, 1796–1895* (Stanford 1989).

"relation between a happening and a structure," that is, "the practical realization of the cultural categories in a specific historical context, as expressed in the interested action of the historical agents, including the microsociology of their interaction."[11] In developing our own approach, we have also made reference to Sahlins's differentiation between the "islands of history" and the *polis*, a comparison that has helped us to articulate the conjuncture at the heart of the concept of the Chinese city [*cheng* and *shi*]. However, this comparison cannot fully capture this dynamic. In a lecture, Sahlins tried to apply his historical approach to imperial China where, as he has argued, the tributary mode continued to reenact, even in the "early modern" contact with the "world system," the cosmology of relationship.[12] I do not doubt that his reconstructed cosmology of the inside-outside relationship can be extended to historical horizons well beyond the early Qing, but I do not intend to transplant it into the "soil" of China where, unlike the case of "the island of history," local history had begun to be written by the "natives" long before the emergence of "the modern world system."[13]

Several millennia prior to its contact with the West, China had already developed a system of writing, and civilization and had developed its own modes of "facing the other." Written Chinese histories have brought with them historical scenarios of both change and continuity. Can the anthropology of history founded on the culture of the "barbarian chieftains" be useful to an ancient civilization such as China?

In the previous chapters, we traveled through a long history where we discovered more specific details of Quanzhou's transformation. In the past, the city as an enclosure and the city as a nexus of social exchange interacted to make history. Its transformations amount to the changing characters of what I have referred to as the two "gestures" of the city, realized in the interactions of agents, the emperors, the magistrates, the merchants, the scholars, and the commoners.

Previous local historical studies including the present one have all focused on the theme of the "bygone prosperity" of Quanzhou. Undoubtedly, the heyday of commerce has its eye-catching characteristics deserving scholarly attention. By leading us to ponder over the fascinating cosmopolitanism of the old town, this theme carries its own intellectual

---

[11] Marshall Sahlins, *Islands of History* (Chicago 1985), p. xiv.

[12] Marshall Sahlins, Cosmologies of capitalism: The Trans-Pacific sector of the "World System," *Proceedings of the British Academy*, lxxiv (1988): 1–51.

[13] If I have understood him correctly, ultimately Sahlins is concerned with anthropology as a human science, in which the interrelationship between "words and things" is differently constituted symbolically in culturally differentiated histories. See Sahlins's well-grounded critique of "rationality" in his reaction to Gananath Obeyeskere's objection to his form of cultural anthropology in his *How "Natives" Think, about Captain Cook, for Example* (Chicago 1995), pp. 148, 190.

inspirations. But in the end, we have chosen a theme different from the dominant voice of the heyday. Guided by the "official" and the "social" maps to the transformative system of *pujing*, we have reviewed the past through a different kind of historical commemoration.

Our narrative began by calling for a reconsideration of the notion of "bygone prosperity." We have been obsessed with a paradox: just when the city had entered its heyday, the restrictive system of *pu* was established. To an extent, *pu*—the earlier version of *pujing*—had laid the localizing spatial framework for the Ming court's civilizing project. After that, changes occurred in this system, the most important ones involving the imperial State, regional officials and elite, and popular re-appropriations of locality.

Quanzhou is one of many regional metropolises of China, all of which have their own distinctive characteristics. In our study, we have focused on a part of urban life—that of the "low places" enclosed within the walls of the regional city. These places may seem excessively local in the present, but in the past they were closely related to supralocal processes—the imperial and macro-regional dynamics that became integral to local social life especially when the city was incorporated more fully by the empire. The advantage of focusing on what we have viewed as the conjuncture of empire and region is that it can begin at the tangible level of local historical specificities and extend from there to larger horizons of space and time.

But in Chinese history, there is a pattern. This so-called pattern is not a line connecting the past and the present via a "one-way street" of time. It contains an element of "mythological time" in the sense of Sahlins's "islands of history," in which a structure of relationship is conceptualized in terms of the shifting tendencies of social categories extended to incorporate twists and turns in history. Nonetheless, a more dynamic perspective of changing time-spaces has caught our attention. In a way, the chronicles of the city could be seen as something resembling the life cycle of an organism: the tail of carp, or a place as a life form that grew, matured, and aged in the cycle of the region. As I argued from the outset, the cycle of the region is but one strand of a much larger history. As a regional metropolis, Quanzhou emerged only when China entered its "late imperial phase," at the point of transition in which the expansion of the empire's tributary system was coupled with an anxious political pursuit of a "Chinese Renaissance." Even within the same period, in a rather linear pattern, as that of the Renaissance, history went down a "spiral road."

Two ways of patterning history from the "natives' point of view" are available. The large-scale history of the dynastic cycle is often conceived of as an alternation between the sagacious and their others, the "confused emperors" [*hunjun*]. From time to time, when a nativistic discourse gains dominance (for example, during the Ming), the "confused emperors" often referred to the late Yuan and the late Qing "barbarian rulers," who harmed the integrity of the civilized world of the Chinese. When a more cosmopolitan culture was advocated, a more self-reflexive mode of history was deployed to honor the great emperors of the Mongols and the Manchus—for example, Hubilie of the Yuan and Kangxi and his successors of the Qing.

Alternatively, from a regional historical perspective, the "fortune" of the city was most sharply reflected in local folklore. The city gained its life and vitality from its *fengshui* propensity. It flourished when it was allowed freedom and withered when it was confined and suppressed by imperial networks of local control. The city was revitalized at times when the loopholes were created in the imperial "net."

In our own narrative, the two perspectives of time and politics are intertwined in a pattern. As an anthropologist, I have hoped to simultaneously exercise in historiography and practice a folkloric display of local worlds to reveal the "structure" of temporalities of the Chinese city. My historical narrative has incorporated elements of the folkloric in which the cycle of the sagacious and the confused emperors is played out in the drama of the Carp. I have also provided a historical comparison with which to relate the cycle to other times and places. In presenting these narratives, I have concentrated on the fusion of different cycles.

The narrative ends in 1896, treating the post-1896 periods merely as an "aftermath" of that year. But neither did the history of *pujing* end in that year, nor did *pujing* cease to play a role in marking out boundaries after the grand sacrifice to ghosts in the late Qing. Intended as a means of redemption for Chinese lives and culture and as a way of transcending the "plate of loose sand," which *pujing* was thought to represent near the end of the empire, the grand sacrifice continued to highlight the internal territorial divisions that have, perhaps to the disappointment of the State, prevailed into the twentieth century. Up to the twenty-first century, the issue of the interrelationship between unity and diversity has thus continued to worry Chinese politicians.

In spite of our concentration on "ancient times," or, particularly, on the period between the thirteenth and the late nineteenth century, we have not turned away from the implications for the present. Just like the local chronicles of prosperity, the history of "low places" like *pujing* also takes in the concurrent historicities of the present. Among these, the most powerful one treats the beginning of time as the end of the "ancient" empire and at the moment of transition to a nation, in which the "Central Kingdom" began to be "condemned" and to "condemn itself" to "modernize." Modern historicities of discontinuity deserve critical reflection, and I seek to provide that by way of structuring time in a different way. The usual forms of "presentism" and "afterology" treat the present as determining the past. Visiting different locations of the past, I have instead explored the borders of local worlds, where we have found a different story.

Great Tradition, Enemy Within

When I was inquiring into the story of *pujing*, some local historians were aware of its historical significance. However, most of them remained satisfied with their own surveys of the materials. From their perspective, the culture of historical Quanzhou amounts to nothing unless it is a cumulative display of prosperity and civilization—a "museum" in which all the different cultural forms, items, products, relics, historical figures, and so on are exhibited as tangible proof of Quanzhou's prosperous past. The spirit of the past, as one of the advocates of *Quanzhouxue* [Quanzhou-ology] puts it, is the cultural vitality of Quanzhou, which not only gave Quanzhou a past but also promises it a new future.[14]

To local historians, "Quanzhou culture" [Quanzhou *wenhua*] matured around the tenth century, when the city became commercialized. "Quanzhou culture" was not of the usual sort. It was characterized by a special kind of "inclusionist ethos" that made possible Quanzhou's absorption of several non-Chinese cultures. It made it possible for the "museum of religions" (including Confucianism) and the "low culture" of folk cults to come together in a unique synthesis. As local historians know well, "Quanzhou culture" in that sense existed only during the golden age of the harbor, chiefly, in the Song and the Yuan Dynasties. Although commerce persisted throughout the imperial period, owing to late Yuan ethnic conflicts and early Ming policy changes, Quanzhou suffered from a drastic turn of fortune, the result of which was the transformation of Quanzhou from a nexus of maritime trade to a camp of imperial offices, official temples, and state cult statues. As local historians sometimes also admit, during the Ming and the Qing, the people of Quanzhou became more "conservative," or, as they now put it, "feudal" [*fengjian*] and "backward" [*luohou*].

Narratives such these can be seen as partially true. However, as I pursued more research among "dead interviewees," I began to have more doubts about what has been taken for granted locally. What has made locals nostalgic for their past has been the expansive moment of maritime trade continued, in the past thirty years, to honor the city as an

---

[14] Fu, Jin Xing, Potuerchu de Quanzhouxue [Quanzhou-ology breaks out of the ground], *Quanzhou Wenshi* [*Quanzhou Culture and History*], 10, 1989: 10–15.

important place. Biases against Quanzhou's "degeneration" have made local historians forgetful of the process whereby the world harbor was transformed, against the wills of local historical actors, into a "backward place."[15]

In today's Quanzhou, at least in the official discourse, the late imperial history of the Ming and the Qing has come to be associated with the growth of local religious activities that are regarded as a manifestation of Chinese "backwardness" and denationalizing "feudalism" and, thus, in opposition to modern Chinese civilization. The distinction between the "progressive" and the "backward" made within the same "Quanzhou culture" leads to the bifurcation of history.

Since the 1980s, the cultural landscapes of Quanzhou have dramatically changed. "Tradition" [*chuantong*], "heritage" [*yichan*], "culture" [*wenhua*], and whatever is simultaneously associated with the greatness of "being Chinese" and "being the people of Quanzhou" are now highly valued by government officials. Concepts of "local worlds" [*xiangtu*],[16] which, according to the non-Chinese critic Prasenjit Duara, emerged in the broader context of "East Asian modernity," have, in the post-Mao era, gained ascendancy in the cultural hierarchy of the state. As sites of "authentic values—embodied particularly in the native place—of a larger formation, such as the nation or civilization,"[17] senses of local places have been promoted together with political sentiments of patriotism. Given this new attitude toward the past, the Bureau of Culture (Wenhua Ju), a department in the municipal government in charge of cultural work, has been assigned to protect relics of Chinese tradition treated as "places of superstitious activities" just a few years ago. In so doing, it has listed some old temples in its cultural projects. Local operatic and ritual performances are organized to sanctify China's national holidays, both old and new. In this same postreform period, most households have re-created their domestic shrines for ancestor and deity worship. In the public spaces of the city's neighborhoods, dozens of temples of different sizes, names, and deities have been rebuilt. Marked out during deity-cult and ghost-worship

---

[15] In 1983, the editorial board of *Quanzhou Wenshi* [*Quanzhou Culture and History*], the major journal for Quanzhou studies, organized a discussion on the decline of Quanzhou's prosperity. But the debates did not end up with historical reflections on the Han ideological projects through which the city was reshaped in the Ming. They focused either on geographic causes or on Mongol repression.

[16] In this study, I have also deployed the concept of "local worlds," but I do not intend to limit its meaning to *xiangtu* [rural soil]. The sense of locality that I seek to "map" also involves those of open extensions, networks, and festivity, which are considered as integral to "local worlds" in Quanzhou.

[17] Prasenjit Duara, Local worlds: The poetics and politics of the native place in modern China, in Huang, Shumin, and Hsu, Chengkuang (eds.), *Imagining China: Regional Division and National Unity* (Taipei 1999), p. 161.

festivals, the old boundaries of *pujing* have survived in the memories of the local people.

However, "traditional culture" has been divided into two parts. Officially, the concept of "superstition" is still used by the mass media to describe the "backward" parts of the same culture. Although a great amount of time has passed, what worried the cadres in Mao's time has continued to make the Dengist reformers anxious. In particular, the system of territorial temples, their deity cults, and the festivals connected with *pujing* have continued to be denounced as manifestations of "feudal superstition."

Why has there been such a tension between old territorial communities and the re-invented traditions? We can find an answer in the very concept of "society" itself. According to Liang Shu Ming, who compared Chinese cults with his notion of a unitary "Occidental religion" [*xifang zongjiao*], the structure of Chinese religion accounts for why the Chinese have had enormous difficulties in establishing their modernity. He argues that the Chinese people have been so divided by their kinship and territorial boundaries that a transcendental order [*chaoyue*], which had been, for centuries prior to the modern age, available in "Western religion" to facilitate societal modernization of Europe, has been entirely lacking in the "religion of China" [*zhongguo zongjiao*]. Liang argues that in order to modernize China, a sense of transcendental order is needed as a cultural prerequisite.[18]

Liang Shu Ming's argument was quite original, because he was one of the first to point out the "symbolic roots" of European bureaucracy that have only recently come to the attention of anthropologists.[19] In his lifetime, however, Liang Shu Ming was uninterested in the scholarly pursuit of precision. His purpose was the advocacy of a theological metaphor of transcendence in China, through which he hoped to change the character of the Chinese into one suitable for a modern national culture.

Not all modern Chinese thinkers and actors perceive the issue in the same way as Liang Shu Ming. But the pursuit of what the great nationalist thinker has called a "transcendental order" has persisted in different aspects of Chinese political life since the early twentieth century. Up to the present, the same tension between *pujing* territorial cult areas and what Liang Shu Ming has referred to as "transcendence" has remained. For example, the revival of "superstition" in Quanzhou has been followed by yearly campaigns forbidding territorial celebrations (despite the fact that efforts to stop "superstitious activities" are often not successful).

---

[18] Liang, Shu Ming, *Zhongguo Wenhua Yaoyi* [*Core Meanings of Chinese Culture*] (Taipei 1983 [1949]).

[19] Michael Hertzfeld, *The Social Reproduction of Indifference: Exploring the Symbolic Roots of Western Bureaucracy* (Chicago 1992).

A decade ago, I wrote a thesis on this problem.[20] I related the "antisuperstition" campaigns to the self-assertion of national culture. I depicted the mutually oppositional festivals in contemporary Quanzhou as consisting of several contesting calendars of ritual—the territorial temple ritual calendars, the annual cycle of the Bureau of Culture's "cultural events", and what can be called the "bureaucratic spectacles" of national holidays.[21]

The government's treatment of *pujing* as part of "feudal superstition" is *pujing*'s most recent fate. But how new is this attitude on the part of the government? An answer to the question demands a historical explanation, and the historical explanation in turn needs to be formulated on the basis of a reconsideration of several issues. In what specific historical processes and for what political reasons did these territorial cult areas emerge and change? In what ways have the connotations of territorial communities changed over time to become "distained" by the modern regimes of the twentieth century and early twenty-first century? From a broader historical perspective, what can account for the two modern regimes' attempts to eliminate "superstition"? Our observation that *pujing* as a system was sometimes official and politically rational and other times treated as "licentious cults" and manifestations of "superstition" leads to

---

[20] I was, then, keenly interested in what I would now call the "ethnographic excavation" of historical commemorations. I focused my attention on the ways in which *pujing* territorial divisions have served to contest two other sorts of spatial concepts. I explored how persistent territorial festivals connected with *pujing* cult areas have existed as a kind of spatial concept in which households and communal "havens" have been constructed in opposition to "the spaces for the local presence of the state." I also investigated the manner in which the newly established Bureau of Culture has treated *pujing* festivals and regional culture.

[21] Territorial festivals, which are based on the old calendars of the gods' birthdays, formulate a ritual calendar in which spatial concepts are implicated with reference to specific localities and families. In contrast, both the annual cycles of the national holidays and the major "cultural events" organized by the Bureau of Culture are based on the state-designated modern and Western-derived "public calendar" [*gongli*], which has located traditional lunar and solar occasions in the new calendar as reference points. They jointly provide a time schedule for work and leisure. However, the annual cycle of "cultural events" that the Bureau of Culture organizes is more about regional tradition, which, as the cadres in the government maintain, is part of China's national tradition. In spite of its regional characteristics, in the official discourse of culture, this tradition has been most closely associated with the heyday of regional development during the Tang, the Song, and the Yuan Dynasties, which also constitutes the core subject matter of Quanzhou studies. The contesting calendars, in which different histories are ritualistically invoked, attest to, in a local way, distinctions, interactions, and contests between the "great and little traditions." From the perspective of modern cultural theory, the politics of culture are bound up with the tension between "modern culture," which has extended into "old societies" and the "little traditions of communities," which have, paradoxically, persisted in the age of modernity.

a more general historical question: why did some "reigns"—including the modern "reign" of Mao—seek to abolish *pujing* while others did not?

Answering such questions is critical not only to the understanding of the geography of public life in the city but also to our patterning of historical trajectories. Thus, I have dedicated many years to studying *pujing*. In the course of my study, I have amassed a sufficient body of archival materials. Some of these materials are found in local gazettes and official dynastic histories, most of which are literary extensions of the official designations of local administration. Other materials include those loosely dispersed in personal writings, stele inscriptions, political proposals, gazettes of customs, and biographic narratives. Among these, some are by well-known authors; others are written by those that have only left obscure traces. My data has also been enriched by ethnographic observation of remaining and reconstructed *pujing* temples in which a vivid sense of religiosity is still strongly felt today. Together these materials constitute a database from which a history of *pujing*'s changing "faces" can be reconstructed.

The boundaries now marked by "superstitious activities" have been out of date since the Republican redistricting of local administration in the 1930s.[22] But if we return to the age of the Yuan, we would see that *pujing* was invented as a brand new system of territorial control, integration, and exploitation. The locals, classified as *Nan Ren* [Southern Peoples] during the Yuan, were colonial subjects ruled by the Mongols and their Persian associates. They lived in these strictly controlled neighborhoods. To them, these arbitrary territorial divisions were administrative weapons of the government. Both the Yuan district organization could, perhaps, also fit into local old estates in "the preceding dynasty" to a certain extent, but they were intended to transcend them. Even in the Ming Dynasty, when the city was in the hands of the Han, what the monarch imagined as good for peace, order, and morality were not derivatives of local people's own senses of place. In short, the territorial segments of *pujing* were imposed from "above," from the court far away. The intended functions of *pujing* were "mutual watch" and "self-government," just like those of the neighborhood committees of the present. These organizations were far from unofficial, deviant, or "superstitious."

---

[22] With the establishment of the modern Chinese nation-state in 1911 and the implementation of the new place administration policy, the imperial *pujing* system was abolished. Between the 1920s and 1940s, *pujing* as an administrative institution was replaced by the Republican *baojia* system. In the earliest phase of Communist rule (1949–1958), a new district [*qu*] and street [*jie*] system replaced the *baojia* system. After "collectivization" and until the end of the Cultural Revolution (1958–1976), urban spatial divisions were modeled on rural communes and brigades. These divisions were finally renamed "street offices" [*jiedao ban*] and "resident's committees" [*juwei hui*] during the Reform Period.

By the Qing, when what were once viewed as "licentious cults" (and now redefined as "superstition") extended into the public realms of the city, *pujing* remained official, orthodox, and rational. Still serving to help collect taxes and organize local self-government, it continued to be described in the Qing gazettes as an administrative apparatus. Some of its popular religious aspects were condemned as "licentious cults," but many other aspects were deployed in the strategic game of the "congregations of gods," the spectacle featuring the regional union of power elites and local thugs. The same story prevailed until the year 1839. Despite the fact that *pujing* divisions were producing so much chaos, conflict, and bloodshed, the scholar-gentry and imperial officials still hoped to harness their military energy to combat the "ocean barbarians" [*yangyi*].

The alternating roles of *pujing* highlight that which has been conceptually "fixed" in modern times was, in the past, dynamic and transformative. In the six centuries in which *pujing* existed as an officially endorsed institution the system was constantly adjusted to a continual and self-renewing pursuit—that of imperial transcendence over locality. It is ironic that this sense of transcendence was expressed in the politics of locality in which civilians were confined to their own neighborhoods.

In imperial times, few emperors enjoyed seeing their subjects moving around the country freely. In the imperial ideal of demography, transcendence worked best when all the people were kept in charted places. Among the emperors, Zhu Yuan Zhang, the Ming monarch, was the most anxious advocate of this model. While his cosmological projection was one of the most fully formed in ancient China, he imposed a policy among the subject populace that ran contrary to his own understanding of cosmic transcendence. He sought to restrict the movement of the bodies of his subjects to within one *li*, which was, of course, not only extremely impracticable but also "de-nationalizing."

Compared to this self-acclaimed native Han emperor, the "enlightened despots" of the Mongols and the Manchus were much less inclined to this dream of a "farm garden" sort of moral order. In both the Yuan and the Qing Dynasties, there were fewer discussions of the mutual watch of subjects. In the Yuan, instead of surveillance, a lot of energy was invested in the direct rule of the Nan Ren colonies. In terms of *pujing*, the Yuan's policy best fits the administrative place theory, and it allowed an extensive scope of class-divided rule. During the Qing, looser control was imposed on places, and local competitions for power were encouraged.

Thus, the only dynasty that sought to find a perfect political language of locality was the Ming. Our interest in Ming Quanzhou partly derives from the observation that the Ming was a time in which the prosperity of commerce gave way to bureaucratic spectacles of power. However, had I not inquired ethnographically into modern cultural politics, I might have not viewed the Ming as so important a transition. Modern Chinese cultural politics have also relied heavily on a planned language of locality, and like the Ming, the modern regime of the People's Republic has been faced with a serious tension between its vision of civilization and "licentious cults" (now termed "feudal superstition"). I now turn to an analysis of the concept of "civilizing process" in an attempt to explain the similarities between the two historically distant "dynasties," and in doing so I hope to find a cultural interpretation in the historical comparison.

"Civilizing Process" and Popular Religion: Comparative Perspectives

The Ming "civilizing Confucianism" involved strong elements of moralism, and such strong elements of moralism made it different from European civilizing missions. "Civilizing Confucianism" in the Ming did not lack an emphasis on a popularized "high culture," nor was it short of militarily and culturally maintained boundaries. However, it was, in the end, not extended into the fields of legal practice. Legal practice was embedded in moral judgments of right and wrong and was therefore subordinated to the "rule of ritual" [li zhi], the designated proper ways of doing things, or what James Watson has called "orthopraxy."[23] Hence, unlike the European "punitive practices" described by Foucault, the Ming legal system was encompassed by the ritual models that I have depicted as "sanctive practices." In the concept of "sanctive practices," gods, ancestral spirits, and ghosts jointly served to govern and judge people in the afterworld. The ethico-moral character of the early Ming "civilizing process" was bound up with the ways in which late imperial China continued to pursue a unified empire, which in Europe gave way to newly formed absolutist regimes of old feudal estates.

Elias argues that a prerequisite development for the civilizing process in Europe took place in the twelfth and thirteenth centuries. It was the addition of a new social group—the bourgeoisie—into the power struggles among different social groups, including the nobility, the church, and the princes. The outcome of these struggles was the establishment of provincial princes as independent kings of different estates and, then, as absolute kingly monarchs, which emerged to ease the tension between the nobility and the newly emergent "bourgeoisie." The civilizing of conduct increased along with the rise of the despots' power to facilitate the formation of a hierarchical social order, with the absolute ruler and the court as its head.

---

[23] James Watson, Rites or beliefs? The construction of a unified culture in late imperial China, in Lowell Dittmer (ed.), *China's Quest for National Identity* (Ithaca 1993), pp. 80–103.

The critical phase of the civilizing process was accomplished in France in a few centuries of development, where, compared to Germany, the barrier between the nobility and the bourgeoisie was weaker and the ties between them were increasingly stronger. Elias describes the process as the following:

> The most influential courtly society was formed, as we know, in France. From Paris, the same codes of conduct, manners, taste and language spread, for varying periods, to all other European courts. This happens not only because France was the most powerful country at the time. It was only now made possible because, in a pervasive transformation of European society, similar social formations, characterized by analogous forms of human relations, came into being everywhere.

Elias continues:

> The absolute-courtly aristocracy of other lands adopted from the richest, most powerful and most centralized country of the time the things which fitted their own social needs: refined manners and a language which distinguished them from those of inferior rank. In France they saw, most fruitfully developed, something born of the similar social situation and which matched their own ideals: people who could parade their status, while also observing the subtleties of social intercourse, making their exact relation to everyone above and below them by their manner of greeting and their choice of words—people of "distinction" and "civility." In taking over French etiquette and Parisian ceremony, the various rulers obtained the desired instruments to express their dignity, to make visible the hierarchy of society, and to make all others, first and foremost the courtly nobility themselves, aware of their dependence.[24]

In the city of Quanzhou, during a corresponding period of time, a new merchant power was also emerging, but it was not a distinct "bourgeoisie" but part of the Yuan Dynasty's race-class system of hierarchy in which non-Chinese merchants such as the powerful Persian Pu Shou Geng gained hegemony over the regional economy. In the late Yuan, efforts were made to establish a separate state in the prefectures of Fujian. But they were made by Persians against the Mongols and by the Han against the Persians and Mongols, and they resulted in the pursuit of a unitary empire desired to end separatist "chaos."

During the Ming, the "Central Kingdom" did not disintegrate into separate regimes governed by an absolute monarch. History ran in a direction contrary to that of Europe. The emperor, the only monarch in a vast continent, sought to establish himself not only as emperor but also as sole king who assumed all the charisma of the sagacious. In Europe,

---

[24] Norbert Elias, *The Civilizing Process* (Oxford 1994), p. 267.

bounded sovereignty became possible when it came as a consequence of the disintegration of a unified historical empire. By contrast, in China, it was in the reunification of the empire, which was first accomplished by the "Sinicized barbarians," the Mongols, and then, further consolidated by the Han-centric imperial state of the Ming, that bounded sovereignty found its foundation. Empire was retained, and the absolutist rule of the monarch was consolidated by extending the bounded sovereignty of the despot-king throughout the whole of empire.

In the Ming, the division between the nobility and the "bourgeoisie" was even less visible. In fact, one may doubt whether they constituted two separate social forces. The Ming situation can more or less be characterized as a valiant failure of both groups in the face of the monarch's autocracy. Certainly, as we have shown, the monarch did seek to establish what the great French Sinologist Jacques Gernet has defined as a "Renaissance" of classical China.[25] Yet he did not do so by presiding over the contesting groups of the nobility and the bourgeoisie. Instead, he tried to realize his dream of the perfect union of the empire by endorsing Neo-Confucian ideals of order as common rules of conduct for the radically diverse social groups of peasants, craftsmen, "industrialists," merchants, and scholar-officials.

The concerns of modern nation-builders had already occupied the imperial rulers from the very beginning of the first Ming emperor's reign. The "integrative revolution," a term many apply to refer to the modern pursuit of national transcendence over "primordial ties,"[26] had been sought after in different ways in pre-Ming China. But even if pre-Ming history is not considered, the Ming, whose "official religion" drew heavily from Song scholastic Neo-Confucianism, possessed the most obvious official civilizing culture. This culture continued to be desired at later stages of history, particularly in the late nineteenth-century discourse of redemption and the twentieth-century revolutions and nation-building projects.

In the twentieth century, transcendence has taken on new characteristics. For instance, the national holidays are a special form of order. In cooperation with workplaces and hierarchical state institutions, they become "bureaucratic spectacles" set aside from traditional ritual. If we adopt Don Handelman's thesis,[27] we would argue that these new spectacles are modern. For Handelman, bureaucratic spectacles are mirrors that reflect the formative power of the statist bureaucracies to shape, discipline, and control social order. As such, they gain meaning mainly

---

[25] See Chapters 4 and 5.

[26] Clifford Geertz, *The Interpretation of Cultures* (New York 1973), pp. 255–310.

[27] Don Handelman, *Models and Mirrors: Towards an Anthropology of Public Events* (Oxford 1998).

by differentiating themselves from traditional ritual, which predicted and monitored change with its own operations. From our perspective, if bureaucratic spectacles are a form of national culture, they would also refer to a special sort of transcendence. In this form of transcendence, the ensuring mechanisms for the displays of the orderly supralocal nation are paradoxically the regionalized work unit and time schedules and the uniquely local chronicles of prosperity.

In modern China, transcendence has also been advocated in the broader scope of "cultural self-awareness" [*wenhua zijue*].[28] However, as Liang Shu Ming suggests, this sense of transcendence derives chiefly from comparative cultural studies that conceptually separate China from the West. Although this conceptual framework for comparison renders China all too different from other cultures, territorial divisions connected with "superstition," the opposite of science and the modern way of life, such as those in the *pujing* system, are regarded as the "unofficial culture" that makes China lacking in integrity and solidarity.

Not to deny that fears of disintegration had existed among the emperors and prefects ever since the "Central Kingdom" began to write its history, we should emphasize the point that from what we have seen in the city of Quanzhou, these worries tended to be more pronounced in the late imperial dynasties. These fears can be partly explained simply by the emperors' pursuit of unifying authority or authorized unity, but the rapid accumulation of such worries in the Ming and the Qing Dynasties should be considered also in the context of the expansion of popular religious cult organizations, which had ironically been inseparable from the Song and the Ming's promotion of the sagacious and the divine.

In our analysis of late imperial China's quest for cosmic knowledge and social order, we have drawn on Gernet's thesis of "the Chinese Renaissance" and Qian Mu's idea of "Civilizing Confucianism."[29] After the "medieval prosperity of foreign religions," the post-Song religious constitutions seemed a lot more Sinicized. The Sinicization of the Buddhist ghost festival in the Song provides a good example.[30] However, what we have observed in the city of Quanzhou suggests a more complex phenomenon. Although Sinicization had already begun by the Northern Song, in the coastal margins of the Central Kingdom, religious coexistence and mutual tolerance developed. Not until the Ming did the forceful imposition of Sinicization exert pervasive influence on local ritual landscapes.

---

[28] Fei, Xiao Tong, Fansi, duihua, wenhua zijue [Reflections, dialogues, and cultural self-awareness], in Ma, Rong and Zhou, Xing (eds.), *Tianye Gongzuo yu Wenhua Zijue* [*Fieldwork and Self-Awareness of Culture*] (Beijing 1998), pp. 38–54.

[29] See Chapter 4.

[30] Stephan Teiser, *The Ghost Festival in Medieval China* (Princeton 1996).

In the city of Quanzhou, the rapid and wide diffusion of popular religious cults in the late Ming was driven paradoxically by the court project of Sinicization. The outcome of the Ming's assertion of official religion was what has often been characterized as "timeless," enduring imperial official cults, as Stephan Feuchtwang outlines:

> The official imperial cults were organized as part of territorial division of the empire, centered on administrative cities down through provinces and prefectures to counties. The objects of the imperial cults were meant to include everything below the level of the county. At each level of the official hierarchy there were, outside the walls of each administrative city, altars to objects which were equivalents of the emperor's own prerogatives: heaven and earth, rivers, mountains, winds, rain, grain. Below the imperial capital, there were the local rivers, mountains, rain and winds, and two altars which had a particular standing in relation to subcounty territorial cults. One was for the ghosts located there, the Altar for Those-Who-Died-Without-Future [Li tan]. Tablets of carved and inscribed words naming each of these categories were kept in the temple of the administrative city's Wall and Moat (City) God Temple. They were taken out of the city to the altars on the prescribed days of their rites.[31]

In the early Ming, these locations were worship platforms established on the borders between local communities of *pujing*. Gradually, they became "public properties" in which popular territorial cults and ghost festivals established themselves in different locales. For the court, all the local halls, temples, pavilions, and altars were to be maintained in line with the projected extension of the civilizing orthodoxy of the state. By the late Ming, however, these spaces had already accommodated all sorts of "licentious cults." Campaigns to eliminate these cults persisted until the end of the Ming. Not until the early Qing, when such regional heroes and academicians as Shi Lang, Fu Hong Ji, Li Guang Di, and Lan Li became the major players in the "theater state," to adopt a term from Geertz,[32] were these cults re-admitted into the officially promoted "congregations of gods."

During the early Qing, Quanzhou seemed to have an opportunity to revitalize what we may call the "Carpist spirit." The regional elites and court academicians brought about a certain degree of compromise between official and local modes of ritual. Yet, even in this historical period, a middle stratum serving to link the local to the monarchy and thereby

---

[31] Stephan Feuchtwang, *The Imperial Metaphor: Popular Religion in China* (London 1992), p. 63. In the previous chapters, I have argued that some of these locations of divinities had existed prior to the Ming and that their cosmological models had been available in the post-Han *jiaosi* system. But their cosmological and religious perfecting started in the early Ming.

[32] Clifford Geertz, *Negara: The Theater State in Nineteenth-Century Bali* (Princeton 1980).

integrate the nation, which was characteristic of European modernity, was not developed in the city.

According to Robert A. Schneider, in Toulouse in southern France, a city with a history of trade similar to that in Quanzhou, in the late fifteenth century and the early sixteenth century, a new elite formed, composed of powerful magistrates belonging to the parliament of Toulouse and wealthy pastel merchants. The cultural and social ties binding this elite to the urban populace persisted for nearly two centuries, and the city's public life maintained its local character. In the late seventeenth century, these vertical ties began to break down. The elite also turned away from local concerns to absolutism and Parisian culture. Simultaneously, social tensions between economically differentiated groups of the rich and the poor increased. The city became cosmopolitan in the eighteenth century, and Schneider describes this process:

> Many elites, especially royal magistrates, began to see themselves as actors on the national, rather than local, political stage, and royal patronage of the local academic movement reinforced this trend. Increasingly the ideal life of the elite was fashioned after the ways of Paris. These and other changes created the conditions for the cosmopolitan city that emerged in the eighteenth century, a city marked by a combination of greater refinement and expanded festive life, and armed surveillance.[33]

In Quanzhou, the late seventeenth century also witnessed the elevation of local elite identities with the supralocal court. These local warlords, the power elite, achieved their status through either the imperial examination system or, more important, military campaigns against the remaining Ming forces. They, like their counterparts in Toulouse, forged ties to connect themselves upward with the court. This bottom-up structure of vertical tie formation, however, did not diminish their relations with regional society, and they did not fashion their lifestyle in accordance with the Manchus in Beijing—who in fact regarded themselves as "barbarians" receiving civilization from the colonized Han. As in Toulouse, festivity in Quanzhou increased and was directly promoted by the elite. This festivity, which Robert Weller has termed "hot and noisy religion," did not result in the making of a cosmopolitan city. Instead, as exemplified by the "congregations of gods," it operated mainly to celebrate competitive regional vitality. Through this show of vitality, the openness of the Qing Empire was also displayed. However, in the end, these rituals became little more than an excuse to show off local strength—as manifested in feuds and "Carpist spirit," which we discussed in Chapter 2.

---

[33] Robert A. Schneider, *Public Life in Toulouse, 1463–1789: From Municipal Republic to Cosmopolitan City* (Ithaca 1989), p. 359.

Conflicts between official and popular "religions" have always emerged soon after the assertion of official religion. And equally explainable was the fact that the post-1839 existence of *pujing* has, as the official discourse in different periods depicted it, been ever more worrying than the previous times. Feuds that began to evolve in the late Ming did not worry the early Qing prefects who were happy to see locals fighting among themselves, unwittingly, to benefit the regional elites' and the court's consolidation of power. Yet by the mid-nineteenth century they were regarded as harmful to the "national solidarity" of the "Central Kingdom." For the whole of the twentieth century, in order to unify the "plate of loose sand" that was China, feuds were deemed ever more serious offenses to national integrity, but they have yet to disappear.

The Fate of Sinological Anthropology

As some elderly witnesses still recollect, from April of 1949 onward, the People's Liberation Army successfully defeated the Kuomintang (KMT) in several battles and reached the Lower Yangze Valley. In Anhai, a garrison-town initially built to guard the frontier of the Ming Dynasty, a group of communist revolutionaries, the Central Fujian Regiment, arrived at a festival for the local goddess Tianhou's birthday. There they mobilized some of the ritual participants, turning the temple festival into a drama of violence by attacking the KMT army's local compounds, and they succeeded in wiping out the KMT army and assuming control of the township.

A few months later, in the City of Quanzhou, the commander of the Communist Central Fujian Regiment sent an agent to the Buddhist monastery of Chengtian Si, the location of the 1896 salvation ritual, where the regional KMT troops were then stationed. The agent persuaded the KMT army commander in Quanzhou to rebel against the KMT. By August of the same year, except for a small number of police and soldiers who had escaped from the city to Jinmen and Taiwan, the few remaining groups of KMT army officers had fled to the mountainous counties of Anxi, Yongchun, and Dehua.[34] On September first, a Temporary People's Government (Linshi Renmin Zhengfu) was established in Quanzhou. Two days later, General Ye Fei, a returned overseas Chinese who had joined the Communist Party of China (CPC), led the Tenth Army of the People's Liberation Army (PLA) into Quanzhou, where he joined the Minzhong Regiment and merged his army with the Temporary People's Government, forming the New Regional Government.

---

[34] There, upon the instruction of Chiang Kai-shek's intelligence organization, they recruited and armed some of the local landlords, farmers, and bandits to fight against the new government in hope of Chiang Kai-shek's return, but the other remaining KMT forces were recruited into the PLA's 87th regiment.

On the first of October, Mao Ze Dong announced to the parading
crowds assembled in Tiananmen Square that "the Chinese people have
now stood up." Prior to his speech, the PLA had assumed control of
all mainland regions other than Tibet. Most ministries and government
organizations were pre-established in the Taihang Mountains on the border
region between Hebei and Shanxi before the Central Party Committee
moved to Beijing. In the mountains, the date of the establishment of New
China had been carefully chosen, and the ceremony of "inspecting the
parading army" [yuebing] in Tiananmen Square and along Lasting Peace
Street (Changan Jie) had been pre-arranged.[35]

While the "sent down to the south" cadres [nanxia ganbu] and
local activists in Quanzhou were busily involved in the intensive labor of
building a new local society, in the new capital city of Beijing, the new
statesmen worked day and night on the construction of a new nation.
Learning from the lesson of the late Ming peasant rebel Li Zi Cheng, who
became a corrupt emperor, the new regime sought to put the country back
on the tracks of "lasting order and long peace" [chang zhi jiu an]. For
this purpose, the principle of "long-term revolution" [changqi geming]
was adopted as a preventative measure against moral decay and dynastic
downfall. At the same time, the new political technologies of the nation-
state were applied to stabilize society.

Coinciding with this transitional moment, a new sort of Chinese
anthropology began to emerge in academic circles of Europe and
America. The British social anthropologist Maurice Freedman, who never
had the chance to visit the mainland in his lifetime, carried out a study
of family and marriage among Chinese living in the British colony of
Singapore under the auspices of the Colonial Social Research Council.[36]
He gathered data from his own experiences among the Chinese migrant

---

[35] In Quanzhou, the PLA soldiers who had been assigned to pacify the mountainous areas
of South Fujian were stationed around the county seats of those areas. There they, as the
PLA regiment that had been the first to reach the south of the Yangze Valley, mobilized
a great number of local young men and women to serve as mediators between them
and local people. Working jointly with the newly recruited and armed local young men,
translators (working to decipher northern and southern tongues), and cadres, they
established new county governments in these areas. Guided by some local young men
deep into the mountains, they chased the KMT officers and their allied "bandits" into
confined areas and finally wiped them out in late 1950. While the military campaign of
"wiping out the bandits" [jiaofei] was under its way, in the prefecture's capital Quanzhou,
a "regiment of frontier defense" was organized to guard the coast. In the urban area, the
Bureau of Public Security [Gong An Ju] was set up. Patrolling the streets of the city, the
new police officers, although they spoke the local language, were led by formal PLA men
sent to the south who spoke northern dialects. Many government offices that the KMT
had left behind were reoccupied by a new generation of cadres who were assigned to the
reform of urban private businesses and the making of a new social fabric.

[36] Maurice Freedman, Lineage Organization in Southeastern China (London 1958), p. iii.

communities overseas and from his study of Sinological works in European languages "on the nature of Chinese society" in the provinces of Fujian and Guangdong. Incorporating what he saw and read into his theory of the Chinese lineage, Freedman offered a new perspective on Chinese social structure typified by South Fujian, where I have worked as a field anthropologist and historian.

Anthropological research has since begun to transcend the localities of China. Between the 1950s and 1970s, during which mainland China was largely closed to the outside, a new phase in the social anthropology of China was created in the West and the extra-territorial Chinese societies of Singapore, Hong Kong, and Taiwan.[37] The beginning was launched with Freedman's endeavor to establish a "Sinological anthropology." Seeking to draw our attention away from the usual place-centric ethnographies, Freedman developed a structural approach, whereby villages were included under the high category of societal "China." His approach to Chinese anthropology was later reexamined in ethnographies of Hong Kong's new territories and Taiwanese villages.[38] But in his lifetime, Freedman insisted on a "supralocal anthropology," which was not far from the notion of "national transcendence."

The kind of anthropology that Freedman envisaged was one in which a full account of the state's politics was taken. While he was not uninterested in modern politics of the state, he could research and read only about "prerevolutionary China." He devoted most of his life to the analysis of "politics in the old state." In his analyses, the "official map" of civilization occupied the central position.

Freedman's anthropology was a historical anthropology without process. He utilized rich secondary sources in his study of the structure of Chinese religion and society, of which he developed a static model. In his later works, he emphasized the intersections between the state and society in history. Yet the intersections were defined as timeless manifestations of a continuing cosmology of "classical China," a "great tradition" that was conceptualized either as a top-down descending pattern of diffusion (J. J. M. de Groot) or as bottom-up ascending courtification of rural culture (Marcel Granet).[39]

Ironically, as the new "supralocal anthropology" of China was emerging, the concept of place became even more heavily emphasized.

---

[37] Anthropological fieldwork in the mainland was replaced by "nationality identification work."

[38] For a critique of Freedman's model, see Allen Chun, *Unstructuring Chinese Society: The Fiction of Colonial Practice and the Changing Realities of "Land" in the New Territories of Hong Kong* (Amsterdam 2000).

[39] Maurice Freedman, On the sociological study of Chinese religion, in Arthur Wolf (ed.), *Religion and Ritual in Chinese Society* (Stanford 1974), pp. 19–41.

In addition to Freedman's emphasis on lineages as a kind of territorial bond, in his path-breaking studies of social structure, G. William Skinner presented a "functional" interpretation of place institutions. Bringing a two-fold theory of Chinese places to the center of his theory, Skinner proposed that certain kinds of "central places" (market towns) in rural China served to economically integrate lower places, such as villages, thus depicting China as a collection of macro-regions.[40] Instead of presenting another form of national transcendence, Skinner offered, instead, a certain federation of macro-regions which transcended local worlds.

Since the publication of Freedman and Skinner's work, some scholars have realized that what was at issue was the interrelationship between unity and diversity. One should not forget, however, that this very problem of unity and diversity, or what we have alternatively conceptualized as a dynamic of integration and territorial "segmentation" and of civilization and "moral decay," was also a major concern of the People's Republic of China (PRC).[41]

Out of what Clifford Geertz has called "a desperate search for ways and means to create a more perfect union,"[42] the newly inaugurated state expended great effort in building local sites for manifesting its own presence. Apart from the more explicit means of rule, certain more implicit mechanisms for creating a new social fabric and order were also deemed necessary. Well before all the work of "socialist transformation" was carried out, the work of institution-building had already been started. Deep in the mountains of Taihang in Hebei, where the Eight Route Army had developed its military force and civil order in the early 1940s, rehearsals for the new governments had been organized. Continued in Zhongnan Hai in Beijing after late September 1949, these rehearsals culminated in the formation of a new central government. As ceremonial processes of rehearsal, in the first three months of the new People's Republic, a lengthy series of meetings was organized in Beijing to discuss the creation of a new national calendar.[43]

As in the old dynastic transitions, the new calendar was issued and distributed all over the country three months later. Meanwhile, in the city

---

[40] G. William Skinner, Marketing and social structure in rural China, *Journal of Asian Studies,* 24, 2-3 (1964–1965): 195–228; 363–399.

[41] In the course of transition from the old Republic to the new People's Republic, revolutionary struggles in Quanzhou often took advantage of the "congregations of gods" in which the masses were mobilized against the KMT. Soon after the revolution succeeded in eliminating the old power structure, "congregations of gods" became the target of campaigns against the "old society." The transition unfolded and brought our academic discussion of "popular religion" and "official cults" into new illuminations.

[42] Geertz, *The Interpretation of Cultures,* p. 277.

[43] *Renmin Shoucen* [*The People's Handbook*] (Shanghai 1951).

of Quanzhou, the PLA who witnessed the outbreak of several feuds[44] sought the help of local intellectuals in formulating a way to eliminate "superstition." In the early 1950s, most of the nation's anthropologists were sent to ethnic minority regions to conduct the work of "nationality identification" [*minzu shibie*], which regarded ethnic religious practices as part of their ethnic identities.[45]

To a great extent, Sinological anthropologists' theoretical concerns have been expressed in a radically different way from the ideological advocacy of the contemporary Chinese state. Nonetheless, the same issue of transcendence or lack thereof seems to have occupied both the minds of anthropologists and Chinese politicians.

Recently, Steven Sangren formulated his understanding of Chinese pilgrimage ritual in a way similar to Victor Turner's notion of the "Christian transcendence of pilgrims." This formulation is central to Sangren's "Chinese sociologics"[46]:

> The transcendence sought and produced in pilgrimage is linked to representations of power employed precisely in producing—that is, structuring—both local society and individuals' senses of themselves . . . the social activities of pilgrimage and local ritual are significant arenas of social production and . . . as such these activities are powerful. This power is in fact immanent in the social activities of pilgrimage and local ritual, even though the activities are founded on the premise that this socially productive power is extrinsic to them. . . .[47]

It is for the very purpose of tackling "transcendence," either critically or uncritically, in anthropological studies of Chinese culture, that constant efforts have been made to accommodate fieldwork and archival findings from local cultural settings to the "great tradition" of Chinese civilization.

For Freedman, the anthropology of China was entirely breaking away from old ethnographies of places, but it actually was not quite so. In the late 1930s and 1940s, when the first generation of native

---

[44] In the transition period, many local people in Quanzhou did not really know how the local society was to be changed. Outside the City of Quanzhou, in the rural township of Shishi (now a prosperous postreform city), the 7th month festival for the ghosts [*pudu*] was being organized. It was soon stopped by the PLA's propaganda workers who declared the feast of ghosts to be incompatible with the first national celebration to be held a few days later in Beijing.

[45] Fei, Xiao Tong, Jianshu wode minzu yanjiu silu [A brief reflection on the lines of thought with which I have studied nationalities], in his *Congshi Qiuzhi Lu* [*Pursuing Knowledge through Practice*] (Beijing 1998), pp. 96–118.

[46] P. Steven Sangren, *Chinese Sociologics: An Anthropological Account of the Role of Alienation in Social Reproduction* (London 2000), pp. 96–118.

[47] Ibid., p. 97.

Chinese anthropologists came to the West to write up their "community studies," Robert Redfield's distinction between "great" and "little traditions" had not yet been fully developed. Nonetheless, four core members of this group were already thinking about representing China by conducting fieldwork in small places and studying little traditions for the sake of representing the great one.[48] These internationally known Chinese anthropologists were engaged in what Allen Chun has aptly called "earthbound anthropologies."[49] All the studies were conducted within the confines of villages. Yet, none of them, most notably those conducted by Fei Xiao Tong, Francis L. K. Hsu, Lin Yue Hua, and, to a lesser extent, Tian Rukang, reflected on the villages as having "senses of place."[50]

Contemporary anthropologists contend that village studies are studies of places.[51] By contrast, for the first generation of native Chinese anthropologists—who also wrote their studies in a foreign language—studies of places were meaningless without reference to the transcending order of China. For studies of villages to be meaningful, the "murder" of place was necessary, a notion succinctly captured in the Maoist era slogan: "Studies of peasants should be targeted at the elimination of peasantry [*yanjiu nongmin, xiaomie nongmin*]. Each of the studies sought to discover the totality of China reflected in the small mirror of the village.[52]

Already by the 1960s, Freedman deemed the earlier ethnographies of China as out-of-date descriptions of villages. After being critiqued for their shortage of classic traditions from the *Book of Poems* and the *Scripture of Rites,* these studies gave way to the bifurcated histories of "oriental despotism" and the African model of segmentation.[53]

---

[48] As Leach argues, Fei Xiao Tong, deriving his observations from a Kaixiangong village, was treating this place as a typical example of how "peasant life in China" changed. Writing in the style of the experimental ethnographic novel, Lin Yue-hua sought to depict Chinese lives as bound up in a culturally peculiar world of geomancy and lineage. Treating a Chinese village like an African tribe, Martin Yang demonstrated a total surrender of China to the ethnology of the ancient social mode. Turning a Bai ethnic minority township into a typical site of Chinese ancestral worship, Francis L. K. Hsu placed his image of China under "the ancestral shadow." Exempting Fei Xiao Tong a little from this criticism in consideration of his loyalty to the Functionalist School of Anthropology, Leach denounces such efforts for their failures to decipher these societies as sites containing a holistic cosmology and/or a "functionally related whole (and 'in its own right')." See Edmund Leach, *Social Anthropology* (London 1982), pp. 122–148.

[49] Chun, *Unstructuring Chinese Society*, pp. 13–46.

[50] Wang, Ming Ming, *Shehui Renleixue yu Zhongguo Yanjiu* [*Social Anthropology and Sinology*] (Beijing 1997), pp. 44–56.

[51] Steven Feld and Keith Basso (eds.), *Senses of Place* (Santa Fe 1996).

[52] Wang, *Shehui Renleixue yu Zhongguo Yanjiu* [*Social Anthropology and Sinology*], pp. 25–64.

[53] Ibid., pp. 65–111.

Sinological anthropologists then turned to the "Chinese religion" for inspiration. Through a mutation of J. J. M. de Groot's top-down model of the *Scripture of Rites* and Marcel Granet's bottom-up model of the *Book of Poetry*,[54] they looked at something that they thought would allow an anthropology of civilization to emerge from the theoretical frontiers of anthropology.

Nevertheless, post-Freedman Sinological anthropology, like the pioneering ethnographies of the 1930s, has been done in villages gradually opened up to outsiders.[55] In an ambitious effort to discover the "Chinese essence" from the bottom up, anthropologists have treated the diversity of peasant cultures as neat correspondences to the diversity of localities and have located, in each of their villages, a peculiarly Chinese cultural logic of gods, ghosts, and ancestors.[56]

As an outcome of this ambitious effort, the project of Robert Redfield, which was hardly mentioned before the 1970s in Chinese anthropology, had become, by the 1980s, a prime target of critique. Writing in the new phase of Chinese anthropology, Catherine Bell and Steven Sangren have applied the insights of Chinese anthropology to develop a critique of the notorious dichotomy of great and little traditions, and paradoxically, they have done so with reference to the conjunction of the Chinese elite[57] and to place-linking pilgrimages.[58] Moreover, as we should also note, the Gramscian idea of hegemony has become influential among the core researchers of "Chinese folk religion."[59]

A notion of a unified religion in China implies, though in a variety of ways, a notion of unified ethnicity.[60] Conversely, heterodox derivatives of a supposed singular "historical metaphor" could convey an alternative order by turning the kingly into the demonic and the demonic into the kingly.[61] In the spirit of that dialectic, in the quest for an alternative culture, recently Myron Cohen has called for "the peripheralization of traditional [Chinese] identity," whereby we are pushed toward a recognition of the heterodox as the center

---

[54] Freedman, On the sociological study of Chinese religion.

[55] Simultaneously, political scientists have revitalized the anthropological tradition of ethnography by using village studies to analyze Mao era and post-Mao political changes.

[56] Arthur Wolf, Gods, ghosts, and ancestors, in his edited *Religion and Ritual in Chinese Society* (Stanford 1974), pp. 131–182.

[57] Catherine Bell, Religion and Chinese culture: Towards an assessment of popular religion, *History of Religions*, 29(1) (1989): 37–57.

[58] P. Steven Sangren, Great and little traditions reconsidered: The question of cultural integration in China, *Journal of Chinese Studies*, 1(5) (1984): 1–24.

[59] Hill Gates and Robert Weller, Hegemony and Chinese folk ideology, *Modern China*, 13(1) (1987): pp. 3–16.

[60] Stephan Feuchtwang, A Chinese religion exists, in Hugh Baker and Stephan Feuchtwang (eds.), *An Old Society in New Settings* (Oxford 1991), pp. 131–161.

[61] Feuchtwang, *The Imperial Metaphor*.

of the Chinese nation and culture.[62] But how? Even though we reject the notion that anthropologists who work in small places should portray their communities as cosmo-political models of the whole of China, Cohen seems to have neglected the observation that dynastic projects of absorbing heritages either from local religious cults such as Tianhou[63] or from ready-made models of mid-level philosophical elitism[64] have been equally productive of heterodoxy.[65]

Tensions between integration and segmentation have constantly been felt among different social groups throughout history, but the problem is not simply that of unity versus diversity but rather how different social forces have dealt with this same problem in different ways in different periods of history.

In retrospect, in approaching the historical questions surrounding changing *pujing* practices, I still have in mind all the questions concerning "transcendence." As I argued from the outset, the present *pujing* ritual practices are the opposite of the transcending civilization of modernity. Some anthropologists who adopt a timeless ethnographic method would immediately conclude from this observation that such "segments," "divisive territorial boundary systems," "superstition," and "disintegration" formulate the enemy of "great tradition," whose ultimate teleology is transcendence. Nonetheless, in our study, more specifically formulated as a question of bureaucracy, ritual, and social action, all the questions of supralocal presence, civilization, transcendence, and politics give way to a single problematic: how can a genealogy of segmenting *pujing* inform an anthropology of civilizing transcendence?

---

[62] Myron Cohen, Being Chinese: The peripheralization of traditional society, in Tu, Weiming (ed.), *The Living Tree: The Changing Meaning of Being Chinese Today* (Stanford 1991), pp. 88–108.

[63] James Watson, Standardizing the gods: The promotion of T'ien Hou (Empress of Heaven) along the South China Coast, 960–1960, in David Johnson, Andrew Nathan, and Evelyn Rawski (eds.), *Popular Culture in Late Imperial China* (Berkeley 1985), pp. 292–324.

[64] Angela Zito, *Of Body and Brush: Grand Sacrifice as Text/Performance in Eighteenth-Century China* (Chicago 1997).

[65] With all the new perspectives of place becoming available there has been a resurgence of village studies in "postreform Chinese anthropology." "Anthropologists don't study villages . . . they study in villages" Geertz, *The Interpretation of Culture*, p. 22. Postreform anthropologists from China and abroad have focused their attention on what has taken place in the villages but not on the issue of "what a village is." As Feuchtwang suggests, "there is a political entity with a centralized government called China that it claims to be and serves as the focal point for claims and counter claims to being truly representative of 'China'" (Stephan Feuchtwang, Local religion and village identity, in Liu, Tao Tao, and Faure, David [eds.], *Unity and Diversity: Local Cultures and Identities in China* [Hong Kong 1996], p. 162). These studies *in* places have continued to work toward representations and counterrepresentations of post-Mao China. Leaving the ambitions of Freedman, Skinner, and other historical anthropologists behind, they situate themselves comfortably in the small shrines of contemporary places.

Throughout imperial times, *pujing* were perceived in different ways by
different social forces. Even as an official institution, they also represented
a "confused" order of things changing with time. From the perspective of
their officially designated functions, *pujing* changed from an institution of
local administration, to a tool of the Ming vision of a perfect union of administration and civilization, and finally to the early Qing warring "Eastern and
Western Buddha alliances." These changes followed revolving patterns of
imperial State politics from Mongol colonialism, to Ming "Renaissance"
and nativism, and then to the Manchu "enlightened despotism."

In term of *pujing*'s role in public city life, a more or less linear line of
"evolution" can be drawn: as territorial cult boundaries, *pujing* were, in the
first instance, districts of local guardian-gods, religious communities, ghost
festivals, and procession rituals. Gradually these boundaries were transgressed
by "congregations of gods," which were pan-city, public, and competitive.
In other words, these communities evolved from more locally confined territorial cult activities to more public displays of power and vitality.

Apart from the changing patterns of boundaries and local control, we
also observe the scenarios of the interactions of different maps of the life
world in the city of Quanzhou as cultural and political imageries of changing
conditions of existence. Here, worth noting is the perspective advanced by
Philip Kuhn, who focuses on the "variations of the common theme" in
Chinese worldviews and politics. Kuhn reveals how events became effective
in bringing together different groups, places, and interpretations into an
arena of conjunction and contestation.[66] Much like Kuhn's example of
the "soul-stealing crisis,"[67] different understandings of *pujing* emerged in
different transitional moments in which ideological, politico-strategic and
ritual discursive responses were made in common as displays of order.

---

[66] Kuhn focuses on the "soul-stealing crisis" around the year 1768, which spread through
   the Chinese continent from the unknown outside to affect many levels of society. As
   Kuhn elegantly described, in responding to the scare, each social group arranged the
   components of sorcery lore to fit its own view of the world. But the different expressions of
   the same event springing from different social roles and life experiences shared a common
   theme, the "danger from persons unknown and unseen." See Philip Kuhn, *Soulstealers:
   The Chinese Sorcery Scare of 1768* (Cambridge 1990), p. 223.
[67] In deciphering the "soul-stealing crisis" in a special moment of late imperial Chinese
   history, Kuhn continues his attempt to offer an interpretation of modern China through
   the historically continuous study of late imperial periods. Like Freedman's version of
   sinological anthropology, Kuhn's analysis obscures the boundary between historical
   events and culture. Although his theory serves as a good reaction to John Fairbank's
   "impact-response" model of modern China, Kuhn forgets the fact that the fluctuating
   and re-ordering of culture and society under different historical circumstances was an
   important characteristic of China's past. A more effective historical narrative should focus
   on one region and extend its scope to a longer duration of historical time. In so doing, it
   is possible for us to make a historically comparative analysis of how different actions and
   interpretations have changed over time.

The pasts of the empire and, subsequently, empire-turned monarchical and national regime were intertwined with the local histories of places, a process that often involved dislocation and relocation, dispossession and repossession. It was to reconstructing these histories that led anthropologists to set out to develop a new ethnographic approach. To a great extent, if the story of *pujing* reveals anything relevant to this, then it is about how to develop an anthropology of "complex society" with complex linkages, locations, and dislocations in history—that is, how, in the anthropology of civilization, "segments" can be shown to co-exist with and involve totalities and, in the same process, totalities can be analyzed through their engagements with "segments."

Our historical specificities have more to them, however, because these interactions have been examined from two mutually complementary perspectives. Observed from a bird's-eye view, the "segments" and "totalities" can be seen as patterns that made up co-present "maps." At the same time, when they are viewed from the inside in greater detail, they become a conglomeration of the life experiences and politics of emperors, officials, scholars, soldiers, peasants, craftsmen, merchants, and smugglers who made history with their different conceptions of order and chaos. As individuals, people were placed in the political-cum-cultural hierarchy of the empire, which led to constant struggles and vicissitudes, including those of court intrigue, regional power struggles, and the symbolic competitions of the "congregations of gods."

In our interpretation, emperors, prefects, Confucian scholars, merchants, local elites, and ordinary households all played a role in the reconfiguration and transformation of *pujing*. In this transformation of *pujing*, "transcendence" as a problematic merged with responses to crises, constituencies of local public order, and displays of strength and vitality. Local folklore more vividly describes these dramas in terms of the interaction between carp and the net. *Pujing*, originating as an imperial net to catch the Carp, sometimes served its originally designated function of "fishing" (the Yuan and the Ming) but sometimes "released Carp" from its entanglements (the early Qing). From the perspectives of nonofficial practices, it underwent a transformation from the net into the carp, expressing nostalgia for the bygone "golden age" and displaying the local geomancy of "good fortune," which the net was, in the beginning, intended to obstruct.

By no means have we meant to suggest that our less linear mode of historical narrative is intended to displace the linear line of "civilizing process" in Europe. What we have sought here has been nothing more than a comparative illustration of Chinese history, which is meaningful for its conceptual utility in clarifying aspects of local history. Yet, for nationalistic intellectuals such as Liang Shu Ming, comparison has become something else. As we mentioned earlier, in the national Chinese pursuit of transcendence, the comparative method has developed into a competitive cultural politics in which the weakness of China has been associated with its lack of modernity and, ironically, dearth of "tradition" as well. The modernity and tradition that have been understood to be "lacking in China" have sounded two distinguished types of culture. Paradoxically, they have been the same "transcendence" that has divided history into the contrasting past and present.

It is at this moment of discursive transition that the city, along with the empire-turned-nation, has entered a different track of history since the twentieth century. Alternating cycles of empire have remained to serve as popular cultural metaphors used to critique the modern "confused emperors" and to call for the long-awaited revitalization of the Chinese culture. Yet, they have also become ever more intolerable to the nation-builders, who would prefer to toss this cycle into the dustbin of history.

The events of the twentieth century have forced us to reconsider the idea of "transcendence." In Sinological anthropology, "transcendence" may simply refer to a cosmological pattern or a political-economic totality that goes beyond local and historical contingencies to "map" the boundaries of the Chinese nation. Yet it is precisely the conceptual boundaries of "transcendence" that anthropologists and historians use to define their research projects and where the politics of modernity also finds its foundation.

As anthropologist Michael Hertzfeld brilliantly argues, transcendence, so closely related to the Weberian notion of the formalism of bureaucracy, has drawn on Judo-Christian and Indo-European concepts of the superiority of mind of over matter and of thinkers over actors. It places rationality above and beyond mere experience. As a productive ethic, stemming from Calvinism, that treats culture as the commutation of historical consciousness, transcendence separates eternal truth from the mere contingencies of society and culture.[68]

The history of transcendence is manifest destiny, "the European spirit marching to the ultimate emancipation of intelligence from gross flesh. Its particular realizations include the idea of perfectly context-free, abstract language and, in the field of bureaucratic administration, a rational Western model untrammeled by 'ecology'—in other words, by whatever is specific to a particular culture."[69] When Liang Shu Ming says that China falls short of transcendence he is thus reiterating Weber's point that an abstracted bureaucratic language is not found in China. When all the campaigners against "superstition" argue that *pujing* represents the backwardness of the Chinese people in Quanzhou, they are also saying something similar.

---

[68] Hertzfeld, *The Social Reproduction of Indifference.*
[69] Ibid., pp. 19–20.

However, Hertzfeld argues that there is a tremendous irony at the heart of this. The idea of transcendence is itself highly contingent. "As a filtering out of eternal verity from the circumstantial or contingent, it is the basis of authority in virtually all ideologies of state: it represents state power as naturally or divinely ordained, depending on available theology."[70] In this sense, what we said earlier, that in the early imperial *pujing* system a strong sense of transcendence could be detected, is true of history.

A Final Note

Today, after centuries of searching, Chinese culture once again is in a desperate quest for a common ground that, as is hoped, might "heal its fractures" left by all the internal and external upheavals of history.[71] Yet, at the same time, China remains a continent of different cultures, each of which continues to serve as the medium through which the sagacious and the ordinary of a particular region or ethnic group express themselves. Whether or not it is possible to reconcile the quest of unity and that of diversity remains a problem. The theoretical contradictions and practical confusions surrounding them continue to affect the complex structure of feeling in "being Chinese."

In the city of Quanzhou, as in other Chinese cities and townships, the bureaucratic spectacles of national celebrations develop on the horizons of mass media and the leisure economy. At the same time, "cultural events" are organized through the combined efforts of local government departments and delegations of local theatrical troupes, senior citizens' associations, trade unions, temple committees, schools, and work units to celebrate the greatness of the city. Historians continue to work under the shadow of "bygone prosperity." More and more monographs, collections, and journals appear in bookstores. Their topics are increasingly wide-ranging, from overseas communication history [*haiwai jiaotong shi*], to gazettes of old Confucian academies, to temple records.[72] Recently, Wang Lian Mao,

---

[70] Ibid., pp. 20–21.

[71] Tu, Wei-ming, Cultural China: The periphery as the center, in his edited *The Living Tree: The Changing Meaning of Being Chinese Today* (Stanford 1991), pp. 1–34.

[72] Native historians' enthusiasm for local maritime cosmopolitanism constantly reminds me of what anthropologists such as Edmund Leach said about history: historians often turn historical records into a charter for what they believe about the present. In Quanzhou, both the local and foreign studies have been promoted as contributions to the subject of "Quanzhouxue" [Quanzhou-ology]. The term *Quanzhouxue* emerged in the mid-1980s, a few years after the implementation of the "open-door policy." Locally, the range of research that the particular term represents has been characterized as the "exemplary study of Chinese tradition of commercial openness." The historical records that scholars of Quanzhouxue have rediscovered have served to highlight the historical transnational networks of trade and cross-cultural communication centered in Quanzhou. Like all sorts of officially organized spectacles, these records have become exhibits and performances of the bygone prosperity of Quanzhou.

one of the most active practitioners of overseas communication history, the curator of the Museum of Overseas Communication History in Quanzhou, proposed to the government that even the lowest-level cultural relics such as *pujing* temples should be preserved as part of local cultural heritage. Encouraged by this principle, a territorial temple containing a slight trace of overseas connections has been turned into a museum.

Where do the boundaries between great and little traditions lie? The problem has perplexed the officials involved in culture work in Quanzhou. While basking in the glory of the traditions, the officials in the Bureau of Culture, who usually also attended "superstitious festivals" in their home *pujing* neighborhoods, also feel a "sadness" [*bei'ai*] toward them. As one of them said in the restricted code of official language: "After more than forty years of cultural reconstruction, we still see backward masses who tie themselves to superstition and by so doing become indifferent to the real culture of the Bureau of Culture." Obviously, such a sense of "sadness," as a continuation of its late Ming and Qing "ancestor" (sadness for the "licentious cults"), has sprung as much from "cultural reality" itself as from the discursive negation of history, on which "great and little traditions" are both based.

In less restricted situations of dialogue, the same officials express more relaxed attitudes toward the cultural situation in Quanzhou. After all, this state of affairs in many ways can be seen as a continuation of the interactive drama of "the Carp and the net." There already exists in Quanzhou the intuition that a civilizing project always has the potential of yielding—intentionally or unintentionally—regional characteristics and unofficial "licentious cults." Since it is impossible for a civilization to incorporate all the meanings of regional cultures such as that of Quanzhou, today's advocates of Chinese civilization are forced to place their faith in the convergence of cultures, to whose revelation, local historical narratives—in the contexts of which this study of *pujing* is situated as a reflexive subject—have made a contribution.

Glossary

An Lu Shan 安禄山
An Shi Zhi Luan 安史之乱
Anbian Guan 安边馆
ansun mincai 暗损民财
A-Ye Gong 阿爷公
badao 霸道
bagua 八卦
Banbi Jiangshan 半壁江山
bantou ye 班头爷
Banzhi Ji 班枝记
Baojia *lianzuo fa* 保甲连坐法
Baojia 保甲
Baosheng Dadi 保生大帝
bao 报
Bashu 巴蜀
Beiyue 北岳
bian qi yisu 变其夷俗
bian 匾
Bing Bu 兵部
Bing Zhi 兵志
bingfa 兵法
Bingma Si 兵马司
Bixia Yuanjun 碧霞元君
bogui 搏龟
Bowuzhi 博物志
budi 步递
buyi zhicai 不义之财
Cai Xiang 蔡襄
Cang Shu 藏书

ce 策
cheng 城
chengshi 城市
Chang Xing 常性
changqi geming 长期革命
chaobai 朝拜
chaoyue 超越
Chen Bu Chan 陈步蟾
Chen Hong Jin 陈洪进
Chen Si Dong 陈泗东
Chen You Ding 陈友定
chengchi 城池
Chengde 成德
Chenghuang 城隍
Chengtian Si 承天寺
chihou 斥侯
chuan bang 船帮
chuanggun 闯棍
chuantong 传统
chujian yudao 除奸御盗
Ciji 慈济
Citong Cheng 刺桐城 (Zaitun)
ci 祠
ci 赐
danwei 单位
daohai bujing 道海不靖
Daoyi Zhilue 岛夷志略
daoyin 导淫
dao 道

305

dapo 打破

dasai shenxiang 大赛神像

Datang Jiaosi Lu 大唐郊祀录

datong 大同

daxing 大姓

Deng Mao Qi 邓茂七

Di Tan 地坛

Di 狄

di 递

didi pu 急递铺

Didu 帝都

ding 顶

Dinghai 丁亥

Dingxiang 顶香

diqi 地气

dizhi 地支

Dong Xi Fo 东西佛

Dong'an Xian 东安县

Dongfanghong Lu 东方红路

Donghu 东湖

Dongmen 东门

Dongyue 东岳

du 都

duanwu jie 端午节

Duli Zhi 都里志

en 恩

ershiba xiu 二十八宿

fanfang 番坊

fang wangchuan 放王船

Fangqiu 方丘

fangshi 方士

fangxiang 坊厢

Fangyu Xunjing 防隅巡警

Fanke 番客

fan 番

fazhi 法治

fa 法

Fei Feng 飞凤

fei huaxia zhi yi 非华夏之仪

feihu qi 飞虎旗

feiwei 非为

Fei Xiaotong 费孝通

Fen Shu 焚书

fengjian 封建

fengshan 封禅

Fengsheng Gong 奉圣宫

Fengsheng 奉圣

Fengti Yi 枫亭驿

fengtiao yushun 风调雨顺

fengyu 封域

Fengzhi Daifu 奉直大夫

fenlei xiedou 分类械斗

Fenyang 汾阳

fenye 分野

Fo Guo 佛国

Fo shengri 佛生日

foxiang 佛香

Fu Hong Ji 富鸿基

Fu Jin Xing 傅金星

fu renzhixing 拂人之性

Fude Zhengshen 福德正神

Fumei Gong 富美宫

Fuqian Pu 府前铺

Fuzhou 福州

gang yin 纲银

gangbo wanguo chuan, shili shizhou ren 港泊万国船, 市井十洲人

gangji 纲纪

gaoshe fanshang 犒设蕃商

geli yuesuo 各立约所

Geng Jingzheng 耿精忠

gongbing 弓兵

gong 工

gong 公

gong 贡

gu hun 孤魂

Gu Jie Gang 顾颉刚

Gu Yan Wu 顾炎武

Guandi Miao 关帝庙

Guangping Wang 广平王

guanjun 官军

guanmi 官米

guanwu 官屋

guanyi 馆驿

guihua 归化

Guilong 龟龙

guizhi 规制
gui 鬼
guji 古迹
guo tai min an 国泰民安
Guo Zao Qing 郭造卿
guojia 国家
guoshi 国势
guo 国
gongshe 公社
Gurong Jing Yuantan Yuanshuai 古榕境元坛元帅
Gushi 固始
gu 贾
haibin zhoulu 海滨邹鲁
haidao 海盗
haidu 海渎
Haiguo Tuzhi 海国图志
Haijiao Guan 海交馆
haijin zhengce 海禁政策
haishen 海神
hai 害
Han Qi 韩琦
Han 汉
Han 汉
He Qiao Yuan 何乔远
He Shen 河神
heihu 黑虎
heipu 黑簿
he 和
He 河
Hong Cheng Chou 洪承畴
Hongmao 红毛
Hu Tianbao 胡天保
Hu Tianmei 胡天妹
hua hui shen wei fali 化鬼神为法吏
hua xiangyin wei xingchang 化乡饮为刑场
huacheng zhi xiao 化成之效
huacheng 化成
huafang 画坊
huafeng lunmo 华风沦没
Huai 淮
huanei 化内

Huang Cheng Xuan 黄承玄
Huang Jue Zi 黄爵兹
Huang Zong Xi 黄宗羲
huangjin shidai 黄金时代
Huanqiu 圜丘
huanren 幻人
Huaqiao 花桥
huawai 化外
huaxia 华夏
huayi zhibian gaoyu junchen zhifen 华夷之辨高于君臣之分
Hui'an Zhengshu 惠安政书
Hui'an 惠安
hui 会
Hui 回
huji 户籍
hunjun 昏君
huojia 火甲
Hushan Wang Xianggong 湖山王相公
huxiang zhiding 互相知丁
Hu 胡
Ji 济
Jia Gu 嘉谷
jiaji renzu 家给人足
Jiali 嘉礼
jiali 家礼
Jiang Fu Cheng 将福成
jiangdu 讲读
Jiangshan 江山
jiangshi 将士
Jiangxia Hou 江夏侯
Jiang 江
jiao 郊
jiaohua zhi ru 教化之儒
jiaohua 教化
jiaoshe 郊社
jiao-si 郊祀
jiao 教
jiazhang 枷杖
jia 甲
jie huotao 戒窝逃
jiedao ban 街道办

jiefen xizheng 解纷息争
jielu 借路
jieshi 戒石
jie 劫
jijiao di 急脚递
jile zhi you 极乐之游
Jin'an 晋安
jingshan ting 旌善亭
jingshen yu xiangren xiangtong 精
　神与乡人相通
Jingtian Zhi 井田制
Jingzhu Gong 境主宫
jing 经
jing 境
Jinjiang 晋江
Jinping 晋平
jiuzhou 九州
Jiuzi Shan 九日山
ji 己
Jubao Jie 聚宝街
Jun 军
junhu 军户
junxun pu 军巡铺
junyao yin 均徭银
junzi 君子
Kaiyuan Si 开元寺
Keju 科举
Koxinga 国姓爷
kuangfu 旷夫
kuang 狂
kuanyu renci 宽裕仁慈
kuhai 苦海
Kun Lun 昆仑
Lan Ding Yuan 蓝鼎元
Lan Li 蓝理
Lei Yu Shan Chuan Chenghuang
　雷雨山川城隍
Leshan Wang 乐山王
Li Bu 礼部
Li Guang Di 李光地
Li Guang Jin 李光缙
Li Zhi 李贽
Li Zi Cheng 李自成

lian baojia 联保甲
Liang Fang Zhong 梁方仲
Liang Shu Ming 梁漱溟
Liangzhang 粮长
Licheng Qu 鲤城区
Licheng 鲤城).
Lifa Zhi Zhi 礼法之治
ligui 厉鬼
Liguo 鲤廓
lijia shen 里甲神
lijiao 礼教
lijia 里甲
Lin Dao Qian 林道乾
Lin Feng 林凤
Lin Hui Xiang 林惠祥
Lin Ze Xu 林则徐
ling 灵
lishe shen 里社神
lishe 里社
Liu Ji 刘基
Liu Xingjun 刘星君
Liu Yao Chun 刘耀椿
liyi 礼仪
liyu xizhu 鲤鱼戏珠
Liyu Yue Longmen 鲤鱼跃龙门
Liyuan 梨园
liyun 礼运
lizhi 礼治
li 礼
li 里
li 理
li 厉
li 利
loufeng 陋风
luanshi 乱世
luan 乱
luocheng 罗城
luofan 落幡
luohou 落后
luwen 律文
luying 绿营
madi 马递
Maiban 买办

majing 马精
manjie doushi shengren 满街都是圣人
Man 蛮
mengfu 盟府
Mengliang Lu 梦梁录
mianzi 面子
Min Shu Chao 闽书抄
Minghuan Ci 名宦祠
Mingjiao 明教
Minglie Wang 明烈王
Mingtang 明堂
Mingzhou 明州
minim 民米
Minsu Zhoukan 民俗周刊
Minxue 闽学
Minyue Guo 闽越国
minzu shibie 民族识别
mixin 迷信
mosu 末俗
Nan Ren 南人
Nan'an 南安
Nanbei Chao 南北朝
nanguo zhi zhuhou 南国之诸侯
Nanwai Zongzheng Si 南外宗正司
nanxia ganbu 南下干部
Nanyang 南洋
Nanyue 南岳
nao 闹
nei luan 内乱
nei 内
nianjie 年节
nong 农
nuo 傩
pai 牌
pai 派
pianmu bude xiahai 片版不得下海
Pingshui Miao 平水庙
Pofu Jiangjun 破腹将军
Pu Shou Geng 蒲寿庚
pu 铺
pubing 铺兵
puce 铺册

pudi 铺递
pudu 普渡
pufei 铺匪
puhu 铺户
pujing 铺境
Puquan 溥泉
pushe 铺舍
pusi 铺司
putu 铺图
Puxiang Zhi 铺乡志
puyi/shili 铺驿/市厘
Puzhu Gong 铺主宫
Qi Ji Guang 戚继光
qi xue 七血
Qian Mu 钱穆
Qiang 羌
qianjie 迁界
qibao 祈报
qihuo 乞火
Qin Shi Huang Di 秦始皇帝
*qing wu zhi sh*u 青乌之术
qingdao qi 清道旗
Qingyuan Pu 清源铺
Qingyuan Shan 清源山
Qingyuan 清源
qinzheng 勤政
qiqiu ping'an 祈求平安
qiya liangshan 欺压良善
qi 祈
quanyang xiaoguo 犬羊小国
Quanzhou 泉州
Quanzhou *de kaifang chuantong* 泉州的开放传统
Quanzhou Ren *ai renao* 泉州人爱热闹
Quanzhou Ren *gege meng* 泉州人个个猛
Quanzhouxue 泉州学
Rang shijie liaojie Quanzhou, *rang* Quanzhou *zouxiang shijie* 让世界了解泉州, 让泉州走向世界, *renqing* 人情
renqi 人气

renwen 人文
renxin 人心
Ri Tan 日坛
Riyue Taibao 日月太保
Rong 戎
Rouyuan 柔远
ruanpeng 软棚
rugong 入贡
ruizhi 锐志
ru 儒
saida 赛答
saihui yingshen 塞会迎神
Sanjiao Pu 三教铺
sanjun siling qi 三军司令旗
Sanwu 三吴
Semu Ren 色目人
Shan Hai Jing 山海经
Shanchuan Tan 山川坛
shanchuan 山川
shang jiaohua 尚教化
Shang Yuan 上元
Shangdi 上帝
shangfeng baisu 伤风败俗
shangsi 上祀
shangwang 伤亡
shangzhou 上州
shang 商
Shanxi 陕西
Sheji Shen 社稷神
Sheji Tan 社稷坛
shejii 社稷
shengjiao 声教
shengshi 盛世
Shengwang 圣王
sheng 生
shenming ting 申明亭
shenming 神明
Shenshang 绅商
sheshen 社神
shexue 社学
she 舍
she 社

She 畲
Shi Lang 施琅
shi zhu 石主
Shibo Si 市舶司
shifu 士夫
Shigu Miao 石鼓庙
shihe nianfeng 时和年丰
shizhe shengcun 适者生存
shi 士
shi 市
shu tongwen, che tonggui 书同文,
  车同轨
shuai qi 帅旗
Shuangzhong 双忠
shui buzai shen, you long ze ling 水
  不在深, 有龙则灵
shuiguan 水官
shuipu 水普
Shuixian 水仙
shuqi 竖旗
shu 熟
sidian buzai 祀典不载
Si Ma Qian 司马迁
sixiang 四象
si 私
su 俗
tagu 他故
taige 抬阁
Taiji Tu 太极图
Taili Tan 太厉坛
Taishan Nainai 泰山奶奶
Taishan Shen 泰山神
Taiyuan 太原
Taizi 太子
Taizu 太祖
Tang Zhonglie Ci 唐忠烈祠
tan 壇
Tao Shao Xi 陶少溪
tawei 他为
Tian Tan 天坛
Tiandu Yuanshuai 田都元帅
Tianhou 天后

tianli 天理

Tianshang Shengmu 天上圣母

Tianxia Junguo Libing Shu 天下郡
国利病书

Tianxia 天下

Tianzi 天子

tiguo jingye 体国经野

tishuai 提帅

ti 体

tongjiao nannu 通交男女

Tongyuan Wang 通远王

tong 同

tu 图

tuanlian 团练

tuqiu 土酋

wai 外

Wang Da Yuan 汪大渊

Wang Fu Zhi 王夫之

Wang Jing 王泾

Wang Shi June 王士俊

Wang Ye Gong 王爷公

Wang Ye 王爷

wangdao zhi ru 王道之儒

Wangdao 王道

wanguo 万国

Wangyun Lou 望云楼

wanmin zhili 万民之利

Wei Yuan 魏源

Wen Tian Xiang 文天祥

wenhua datai jingji changxi 文化
搭台，经济唱戏

Wenhua Ju 文化局

wenhua 文化

Wenling Jiushi 温陵旧事

Wenling 温陵

wenmiao 文庙

Wenwu Zunwang 文武尊王

Wenxiang Miao 文相庙

wenyi 文艺

wokou 倭寇

wopu 窝铺

wo 倭

Wu Di 武帝

wu lun 五伦

Wu Zao Ting 吴藻汀

Wu Zeng 吴增

Wu Zhenren 吴真人

Wu Zi Mu 吴自牧

Wudai Shiguo 五代十国

wufang qi 五方旗

wufu 五服

wulai 无赖

Wulin Jiushi 武林旧事

wuma buneng shi 无马不能师

wumiao 武庙

Wurong 武荣州

wuwei 无为

wuyin tonggu 五音铜鼓

wuyi 武艺

Xi Fo 西佛

Xia Yuan 下元

Xiaji Shi 县级市

Xiamen 厦门

xiang 乡

xiang 厢

xiang yinjiu 乡饮酒

xiangbei 相背

xiangbing 乡兵

xiangfu 相附

Xianggong Ye 相公爷

xianghui 香会

xiangquan xiang 相劝相规

xiangshen 乡绅

xiangtu 乡土

Xiangxian Ci 乡贤祠

xiangyong 乡勇

xiangyou xiangxu 相友相恤

xiangyue 乡约

xiangzu jituan 乡族集团

Xiannong Tan 先农坛

xianwang zhi jiao 先王之教

Xianzhen 县镇

xian 献

Xiao Wang Zhi 萧望之

xiaojia 小甲
xiaoren 小人
xiao 孝
xiaozhang 消长
xiasi 下祀
xieshu 邪术
xifang zongjiao 西方宗教
xingshi 形势
xingye 星野
xingzheng quhua 行政区划
xing 性
xiong'e manying 凶恶满赢
Xiting 溪亭
Xiyue 西岳
xuan jiaohu yu haiwai zhu fanguo
宣教化于海外诸番国
xue 穴
xunjing pu 巡警铺
xunshi qi 巡视旗
yacheng 衙城
yangyi 洋夷
yanjiu nongmin, xiaomie nongmin
研究农民，消灭农民
yanpai 衍派
Yan Xi Ju 延禧局
yaofu 妖服
yaoyi 徭役
Ye Chun Ji 叶春及
Ye Fei 叶飞
ye 野
yegui 野鬼
yi hai wei tian 以海为田
yi yifeng zhizhi 以夷风制治
Yi 夷
yichang 谊长
yichan 遗产
yigui 疫鬼
yiguo ruokuang 一国若狂
yili 义礼
yili 议礼
yinci 淫祠
Yinglie Hou 英烈侯
yingshen saihui 迎神赛会

yinyang 阴阳
yipan sansha 一盘散沙
yipu 驿铺
yiqiang furuo 抑强扶弱
yiren 艺人
yitan sishui 一潭死水
Yitiaobian Fa 一条鞭法
yiwei 异为
yizhi duiwai 一致对外
yizhuang 义庄
yi 义
yi 邑
Yongchun 永春
Yongjia Zhi Luan 永嘉之乱
Yongle Huangdi 永乐皇帝
Yongzhen 永贞
youdou 游惰
youfang zhengjiao 有妨正教
youguo bifa 有过必罚
youhuan birang 有患必禳
youhun sanpo 游魂散魄
youqiu bidao 有求必祷
youyi 邮驿
Yu Dayou 俞大猷
Yu Li Zi 郁离子
Yuanmiao Guan 元庙观
Yue Tan 月坛
Yue 越
yuebing 阅兵
Yuedi 越地
yuefu 约副
Yuegang 月港
yuesuo 约所
yuexiu 月宿
yuezan 约赞
yuezheng 约正
Yue 粤
yun 运
Yushi 雨师
yu 隅
yu 欲
Zengjing Xiang 曾井巷
Zhang Tianshi 张天师

Zhangpu youji 漳浦游击
Zhangzhou 漳州
zhanhu 站户
Zhao Ru Guo 赵汝适
Zhao Tianjun 赵天君
zhaohui 昭惠
zhaolai yuanren 招徕远人
Zhen Dexiu 真德秀
Zheng Cheng Gong 郑成功
Zheng He 郑和
Zheng Zhi Long 郑芝龙
zhengli 争利
zheng 正
Zhenlie Jiexiao Ci 贞烈节孝祠
zhiyue 知约
zhi 智
Zhong Guo 中国
Zhong Yuan 中元
zhongguo zongjiao 中国宗教
zhonghui zhi suo 众会之所
Zhongshan Lu 中山路
Zhongshu 中书
zhongsi 中祀
Zhongyi Xiaolian Ci 忠义孝廉祠

zhongyuan 中原
Zhongyue 中岳
Zhou De Xing 周德兴
Zhou Guan 周官
Zhou Mi 周密
Zhou Yi 周易
Zhou 周
Zhu Xi 朱熹
Zhu Yuan Zhang 朱元璋
Zhuang Wei Ji 庄为玑
Zhuang Yong Bin 庄用宾
zhuan 专
Zhufan Zhi 诸蕃志
Zhuge gu 诸葛鼓
Zhuling 朱陵
Zhuwenzi Zhai 朱翁子寨
zhuyi 逐疫
Zhuzi guohua 朱子过化
zhu 祝
zicheng 子城
ziyou 自由
zongjia 总甲
zui 罪
zuzheng 族正

Bibliography

Primary Sources

Anxi Xianzhi [*Anxi County Gazette*], compiled by Zhuang, Cheng. 1985 [1757]. People's Publishing House, Fuzhou.

Cai, Xiang. 1996 [1011]. Xiu yi ji [Inscription of re-amendment of a courier-post station], in *Cai Xiang Ji* [*The Collection of Writings by Cai Xiang*], Ancient Archives Press, Shanghai, pp. 495–496.

Chang, Shuo. 2000 [805]. *Datang Kaiyuan Li* [*The Kaiyuan Rituals of the Great Tang Dynasty*], Nationality Press, Beijing.

Chen, Bu Chan. 1992a [1839]. Shang daguancha Quanzhou Dong Xi Fo ce (A formula presented upward to his superior observer concerning the problem of Dong Xi Fo in Quanzhou), in *Fengzhou Jigao* [*A Collection of Manuscripts from Fengzhou*], compiled by Chen, Guo Shi, Office of Local Gazetteers, Nan'an, pp. 466–467.

———. 1992b [1839]. Cewen xiedou luqiang shi [Questions and answers concerning feuding, kidnapping, and robbery], in *Fengzhou Jigao* (*A Collection of Manuscripts from Fengzhou*), compiled by Chen, Guo Shi, Office of Local Gazetteers, Nan'an, pp. 467–469.

Chengtian Si Temple. 1896. *Muquan Chengtian Wangyuan Pudu* [*Pamphlet Soliciting Contributions to the Great Universal Salvation Ceremony at the Temple of Chengtian Si*], Xiamen University Library, Xiamen.

Chongwu Suocheng Zhi [*Records of Chongwu Garrison Town*], compiled by Zhu, Tong. 1987 [1542]. People's Publishing House, Fuzhou.

Cultural Bureau. 1990. *Quanzhou Wenhuaju Gongzuo Huibao* [*A Work Report of Cultural Bureau in Quanzhou*], Cultural Bureau, Municipal Government, Quanzhou.

Dean, Kenneth, and Zheng, Zhen Man (eds.). 2003. *Fujian Zongjiao Beiming Huibian: Quanzhoufu Fence* [*Epigraphical Materials on the History of Religion in Fujian: Quanzhou Region*] 3 Vols., People's Publishing House, Fuzhou.

Dehua Xianzhi [*Dehua County Gazetteer*], compiled by Lu, Ding Mei. 1987 [1746]. Office of Local Gazetteers, Dehua.

315

316

Fengsu Zhi [Record of local customs], *Quanzhou Fuzhi* [*Quanzhou Prefecture Gazette*], compiled by Yang Ming, Qian. 1985 [1612]. *Quanzhou Jiufengsu Ziliao Huibian* [*A Collection of Materials on Old Customs in Quanzhou*], Office of Local Gazetteers, Quanzhou, pp. 6–24.

Fengzhou Jigao [*A Collection of Manuscripts from Fengzhou*], compiled by Chen, Guo Shi. 1992 [1904]. Office of Local Gazetteers, Nan'an.

Fujian Research Institute of Arts. 1983. *Fujian Xishi Lu* [*Historical Materials of Fujian Operas*], People's Publishing House, Fuzhou.

Gao, Yang Wen (ed.). 2001. *Qi Jiguang Wenji* [*The Collection of Writings by Qi Jiguang*], Chinese Bureau of Books, Beijing.

He, Qiao Yuan. 1994 [1628–1632]. *Min Shu* [*The Book of Fujian*], People's Publishing House, Fuzhou.

Huang, Bai Ling. 1982. *Jiuri Shan Zhi* [*The Gazette of the Nine Suns Mountain*], Cultural Bureau and Relics Management Committee, Quanzhou.

Hui'an Xianzhi [*Hui'an County Gazette*], compiled by Wu, Yu Ren. 1985 [1803]. Office of Local Gazetteers, Hui'an.

Jinjing Xianzhi [*Jingjing County Gazette*], compiled by Fang, Ding. 1945 [1765]. Committee of Archival Materials, Jinjiang.

———. compiled by Zhou, Xue Zeng. 1990 [1830]. People's Publishing House, Fuzhou.

Lan, Ding Yuan. 1995 [1732]. Shuzu Fujian tidu Yishan Gong jiazhuan [A family biography of Yishan Gong (Lan Li), the governor of Fujian], in *juan* 6 of his Luzhou Chuji (The primary collection of Master Luzhou), included in his *Luzhou Quanji* [*A Collection of Works by Mr. Luzhou*] 2 Vols., Xiamen University Press, Xiamen, Vol. 1, pp. 139–147.

Li, Guang Di. 1995 [1690–1719]. *Rongcun Yulu, Rongcun Xu Yulu* [*Quotations of Mr. Rongcun, Continued Quotations of Mr. Rongcun*], Chinese Bureau of Books, Beijing.

Lian, Heng. 1983 [1920–1921]. *Taiwan Tongzhi* [*The Comprehensive Gazetteer of Taiwan*], Commercial Press, Beijing.

Liang, Ting Lan. 1959 [1850]. *Yifen Wenji* [*Stories and Records of the Moods of the Barbarians*], Chinese Bureau of Books, Beijing.

Lin, Long Hai. 1993. *Quanzhou Jianzhi Zhi* (*The Gazetteer of Quanzhou's Local Administrative Distribution*), Strait Arts Press, Fuzhou.

Liu, Ya Zi. 1994. *Nanming Shiliao* [*Historical Materials of the Southern Ming*], People's Publishing House, Shanghai.

Long, Wen Bing. 1956 [1887]. *Ming Hui Yao* [*A Collection of Descriptions of Major Events during the Ming*], Chinese Bureau of Books, Beijing.

Ming Shi [*The History of the Ming Dynasty*], compiled by Zhang, Ting Yu. 1974 [1739]. The Chinese Bureau of Books, Beijing.

Mingkan Minnan Xiqu Xuanguan Xuanben Sanzhong [*Three Selected Plays of the Ming Editions of Minnan Local Opera*], compiled by Peter Van der Loon. 2003. Drama Press, Beijing.

Museum of Maritime Communication History. 1983. *Quanzhou Haiwai Jiaotong Shiliao Huibian* [*A Collection of Materials of Quanzhou's Overseas Communication History*], Chinese Society for Historical Studies of Maritime Communication, Quanzhou.

Nanwai Tianyuan Zhaoshi Zupu [*The Genealogy of the Zhao Family of Tianyuan Origin of the Southern Capital Branch*], Research Association of the Southern Capital Branch of the Zhao Clan. 1994. Quanzhou.

Nian, Liang Tu. 2002. *Jinjiang Beike Xuan* [*Selected Stele Inscriptions in Jinjiang*], Xiamen University Press, Xaimen.

Office of Local Gazetteers. 1985a. *Quanzhou Jiufengsu Ziliao Huibian* [*A Collection of Materials on Old Customs in Quanzhou*], Municipal Government, Quanzhou.

———. 1985b. *Quanzhou Fangyu Jiyao* [*Main Materials of Quanzhou Historical Geography*], Municipal Government, Quanzhou.

———. 1999. *Licheng Qu Zhi* [*The Gazette of the Borough of Carp City*], Chinese Social Science Press, Beijing.

Office of Place Names. 1983. *Quanzhou Diming Zhi* [*The Gazette of Place Names in Quanzhou*], Office of Place Names, Quanzhou.

Qi, Ji Guang. 2001a [1567]. Shang yingzhao chenyan yipuenshang shugao [A treatise handed over to his majesty on broadly delivering bestowals and awards], in Gao, Yang Wen (ed.), *Qi Jiguang Wenji* [*The Collection of Essays by Qi Jiguang*], Chinese Bureau of Books, Beijing, pp. 23–33.

———. 2001b [1567]. Jibie min zhang yici zhenwang jiangshi [A eulogy read in a farewell ceremony held at the memorial halls for martyred commanders and officers], in Gao, Yang Wen (ed.), *Qi Jiguang Wenji* [*The Collection of Essays by Qi Jiguang*], Chinese Bureau of Books, Beijing, pp. 189–190.

Quanzhou Fuzhi [*Quanzhou Prefecture Gazette*], compiled by Yang Ming, Qian. 1612. Quanzhou.

———. compiled by Huai Yin, Bu, and Huang, Ren. 1870 [1763]. Keban edition by Zhang Zuo Biao, Office of Local Gazetteers, Quanzhou.

Qing Shilu Taiwan Shi Ziliao Zhuanji [*A Special Collections of Materials on Taiwan History in the Book Facts Record of the Qing*], compiled by Zhang, Ben Zheng. 1993. People's Publishing House, Fuzhou.

Shi, Hong Bao. 1985 [1857]. *Min Zaji* [*Miscellaneous Notes on Fujian*], People's Publishing House, Fuzhou.

Si Ma, Qian. 1959 [unclear]. *Shi Ji* [*Historians' Records*], Chinese Bureau of Books, Beijing.

Tianhougong Temple. 1990. *Quanzhou Tianhou Gong Jianjie* [*A Brief Introduction to the Tianhou Temple of Quanzhou*], Museum of Fujian-Taiwan Relations, Tianhou Gong Temple, Quanzhou.

van der Loon, Peter. 2003. *Ming Kan Minnan Xiqu Xuanguan Xuben Sanzhong* [*The Ming Editions of Three Play Scripts of Minnan Regional Operas*], Chinese Drama Press, Beijing.

Wang, Jing. 2000 [805]. *Datong Jiaosi Lu* [*The Record of Suburban Ceremonies in the Great Tang Dynasty*], Nationality Press, Beijing.

Wang, Yang Ming. 1992 [1572]. Nangan Xiangyue [Community pact in South Jiangxi], in his *Wang Yang Ming Quanji* [*The Collection of Writings by Wang Yang Ming*], Vol. 1, Shanghai Guji Chubanshe, Shanghai, pp. 599–603.

Wang, Zhi Chun. 1989 [1879]. *Qingchao Rouyuan Ji* [*A Record of the Qing Dynasty's History of Cherishing Afar*], Chinese Bureau of Books, Beijing.

Wu, Tan. 1992 [1779]. *Daqing Luli Tongkao* [*The Comprehensive Survey of Laws and Regulations in the Great Qing*], The Chinese University of Politics and Law Press, Beijing.

Wu, Wen Liang. 2005 [1957]. *Quanzhou Zongjiao Shike* [*Epigraphical Materials of Religions in Quanzhou*], Science Press, Beijing.

Wu, Zi Mu. 2001 [1270]. *Mengliang Lu* [*Records of Mengliang*], Friendship Press, Jinan.

Xiamen Zhi [*The Gazette of Xiamen*], compiled by Zhou, Kai. 1996 [1840]. Lujiang Press, Xiamen.

Ye, Chun Ji. 1987 [1672]. *Hui'an Zhengshu* [*Hui'an County Political Manual*], People's Publishing House, Fuzhou.

Yu, Ji Deng. 1995. (Reprint of the original Ming undated edition) *Huangming Diangu Jiwen* [*Records of the Ming Emperors' Literary Quotations*], Reference Books Press, Beijing.

Yuan Shi [*Yuan History*], compiled by Song, Lian. 1983 [1371]. Chinese Bureau of Books, Beijing.

Zeng, Huan Zhi, and Fu, Jin Xing. 1986. *Quanzhou Tonghuai Guanyue Miao Zhi* [*The Gazette of the Temple of Guandi and Yue Fei at Tonghuai in Quanzhou*], United Front Department, Quanzhou.

Zhou, Mi. 2001 [1242–1252]. *Wulin Jiushi* [*Old Things in Wulin*], Friendship Press, Jinan.

Zhuang, Wei Ji. 1985. *Jinjiang Xinzhi* [*The New Gazette of Jinjiang*], Office of Local Gazetteers, Quanzhou.

Zhuo, Zheng Ming. 1996. *Quanzhou Huaqiao Zhi* [*The Gazette of Overseas Chinese from Quanzhou*], Chinese Social Science Press, Beijing.

Secondary Sources

Abu-Lughod, J. 1989. *Before European Hegemony: The World System in A.D. 1250*, Oxford University Press, New York.

Ahern, E. 1981. *Chinese Ritual and Politics*, Cambridge University Press, Cambridge.

Anagnost, A. 1987. Politics and magic in contemporary China, *Modern China* 13(1): 40–62.

Anderson, B. 1991. *Imagined Communities: Reflections on the Origin and Spread of Nationalism*, Verso, London.

Andrade, T. 2004. The Company's Chinese pirates: How the Dutch East India Company tried to lead a coalition of pirates to war against China 1621–1662, *Journal of World History* 15(4): 415–444.

Appadurai, A. 1988. Introduction: Place and voice in anthropological theory, *Cultural Anthropology* 3(1): 16–20.

Arendt, H. 1958. *The Human Condition*, University of Chicago Press, Chicago.

Barlow, T. (ed.). 1997. *Formations of Colonial Modernity in East Asia*, Duke University Press, Durham and London.

Bell, C. 1989. Religion and Chinese culture: Towards an assessment of popular religion, *History of Religions* 29(1): 37–57.

Benevolo, L. 1993. *The European City*, Blackwell, Oxford.

Bhabha, H. 1990. DissemiNation: Time, narration, and the margins of the modern world, in H. Bhabha (ed.), *Nations and Narration*, Routledge, London, pp. 291–322.

Bourdieu, P. 1979. *Outline of a Theory of Practice*, Cambridge University Press, Cambridge.

Brook, T. 1985. The spatial structure of Ming local administration, *Late Imperial China* 6(1): 1–55.

———. 1998. *The Confusions of Pleasure: Commerce and Culture in Ming China*, University of California Press, Berkeley and Los Angeles.

Casey, E. S. 1996. How to get from space to place in a fairly short stretch of time: Phenomenological prolegomena, in S. Held and K. H. Basso (eds.), *Senses of Place*, School of American Research Press, Santa Fe, pp. 13–52.

Chaffer, J. 2001. The impact of the Song imperial clan on the overseas trade of Quanzhou, in A. Schotttenhammer (ed.), *The Emporium of the World: Maritime Quanzhou, 1000–1400*, Brill, Leiden, pp. 13–46.

Chen, C. 1990. Orthodoxy as a mode of statecraft: The ancient concept of Cheng, in Liu, Kwang-ching (ed.), *Orthodoxy in Late Imperial China*, University of California Press, Berkeley and Los Angeles, pp. 27–52.

Chen, C. C. 1998. Quanzhou "yuesuo" kaocha [An investigation into Quanzhou's community pact halls], *Mintai Minsu* [*Fujian and Taiwan Folklore*], Vol. 2, pp. 37–46.

Chen, C. C. and Lin, S. L. 1990. *Quanzhou Jiu Pujing Jilue* [*A Brief Survey of Old Pujing in Quanzhou*], United Front Department and Office of Local Gazetteers, Quanzhou.

Chen, C. N. 1994 [1987]. *Taiwan de Zhongguo Chuantong Shehui* [*Traditional Chinese Society in Taiwan*], Yunchen Cultural Enterprise, Inc., Taipei.

Chen, D. S. 1985. Wenling suishi ii [Notes on seasonal customs in Warm Hills (Quanzhou)], in *Quanzhou Jiu Fengsu Ziliao Huibian* [*A Collection of Materials on Old Customs in Quanzhou*], Office of Local Gazetteers, Quanzhou, pp. 84–96.

Chen, D. X. 1980. Quanzhou tixian mu'ou yishu fazhan chutan [A preliminary investigation into the historical development of string puppets in Quanzhou], *Quanzhou Wenshi* [*Culture and History in Quanzhou*], 2-3, pp. 68–91.

Chen, G. 1988. Quanzhou shi jianzhi yange [The evolution of local administration in Quanzhou], *Quanzhou Wenshi Ziliao* [*Cultural and Historical Materials in Quanzhou*], 4, pp. 34–39.

Chen, G. B. 1994. Ming Longwan Nianjian Ye Chunji zai Hui'an Xian hui Yinci yuanyi chuyi [A preliminary study of the question why Ye Chunji sought to destroy licentious cults in Hui'an county in the Longqing and Wanli Reigns of the Ming], *Quanzhou Daojiao Wenhua* [*Daoist Culture in Quanzhou*], 1, pp. 34–37.

Chen, G. Q. (ed.). 1990. *Chongwu Yanjiu* [*Studies of Chongwu*], Social Science Press, Beijing.

Chen, J. Y. 1997, Dubei santi (Three discussions on three stele inscriptions), *Mintai Minsu* [*Fujian and Taiwan Folklore*], 1, pp. 65–73.

Chen, K. L. 1990, *Qingdai Taiwan Yimin Shehui Yanjiu* [*A Study of Migrant Societies in Taiwan in the Qing Dynasty*], Xiamen University Press, Xiamen.

Chen, S. S. 1997. *Huaiyi yu Yishang: Mingdai Haiyang Liliang Xingshuai Yanjiu* [*Cherishing the Barbarians and Repressing the Merchants: A Study of the Surge and Decline of Maritime Power in the Ming Dynasty*], People's Publishing House, Jinan.

Chen, S. D. 1981. Lun Li Guangjin de zhongshang qingxiang [On Li Guangjin's tendency to emphasize commerce], *Quanzhou Wenshi* [*Culture and History in Quanzhou*], 5, pp. 6–7.

———. 1982. Lue lun Mingdai Fujian yanhai de fan zousi cuoshi [A brief essay on the anti-smuggling policies in Fujian during the Ming], *Quanzhou Wenshi* [*Culture and History in Quanzhou*], 6-7, pp. 125–127.

———. 1990. Qianyan (Preface), to Chen, C. C., and Lin, S. L., *Jiu Pujing Jilue* [*An Investigation into the Old Pujing in Quanzhou*], United Front Department, Quanzhou, pp. 1–2.

———. 1991. Quanzhou haiwai jiaotong yu haishen xinyang [Overseas communication and maritime cults in Quanzhou], in *China and the Maritime Silk Roads*, 2 Vols., People's Publishing House, Fuzhou, Vol. 1, pp. 360–374.

Chen, Y. D. 1980. Quanzhou Gucheng Takan [Field Research into Quanzhou's Ancient City Sites], *Quanzhou Wenshi* [*Culture and History in Quanzhou*], 2-3, pp. 1–13.

———. 1987. Quanzhou wuyue [The five great peaks in Quanzhou], *Quanzhou Wenshi Ziliao* [*Cultural and Historical Materials in Quanzhou*], 3, pp. 145–151.

Chen, Z. Q. 1980. Lun Quanzhou nanwai zongzhengsi [A treatise on the Southern Branch of the Royal Clan in Quanzhou], *Quanzhou Wenshi* [*Culture and History in Quanzhou*], 4, pp. 70–74.

Cheng, X. C. 1987. *Zhongguo Difang Zhengfu* [*China's Local Government*], Chinese Bureau of Books, Hong Kong.

Ch'u, T. 1962. *Local Government in China under the Ch'ing*, Harvard University Press, Cambridge, MA.

Chuan, H. S. 1934. Songdai dushi de ye shenghuo [Night life in the urbanities of the Song], *Shihuo* [*Economic History*] 1(1): 23–28.

Chun, A. 2000. *Unstructuring Chinese Society: The Fiction of Colonial Practice and the Changing Realities of "Land" in the New Territories of Hong Kong*, OPA, Amsterdam.

Clark, H. 1991a. *Community, Trade, and Networks: Southern Fujian Province from the Third to the Thirteenth Century*, Cambridge University Press, Cambridge.

———. 1991b. Quanzhou maoyi he Quanzhou shibosi de sheli [Quanzhou trade and the establishment of the Trade Superintendantcy in Quanzhou], in *China and the Maritime Silk Roads*, 2 Vols., People's Publishing House, Fuzhou, Vol. 1, pp. 375–394.

———. 2000. Overseas trade and social change in Quanzhou through the Song, in A. Schottenhammer (ed.), *The Emporium of the World: Maritime Quanzhou, 1000–1400*, Brill, Leiden, pp. 47–94.

Cohen, B. 2004. *The Bernard Cohen Omnibus: An Anthropologist among the Historians and Other Essays*, Oxford University Press, New Delhi.

Cohen, M. 1991. Being Chinese: The peripheralization of traditional society, in Tu, W. M. (ed.), *The Living Tree: The Changing Meaning of Being Chinese Today*, Stanford University Press, Stanford, CA, pp. 88–108.

———. 1993. Cultural and political inventions in modern China: The case of the Chinese "peasant," in Tu, W. M. (ed.), *China in Transformation*, Harvard University Press, Cambridge, MA, pp. 151–170.

Comaroff, J., and Comaroff, J. 1992. *Ethnography and the Historical Imagination*, Westview, Boulder, CO.

Corradini, P. 1994. Italians in Quanzhou during the Yuan Dynasty, in *China and the Maritime Silk Roads*, 2 Vols., People's Publishing House, Fuzhou, Vol. 1, pp. 32–39.

Dean, K. 1993. *Taoist Ritual and Popular Cults in Southeast China*, Princeton University Press, Princeton, NJ.

DeGlopper, D. 1974. Religion and ritual in Lukang, in A. Wolf (ed.), *Religion and Ritual in Chinese Society*, Stanford University Press, Stanford, CA, pp. 43–71.

de Groot, J. J. M. 1892. *The Religious System of China*, Vol. 1, Brill, Leiden.

Dell'Orto, A. 2002. *Place and Spirit: Tidi Gong in the Stories, Strategies, and Memories of Everyday Life*, Routledge-Curzon, London.

Duara, P. 1995. *Rescuing History from the Nation: Questioning Narratives of Modern China*, University of Chicago Press, Chicago.

———. 1997. Nationalists among transnationals: Overseas Chinese and the idea of China, in A. Ong and D. Nonini (eds.), *Ungrounded Empires: The Cultural Politics of Modern Chinese Transnationalism*, Routledge, London, pp. 39–60.

———. 1999. Local worlds: The poetics and politics of the native place in modern China, in Huang, S., and Hsu, C., (eds.), *Imagining China: Regional Division and National Unity*, Academia Sinica, Taipei, pp. 161–200.

Duncan, J. S. 1990. *The City as Text: The Politics of Landscape Interpretations in the Kandyan Kingdom*, Cambridge University Press, Cambridge.

Dutton, M. 1988. Policing the Chinese household, *Economy and Society* 17(2): 195–224.

Eberhard, W. 1957. The political function of astronomy and astronomers in Han China, in J. K. Fairbank (ed.), *Chinese Thought and Institutions*, University of Chicago Press, Chicago, pp. 33–70.

Ebrey, P. B. 1986. The early stages in the development of descent group organization, in P. B. Ebrey and J. L. Watson (eds.), *Kinship Organization in Late Imperial China, 1000–1940*, University of California Press, Berkeley and Los Angeles, pp. 16–61.

Elias, N. 1983. *The Court Society*, Pantheon House, New York.

———. 1994. *The Civilizing Process*, Blackwell, Oxford.

Elman, B. A. 1999. *Classicism, Politics, and Kinship: The Ch'ang-chou School of New Text Confucianism in Late Imperial China*, University of California Press, Berkeley and Los Angeles.

Elvin, M. 1985. Between the earth and heaven: Conceptions of the self in China, in M. Carrithers, S. Collins, and Steven Lukes (eds.), *The Category of the Person: Anthropology, Philosophy, History*, Cambridge University Press, Cambridge, pp. 156–189.

———. 1990. The Double-Disavowal: The attitudes of radical thinkers to the Chinese tradition, in D. S. Goodman (ed.), *China and the West: Ideas and Activities*, Manchester University Press, Manchester, pp. 3–29.

Eshrick, J., and Rankin, M. (eds.). 1990. *Chinese Local Elites and Patterns of Dominance*, University of California Press, Berkeley and Los Angeles.

Farmer, E. 1990. Social regulations of the first Ming emperor: Orthodoxy as a function of authority, in Liu, K. (ed.), *Orthodoxy in Late Imperial China*, University of California Press, Berkeley and Los Angeles, pp. 103–152.

Faure, D. 1999. The emperor in the village: Representing the state in South China, in J. P. McDermott (ed.), *State and Court Ritual in China*, Cambridge University Press, Cambridge, pp. 267–298.

Faure, D., and Siu, H. (eds.) 1995. *Down to Earth: The Territorial Bonds in South China*, Stanford University Press, Stanford, CA.

Fei, X. T. (Fei, Hsiao-tung). 1939. *Peasant Life in China*, Routledge, London.

———. 1953. *China's Gentry: Essays in Rural-Urban Relations*, University of Chicago Press, Chicago.

———. 1998a. Jianshu wode minzu yanjiu silu [A brief reflection on the lines of thought with which I have studied nationalists], in his *Congshi Qiuzhi Lu* [*Persuing Knowledge through Practice*], Beijing University Press, Beijing, pp. 119–136.

———. 1998b. Fansi, duihua, wenhua zijue [Reflections, dialogues, and self-awareness of culture], in Ma, R., and Zhou, X. (eds.), *Tianye Gongzuo yu Wenhua Zijue* [*Fieldwork and Self-Awareness of Culture*], Qunyan Press, Beijing, pp. 38–54.

Feld, S., and Basso, K. H. (eds.). 1996. *Senses of Place*, School of American Research Press, Santa Fe, NM.

Feng, T. Y. 1998. *Mingqing Wenhuashi Sanlun* [*Essays on the Cultural History of the Ming and the Qing*] (2nd ed.), Central China University of Science and Technology Press, Wuhan.

Feuchtwang, S. 1974a. City temples in Taipei under three regimes, in G. W. Skinner and M. Elvin (eds.), *The Chinese City between Two Worlds*, Stanford University Press, Stanford, CA, pp. 263–302.

———. 1974b. Domestic and communal worship, in A. Wolf (ed.), *Religion and Ritual in Chinese Society*, Stanford University Press, Stanford, CA, pp. 103–130.

———. 1975. Investigating religion, in M. Bloch (ed.), *Marxist Analyses of Social Anthropology*, Malaby Press, London, pp. 61–82.

———. 1991. A Chinese religion exists, in S. Feuchtwang and H. Baker (eds.), *An Old Society in New Settings*, JASO, Oxford, pp. 131–161.

———. 1992a. *The Imperial Metaphor: Popular Religion in China*, Routledge, London.

———. 1992b. Boundary maintenance: Territorial altars and areas in rural China, *Cosmos* 8: 93–109.

———. 1996. Local religion and village identity, in Liu, T., and D. Faure (eds.), *Unity and Diversity: Local Cultures and Identities in China*, Chinese University of Hong Kong Press, Hong Kong, pp. 161–176.

Fiskesjo, M. 1999. On the "raw" and the "cooked" barbarians of imperial China, *Inner Asia* 1(1): 139–168.

Foucault, M. 1977. *Discipline and Punish: The Birth of the Prison*, Penguin Books, London.

Freedman, M. 1958. *Lineage Organization in Southeastern China*, Athlone, London.

———. 1963. A Chinese phase in social anthropology, *British Journal of Sociology* 14(1): 1–19.

———. 1966. *Chinese Lineage and Society: Fukien and Kwangtung*, Athlone, London.

Freedman, M. 1974. On the sociological study of Chinese religion, in A. Wolf (ed.), *Religion and Ritual in Chinese Society*, Stanford University Press, Stanford, CA, pp. 19–41.

———. 1979 [1974]. The politics of an old state: A view from the Chinese lineage, in G. W. Skinner (ed.), *The Study of Chinese Society: Essays by Maurice Freedman*, Stanford University Press, Stanford, CA, pp. 334–350.

Fu, J. X. 1989. Potuerchu de Quanzhouxue [Quanzhou-ologue breaks out from the ground], *Quanzhou Wenshi* [*Culture and History in Quanzhou*] 10: 2–15.

———. 1992. *Quanshan Caipu* [*Picking Up Jades in the Mountains of Quanzhou*], Office of Local Gazetteers, Quanzhou.

———. 1994. *Quanxian Zhuzuo Shuping* [*Reviews of Works by the Sagacious from Quanzhou*], Lujiang Press, Xiamen.

———. 1981. Mingdai Quanzhou Anping shangren shiliao jibu: Du Li Guangjin Jingpi Ji yu He Qiaoyuan Jingshan Quanshu liangshu zhaji [Additional materials concerning Anping merchants in Quanzhou: Reading Jingbi Ji by Li Guangjin and Jingshan Quanji by He Qiaoyuan], *Quanzhou Wenshi* [*Culture and History in Quanzhou*] 5: 1–5.

Fu, Y. L. 1989. *Fuyiling Zhishi Wushi Nian* [*Fu Yiling's Papers on the Study of History: 50 Years of Efforts*], People's Publishing House, Shanghai.

Fu, Z. W. 1983. Songdai Quanzhou Shibo Shi sheli wenti tantao [An inquiry into some issues concerning the establishment of Trade Superintendents in Quanzhou in the Song Dynasty], *Quanzhou Wenshi* [*Culture and History in Quanzhou*] 8: 1–10.

Gao, L. Y., and Chen, Q. 1986. *Fujian Zhuzi Xue* [*The Fujian School of Zhu Xi's Philosophy*], People's Publishing House, Fuzhou.

Gao, X. 1995. *Kang Yong Qian Sandi Tongzhi Sixiang Yanjiu* [*A Study of Kangxi, Yongzheng, and Qianlong Emperors' Ideas of Political Rule*], Renmin University Press, Beijing.

Gates, H. 1996. *China's Motor: A Thousand Years of Petty Capitalism*, Cornell University Press, Ithaca, NY.

Gates, H., and Weller, R. 1987. Hegemony and Chinese folk ideology, *Modern China* 13(1): 3–16.

Geertz, C. 1973. *The Interpretation of Cultures*, Basic Books, New York.

Gellner, E. 1983. *Nations and Nationalism*, Blackwell, Oxford.

Gernet, J. 1982 [1972]. *A History of Chinese Civilization*, Cambridge University Press, Cambridge.

Giddens, A. 1985. *The Nation-State and Violence*, Polity, Cambridge.

Goody, J. 1998. *Food and Love: A Cultural History of East and West*, Verso, London.

Guo, S. L. 2000. *Xichao Jidang Xia de Wanqing Dilixue* [*Late Qing Geography under Western Tides*], Beijing University Press, Beijing.

Granet, M. 1975. *The Religion of the Chinese People*, Blackwell, Oxford.

Gu, J. G. 1928a. Quanzhou de Tudi shen [Locality gods in Quanzhou], *Minsu Zhoukan* [*Folklore Weekly*], March 28th and April 4th, 1928.

———. 1928b. *Miaofeng Shan* [*The Miaofeng Mountain*], Folklore Series of Institute of Linguistics and History, National Chongshan University, Guangzhou.

———. 1988 [1930]. *Zhongguo Shanggushi Jiangyi* [*Lectures on the Study of Classical Chinese History*], Chinese Bureau of Books, Beijing.

Gu, J. G. 1998 [1955]. *Qinhan de Fangshi yu Rusheng* [*Necromancers and Confu-cians in Chin and Han Dynasties*], Ancient Archives Press, Shanghai.

Gu, J. G., and Shi, N. H. 2000 [1939]. *Zhongguo Jiangyu Yange Shi* [*History of the Changes of China's Borders*], Commercial Press, Beijing.

Gu, Y. W. 1994 [1670]. *Rizhi Lu* [*Record of Daily Accumulated Knowledge*], Yuelu Mountain Publishing, Changsha.

———. 1985[1639]. *Tianxia Junguo Libing Shu* [*A Book of the Advantages and Disadvantages of Regions in China*], juan on Quanzhou, Office of Local Gazetteers, *Quanzhou Fangyu Jiyao*, Office of Local Gazetteers, Quanzhou, pp. 191–248.

Handelman, D. 1998. *Models and Mirrors: Towards an Anthropology of Public Events*, Berghahn Books, Oxford.

Harrell, S. 1987. The concept of fate in Chinese folk ideology, *Modern China* 13(1): 90–110.

He, T. S. 1987. Licheng jiexiang jianshe huigu [A look backward on the construction of urban streets and lanes], *Quanzhou Licheng Wenshi Ziliao* [*Cultural and Historical Materials in the Carp City of Quanzhou*], 9, pp. 123–128.

Hertzfeld, M. 1992. *The Social Reproduction of Indifference: Exploring the Symbolic Roots of Western Bureaucracy*, University of Chicago Press, Chicago.

Hevia, J. 1995. *Cherishing Men from Afar: Qing Guest Ritual and the Macartney Embassy of 1793*, Duke University Press, Durham.

Hostetler, L. 2001. *Qing Colonial Enterprise: Ethnography and Cartography in Early Modern China*, University of Chicago Press, Chicago.

Hou, W. L. 1956. *Zhongguo Zaoqi Qimeng Sixiang Shi* [*A History of Early Enlightenment Ideas in China*], People's Publishing House, Beijing.

Hsu, F. L. K. 1948. *Under the Ancestors' Shadow: Chinese Culture and Personality*, Routledge, London.

Hua, Y. G. 1998. *Xihan Lixue Xinlun* [*A New Treatise on the Thought of Ritual in Western Han Dynasty*], Social Science Academy Press, Shanghai.

Huang, R. 1974. *Taxation and Government Finance in Sixteenth-Century China*, Cambridge University Press, Cambridge.

Huang, S. 1989. *The Spiral Road: Changes in a Chinese Village through the Eyes of a Communist Party Member*, Westview, Boulder, CO.

Jenner, W. 1992. *The Tyranny of History: The Roots of China's Crisis*, Penguin Books, Harmondsworth.

Jia, H. H. 2003. Songdai chengshi xiangzhi yanjiu [A study of the xiang institution in the Song dynasty], in *Hou Ren Zhi Shi Jiushi Shoucheng Jinian Wenji Jing* [*A Collection of Essays in Honoring the Ninetieth Birthday of Professor Hou Ren Zhi*], The Center for Historical Geography of Peking University, Academic Press, Shanghai, pp. 26–48.

Jing, J. 1999. Villages dammed, villages repossessed: A memorial movement in Northwestern China, *American Ethnologist* 26(2): 324–343.

Jordon, D. 1972. *Gods, Ghosts, and Ancestors: Folk Religion in a Taiwanese Village*, University of California Press, Berkeley and Los Angeles.

Katz, P. 1995. *Demon Hordes and Burning Boats: The Cult of Marshal Wen in Late Imperial Chekiang*, State University of New York Press, Albany, NY.

Ke, J. R. 1985. Quanzhou Pudu fengsu kao [An investigation of pudu cus-toms in Quanzhou], in *Quanzhou Jiu Fengsu Ziliao Huibian* [*A Collection of*

Materials of Old Customs in Quanzhou], Office of Local Gazetteers, Quanzhou, pp. 143–150.

Kirby, W. C. 2000. Engineering China: Birth of the developmental state, 1928–1937, in Yeh, Wen-hsin (ed.), *Becoming Chinese: Passages to Modernity and Beyond*, University of California Press, Berkeley and Los Angeles, pp. 137–160.

Kuhn, P. A. 1980 [1970]. *Rebellion and Its Enemy in Late Imperial China: Militarization and Social Structure, 1796–1864*, Harvard University Press, Cambridge, MA.

————. 1990. *Soulstealers: The Chinese Sorcery Scare of 1768*, Harvard University Press, Cambridge, MA.

La Fontaine, J. S. 1998. *Speak of the Devil: Tales of Satanic Abuse in Contemporary England*, Cambridge University Press, Cambridge.

Lamley, H. J. 1990. Lineage feuding in Southern Fujian and Eastern Guangdong under Qing rule, in J. Lipman and S. Harrell (eds.), *Violence in China: Essays in Culture and Counterculture*, State University of New York Press, Albany, NY, pp. 27–64.

Leach, E. 1982. *Social Anthropology*, Fontana, London.

Lemoine, J. 1989. Ethnologists in China, *Diogenes*, 177, pp. 83–111.

Leonard, K. J. 1984. *Wei Yuan and China's Rediscovery of the Maritime World*, Council on East Asian Studies, Harvard University Press, Cambridge, MA.

Levi-Strauss, C. 1997 [1973]. *Tristes Troipiques*, The Modern Library, New York.

Li, Y. K. 1989. Shilun lishishang Quanzhou de xiedou [A preliminary treatise on feuds in historical Quanzhou], *Quanzhou Wenshi* [*Culture and History in Quanzhou*], 10, pp. 132–138.

————. 1995. *Quanzhou Haiwai Jiaotong Shilue* [*A Sketch History of Quanzhou's Overseas Communication*], Lujiang Press, Xiamen.

————. 1998. Mingqing shiqi Quanzhou tuixing xiangyue ruogan wenti [Some issues related to the promotion of *xiangyue* in Quanzhou in the Ming and the Qing], *Mintai Minsu* [*Fujian and Taiwan Folklore*], 2, pp. 5–17.

Liang, F. Z. 1956. *Mingdai Liangzhang Zhidu* [*Grain Head System in the Ming Dynasty*]. People's Publishing House, Shanghai.

Liang, S. M. 1983 [1949]. *Zhongguo Wenhua Yaoyi* [*Core Meanings of Chinese Culture*], Wunan Books, Taipei.

Lin, H. X. 1993 [1936]. *Zhongguo Minzu Shi* [*History of Nationalities in China*], 2 Vols., Commercial Press, Beijing.

Lin, M. R. 1993. *Taiwan Ren de Shehui yu Xinyang* [*Taiwanese Society and Beliefs*], Independent Evening Paper Press, Taipei.

Ling, S. S. 1963. Beiping de fengshan wenhua [The sacred enclosures and stepped pyramidal platforms of Peiping], *Bulletin of Institute of Ethnology, Academia Sinica* 16: 1–100.

————. 1964. Zhongguo gudai she zhi yuanliu [Origin of the *she* in ancient China], *Bulletin of Institute of Ethnology, Academia Sinica* 17: 1–44.

————. 1965. Zhongguo de fengshan yu lianghe liuyu de 1kunliu wenhua [A comparative study of the ancient Chinese *fengshan* and the zuggurat in Mesopotamia], *Bulletin of Institute of Ethnology, Academia Sinica* 19: 1–51.

Liu, H. R. 1997. Xishen Xianggong Ye zai Quanzhou de fengsi [Local Worship of the Opera God Xianggong Ye in Quanzhou], *Mintai Minsu* [*Fujian and Taiwan Folklore*], 1, pp. 145–164.

Liu, K. (ed.). 1990. *Orthodoxy in Late Imperial China*, University of California Press, Berkeley and Los Angeles.

Liu, S. H. 1996. Lun Bixian Yuanjun xingxiang de yanhua jiqi wenhua neihan [On the evolution and cultural significance of the cult of the Prime Monarch of Azure Clouds], in Liu, X. C. (ed.), *Miao fengshan: Shiji Zhijiao de Zhongguo Minsu Liubian* [*Miaofeng Shan: The Changes of Chinese Folk Customs at the Transition of the Century*], Urban Press, Beijing, pp. 60–68.

Liu, Z. W. 1997. *Zai Guojia yu Shehui Zhijian: Mingqing Guangdong Lijia Fuyi Zhidu Yanjiu* [*Between the State and Society: A Study of Lijia Taxation-Labor Service Institution in Guangdong in the Ming and the Qing*], Zhongshan University Press, Guangzhou.

Lowenthal, D. 1998. *The Heritage Crusade and the Spoils of History*, Cambridge University Press, Cambridge.

Luan, C. X. 1998. *Mingdai Huangce Yanjiu* [*A Study of Huangce in the Ming*], Social Science Press, Beijing.

Luo, D. Y. 1998. *Ming Taizu Lifa Zhizhi Yanjiu* [*A Study of Taizu Emperor's Rule of Ritual and Law in the Ming*], Higher Education Press, Beijing.

Lyle, E. 1990. Introduction, to her edited *Archaic Cosmos: Polarity, Space and Time*, Polygon, Edinburgh.

Madsen, R. 1984. *Morality and Power in a Chinese Village*, University of California Press, Berkeley and Los Angeles.

McDermott, J. P. (ed.). 1999. *State and Court Ritual in China*, Cambridge University Press, Cambridge.

McKnight, B. K. 1971. *Village and Bureaucracy in Southern Song China*, University of Chicago Press, Chicago.

Menzies, G. 2003. *1421: The Year China Discovered the World*, Bantam Books, London.

Meyer, J. F. 1976. *Beijing as a Sacred City*, Asian Folklore and Social Life Monographs 81, The Oriental Culture Service, Taipei.

Murray, D. H. 1987. *Pirates of the South China Coast, 1790–1810*, Stanford University Press, Stanford, CA.

Naquin, S. 1992. The Peking pilgrimage to Miaofeng Shan: Religious organizations and sacred sites, in S. Naquin and C. Yu (eds.), *Pilgrims and Sacred Sites in China*, University of California Press, Berkeley and Los Angeles, pp. 333–337.

Needham, J. 1981. *The Shorter Science and Civilization in China*, Vol. 2, abridged, C. A. Ronan, Cambridge University Press, Cambridge.

North, D. 1981. *Structure and Change in Economic History*, W. W Norton, New York.

Ohnuki-Tierney, E. 1990. Introduction, to her edited *Culture through Time: Anthropological Approaches*, Stanford University Press, Stanford, CA, pp. 1–25.

Ong, A., and Nomini, D. (eds.). 1997. *Ungrounded Empires: The Cultural Politics of Modern Chinese Transnationalism*, Routledge, London.

Ownby, D. 1996. *Brotherhoods and Secret Societies in Early and Mid-Qing*, Stanford University Press, Stanford, CA.

Pearson, R., Li, M., and Li, G. 2000. Port city and hinterland: Archaeological perspectives on Quanzhou and its overseas trade, in A. Schottenhammer (ed.),

The Emporium of the World: Maritime Quanzhou, 1000–1400, Brill, Leiden, pp. 177–236.

Pusey, J. 1983. *China and Charles Darwin*, Harvard University Press, Cambridge, MA.

Qian, M. 1939. *Guoshi Dagang* [*Outline of National History*], Commercial Press, Shanghai and Beiping.

Rawski, E. 1985. Economic and Social Foundations of Late Imperial China, in A. Nathan, D. Johnson, and E. Rawski (eds.), *Popular Culture in Late Imperial China*, University of California Press, Berkeley and Los Angeles, pp. 3–33.

Redfield, R. 1941. *The Folk Culture of Yucatan*, University of Chicago Press, Chicago.

Rowe, W. 1989. *Hankow: Conflict and Community in a Chinese City, 1796–1895*, Stanford University Press, Stanford, CA.

Ruan, Dao Ting, He, Jian Hun, and You, Guo Wei. 1962. Luetan Quanzhou Dongxi Fu Xiedou [A brief treatise on Dongxi Fu and feuds in Quanzhou], *Quanzhou Wenshi Ziliao* [*Cultural and Historical Materials in Quanzhou*], 7, pp. 40–51.

Sahlins, M. 1981. *Historical Metaphors and Mythical Realities: Structure of the Early History of the Sandwich Islands Kingdom*, University of Michigan Press, Ann Arbor.

———. 1985. *Islands of History*, University of Chicago Press, Chicago.

———. 1988. Cosmologies of capitalism: The trans-pacific sector of the "world system," *Proceedings of the British Academy*, lxxiv, pp. 1–51.

———. 1995. *How "Natives" Think, about Captain Cook, for Example*, University of Chicago Press, Chicago.

———. 2000. *Culture in Practice*, Zone Books, New York.

Said, E. 1978. *Orientalism*, Penguin, New York.

Sands, B., and Myers, R. H. 1986. The spatial approach to Chinese history: A test, *Journal of Asian Studies* 45(3): 721–743.

Sangren, P. S. 1984. Great and little traditions reconsidered: The question of cultural integration in China, *Journal of Chinese Studies* 1(5): 1–24.

———. 1987. *History and Magical Power in a Chinese Community*, Stanford University Press, Stanford, CA.

———. 2000. *Chinese Sociologics: An Anthropological Account of the Role of Alienation in Social Reproduction*, Athlone, London.

Schipper, K. 1993. *The Taoist Body*, University of California Press, Berkeley and Los Angeles.

Schottenhammer, A. (ed.). 2001. *The Emporium of the World: Maritime Quanzhou, 1000–1400*, Brill, Leiden.

Shepherd, J. 1993. *Statecraft and Political Economy on the Taiwan Frontier, 1600–1800*, Stanford University Press, Stanford, CA.

Shiba, Y. 1970. *Commerce and Society in Sung China*, Center for Chinese Studies, Ann Arbor, MI.

Schneider, R. A. 1989. *Public Life in Toulouse, 1463–1789: From Municipal Republic to Cosmopolitan City*, Cornell University Press, Ithaca, NY.

Shue, V. 1988. *The Reach of the State: Sketches of Chinese Body Politic*, Stanford University Press, Stanford, CA.

Siu, H. 1995. Subverting lineage power: Local bosses and territorial control in the 1940s, in D. Faure and H. Siu (eds.), *Down to Earth: Territorial Bonds in South China*, Stanford University Press, Stanford, CA, pp. 188–208.

Siu, H., and Faure, D. 1995. Introduction, to their edited *Down to Earth: Territorial Bonds in South China*, Stanford University Press, Stanford, CA, pp. 1–20.

Sjoberg, G. (1960), *The Preindustrial City: Past and Present*, The Free Press, New York.

Skinner, G. W. 1964–1965. Marketing and social structure in rural China (two parts), *Journal of Asian Studies* 24(2): 195–228; 363–399.

———. 1977. Cities and the hierarchy of local systems, in G. W. Skinner (ed.), *The City in Late Imperial China*, Stanford University Press, Stanford, CA, pp. 275–353.

———. 1985. Presidential address: The structure of Chinese history, *Journal of Asian Studies* 44(2): 271–292.

Smith, R. 1991. *Fortune-Tellers and Philosophers*, Westview, Boulder, CO.

———. 1996. *Chinese Maps*, Oxford University Press, Hong Kong.

So, K. L. 1991. *Tang Song Shidai Minnan Quanzhou Shidi Lungao* [*Papers on the Historical Geography of Quanzhou, South Fujian during the Tang and Song Periods*], Commercial Press, Taipei.

———. 2000. *Prosperity, Region, and Institutions in Maritime China: The South Fukien Pattern, 946–1368*, Harvard University Asia Center, Cambridge, MA.

Southall, A. 1998. *The City in Time and Space*, Cambridge University Press, Cambridge.

Strand, D. 1989. *Rickshaw Beijing: City People and Politics in the 1920s*, University of California Press, Berkeley and Los Angeles.

———. 2000. "A high place is better than a low place": The city in the making of modern China," in Yeh, W. (ed.), *Becoming Chinese: Passages to Modernity and Beyond*, University of California Press, Berkeley and Los Angeles, pp. 98–136.

Su, S. B. (ed.). 1996. *Hong Chengchou Yanjiu* [*Studies of Hong Chengchou*], Social Science Press, Beijing.

Su, T. 1982. Dageming hou Quanzhou sanci pomi yundong [Three anti-superstitious movements in Quanzhou after the Xinhai Revolution], *Quanzhou Wenshi Ziliao* [*Cultural and Historical Materials in Quanzhou*], 13, pp. 172–180.

Taylor, R. 1990. Official and popular religion and the political organization of Chinese society in the Ming, in Liu, K. (ed.), *Orthodoxy in Late Imperial China*, University of California Press, Berkeley and Los Angeles, pp. 126–157.

Teiser, S. 1996. *The Ghost Festival in Medieval China*, Princeton University Press, Princeont, NJ.

Tu, W. M. 1991. Cultural China: The periphery as the center, in his edited *The Living Tree: The Changing Meaning of Being Chinese Today*, Stanford University Press, Stanford, CA, pp. 1–34.

Wakeman, F. 1985. *The Great Enterprise: The Manchu Reconstruction of Imperial Order in Seventeenth-Century China*, 2 Vols., University of California Press, Berkeley and Los Angeles.

Waldron, A. 1990. *The Great Wall of China: From History to Myth*, Cambridge University Press, Cambridge.

Wallerstein, I. 1974. *The Modern World System*, Academic Press, New York.

Wang, G. W. 1991. *China and the Chinese Overseas*, Times Academic Press, Singapore.

Wang, H. 1997. The fate of "Mr. Science" in China: The concept of science and its application in modern Chinese thought, Tanie Barlow (ed.), *Formation of Colonial Modernity*, Duke University Press, Durham, NC, pp. 21–82.

Wang, H. Z. 1991. *Hong Chengchou Zhuan* [*The Biography of Hong Chengchou*], Red Flag Press, Beijing.

Wang, L. M. 1980a [1963]. Quanzhou chaicheng pilu yu shizheng gaikuan [The destruction of city walls and the paving of new roads in Quanzhou's urban planning], *Quanzhou Wenshi* [*Culture and History in Quanzhou*], 2-3, pp. 33–39.

———. 1980b. Pu Shou Geng tusha nanwai zongzi kao [An investigation into Pu Shougeng's massacre of the Song Royal Clan], *Quanzhou Wenshi* [*Culture and History in Quanzhou*], 4, pp. 75–82.

———. 1994. Quanzhou haiwai jiaotong shi yanjiu gaishu [A survey of historical studies of overseas communication in Quanzhou], in *China and the Maritime Silk Roads*, 2 Vols., People's Publishing House, Fuzhou, Vol. 2, pp. 18–30.

———. 1999. Quanzhouxue yu haijiaoshi chiyi [A preliminary discussion on Quanzhou-ologue and overseas communication history], *Haijiaoshi Yanjiu* [*Maritime Communication History Research*], 2, pp. 1–11.

Wang, M. K. 1997. *Huaxia Bianyuan: Lishi Jiyi yu Zuqun Rentong* [*The Peripheries of Huaxia: Historical Memory and Ethnic Identity*], Yunchen Series, Taipei.

Wang, M. M. 1987. Tangsong renkou de zengzhang yu Quanzhou gang de boxing [The increase of population and the surge of Quanzhou harbor in the Tang and the Song], *Fujian Renkou* [*Fujian Demography*], 1, pp. 1–10.

———. 1993. Flowers of the State, Grasses of the People: Yearly Rites and Aesthetics of Power in Quanzhou in the Southeastern Coastal Macro-region of China, Ph. D. thesis, University of London, London.

———. 1994. Quanzhou: The Chinese city as cosmogram, *Cosmos* 16(1): 3–25.

———. 1995. Place, administration, and territorial cults in late imperial China: A case study from South Fujian, *Late Imperial China* 16(2): 33–78.

———. 1997. *Shehui Renleixue yu Zhongguo Yanjiu* [*Social Anthropology and Sinology*], Sanlian Books, Beijing.

———. 1999. *Shiqu de Fanrong: Yizuo Laocheng de Lishi Renleixue Kaocha* [*The Bygone Prosperity: A Historical Anthropology of an Old City, Quanzhou*], People's Publishing House, Hangzhou.

———. 2002. *Renleixue shi Shenma?* [*What Is Anthropology?*], Beijing University Press, Beijing.

———. 2004a. Mapping "chaos": The Dong Xi Fo feuds of Quanzhou, 1644–1839, in S. Feuchtwang (ed.), *Making Place: State Projects, Globalisation and Local Responses*, University London College Press, London, pp. 33–60.

———. 2004b. Tianxia zuowei shijie tushi [All Under Heaven as a world model], *Niandu Xueshu* [*Annual Academic Review*], 3, pp. 1–66.

Watson, J. L. 1985. Standardizing the gods: The promotion of T'ien Hou (Empress of Heaven) along the South China Coast, 960–1960, in D. Johnson, A. Nathan, and E. Rawski (eds.), *Popular Culture in Late Imperial China*, University of California Press, Berkeley and Los Angeles, pp. 292–324.

———. (ed.). 1988. *Death Ritual in Late Imperial and Modern China*, University of California Press, Berkeley and Los Angeles.

———. 1989. Self-defense corps, violence and the bachelor sub-culture in South China: Two case studies, *Proceedings on the Second International Conference on Sinology*, Academia Sinica, Taipei, pp. 209–222.

———. 1993. Rites or beliefs? The construction of a unified culture in late imperial China, in L. Dittmer (ed.), *China's Quest for National Identity*, Cornell University Press, Ithaca, NY, pp. 80–103.

Weber, M. 1951. *The Religion of China*, The Free Press, New York.

Weller, R. 1987. *Unities and Diversities in Chinese Religion*, Macmillan, London.

———. 1994. *Resistance, Chaos, and Control in China*, University of Washington Press, Seattle.

Wolf, A. 1974. Gods, ghosts, and ancestors, in his edited *Religion and Ritual in Chinese Society*, Stanford University Press, Stanford, CA, pp. 131–182.

———. (ed.) 1974. *Religion and Ritual in Chinese Society*, Stanford University Press, Stanford, CA.

Wolf, E. R. 1982. *Europe and the People without History*, University of California Press, Berkeley and Los Angeles.

Wu, C. M. 1999. *Zhongguo Dongnan Tuzhu Minzu Lishi yu Wenhua de Kaoguxue Kaocha [Archaeological Investigations into the History and Culture of the Aborigines in Southeast China]*, Xiamen University Press, Xiamen.

Wu, H. 2000 [1963]. *Zhu Yuanzhang Zhuan [The Biography of Zhu Yuanzhang]*, Hundred Flowers Art Books, Tianjin.

Wu, J. Q. 1981. Song Yuan nanxi zai Quanzhou de huo wenwu: Liyuanxi qianshi [The living relic of the Song-Yuan Southern Opera: Some Understanding of Liyuanxi Opera], *Quanzhou Wenshi [Culture and History in Quanzhou]*, 5, pp. 36–59.

Wu, Q. 1984. Quanzhou baojia de jianli he xiangzhenbao quhua [The establishment of *baojia* and the divisions of *xiang, zheng* and *bao* in Quanzhou], *Quanzhou Wenshi Zhiliao [Cultural and Historical Materials in Quanzhou]*, 16, pp. 117–138.

Wu, Y. X. 1993. *Quanzhou Zongjiao Wenhua [Religious Culture in Quanzhou]*, Pujiang Press, Xiamen.

———. 1994. Quantai "pudu" fengsu kao [An investigation into the Pudu festival in Quanzhou and Taiwan], *Quanzhou Daojiao Wenhua [Daoist Culture in Quanzhou]*, 1, pp. 19–24.

———. 2002. Lun Yuanmo Quanzhou Yisibaxi zhanluan [On the military chaos of Ispahan in Quanzhou by the end of the Yuan dynasty], *Quanzhou Gang yu Haishang Sichou Zhi Lu [The Port of Quanzhou and the Maritime Silk Road]*, Social Science Press, Beijing, pp. 311–323.

Wu, Z. 1985. Quansu Jichi Pian [Critical poets of Quanzhou customs], in *Quanzhou Jiu Fengsu Ziliao Huibian [Collection of Materials of Old Customs in Quanzhou]*, Office of Local Gazetteers, Quanzhou, pp. 97–125.

Wu, Z. T. 1957 [1940]. *Quanzhou Minjian Chuansuo Ji* [*A Collection of Folk Tales and Legends in Quanzhou*] 4 Vols., People's Publishing House, Fuzhou.

———. 1985. Quanzhou Dongxi Fo [The Eastern and Western Cult Factions in Quanzhou], in *Quanzhou Jiu Fengsu Ziliao Huibian* [*Collection of Materials of Old Customs in Quanzhou*], Office of Local Gazetteers, Quanzhou, pp. 165–171.

Xie, F. 1990. Shiliu shiqi shiji zhongguo haidao yu haishang sichou zhi lu [Chinese pirates and the Maritime Silk Route in the sixteenth and the seventeenth centuries], in *China and the Maritime Silk Roads*, 2 Vols., People's Publishing House, Fuzhou, Vol. 1, pp. 46–54.

Xie, G. Z. 1982. Qingchu Dongnan yanhai qianjie kao [An Investigation of Qianjie in the southeastern coast of China], in his *Mingqing Zhiyi Dangshe Yundong Kao* [*Studies of Movements of Factions and Associations in the Ming and Qing Dynasties*], Chinese Bureau of Books, Beijing, pp. 237–269.

Xu, S. M. 1992. *Li Guangdi Zhuanlun* [*The Biography with Comments of Li Guangdi*], Xiamen University Press, Xiamen.

Yan, Y. 1996. *The Flow of Gifts: Reciprocity and Social Networks in a Chinese Village*, Stanford University Press, Stanford, CA.

Yang, C. K. 1961. *Religion in Chinese Society*, University of California Press, Berkeley and Los Angeles.

Yang, G. Z. 1998. *Min Zai Haizhong* [*Fujian in the Sea*], Higher Education Press, Nanchang.

Yang, H. X. 1986. Zhongguo Gudai Chengshi Jianshe [The construction of ancient Chinese cities], in *Zhongguo Gudai Jiaozhu Kexue Lunwenji* [*A Collection of Papers on Ancient Chinese Architectural Sciences*], Foresight Press, Beijing, pp. 6–33.

Yang, K. 1993. *Zhongguo Gudai Ducheng Zhidushi Yanjiu* [*Institutional Historical Studies of Ancient Chinese Capitals*], Ancient Archives Press, Shanghai.

Yang, L. S. 1957. The concept of *pao* as a basis for social relations in China, in J. K. Fairbank (ed.), *Chinese Thought and Institutions*, University of Chicago Press, Chicago, pp. 269–290.

Yang, M. C. 1945. *A Chinese Village: Taitou, Shantung Province*, Columbia University Press, New York.

Yang, Q. J. 1996. Hong Cheng Chou zhuanji liuzhong bikan [A comparative analysis of six biographies of Hong Cheng Chou], in Su, Shuang Bi (ed.), *Hogn Cheng Chou Yanjiu* [*Studies of Hong Cheng Chou*], Chinese Social Science Press, Beijing, pp. 238–254.

Yang, X. K. 1987. *Zongzhou Shehui yu Liyue Wenming* [*Society and Cermonial Civilization in the Zhou Dynasty*], People's Publishing House, Beijing.

Yeh, W. 2000. Introduction, to his edited *Becoming Chinese: Passages to Modernity and Beyond*, University of California Press, Berkeley and Los Angeles, p. 1–30.

———. (ed.). 2000. *Becoming Chinese: Passages to Modernity and Beyond*, University of California Press, Berkeley and Los Angeles.

Zang, R. 1997. *Zhongguo Gudai Yizhan yu Youchuan* [*Courier Stations and Postal Transmission in Ancient China*], Commercial Press, Beijing.

Zeng, J. M. 1994. Qiantan Quantai "wangye" xinyang [An informal discussion on the cults of Wang Ye in Quanzhou and Taiwan], *Quanzhou Daojiao Wenhua* [*Daoist Culture in Quanzhou*], 1, pp. 46–49.

Zhang, J. J. 1935. Songshi nandu hou de dushi shenghuo [Urban life after the Song court moved to the South], *Shihuo [Economic History]*, 1(10): 36–43.

Zhang, X. L. 1935. Mingdai hukou taiwang yu tiantu huangfei juli [Some examples of escaping households and deserted fields in the Ming], *Shihuo [Economic History]* 3(2): 50–53.

Zhao, S. Y. 1996. Guojia zhengsiyu minjian xinyang de hudong: yi jingshi deDing yu dongyuemiao wei ge'an [The interaction between orthodox rituals and folk beliefs: A case study of the dings in Beijing], *Beijing Shifan Daxeu Xuebao [Beijing Normal University Bulletin]*, 6, pp. 1–15.

Zheng, G. D. 1993. *Quanzhou Daojiao [Daoism in Quanzhou]*, Lujiang Press, Xiamen.

Zheng, G. N. 1998. *Zhongguo Haidao Shi [History of Chinese Piracy]*, East China Normal University Press, Shanghai.

Zheng, Y. J. 1978. *Zheng He Xia Xiyang [Zheng He Paid Visits to the Western Oceans]*, Ocean Press, Beijing.

Zheng, Y. T., and Wang, X. S. 1994. *Zhongguo Chenghuang Xinyang [Chinese Beliefs in the City God]*, Sanlian Books, Shanghai.

Zheng, Z. M. 1998a. Qingdai minnan xiangzu xiedou de yanbian [The changes of lineage feuds in South Fujian in the Qing], *Zhongguo Shehui Jingjishi Yanjiu [Chinese Socio-Economic History Research]*, 1, pp. 16–23.

———. 1998b. Minghouqi Fujian difang xingzheng de yanbian: jianlun Ming zhongye de caizheng gaige [The transformation of local administration in late Ming Fujian: Also commenting on the financial reform in mid-Ming], *Zhongguo Shi Yanjiu [Chinese History Research]*, 1, pp. 147–157.

Zhou, G. Z. (ed.). 1990. *Fujian Haifang Shi [History of Coastal Defense in Fujian]*, Xiamen University Press, Xiamen.

Zhou, J. L. 1984. Huaqiao touzi yu Quanzhou gongshangye [Overseas Chinese investments and Quanzhou's industry and commerce], *Quanzhou Wenshi Ziliao [Cultural and Historical Materials in Quanzhou]*, 16, pp. 1–17.

Zhou, Z. H. 1990. *Tiguo Jingye Zhidao [The Way of Controlling the Country and the Wilderness]*. Chinese Bureau of Books, Hong Kong.

Zhu, S. H. (ed.). 1994. *Zhongguo Gudai Zhi'an Zhidu Shi [The Institutional History of Chinese Public Security Management]*, Henan University Press, Zhengzhou.

Zhu, W. G. 1979. Yuanmo roulin Xing Quan de Yisafahanh bingluan [The military chaos of Yisfahang at the end of the Yuan and its harm in Xinghua and Quanzhou], *Quanzhou Wenshi [Culture and History in Quanzhou]*, 1, pp. 1–10.

Zhuang, J. H. 1996. *Haiwai Jiaotong Shiji Yanjiu [Archaeological Studies of Overseas Communication History]* Xiamen University Press, Xiamen.

Zhuang, W. J. 1980a. Quanzhou lidai chengzhi tansuo [An investigation of city sites in the historical periods of Quanzhou], *Quanzhou Wenshi [Culture and History in Quanzhou]*, 2-3, pp. 14–28.

———. 1980b. Yuanmo waizu panluan yu Quanzhou gang de shuailuo [The rebellions of foreign ethnic groups at end of the Yuan and the decline of Quanzhou harbor], *Quanzhou Wenshi [Culture and History in Quanzhou]*, 4, pp. 19–26.

Zhuang, W. J. 1991. Quanzhou songchuan wei Pujia Sichuan kao [The belonging of the Song boat in Quanzhou to the family of the Pus: An investigation], in *China and the Maritime Silk Roads,* 2 Vols., People's Publishing House, Fuzhou, Vol. 1, pp. 344–353.

Zito, A. 1987. City gods, filiality, and hegemony in late imperial China, *Modern China* 13(3): 333–371.

———. 1997. *Of Body and Brush: Grand Sacrifice as Text/Performance in Eighteenth-Century China,* University of Chicago Press, Chicago.

INDEX

A

Abu-Lughod, Janet, 19, 34
Ahern, Emily, 187
All Under Heaven, 74, 78, 119, 124, 147, 149, 150, 223, 244, 262; *see* Tianxia
Altar for Soil and Grain, 143
Altar for the God of Agriculture (Xiannong Tan), 214, 311
Altar of State Worship (Sheji Tan), 149, 310
Amif-eddin, 104
Analects, 17, 66; Lun Yu, 246
Andreas, 85
An-Shi Chaos (An Shi Zhi Luan), 76, 305
Appadurai, Arjun, 52
Arendt, Hannah, 23
Asiatic mode of production, 74–75; *see* feudal mode of production

B

badao, 124–125, 305; see *wangdao*
bantou ye, 187, 305
Baojia, 51, 125, 174–176, 226, 242, 246, 283, 305; xianzhen, 51, 311
Baosheng Dadi, 190–191, 240, 305
Barlow, Tanie, 56
begging fire [efficacy] (qihuo) ceremony, 217, 309
Bell, Catherine, 297
Bing Bu [Ministry of Armies], 98, 305
Bingma Si [Office of Soldiers and Horses], 106, 305
Bixia Yuanjun [Prime Monarch of Azure Clouds], 204, 305
boundary removal policy, 64
Bourdieu, Pierre 141, 206

Brook, Timothy, 33, 39, 43, 106, 111, 126–127, 169, 179, 201, 205
Buddhism, 86, 88, 99, 114, 270
Bureau of Construction Affairs (Gong Wu Ju), 264
Bureau of Culture (Wenhua Ju), 280, 311
Bureau of Li [Ritual], 127; *see* Minister of Rites (Li Bu)
Bureau of Urban Construction Affairs (Shi Zheng Ju), 265, 269
Bureau of Yue [Music], 127

C

Cai Xiang, 100, 235, 305
Carp City, 28, 30–31, 34, 54, 77, 201
Catholicism, 85
Celestial Altar (Tian Tan), 143, 310
Central Kingdom, 47, 64–65, 69, 71–72, 75, 78–79, 86, 98, 105, 113, 118, 120–122, 124, 131, 141, 159, 170, 192, 252, 255, 257, 278, 286, 288, 291
Ch'u, T'ung-tsu, 43
Chaffer, John, 80–81
Chang Gun, 235
Chang Xing, 138, 143–144, 151, 153, 202, 204, 305
chaotic (*luan*), 11, 69, 199, 221, 228; chaotic ages (*luanshi*), 76
Chen Bu Chan, 217–220, 228–229, 233–237, 245–248, 305
Chen Chui Cheng, 42, 96, 188
Chen Guo Hui, 266
Chen Hong Jin, 204, 305
Chen Si Dong, 42, 89–90, 96, 170, 172, 305
Chen You Ding, 63, 104, 130, 305
Chen Yun Dun, 87, 144–145, 204

About the Author

Mingming Wang is Professor of Anthropology at Peking University. He is also director of the National Center for Anthropological and Ethnological Inquiries located at Central Minzu University in Beijing and founder and chief editor of *Chinese Review of Anthropology*. He has a Ph.D. from University of London and is author of many articles and books on Chinese anthropology, history, and sociology in both Chinese and English, including *Social Anthropology and Sinology* (1997, in Chinese), *Grassroots Charisma* (2001, in English, co-authored with Stephan Feuchtwang), *Beyond Rural China* (2003, in Chinese), *The West as Other* (2007, in Chinese), and *The Intermediaries: "Tibetan-Yi Corridor" and the Reformation of Anthropology* (2008, in Chinese). He also writes political comments and travel logs.